Author in field

Afoot and Afield in
San Diego County

Jerry Schad

Wilderness Press
Berkeley

Photos by the author
Design by Thomas Winnett
Cover design by Tom Ridge
Library of Congress Card Catalog Number 85-41053
International Standard Book Number 0-89997-057-5
Manufactured in the United States of America
Published by Wilderness Press
        2440 Bancroft Way
        Berkeley, CA 94704

        Write for free catalog

Library of Congress Cataloging-in-Publication Data

Schad, Jerry.
    Afoot and afield in San Diego County.

    Includes index.
        1. Hiking--California--San Diego County--Guide-books.
2. Backpacking--California--San Diego County--
Guide-books. 3. San Diego County (Calif.)--
Description and travel--Guide-books. I. Title.
GV199.42.C22S2669 1986   917.94'980453   85-41053
ISBN 0-89997-057-5

ACKNOWLEDGMENTS

Many people have offered their time, talents, and knowledge during the various phases of producing this book. I would like to thank Mike Fry, Don Endicott, Nick Soroka, Bob and Sharon Hartman, Jane Rauch, Jim Sugg, Bill Becker, Gene Troxell, Janet Leavitt, Pete and Cinde Nowicki, and my wife, René, for sharing adventures with me on the trail, and for helping with transportation during the past year. During the information-gathering phase, George Leetch and Uel Fisk shared their knowledge of some of the more obscure parts of the county. Several people associated with local parks and public agencies have been of assistance too; among them, Manfred Knaak, Paul Remeika, Torrey Lystra, Norm Machado, Greg Greenhoe, Susan Blankenbaker, George Kowatch, Jack Shu, and Russ Kaldenberg. Shannon O'Dunn and Mitch Beauchamp reviewed parts of the manuscript, and Cathey Byrd prepared the symbols that appear at the top of every trip description. Tom Winnett and Jeff Schaffer offered sound advice concerning the drawing of the maps; and Tom, in his usual meticulous way, superbly edited the text. Portions of this manuscript were derived from an earlier series of articles written by me for *San Diego Home/Garden* magazine; appreciation is extended to editor Peter Jensen for permission to reprint this material. Final appreciation goes to my wife, René, for patience and encouragement during a period in which I seemed to be either somewhere in the mountains, or sequestered in a back corner of the house with my word processor.

Jerry Schad
San Diego, California
March 1986

PREFACE

Hiking and backpacking are just two of the many satisfying recreational pursuits enjoyed year-round by those fortunate enough to live under the sunny skies in the equable climate of the San Diego region. Few hikers, however, realize how broad the spectrum of opportunity really is. On one end of this spectrum lie San Diego County's coastal canyons and mountain parks, some laced with well-marked hiking and bridle trails. The other end is obscure, containing vast stretches of undeveloped land in the county's public domain, including many of our newest state and federal wilderness areas. There are few or no trails in these areas, but the potential for unconfined exploration there is almost unlimited.

No single information source has attempted to exhaust even one end of the above-mentioned spectrum—until now. My goal in writing this book was to bring into sharp focus virtually every hike worth taking in the public lands of the county—hikes ranging in difficulty from short, self-guiding nature trails, to peak climbs and canyon treks that would challenge even the most skilled adventurer.

No stone was left unturned in an attempt to deliver current and accurate information for each trip in this book, but, alas, certain compromises concerning the completeness and overall scope of the book were necessarily made. Some of the longer and some of the more technically difficult (cross-country) routes hiked during the information-gathering phase were rejected for inclusion as being either too tedious or unacceptably hazardous.

Conspicuously absent is a complete log of San Diego County's share (about 120 miles) of the Pacific Crest Trail, the West's best-known long-distance footpath. Since this information is adequately treated in other publications, I chose to highlight only the most scenic parts of the PCT in this book. In several of the trip descriptions, the PCT is used as a means to reach another trail or some interesting off-trail destination. (It should be noted that, while some parts of the PCT are indeed very scenic, there are other segments that are very tedious and boring. One stretch through the semidesert San Felipe Hills winds 24 miles with scarcely a change of scenery, and no water.)

In geographical scope, this book encompasses all public lands (and a few private lands on which the public is welcome) within San Diego County, with the exception of some areas not easily reached from the San Diego area, but rather geographically related to other counties. These include the San Mateo Canyon Wilderness, a small part of which intrudes into San Diego County north of Camp Pendleton; the San Onofre State Beach area adjacent to the southern Orange County coastline; and Bucksnort Mountain, accessible by way of the PCT from the vicinity of Anza in Riverside County. On the other hand, some areas in Riverside and Imperial counties, adjacent to or part of Anza-Borrego Desert State Park, were included in this book because of their ease of access from the San Diego area.

About 80 percent of the trips in this book were hiked at least once by me during 1985; others earlier. Roads and trails can and do change every year, however. An expansion of recreational opportunity during the next several years is expected as new county and city parks are developed in and near the urban areas. New trails will be built in the Cleveland National Forest and in the state parks. Periodic updates and new editions of this book are planned for the future. You can keep me apprised of recent developments and/or changes by writing me in care of Wilderness Press.

Contents

Foothills and Mountains

The Desert

Appendices

Index

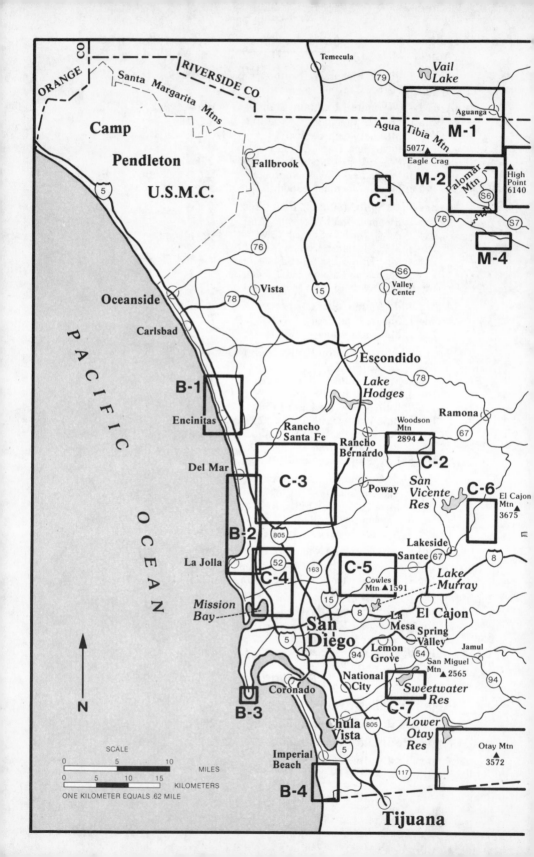

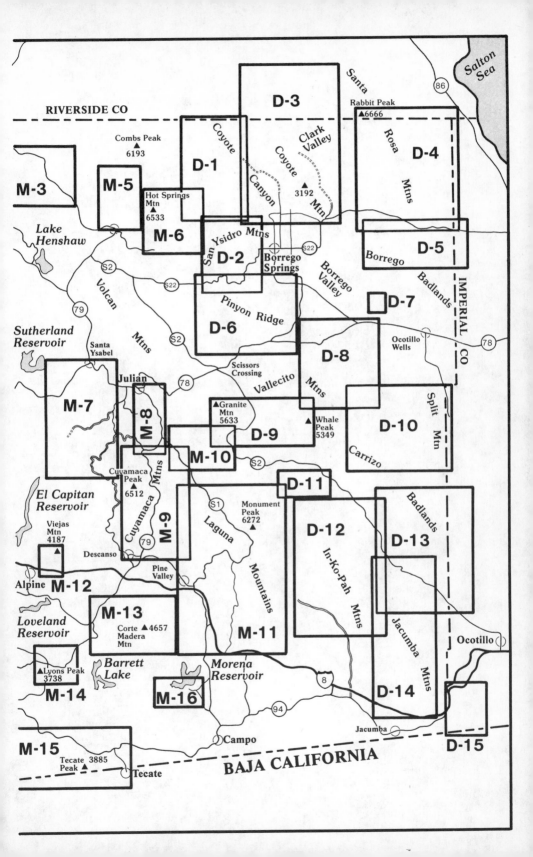

INTRODUCING SAN DIEGO COUNTY

The San Diego region is special in that no simple description can ever hope to characterize it. Lacking any single, overpowering symbol (except, of course, the almost perpetually sunny weather), it revels instead in its remarkable diversity. The blue ocean, the tranquil bays, the sparkling beaches, the sun-splashed coastal mesas, and the rugged little coastal canyons that most San Diegans live with every day are but a small part of the whole. Beyond lies a beautiful and varied backcountry area of boulder-strewn foothills, pine-clad mountains and vast desert spaces.

For hikers, backpackers, and explorers of the great outdoors, this diversity is good news. San Diego County offers a greater variety of experiences and more opportunities to practice an unconfined type of recreation than any other similar-sized area in the United States. Of the county's 4255 square miles, more than one-third, or a total of approximately 1550 square miles, is public land open to recreational use. Included in this total are several state parks (chiefly Anza-Borrego Desert State Park), 802 square miles; the Cleveland National Forest, 438 square miles; land in the public domain administered by the federal Bureau of Land Management, 283 square miles; and numerous county and city parks.

With the expenditure of less than two hours' driving time and one or two hours' walk, a San Diego urbanite can reach any of a dozen totally different natural environments, ranging from snowy mountain peaks and fern-bedecked streams to sculpted desert badlands. Nowhere else in America is such a broad range of natural environments so close and conveniently located, and so available year-round, to a large population.

In the next few pages, we'll introduce you to some of the remarkable aspects of San Diego County's climate, landforms, and flora and fauna. Following that, you'll find some notes about safety and courtesy on the trail, and some tips on how to get the most out of this book. After perusing these chapters, you can dig into, or simply browse through, the heart of this book—176 detailed descriptions of hiking routes from the coast to the Anza-Borrego Desert. Happy reading—and happy hiking!

A Land For All Seasons

A good, descriptive summary of San Diego County's many climates might take the form of just two phrases: "warm and sunny," and "winter-wet, summer-dry." A more detailed analysis would show that there are many variations within this pattern. The distribution of these climates is somewhat easy to picture geographically, since they tend to run in strips parallel to the county's coastline and its roofline—the Peninsular Ranges.

Without resorting to technical classification schemes, let's divide the county into five climate zones:

The westernmost zone, extending inland several miles across the coastal plain, is largely under the moderating influence of the Pacific Ocean. This climate is characterized by mild temperatures that are relatively unvarying, both daily and seasonally. Average Fahrenheit temperatures range from the mid-60s/mid-40s (daily highs/lows) in winter, to mid-70s/mid-60s in summer. Rainfall averages about 10 inches annually. Surprisingly, this climate is not the classic "Mediterranean climate" most people associate with coastal San Diego County and Southern California. It is too dry. True Mediterranean climate more closely matches that of the next zone.

The next zone, about 20–40 miles wide, covers the inland valleys and western foothills of the Peninsular Ranges. This area, which is only partly under the influence of moderating ocean breezes, experiences more extreme temperatures: low 70s/high 30s in winter to high 80s/high 50s in summer. Precipitation averages about 15 inches annually.

The next zone east, the coolest, encompasses the highest elevations of San Diego County: the forested heights of the Palomar, Cuyamaca, Laguna and other similar mountains that form the backbone of the Peninsular Ranges. Winter temperatures average high 40s/low 30s, while summer temperatures average low 80s/high 50s. Precipitation, in the form of both rain and snow, averages about 30 inches annually.

Farther east still, on the desert-facing slopes of the mountains, is a narrow strip characterized by a "high desert" climate. This zone also includes the tops of several eastern spurs of the Peninsular Ranges that extend into the desert. Temperatures range from the low 60s/low 30s in winter to the high 90s/low 60s in summer. Precipitation averages about 10 inches per year.

The easternmost zone includes the "low desert"—below about 3000 feet elevation. This area is almost completely cut off from the moderating influence of the ocean, and it experiences a relatively extreme "continental" type of climate. Temperatures range from the low 70s/low 40s in winter to 100-plus/high 60s in summer. Average precipitation is five inches or less.

No discussion of San Diego County climates would be complete without mention of some of the remarkable extremes of

temperature and precipitation recorded within in the county over the past century.

The highest official temperature ever recorded in the county was a modest 121 degrees at Borrego Springs. Since certain areas of the low desert outside of Borrego Springs regularly experience temperatures averaging five degrees higher, however, it can be presumed that shade temperatures above 120 degrees are not uncommon.

At times even the coastal area can heat for a few days to temperatures in excess of 100 degrees. This situation is known as a "Santa Ana condition," and it occurs when an air mass moves southwest from a high-pressure area in the interior U.S. out toward, say, San Diego County. As the air flows down mountain slopes, it compresses, and this causes it to warm and to dry. During a strong Santa Ana condition, common in late summer and early fall, San Diego or Imperial Beach or some other coastal weather station will sometimes record the highest temperature in the nation!

The lowest temperatures, and the only subzero temperatures, recorded in the county so far, were -4 and -1 degree readings at Cuyamaca Rancho State Park.

Although San Diego County and all of Southern California lies in a belt of generally dry climate, both are susceptible to monster deluges as well as prolonged droughts. Annual precipitation totals measured at San Diego over the past 135 years have ranged from three inches to 26 inches; and Palomar Mountain, the wettest spot in the county, once received a total of 82 inches. Occasionally, a *chubasco,* or tropical storm, from Mexico will move into the desert or mountains, resulting in intense, localized downpours. A century ago, one such storm dumped 16 inches of rain on the border town of Campo in 24 hours, 11.5 inches of that total in a single 80-minute-period! In 1976, another *chubasco,* Hurricane Kathleen, wreaked havoc in southeastern San Diego County, rearranging watercourses and destroying roads, a railroad line, and half a desert town.

Lower Penasquitos Canyon

No San Diegan should complain about the monotony of the weather along the coast ("Ho hum, just another day in paradise"). The mountains beckon with a full range of seasons, complete with spring wildflowers, autumn color and winter snows, while the desert usually offers the kind of pure, almost liquid sunshine and dry heat only seldom experienced near the coast.

A good knowledge of our local climates will help you get the most out of your hiking adventures. Seasonal recommendations are included for hikes in this book (under "Best Times"), but feel free to take the easy and moderate trips any time of year. After all, who says the best temperatures for hiking should always be in the moderate registers of the thermometer?

Reading the Rocks

Some geographers think of San Diego County as being divided into three "geo-morphic provinces." These provinces are not unique to San Diego County, but extend into neighboring counties and into Baja California.

The first, bounded by the curving shoreline of the Pacific Ocean and stretching no more than a few miles inland, is the *Coast province*. It has the form of a terraced plain, in places intricately dissected by steep-sided canyons and arroyos. This is the familiar "canyon-and-mesa" topography on which most of urban and suburban San Diego lies.

The second, the *Peninsular Ranges province*, consists of a series of discontinuous mountain ranges, some more than 6000 feet high. The ranges are generally parallel to one another, generally trend northwest-southeast, and are interspersed with high, sometimes narrow valleys. The bulk of San Diego County's land surface is included in this province, along with all the county's higher elevations. The province stretches north to include the San Jacinto Mountains in Riverside County and south to the tip of the Baja peninsula. The Peninsular Ranges and the Sierra Nevada range to the north are similar in topography: in rough form both are huge, tilted blocks of granitic rock, with steep east escarpments and more gradual west slopes.

The third province is called the Salton Trough. This large depression holds the Salton Sea, and most geologists would say it lies outside San Diego County. However, to this province geographers would add the low-desert landscape of Anza-Borrego Desert State Park in the northeastern corner of the county.

The geomorphic provinces themselves are very complex. Within even a single mountain range or coastal canyon or desert basin, there may exist a dazzling variety of small-scale landforms and underlying rock types. One might want to ask: how did San Diego County's surface get to be so con-voluted; and what processes were respon-sible for the presence of so many different kinds of rock in the county today?

First, it is important to note that Cali-fornia, Oregon, Washington, British Colum-bia and Alaska are composed largely of rock formations that were transported to their current locations from either the west or the south. This migration was accomplished by the formations riding "piggyback" atop large and small plates which, taken all together, form the earth's crust. Such grand-scale movements are still occurring today. For example, California's famous San Andreas Fault is actually just a boundary between two large plates that are gliding past each other. San Diego lies on the oceanic plate, which is drifting north with respect to the continental plate at a rate of about 2¼ inches per year. If this rate continues, then in 14 million years, San Diego will have drifted far enough north to pass San Francisco, which lies on the con-tinental plate. Future hikers—bring your overcoats!

With the above in mind, we begin the geologic story, as painted in broad brush strokes, back about 150 million years ago. At that time, most of present-day location of San Diego County, along with much of western North America, was below sea level. Then, over 2000 miles to the south or southwest, a mountain-building cycle began, as an arc of volcanic islands grew in the ocean. For 50 million years or so, the volcanoes spread lava and ash over a wide area. By the end of this volcanic episode, about 100 million years ago, the arc of volcanic islands had migrated close to the mainland, and the two land masses were now separated by a narrowing, shallow sea. After the sediments of the shallow sea floor were uplifted, they were eroded away and de-posited in deltas near the coast or offshore. Erosion also carried away the debris from the island-arc volcanoes, exposing and attacking deeper layers that had been metamorphosed by heat and pressure generated as the volcanic islands slowly rammed into the mainland.

Still more debris arriving along the coast came from a volcanic area far inland that had evolved in response to the oceanic plate carrying the island-arc volcanoes. The edge of this oceanic plate was diving beneath the mainland plate, and its rock melted when it reached a certain depth, creating magma. This magma rose within the crust, and parts of it solidified before reaching the surface, crystallizing to form granitic rock. But some magma broke through to the surface, and spewed lava and ash far and wide, con-structing a volcanic landscape. (A similar process of volcanism, caused by an offshore, northward-migrating, diving plate, is occur-ring today in the Cascade Range of Wash-ington, Oregon and northern California.) Much of the debris from the mainland volcanic area was in the form of erosion-resistant rhyolitic rock. It seems that during one particular period lasting several million years, cobbles of this rhyolitic rock came to our area by way of a single large river, which once flowed west through today's state of Sonora, Mexico.

Erosive forces continued to nibble away

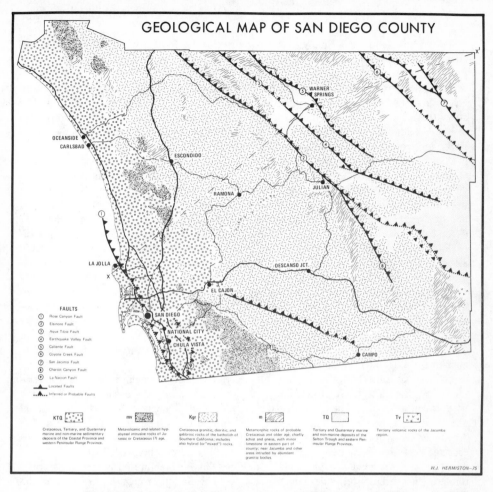

GEOLOGICAL MAP OF SAN DIEGO COUNTY

OCEANSIDE
CARLSBAD

ESCONDIDO

WARNER
SPRINGS

RAMONA

JULIAN

LA JOLLA

DESCANSO JCT.

EL CAJON

SAN DIEGO

NATIONAL CITY

CHULA VISTA

CAMPO

FAULTS
1. Rose Canyon Fault
2. Elsinore Fault
3. Aqua Tibia Fault
4. Earthquake Valley Fault
5. Caliente Fault
6. Coyote Creek Fault
7. San Jacinto Fault
8. Chariot Canyon Fault
9. La Nacion Fault
— Located Faults
▲▲ Inferred or Probable Faults

KTQ — Cretaceous, Tertiary, and Quaternary marine and non-marine sedimentary deposits of the Coastal Province and western Peninsular Range Province.

mv — Metavolcanic and related hypabyssal intrusive rocks of Jurassic or Cretaceous (?) age.

Kgr — Cretaceous granitic, dioritic, and gabbroic rocks of the batholith of Southern California; includes also hybrid (or "mixed") rocks.

m — Metamorphic rocks of probable Cretaceous and older age, chiefly schist and gneiss, with minor limestone in eastern part of county; near Jacumba and other areas intruded by abundant granitic bodies.

TQ — Tertiary and Quaternary marine and non-marine deposits of the Salton Trough and eastern Peninsular Range Province.

Tv — Tertiary volcanic rocks of the Jacumba region.

W.J. HERMISTON–75

Simplified geologic map and profile of San Diego County. Line XX' on the geologic map locates the cross section of the geologic profile. From *San Diego: An Introduction to the Region*, Philip Pryde, ed., © 1976, 1984 by Kendall/Hunt Publishing Company. Reprinted by permission of Kendall/Hunt Publishing Company.

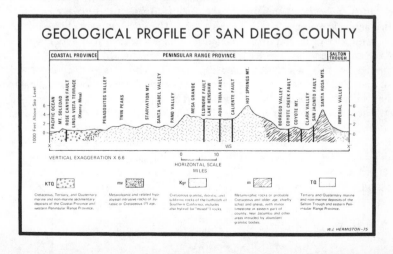

GEOLOGICAL PROFILE OF SAN DIEGO COUNTY

COASTAL PROVINCE | PENINSULAR RANGE PROVINCE | SALTON TROUGH

1000 Feet Above Sea Level

PACIFIC OCEAN
MT. SOLEDAD
ROSE CANYON FAULT
LINDA VISTA TERRACE (Kearny Mesa)
PENASQUITOS VALLEY
TWIN PEAKS
STARVATION MT.
SANTA YSABEL VALLEY
PAMO VALLEY
MESA GRANDE
ELSINORE FAULT
LAKE HENSHAW
AQUA TIBIA FAULT
CALIENTE FAULT
HOT SPRINGS MT.
BORREGO VALLEY
COYOTE CREEK FAULT
COYOTE MT.
CLARK VALLEY
SAN JACINTO FAULT
SANTA ROSA MTS.
IMPERIAL VALLEY

WS

VERTICAL EXAGGERATION X 6.6

0   10
HORIZONTAL SCALE
MILES

KTQ — Cretaceous, Tertiary, and Quaternary marine and non-marine sedimentary deposits of the Coastal Province and western Peninsular Range Province.

mv — Metavolcanic and related hypabyssal intrusive rocks of Jurassic or Cretaceous (?) age.

Kgr — Cretaceous granitic, dioritic, and gabbroic rocks of the batholith of Southern California; includes also hybrid (or "mixed") rocks.

m — Metamorphic rocks of probable Cretaceous and older age, chiefly schist and gneiss, with minor limestone in eastern part of county; near Jacumba and other areas intruded by abundant granitic bodies.

TQ — Tertiary and Quaternary marine and non-marine deposits of the Salton Trough and eastern Peninsular Range Province.

W.J. HERMISTON–75

at the volcanic landscape, finally exposing, after perhaps 20 million years (80 million years ago), the underlying granitic rock, which had originally solidified about three to nine miles below the earth's surface. In time, an increasing amount of the large granitic mass, or batholith, was exposed, and the landscape acquired a different look, perhaps like that of today's mostly granitic San Diego County. The vegetation, however, was very different, in part because plants back then were different, but more important, because this area was still well south of us, located in a tropical clime.

By about 40 million years ago the assemblage of volcanic rocks and granitic rocks plus sediments from both rock types had migrated far enough north to be located immediately west of the present-day state of Sonora, on the mainland of Mexico. Later, a "mere" 10 million years ago, the Gulf of California began to form as an inlet between mainland Mexico and the sliver of land that would become Baja California.

Today, San Diego County—riding on what is known as the Pacific Plate—continues to drift northwest relative to the "mainland" North American Plate. To the east and northeast is the boundary between the two plates, the great San Andreas Fault, running beneath the eastern side of the Salton Trough and under the Gulf of California. In the county's midsection, the granitic mass continues to rise, building up mountains faster than erosive forces are currently tearing them down.

We can now begin to understand the simplified geologic map and profile on page 5. The granitic rocks, and their related dioritic and gabbroic rocks, which are rich in iron, magnesium and calcium, encompass most of the Peninsular Ranges province (including what we generally call our foothills and mountains). Together all are part of the Southern California batholith—the vast mass of rock that crystallized deep beneath a tropical volcanic landscape about 100 million years ago.

Exposed on the western edge of the Peninsular Ranges province, and poking up in places through the coastal plain, is a belt of distinctly older metavolcanic rocks. This is a resistant remnant of the lava and ash that spewed out of the island volcanoes 150 million years ago, later to be metamorphosed when the islands collided with the mainland.

In the Coast province we find sedimentary deposits, both marine and nonmarine (river deposits) which were laid down in various periods from about 80 to 2 million years ago. The marine sediments are typically seen near the coast, the nonmarine sediments farther inland. In many locales you'll see exposures of sandstone, shale, and conglomerate. The rhyolitic cobbles so widely seen today on the beaches and in thick conglomerate beds through much of metropolitan San Diego were not formed where they lie today. They are the water-worn pieces of volcanic rock delivered by the aforementioned large river.

The Coast province deposits are relatively soft and easily eroded. They exhibit a record of changing sea levels and gradual uplift in the form of wave-cut terraces. The terraces themselves are in many places deeply cut by drainage channels—the coastal canyons—which are fairly recent features.

The Salton Trough, an extension of the Gulf of California, lies buried in sediments as much as four miles thick, deposited in relatively recent times, the last few million years. These sediments have been carved into spectacular forms in the badland areas of the Anza-Borrego Desert.

The geologic map shows two other less common general rock types: some volcanic rock exposures in the southeast corner of the county, and several much more widespread bands of metamorphosed sedimentary rocks. The volcanic rocks are about 20 million years in age, and mark the only period of isolated volcanic activity in the county since the great batholith cooled. The metamorphosed sedimentary rocks, which may be 100 to 300 million years old, are the altered remnants of mud, lime and sand layers deposited on a sea floor. This category includes the Julian schist, the presence of which is associated with pockets of ore containing gold and other valuable minerals.

Both the geologic map and the geologic profile show several sympathetic (splinter) faults associated with the San Andreas Fault. Because of these, the land surface of the county does not move as a solid unit toward the northwest, but rather creeps differentially. Vertical and horizontal movements along these faults have fractured the Peninsular Ranges province into a series of separate blocks (mountain ranges), most of them tilted in the characteristic west-dipping fashion.

More finely detailed—and colorful—geologic maps can give a more vivid picture

Toro Peak from Collins Valley

of San Diego County's geological com-
plexities. Refer to Appendix 2 for these and
other sources of information about the
county's fascinating geology.

Native Gardens

Nearly 2000 species of wild plants grow
within the boundaries of San Diego County.
Few counties in the United States can boast
an equal or greater number. Of this total, only
about 200 are non-native (naturalized)
plants from other places in the United States
or other parts of the world.

There are two reasons for this plethora of
plants. One reason has to do with physical
factors: topography, geology, soils, and climate. The sheer complexity of the interrela-
tionships among these factors has produced a
wide range of possible physical habitats.

The second reason is San Diego County's
strategic location between two groups of
flora: a southern group represented by
drought-tolerant plants characteristic of Baja
California, and a northern group represented by moisture-loving plants typical of
the Sierra Nevada and California's north
coastal ranges. As the climate has changed,
seesawing from cool and wet to warm and dry
over the past million years or so, species from
both groups have invaded the county. Once
established, many of these species have
remained in protected niches even as the
climate turned unfavorable for them. Some
have survived unchanged over the ages;
others have evolved into unique forms. Many
are present only in very specific habitats
within the county.

Most of San Diego County's natural
vegetation can be categorized into six general
groupings, which botanists often call plant
communities or plant associations. In a
broader sense, these are biological communities, which include animals as well as
plants. These plant communities are briefly
described below in the order you would
encounter them if you were to drive east from
the coast, over the crest of the highest
mountains, and into the desert.

The *sage-scrub* (or coastal-sage-scrub)
community lies mostly below 1500 feet
elevation, and extends east from the coastline to the foothills and lower slopes of the
mountains. The more-open sage-scrub community intermixes readily with the dense
chaparral community, especially on north
slopes and in canyons along the coastal strip.
The dominant species are small shrubs,
typically California sagebrush, white sage,
black sage, and California buckwheat. Two
larger shrubs often present are laurel sumac
and lemonade berry, which like poison oak
are members of the sumac family. Interspersed among the somewhat loosely distributed shrubs are a variety of grasses and
wildflowers.

The *chaparral* community is commonly
found between 1000 and 4500 feet elevation
on the west slopes of the mountains, and
between 4000 and 5000 feet on some of the
east slopes. It is also found in a few areas
along the coast. Vast areas of San Diego
County are carpeted by almost unbroken
stretches of chaparral. The dominant species
are chamise, ribbonwood, manzanita, scrub
oak, and various forms of ceanothus ("wild
lilac"). These species are tough, intricately
branched shrubs with deep root systems that
help the plants survive during the long, hot
summers. Chaparral is sometimes referred to
as an "elfin forest"—a literal description of a
mature stand. Without the benefit of a trail,
travel through mature chaparral, which is
typically 5 to 15 feet high, is almost impossible.

The *southern oak woodland* community
is found in scattered locations throughout
San Diego County in areas from the foothills
to just below the crests of the mountains. The
indicator species are broadleaf trees, such as
black oaks and various live oaks. These are
intermixed with abundant grasses and sometimes a sparse growth of chaparral shrubs.
The southern oak woodland is very "parklike" in appearance, especially in the spring
with the new growths of grass and wildflowers.

Jeffrey pine forest in Laguna Mountains

The *coniferous forest* (or ponderosa-pine forest) community exists only at the highest elevations of San Diego County—generally above 4500 feet. The common coniferous trees include the ponderosa, Jeffrey, Coulter and sugar pines; white fir; incense-cedar, and big-cone Douglas-fir. These are often intermixed with live and black oaks, various chaparral shrubs, grasses and wildflowers. This is, of course, the type of plant community most people associate with "the mountains."

The *pinyon-juniper woodland* community covers parts of the east-facing slopes of the county's higher ranges, such as the Laguna Mountains. It also exists in the form of botanical "islands" on the crests of the arid Vallecito Mountains and the Santa Rosa Mountains (within San Diego County). The two principal species are rather stunted conifers, the one-leaved pinyon pine and the California juniper. Other plants belonging to this community have rather small, leathery or rigid leaves—a water-conservation feature which is so necessary in the high desert.

The *desert shrub* (or creosote-bush scrub) community covers the desert floor and extends up the east slopes of the mountains to about 2000 feet in elevation. The indicator plant is the creosote bush, a plant not only abundant in our local Colorado Desert (a subdivision of the Sonoran Desert), but throughout the entire Sonoran and Mojave deserts. Ocotillo, many kinds of cacti, and a wide variety of drought-tolerant shrubs are also common. Displays of annual and ephemeral wildflowers are unpredictable but often spectacular.

Aside from the six fairly widespread communities above, there are others that are much more restricted in area: *rocky shore, coastal strand, coastal salt marsh, freshwater marsh, riparian woodland, mountain meadow, desert wash,* and *alkali sink.*

Of these plant communities, the riparian (streamside) woodland, covering less than one-fifth of one percent of the county's land area, is considered the most valuable. Not only is this kind of environment essential for the continued survival of many kinds of birds and animals, it is also very appealing to the senses. Massive live oaks, sycamores and cottonwoods, and a screen of water-hugging willows are the hallmarks of the riparian woodland. Much of this habitat is being threatened by urbanization and attendant development of water resources.

San Diego County has more than its share of rare, endangered, unique, or otherwise unusual species of vegetation. Best known are the Torrey pine, the California fan palm, and two kinds of cypress.

Torrey pines are found in picturesque groves on the eroded bluffs overlooking the Pacific Ocean at Torrey Pines State Reserve, near Del Mar. These trees were widespread at one time, but an increase in aridity has caused their natural range to retreat to just this site and one other—the east end of Santa Rosa Island, which lies off the coast of Santa Barbara. Overzealous collection of the trees' large edible nuts by Indians may also have contributed to its decline. Fog drip from the Torrey pine's long needles apparently provides the extra moisture it needs for its survival.

California fan palms exist in a similarly narrow niche. They are relicts from a time when today's desert was semitropical. Increasing aridity forced them to retreat to canyons and arroyos that have an uninterrupted supply of surface or subsurface water. Their range extends across the Colorado Desert (which includes the Anza-Borrego Desert) into the southern reaches of the Mojave Desert and into Baja California.

The cypresses also have retreated to "arboreal islands." The rare Cuyamaca cypress now is restricted to a small area of chaparral-covered slopes about one mile south of Cuyamaca Peak, while the range of the more widely distributed Tecate cypress includes three San Diego County locations (Otay Mountain, Tecate Peak-Potrero Creek, and Guatay Mountain), one Orange County location, and several more in Baja California.

Early-to-mid spring is the best time to appreciate the cornucopia of San Diego County's native plants. Many of the showiest species—spring wildflowers, for example—burgeon at this time, and other plants exhibit fresh new growth. Peak periods for wildflowers vary according to elevation. The low desert blooms most profusely during a rather short period centered on late March or early April; coastal areas and foothills are usually best in April; and the highest mountains are best in late April and May. Irregular summer desert thunderstorms occasionally give rise to a second period of blooming in fall in the desert and along the east-facing mountain slopes.

For more information about the wildflowers, shrubs, trees and other flora of San Diego County, see Appendix 2—Recommended Reading.

Desert sunflowers in Borrego Valley

Creatures Great and Small

One's first sighting of a mountain lion, a bighorn sheep, a bald eagle, or any other seldom-seen form of wildlife is always a memorable experience. Because of the diversity and the generally broad extent of its habitats, San Diego County plays host to a healthy population of indigenous creatures, including a number of rare or endangered species. People willing to stretch their legs a bit and spend some time in the areas favored by wild animals will eventually be rewarded by some kind of close visual contact.

The most numerous large creature in the county is the mule deer, with a population of at least several thousand. The deer prefer areas of mixed forest and scattered chaparral, especially at the highest elevations in the county, but they can also be seen in the coastal canyons and on desert-facing slopes with moderate growths of vegetation. Deer like to have a protective screen of vegetation near them at all times, and are seldom found in the open areas of the desert. In places like Cuyamaca Rancho State Park, where the deer are protected from hunting, it is uncommon *not* to see any while out hiking the trails.

The mountain lion, once hunted to near-extinction in California, has made a comeback as a protected species. One estimate a decade ago pegged the county population at about 20 individuals, but that number may be five times greater today. Mountain lions not only have a large territorial range (up to 100 square miles); they also inhabit virtually every natural habitat in the county. Secretive in nature, they are seldom observed. Because of their wide-ranging travels, however, tracks and other signs of the mountain lion are quite frequently seen.

The county's most interesting large mammal is the endangered peninsular (desert) bighorn sheep. Some 500 of these agile animals maintain a tenuous existence on the steep slopes and rocky crags of the Anza-Borrego Desert. Unlike mule deer, the bighorn sheep prefer open, rugged terrain, on which they are capable of escaping from almost any predator. They are also superbly adapted to surviving on meager supplies of water and coarse desert vegetation. Bighorn sheep tend to keep a safe distance from human activity, but sometimes seem possessed of a kind of curiosity about humans. Once accustomed to a hiker's presence, a sheep may approach quite closely and make a surprise "appearance." After three or four seconds of eye contact, the animal turns and disappears.

The county's mammals also include the coyote, which has adapted to a broad range of habitats, including the margins of suburbia; the bobcat, a creature sometimes mistaken for a mountain lion, but smaller and much more common; the gray fox of mountain habitats and the kit fox of desert habitats; the opossum; the skunk; the raccoon; and various rabbits, squirrels, woodrats and mice.

Among the commonly seen reptiles are rattlesnakes, which we will discuss in the next section.

The variety of bird life in San Diego County is outstanding, not only because of the great diversity of habitats, but also because the county lies along the Pacific Flyway route of spring-fall bird migration and serves as an important wintering area for waterfowl. The undeveloped areas of the county support several species of rare or endangered birds, including the southern bald eagle, the peregrine falcon, the light-footed clapper rail, the California least tern and the least Bell's vireo.

Mule deer, Cuyamaca Mountains

Health, Safety and Courtesy

Good preparation is always important for any kind of recreational pursuit. Hiking the San Diego backcountry is no exception. Although most of the county's natural environments are seldom hostile or dangerous to life and limb, there are some pitfalls to be aware of.

An obvious safety requirement is being in good health. Some degree of physical conditioning is always desirable, even for those trips in this book designated as easy or moderate (rated * and ** in difficulty). The more challenging trips (rated ***, **** or *****) require increasing amounts of stamina and technical expertise. Running, bicycling, swimming, aerobic dancing, or any similar exercise that develops both the leg muscles and the aerobic capacity of the whole body are recommended as preparatory exercise.

For long trips over rough, cross-country terrain (there are several of these in this book) there is no really adequate way to prepare other than practicing the activity itself. Start with easy- or moderate-length cross-country trips first to accustom the leg muscles to the peculiar stresses involved in "boulder-hopping" or "non-technical climbing" (scrambling over steep terrain), and to acquire a good sense of balance. As we note later, sturdy hiking boots are always recommended for such travel, primarily from a safety standpoint.

Since all hiking in San Diego County is below about 6500 feet elevation, serious health complications due to high altitude are rare. Most sea-level dwellers will, of course, notice some loss of energy and a greater respiration rate in the higher mountain areas.

An important aspect of preparation is the choice of equipment and supplies. The essentials you should carry with you at all times in the backcountry are the things that would allow you to survive, in a reasonably comfortable manner, one or two unscheduled nights out. It's important to note that no one ever plans these nights! No one plans to get lost, injured, stuck, or pinned down by the weather. Always do a "what if" analysis for a worst-case scenario, and plan accordingly. These essential items are your safety net; keep them with you on day hikes, and take them with you in a small day pack if you leave your backpack and camping equipment behind at a campsite.

Chief among the essential items is *warm clothing.* Inland San Diego County is characterized by wide swings in day and night temperatures. In mountain valleys susceptible to cold-air drainage, for example, a midday temperature in the 70s or 80s is often followed by a subfreezing night. Carry light, inner layers of clothing consisting of polypropylene or wool (best for cool or cold weather), or cotton (adequate for warm or hot weather, but very poor for cold and damp weather). Include a thicker insulating layer of "pile" (polyester fiberpile), wool, or down to put on whenever needed, especially when you are not moving around and generating heat. Add to this a cap, gloves, and a waterproof or water-resistant shell (a large trash bag will do in a pinch)—and you'll be quite prepared for all but the most severe weather experienced in San Diego County.

In hot, sunny weather, sun-shielding clothing may be another "essential." This would normally include a sun hat and a light-colored, long-sleeve top.

Water, and to a lesser extent, *food* are next in importance. If water isn't immediately available, carry a generous supply. In the arid San Diego backcountry, you'll need to drink up to a gallon of water during a full day's hike in 70- or 80-degree temperatures; and up to two or three gallons per day in summer desert conditions (hiking in these latter conditions is *not* recommended!) Food is needed to stave off hunger and keep energy stores up, but it is not as essential as water in a survival situation.

Down the list further, but still "essential," are a *map* and *compass, flashlight, fire-starting devices* (examples: waterproof matches or lighter, and candle), and *first-aid kit.*

Items not always essential, but potentially very useful and convenient, are sunglasses, pocket knife, whistle (or other signalling device), sunscreen, and toilet paper.

The essential items mentioned above should be carried by every member of a hiking party, because individuals or splinter groups may end up separating from the party for one reason or another. If you plan to hike solo in the backcountry, being well-equipped is very important. If you hike alone, be sure to check in with a park ranger or leave your itinerary with a responsible person. In that way, if you do get stuck, help will probably come to the right place—eventually.

Taking children on hiking outings involves a special kind of responsibility. San Diego-based "Project Hug-a-Tree" (see Appendix 4) can provide you with information about training and outfitting a child to cope with the possibility of getting lost in the wilderness.

Other than getting lost or pinned down by a rare sudden storm, the four most common hazards found in the San Diego backcountry are loose rocks and/or steep terrain, spiny plants, rattlesnakes, and poison oak. Cross-country hiking in the desert, and to a lesser extent in the mountains and the foothills, frequently involves travel over exposed rock on steep slopes. The erosive forces of flowing water, the freezing and melting of ice, and even brush fires tend to fracture the rock into chunks anywhere in size from house-size to small pebbles. Middle-sized boulders, often poorly anchored, are probably the most dangerous. Before you step on a boulder or pull on it with your hands, try to judge its stability.

Smaller pebbles that act like ball bearings underfoot are often a problem on desert slopes, especially where cacti and the desert agave grow. The agave plant (also known as century plant) consists of a rosette of fleshy leaves each tipped with a rigid thorn containing a mild toxin. A headlong fall into either an agave or one of the more vicious kinds of cacti could easily make you swear off desert travel permanently. It's best to give these devilish plants as wide a berth as possible.

Most desert hikers will sooner or later suffer punctures by thorns or spines. This is most likely to happen during close encounters with the cholla ("jumping") cactus, whose spine clusters readily break off and attach firmly to your skin, clothes or boots. A comb can be used to gently pull away the spine clusters, and tweezers or lightweight pliers can be used to remove any individual embedded spines.

Rattlesnakes are common in all parts of San Diego County. Seldom seen in either cold or very hot weather, they favor temperatures in the 75–90° range—spring and fall in the desert and coastal areas, and summer in the mountains. Most rattlesnakes are as interested in avoiding contact with you as you are with them. Watch carefully where you put your feet, and especially your hands, during the warmer months. In brushy or rocky areas where sight distance is short, try to make your presence known from afar. Tread with heavy footfalls, or use a stick to bang against rocks or bushes. Rattlesnakes will pick up the vibrations through their skin and will usually buzz (unmistakably) before you get too close for comfort.

Poison oak grows profusely along many of the county's canyons below 5000 feet. It is often found on the banks of streamcourses in the form of a bush or vine, and seems to prefer the semi-shade of live and scrub oaks. Occasionally it is seen along well-used trails. Learn to recognize its distinctive three-leaved structure, and avoid touching it with skin or clothing. Since poison oak loses its

Diamondback rattlesnake

should be regarded as unsafe for drinking without purification. This excludes, of course, developed water sources in state and county parks. Chemical (iodine or chlorine) treatment and filtering are the most convenient purification methods, but secondary in effectiveness to boiling. A bigger problem, of course, is the availability of the water itself. Most watercourses and many springs in San Diego County are intermittent. Even some streams shown as "permanent" on topographic maps do occasionally dry up.

Deer-hunting season in San Diego County usually runs for the month of October. Hunting activity takes place over much of the Cleveland National Forest at this time. Although conflicts between hunters and hikers are rare, you may want to confine your mid-autumn explorations to state and county parks, and wilderness areas where hunting is not permitted.

There is always some risk in leaving a vehicle unattended. Automobile vandalism and burglary are not as common in San Diego County as in backcountry areas around Los Angeles, but they are certainly

Poison-oak leaves

leaves during the winter months (usually January, February, and part of March in San Diego County), but still retains some of the toxic oil in its stems, it can be extra hazardous at that time because it is harder to notice.

Some boulder-hopping trips in this book are routed directly down streamcourses where poison oak thickets are impossible to avoid. On these trips, you might consider taking along small garden clippers and gloves. Seldom is any major pruning necessary; just a snip here and there. Thick pants (jeans) and a long-sleeve shirt will serve as a fair barrier against the toxic oil of the poison-oak plant. Do, of course, remove these clothes as soon as the hike is over, and make sure they are washed carefully afterward.

Here are a few more safety tips:

Most free-flowing water in San Diego

not unknown. Troublesome spots include the more remote corners of the Cleveland National Forest and areas near the international border. Undocumented aliens are usually responsible for theft of "survival" items—food, water, clothing. Fortunately these break-ins almost never involve an element of vandalism. Report all theft and vandalism of personal property to the county sheriff, and report vandalism of public property to the appropriate park or forest agency.

Obviously it is unwise to leave valuable property in an automobile. To prevent theft of the car, you can remove your car's distributor rotor, or use some other method of disabling the ignition system.

Whenever you travel the backcountry, you take on a burden of responsibility— keeping the wilderness as you found it. Aside from common-sense prohibitions against littering, vandalism, and inappropriate fires, there are some less obvious guidelines every hiker should be aware of. We'll mention a few:

Never cut trail switchbacks. This practice breaks down the trail tread and hastens erosion. Try to improve designated trails by removing branches, rocks, or other debris; but *don't* do this for unofficial trails or cross-country routes. Report any trail damage and misplaced or broken signs to the appropriate ranger office. (Cleveland National Forest has a form for this purpose.)

When off trail, resist the temptation to build cairns or ducks (rock piles) as trail markers, except when absolutely necessary for route-finding. It is disappointing to follow a remote canyon or ridge, or a well-beaten trail, mindlessly littered with unnecessary markers. On the other hand, don't knock over cairns and ducks unless they are obviously recent and superfluous constructions. Many of the ancient Indian and early settlers' trails are marked by cairns and ducks of possible archeological interest.

Be a "no trace" camper. Camp well away from water (there are a variety of reasons for this) and leave your campsite as you found it—or leave it in an even more natural condi-

tion. Because of the danger of wildfire, campfires are seldom allowed outside of developed campgrounds in San Diego County.

Collecting specimens of minerals, plants, animals, or historical objects is prohibited in state and county parks, and in the national forest. Collecting may be allowed in other jurisdictions—check first.

It is impractical to review here all the specific rules associated with the use of public lands in San Diego County. You, as a visitor, are responsible for knowing them, however. Refer to Appendix 4 for sources of information.

Foster Point Monument

Using This Book

Whether you wish to use this book as a reference tool or as a guide to be read cover to cover, you should take a few minutes to read this section. Herein we explain the meaning of the special symbols and other bits of capsulized information which appear before each trip description, and describe the way in which trips are grouped together geographically.

One way to expedite the process of finding a suitable trip, especially if you're unfamiliar with hiking opportunities in San Diego County, is to turn to Appendix 1, "Best Hikes." This is a cross-reference of several dozen of the most highly recommended hikes described in this book.

Each of the 176 hiking trips belongs to one of 42 "areas." Each area has its own introductory text and map. The areas are coded according to "regions" within San Diego County. Areas B-1, B-2, B-3, etc., are in the Beaches and Bays region of the county. Areas C-1, C-2, etc., are in the Coastal Strip region. Letter M in the area designation refers to the Foothills and Mountains region, and letter D refers to the Desert region. The index map of the whole county on pages xii, xiii shows the coverage of each area map, and the Table of Contents lists the page numbers for each region, area, and trip.

The introductory text for each area includes any general information about the area's history, geology, plants and wildlife not included in the trip descriptions. Important information about possible restrictions or special requirements (wilderness permits, for example) appears here too, and you should review this material before embarking on a hike within a particular area.

The beginning of each area section contains an area map. On most of these maps, more than one hiking route (trip) is plotted,

the numbers in the squares corresponding to trip numbers in the text. These boxed numbers refer to the start/end points of out-and-back and loop trips. The point-to-point trips have two boxed numbers indicating separate start and end points. For some hikes, the corresponding area map alone is complete enough and fully adequate for navigation; for others hikes, more detailed topographical or other maps are recommended. A legend for the area maps appears on page 19.

The following is an explanation of the small symbols and capsuled information appearing at the beginning of each trip description. If you are simply browsing through this book, these summaries alone can be used as a tool to eliminate from consideration hikes that are either too difficult, or perhaps too trivial, for your abilities or desires.

Symbols:

 Easy Terrain: roads, trails and easy cross-country hiking

 Moderate Terrain: cross-country boulder hopping and easy scrambling

 Difficult Terrain: nontechnical climbing required (**WARNING: THESE TRIPS SHOULD BE ATTEMPTED ONLY BY SUITABLY EQUIPPED, EXPERIENCED HIKERS ADEPT AT TRAVELING OVER STEEP OR ROCKY TERRAIN REQUIRING THE USE OF THE HANDS AS WELL AS THE FEET.**)

Only *one* of these three symbols appears for a given trip, indicating the general character of the terrain encountered. A trip almost entirely on roads and trails, but including a short section of boulder hopping or perhaps nontechnical climbing, for example, will be rated as easy terrain, and the difficulties will be duly noted in the text. As the symbols suggest, light footwear (running shoes) is appropriate for easy terrain, while sturdy hiking boots are recommended for more difficult terrain.

Nontechnical climbing includes everything up to and including Class 3 on the rock-climber's scale. While ropes and climbing hardware are not normally required, a hiker should have a good sense of balance, and enough experience to recognize dangerous moves and situations. The safety and stability of heavy hiking boots are especially recommended for this kind of trip. Hazards may include loose or slippery rocks and rattlesnakes (don't put your hands in places you can't see clearly).

 Bushwhacking: cross-country travel through dense brush. This symbol is included for trips requiring a substantial amount of off-trail "bushwhacking." Wear long pants and be especially alert for rattlesnakes.

Only one of these two symbols appears:

 Marked Trails/Obvious Routes

 Navigation by Map and Compass Required (**WARNING: THESE TRIPS SHOULD BE ATTEMPTED ONLY BY HIKERS SKILLED IN NAVIGATION TECHNIQUES.**)

Unambiguous cross-country routes—up a canyon, for example—*are* included in the first category. The hiker, of course, should never be without a map, even if there are marked trails or the route seems obvious.

 Point-to-Point Route

 Out-and-Back Route

 Loop Route

Only one of these symbols appears, reflecting the trip as described. There is some flexibility, of course, in the way in which a hiker can actually follow the trip.

 Suitable for Backpacking

Trips suitable for backpacking. Not all are: some trails are closed at night, and in some parks and jurisdictions overnight trail camping is prohibited or confined to areas not on the route.

Capsulized Summaries:

Distance: An estimate of total distance is given. Out-and-back trips include the sum of the distances of the out and back segments.

Total Elevation Gain/Loss: This is an estimate of the sum of all the vertical gain segments and the sum of all the vertical loss segments along the total length of the route (both ways for out-and-back trips).

Hiking Time: This figure is for the average hiker, and includes only the time spent in motion. It does not include time spent for rest stops, lunch, etc. Fast walkers can complete the routes in perhaps 30% less time, and slower hikers may take 50% longer. We assume the hiker is traveling with a light day pack. Some hikes in this book can take well over 12 hours, and so for the average hiker are more appropriate for overnight backpacking.

Optional/Recommended/Required Map(s): If no recommended or required map is given, then either the appropriate area map in this book or the optional map stated will suffice. Persons familiar with the terrain in a particular trip area may be able to do without a recommended map, as long as some other map is substituted. A required map is one that is essential to the successful navigation of a particular trip route. Most maps, whether optional, recommended or required, are U.S. Geological Survey 7.5-minute series topographic maps. These are the most complete, accurate, and up-to-date maps of the physical features of San Diego County. In some cases, the older 15-minute series maps may be substituted, but at a sacrifice in scale and detail. Even the most up-to-date topo maps (usually revised by aerial survey) omit some well-established trails and other features, so it is important to compare them with the area maps given in this book. For more information about maps, and a list of local sources, see Appendix 4.

Best Times: Because of the extreme heat, the longer desert trips in this book should generally be avoided during any period except the one recommended here. Trips elsewhere in San Diego County are usually safe enough at other than "Best" times, but simply less rewarding.

Difficulty: This overall rating takes into account the length of the trip and the nature of the terrain. The following are general definitions of the five categories:

*   **Easy.** Suitable for every member of the family.

**   **Moderate.** Suitable for all physically fit people.

***   **Moderately Strenuous.** Long length, substantial elevation gain, and/or difficult terrain. Suitable for experienced hikers only.

****   **Strenuous.** Full day's hike (or backpack) over long and often difficult route. Suitable only for experienced hikers in excellent physical condition. A few shorter trips over extremely difficult terrain are included in this category.

*****   **Very Strenuous.** Long and rugged route in extremely remote area. Usually requires at least two days. Suitable only for experienced hikers/climbers in top physical condition.

Two final notes:

In the trip descriptions, mileages along the highways (example: "mile 17.4") are keyed to the mile markers posted every half mile or every mile along San Diego County's state and county highways.

We have omitted addresses and telephone numbers of parks, preserves, and agencies mentioned in the body of this book. An up-to-date listing, however, appears in Appendix 4.

MAP LEGEND

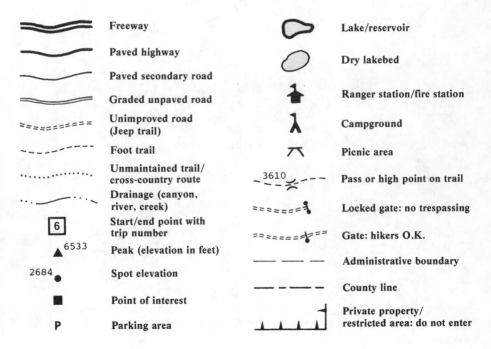

Freeway		Lake/reservoir	
Paved highway		Dry lakebed	
Paved secondary road		Ranger station/fire station	
Graded unpaved road		Campground	
Unimproved road (Jeep trail)		Picnic area	
Foot trail		Pass or high point on trail	
Unmaintained trail/ cross-country route		Locked gate: no trespassing	
Drainage (canyon, river, creek)		Gate: hikers O.K.	
Start/end point with trip number		Administrative boundary	
Peak (elevation in feet)		County line	
Spot elevation		Private property/ restricted area: do not enter	
Point of interest			
Parking area			

Blacks Beach

BEACHES AND BAYS

Area B-1: North County Coast

North County's almost unbroken line of beaches face the Pacific along a gentle arc about 20 miles long. Just behind this is a string of cities and towns. North to south, these are Oceanside, Carlsbad, Leucadia, Encinitas, Cardiff by the Sea, Solana Beach, and Del Mar. Compared to the more densely crowded coastal areas from La Jolla south, life is a bit slower in these communities. The locals take their beach-going and ocean-watching seriously. Some have chosen to live, at some peril, on the very brink of the cliffs overlooking the Pacific.

The popular term "North County" really refers to a middle segment of San Diego County's long coastal plain, not the northernmost part. From a strictly geographical point of view, the northernmost quarter actually lies in Camp Pendleton, a U.S. Marine Corps base. Public access to the coastline within Camp Pendleton is normally allowed only at San Onofre State Beach—a strip of bluff and beach leased by the state from the federal government (San Onofre is not covered in this book).

Many of the beaches along the North County Coast are included in state or county parks. Access to all is by way of the old coast highway (County Highway S-21) wherever it fronts the sand, and elsewhere by stairways down the bluffs. Where private property extends to the beach, public passage is allowed below the mean high tide line along the beach itself.

Unfortunately for beach-goers, hikers, and coastal residents alike, the North County coastline is subject to some of the most rapid erosion anywhere along the California coast.

There are several reasons for this. The supply of sand formerly brought to the coast by free-flowing streams is now partly cut off by dams. A jetty built to protect an artificial harbor north of Oceanside now retards the natural flow of beach sand southward along the coast. Also, powerful winter storms during the past several years have moved vast amounts of sand to offshore sandbars, and full replenishment by the gentle summer waves has not been accomplished. Because the beaches have shrunk in width, the bluffs behind many of the beaches are more often under attack during high tides and storms than before, and the bluffs themselves are composed of weak sandstones. A final factor is the intensive development of the blufftops as sites for view homes; this disturbs the normal drainage patterns and seems to be increasing the rate of retreat of the coastline.

Whether the destiny of the North County coastline is to become a series of broken cliffs and pocket beaches or a somewhat stable continuous strand of sand is not known. For the moment, at any rate, a hiker can still travel its length—at low tide—without donning a snorkel and fins.

Trip 1: South Carlsbad to Cardiff

Distance	5.5 miles
Total Elevation Gain/Loss	(Flat)
Hiking Time	3 hours
Optional Maps	USGS 7.5-min *Encinitas;* street map
Best Times	All year
Difficulty	**

The finest beaches, some of the nicest surf, and the most instructive vistas along the North County coastline are seen on this beach walk. Your visit should coincide with low tide—or at least an ebb tide. During high tide, passage is restricted in at least two places by the wash of the breakers.

If you plan to walk north to south, leave one car in the parking area at Cardiff State Beach (opposite San Elijo Lagoon), and take the other to the south end of South Carlsbad State Beach (0.1 mile north of La Costa Avenue), where roadside parking is available.

Start by walking south along the sandy or cobbled shore. Steep bluffs rise on the left. The bulk of these bluffs is a 50-million-year-old sandstone derived from lagoon and sandbar deposits. As the sandstone erodes away, cobbles embedded in it are released and deposited at the tide line by wave action. Most of the cobbles on this beach are metavolcanic rocks from distant sources, but some are granitic rocks apparently transported from the local Peninsular Ranges. All show the effects of prolonged tumbling and polishing.

In the next two miles you'll see many graphic illustrations of the fragility of the coastal cliffs. In winter, storm waves crash directly against the base of the cliffs, and tug at the lower underpinnings of the many private stairways that zigzag down to the beach. Some of these stairways now have elaborate counterbalance mechanisms to raise and lower them to beach level. The cliffs are fluted with both old and fairly recent landslides, including one great semicircular feature perhaps 40 years old, now almost completely revegetated.

Blufftop property owners have used every strategy imaginable to hold and stabilize the cliff faces, including the installation of elaborate retaining walls and terraces, and the use of flexible pipes to channel runoff. Some have coated the cliff faces with gunite or other impervious materials, and others have tried to plant and maintain erosion-resistant vegetation on the tops and faces of the bluffs. Overwatering is a constant problem: excess irrigation water constantly per-

North County Coast

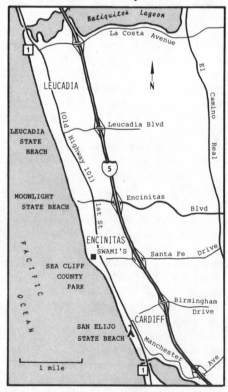

colates into the porous sandstone, and oozes from the cliffs at beach level, further weakening them.

At 2.8 miles from the starting point, the cliffs draw back and the sand widens. This is Moonlight State Beach, a popular sunbathing beach complete with the usual amenities (water, restrooms and a snack bar).

As you continue south, the strip of sand narrows again and you pass the "tightest" spot along this hike, an area just below the ornate Self Realization Fellowship, colloquially known as "Swami's." During a winter storm in 1941, a section of cliff collapsed here, taking with it one of the temples above. The Self Realization Fellow-

ship, at its own expense, installed a barrier of riprap (large chunks of irregularly shaped, resistant rock) at the shoreline to forestall further erosion. The ocean bottom off Swami's gives rise to long combers that are renowned among local surfers.

South of Swami's the strip of sand widens. This is Sea Cliff County Park, accessible from the blufftop by a long, wooden stairway. The beach remains fairly wide as you continue into San Elijo State Beach, with its popular campground on low bluffs above. When these bluffs dwindle to nothing and you cross the inlet to San Elijo Lagoon, the parking area for Cardiff State Beach lies just beyond.

Area B-2: Torrey Pines/La Jolla

Here is the San Diego coastline at its unspoiled best, with clean beaches, dramatic cliffs, and an unlikely forest of rare trees. Walking the wild stretch of beach from Del Mar to La Jolla Shores is more akin to adventuring than simply beachcombing. Exploring the caves at La Jolla Cove or looking out from the bluff tops at Torrey Pines State Reserve is a sure way to forget that just inland lies a part of the eighth largest city in America.

The weather, of course, is generally good the year round, but try to avoid this area at times when warmer weather means more

tourists—summer afternoons especially. Avoid by all means the traffic gridlock during weekday afternoon rush hour in the area between La Jolla and La Jolla Shores. If it's solitude you're looking for, you'll find it merely by venturing out at unconventional times or during the rare spells of bad weather.

Torrey Pines Road, La Jolla Shores Drive, and North Torrey Pines Road are the major streets closest to the coast; access to the beaches and coastline is frequent along these, except where cliffs intervene.

Trip 1: La Jolla Shores to Torrey Pines Beach

Distance	5 miles
Total Elevation Gain/Loss	(Flat)
Hiking Time	2½ hours
Optional Maps	USGS 7.5-min *La Jolla, Del Mar;* or street map
Best Times	All year
Difficulty	**

There are only a few places along the southern California coastline where a person can hike for miles in a single direction and not catch sight of a highway, railroad tracks, powerlines, houses, or other signs of civilization. The Torrey Pines beaches are one such place. Here, for a space of about three miles, sharp cliffs front the shoreline, and cut off the sights and sounds of the world beyond.

Plan to do this beach walk at low tide. High tides—especially in winter—could force you to walk on cobbles at the base of the cliffs or oblige you to wade in the surf. Beach sand is often carried away by the scouring action of the winter waves, but is usually replenished by currents as summer approaches.

A good place to begin this walk is La Jolla Shores Beach. Park near the grassy area called Kellogg Park. (Leave another car at the entrance to Torrey Pines State Reserve if you do this trip one-way. A fee is assessed for parking at the Reserve parking area, but free parking—if you can get it—is available nearby along the shoulder of North Torrey Pines Road.)

From Kellogg Park, head north under Scripps Pier and continue to the point where the sand ends and the rocks begin. At low tide there are interesting tide pools to explore here. These are part of an underwater preserve that extends from La Jolla to Del Mar. All forms of marine life here are protected by law. This rocky area is normally one of only two or three places along the route where shoes are desirable, if not actually needed. Otherwise, you can just go barefoot on the fine sand.

Beyond the tide pools, you may notice that some beach-goers have doffed more than just shoes. You're now on Torrey Pines City Beach, also known as Black's Beach, San Diego's unofficial nude-bathing spot. The city rescinded a "clothing optional" policy for this beach in the late 70s, but old traditions die hard.

At about 1.5 miles from Kellogg Park, a service road comes down through a break in the bluffs; the top end connects with La Jolla Farms Road, where streetside parking is available. This road is the only safe way to climb out to the top of the cliffs in the midportion of this hike. North of here, two precipitous trails ascend to the Glider Port area, but these are dangerous even to experienced climbers—several fatalities have occurred in recent years. The unstable cliffs along this stretch have suffered some big landslides recently, and some areas may be marked off as closed zones.

Sailplanes once launched from the Glider Port, but they've been replaced by hang gliders. This is one of the best areas in the state for that sport, and it's a thrilling diversion to watch these kites plying the updrafts along the cliffs.

Let's not forget the thrill of jumping in the surf, too. Water temperatures are often up into the low 70s in late summer. Remember, though, that rip currents are common here, and usually you swim at your own risk. Lifeguards patrol some areas of the beach during busy periods.

At about four miles from your starting point, you'll come to Flat Rock. If you don't mind wading, you can pass between this rock and the steep sandstone fin coming down from the bluffs of Torrey Pines State Reserve. Otherwise, follow the narrow trail cut into the cliff above the water's edge. Beach Trail goes up the next gully to the right and connects with several blufftop trails in the reserve.

In the fifth and last mile, the narrow beach is squeezed between sculpted sedimentary cliffs on one side and crashing surf on the other. These are the tallest cliffs in western San Diego County. A close look at the faces reveals a slice of geologic history: the greenish siltstone on the bottom, called the Del Mar Formation, is older than the buff or rust-colored Torrey Sandstone above it. Higher still is a thin cap of reddish sandstone, not easily seen from the beach—the Linda Vista Formation.

Finally, the beach widens, the cliffs fall back and diminish in height, and you arrive at the entrance to Torrey Pines State Reserve.

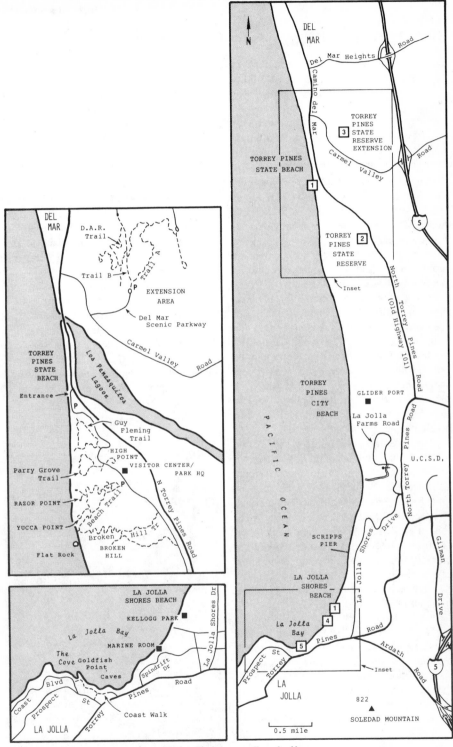

Torrey Pines/LaJolla

Trip 2: Torrey Pines State Reserve Trails

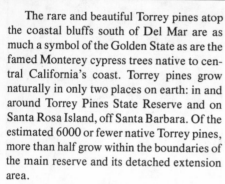

Distance	0.5- to 1-mile loops
Recommended Map	Torrey Pines State Reserve trail map
	(available at the office/museum)
Optional Map	USGS 7.5-min *Del Mar*
Best Times	All year
Difficulty	* to **

The rare and beautiful Torrey pines atop the coastal bluffs south of Del Mar are as much a symbol of the Golden State as are the famed Monterey cypress trees native to central California's coast. Torrey pines grow naturally in only two places on earth: in and around Torrey Pines State Reserve and on Santa Rosa Island, off Santa Barbara. Of the estimated 6000 or fewer native Torrey pines, more than half grow within the boundaries of the main reserve and its detached extension area.

Torrey Pines State Reserve would be botanically noteworthy even without its famous pines; within its roughly 1000 acres are 331 identified species of plants. Vegetation types represented here include sage scrub, chaparral, and salt marsh.

If you're interested in identifying plants and wildflowers typical of the coastal region, and many others common to inland regions, the reserve is simply the best single place to go in San Diego County. Excellent interpretive facilities at the reserve's museum make this an easy task. Besides the exhibits, you can browse through several notebooks full of captioned photographs of common and rare plants within the reserve. You can also visit the native plant gardens surrounding the museum building and at the head of Parry Grove Trail.

If you visit the reserve several times during February through June, you'll be able to follow the succession of flowering as the spring season progresses; be sure to pick up the current monthly wildflower map if you're here at this time.

A good network of trails over the eroded bluffs will take you nearly everywhere in the reserve, except into most canyon bottoms.

It's important that you stick to these trails and eschew shortcuts and cross-country travel. The thin soils are easily eroded without the protection of healthy vegetation. As you'll plainly see, there are already enough occurrences of erosion here, both natural and man-made.

The entrance to the reserve is on North Torrey Pines Road (also known as old Highway 101, the former coast highway), at the base of the long grade up to Torrey Pines Mesa. Past the entrance, a paved road goes up to a parking area adjacent to the reserve office and museum. From here, you can walk to the beginning of any of the trails in 10

Torrey Pines and Torrey sandstone

minutes or less. If this parking area is full, you'll have to leave your car in the lower parking lot down near the entrance, or along the highway shoulder fronting Torrey Pines State Beach. Still another possibility is to park along the frontage road next to Torrey Pines Golf Course and walk into the reserve from the south.

The reserve has a carrying capacity of about 400 people. When this level is reached, as on occasional weekend afternoons, further entry may be restricted.

After a stop at the museum for a bit of educational browsing, you might first explore nearby High Point, where your gaze encompasses the intriguing but currently off-limits section of the reserve known as East Grove. East Grove experienced a wildfire in 1972, and young Torrey pines are now establishing a foothold on the bluffs and canyons below.

Next you might head south on the concrete roadbed of the "old" old coast highway (closed to traffic) and pick up the Broken Hill Trail. The two east branches of this trail wind through thick chaparral and connect with a spur trail leading to Broken Hill Overlook. You'll be able to step out (very carefully) onto a precipitous fin of sandstone and peer over to see what, except for a few Torrey pine trees here and there, looks like desert badlands. A third (west) branch of the Broken Hill Trail winds down a slope festooned with wildflowers and connects with the Beach Trail at a point just above the latter's cliff-hugging descent to the beach.

The heavily used Beach Trail originates at the parking lot near the museum and intersects with trails to Yucca Point and Razor Point. Fenced viewpoints along both of these trails offer views straight down to the sandy beach and surf.

You've saved some of the best for last: the Parry Grove and Guy Fleming loop trails. Here, on the headlands standing against the prevailing westerly winds, the Torrey pines grow largest and thickest. Perhaps this dense cluster of trees is here because of the ability of the cliff topography to wring out moisture-laden air from incoming winter storms. Or maybe it's due to fog droplets collecting on the long needles of the Torrey pine trees— a convincing theory indeed, if you've ever strolled beneath these gnarled giants in a soupy morning fog without your umbrella.

The Guy Fleming Trail is mostly flat, while the Parry Grove Trail starts with a steep descent on stairsteps. In spring the sunny slopes along the Guy Fleming Trail come alive with phantasmagoric wildflower displays; in a good breeze as many as 20 different shades of color dynamically intermix with the colors of earth, sea and sky.

The Torrey Pines trails can be enjoyed the year round, but they're open only during daylight hours. Ranger-led walks are featured on weekends. You can't picnic in the reserve, but after you do your hiking, you can use the tables or the beach down near the entrance. Do take water along on the trails if it's a hot day. Also bring binoculars: the soaring ravens and the red-tailed and sparrow hawks are interesting to watch, as are hang-gliding humans overhead.

Trip 3: Torrey Pines Extension Trails

Distance	0.5- to 1-mile out-and-back trails
Optional Map	USGS 7.5-min *Del Mar*
Best Times	All year
Difficulty	*

Thanks to public donations for land acquisition, an area of natural bluffs and

Torrey pine groves just south and east of Del Mar is now only surrounded—not overwhelmed—by new housing developments. This is the Torrey Pines State Reserve Extension.

The extension area is farther removed from the ocean than the main reserve, but in many respects is equally interesting. Gnarled and twisted Torrey pines cling to stark, eroded sandstone walls here as they do along the Guy Fleming and Parry Grove trails. But here you can find a peacefulness often lacking over there.

The best place to begin a hike in this area is the terminus of Del Mar Scenic Parkway. This is off Carmel Valley Road, 1.1 miles west of Interstate 5, and 0.4 mile east of Camino del Mar. Street parking is abundant.

Nature trail "A" winds up through a sage-filled basin dotted with a few Torrey pines, and climbs to the top of a ridge capped with reddish rock. This cap is part of the familiar Linda Vista Formation, well represented on many of the mesas of San Diego. More trails penetrate the area east of Trail "A."

Trail "B" goes up a draw toward Del Mar Heights, but also gives access to the D.A.R. (Daughters of the American Revolution) Trail on a linear ridge, made of Torrey Sandstone, to the west. From the Torrey-pine-shaded south prow of this ridge, you can look across Penasquitos Marsh to the bluffs of the main reserve, and out to the ocean. West of this ridge a spur trail descends into an intimate little hollow with picturesque sandstone exposures and twisted Torrey pines.

Little use means less maintenance, so the trails in the extension area tend to be poorly marked and hard to follow. Nature buffs won't mind though.

Trip 4: La Jolla Caves

Distance	1 mile round trip
Total Elevation Gain/Loss	(Flat)
Hiking Time	50 minutes (round trip)
Optional Map	USGS 7.5-min *La Jolla;* or street map
Best Times	Extreme low tides; any time of year
Difficulty	**

South of La Jolla Shores Beach, the wide strip of sand is replaced by cobbles and wave-washed cliffs. Offshore of this point, a major submarine canyon, La Jolla Canyon, swallows the sand that normally would migrate slowly southward along the coastline. This is the reason why sandy beaches are the exception rather than the rule from La Jolla all the way to Pacific Beach.

La Jolla itself lies on a shelf along the base of Soledad Mountain, an uplifted block of fairly resistant sandstone. The precipitous north flank of this shelf faces the usually calm and deep waters of La Jolla Bay. Here, wave action from infrequent storms has gouged out a series of sea grottos, known as the La Jolla Caves.

The westernmost cave, at Goldfish Point, is well-known among tourists and natives

LaJolla Caves

alike; it can be reached from above by a long stairway that begins inside the La Jolla Cave Curio Shop and passes through a man-made tunnel. The half-dozen or so other grottos in the series are usually accessible only by water. Extreme low tides (minus 1.5 feet or less), however, can bring some of these within easy reach of hikers.

Check tide tables for the most favorable low tides, and begin your hike about 30 minutes before predicted low. Start from the south end of La Jolla Shores Beach, or from the public beach access alongside the Marine Room restaurant on Spindrift Drive.

Work your way south over the cliff-hugging cobbles, or across the newly exposed tide pools, taking care not to step on the slippery, green rocks. The tide-pool areas in particular show much evidence of "biological erosion"—that is, the breakdown of the structure of the rock itself by the chemical secretions of urchins, barnacles and other sea creatures. As you walk along, you'll hear rasping noises as crabs, startled by your approach, retreat hastily into crevices. Occasionally you can find an octopus in one of the deeper tide pools.

The biggest grotto is enormous—about 50 feet high—at its entrance, but it pinches in toward the rear. The sandstone walls are stained with a rainbow of colors: red and orange from iron oxide, greens and grays from plant life, and purple from iodine in kelp. In the back of the cave is a low passage leading to an adjacent grotto. Enjoy, but don't forget about the incoming tide!

Brown pelicans at LaJolla Bay

Trip 5: La Jolla Coast Walk

Distance	0.5 mile round trip (to Goldfish Point)
Total Elevation Gain/Loss	100'/100'
Hiking Time	20 minutes (round trip)
Optional Map	USGS 7.5-min *La Jolla;* or street map
Best Times	All year
Difficulty	*

A stunning perspective of La Jolla Bay and the sparkling La Jolla Shores coastline is afforded on this short walk along the cliff-tops. You'll be walking directly above the La Jolla Caves, on or near the very brink of a 100-foot drop to the bay's calm surface.

An interesting if obscure place to begin is the small parking area (room for two cars only) at the east end of Coast Walk. This is reached by a short spur street, signed COAST WALK, that intersects Torrey Pines Road at a point 200 yards east of the traffic signal at Prospect Place.

From the tiny parking area, a cliff-hugging dirt path guides you just below the back yards of several palatial houses. A footbridge and steps span a ravine plunging directly to the blue-green waters below. Just beyond that ravine, a short spur path goes up some steps to the intersection of Prospect Place and Park Row. Keep straight. In about 200 yards you arrive at a grove of graceful Torrey pines on Goldfish Point. Although

these trees grow naturally just up the coast at Torrey Pines State Reserve, they were planted here.

The path ends just beyond the pine grove, next to the La Jolla Cave Curio Shop. Many walkers, of course, like to continue by following the paved sidewalk past the pocket beach of La Jolla Cove and around the periphery of Scripps Park. Goldfish Point itself is a good place to sit and relax. You can watch the swimmers, snorkelers and divers below as they float or glide through the often glassy water. If you climb down to the edge of the water, you can look across the face of the cliffs to the east and make out the openings to several of the caves.

Evening strolls along Coast Walk are spectacular, especially during rare periods when the "red tide" (plankton) blooms and produces bioluminescence in the churning water below. Watch your step, though, night or day. Most of the cliff edges are not protected by fencing.

Area B-3: Cabrillo National Monument

The long, south-pointing peninsula of Point Loma and the spectacular curving shoreline of San Diego Bay are two of the principal elements responsible for San Diego's legendary beauty. The peninsula itself is an elongated block of sandstone uplifted about 400 feet above sea level by fault action. It serves as a natural breakwater for the once-shallow (now dredged) bay behind it. South and east of the peninsula, sand has migrated onshore to form the long bar called the Silver Strand. North Island, at the north tip of this natural sandbar, and nearby Harbor and Shelter islands, are fill areas created in the dredging process.

Most of the south half of the Point Loma peninsula is reserved for military uses. Perched on its end, centered on the highest promontory, is one of America's smallest (144 acres) national monuments—Cabrillo. Because of its location adjacent to the city of San Diego, Cabrillo is now ranked as the busiest national monument in the country.

Whether you're a tourist or not, the view alone is worth the almost obligatory visit here. On the clearest winter days, you can see all the way to San Clemente Island, 70 miles offshore, and to the snow-capped summits of the San Bernardino Mountains, 100 miles north. Other attractions are the

whale-watching overlook, the old and new lighthouses, the Visitor Center with its panoramic vista of the bay, and the cityscape, and a tidepool area located on the west (Pacific) shore. The one "trail" in the monument—the Bayside Trail—is described below.

Because the access road into the monument passes through a military reservation, visiting time is limited to the daylight hours, generally after 9 a.m. See Appendix 4 for more information.

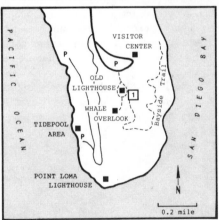

Cabrillo National Monument

Point Loma tidepools

Trip 1: Bayside Trail

	Distance	2.0 miles (round trip)
	Total Elevation Gain/Loss	320'/320'
	Hiking Time	70 minutes (round trip)
	Optional Map	USGS 7.5-min *Point Loma*
	Best Times	All year
	Difficulty	*

Coastal sage scrub and chaparral vegetation are highlighted along this trail, but this is not what makes it worth taking. It is worth taking for the wonderful, unobstructed views of San Diego Bay, the Silver Strand, the skyline of San Diego, and more. You'll double your pleasure if you walk this trail on a crystal-clear day, typical of the period December through March.

The trail begins just east of the old lighthouse, not far from the Visitor Center. The self-guiding leaflet available here describes the flora, the geology, and some of the military uses of the area. The trail is simply an old asphalt road that descends gradually in a rough semicircular arc to a point about 300 feet below and east of the Visitor Center lookouts.

Point Loma's bay slope is honeycombed with the ruins of a World War II defense system of mortars, observation bunkers,

generators and searchlights. You will see some of these remains along the trail. At the point where the trail ends (or rather runs into off-limits Navy property), you'll still be about 90 feet above the water surface. This is a good place to observe the sailboats and ships maneuvering in and out of the bay's entrance, which is protected on the far side by Zuniga jetty. There are also aerial acrobatics to watch, courtesy of gulls, terns, and pelicans—and even aircraft performing takeoffs and landings at the North Island Naval Air Station across the bay.

Return to the lighthouse the same way you came. Tempting as they may be, don't take shortcuts—the vegetation is easily trampled and the soil eroded by one footprint too many. Besides, off-trail exploration is strictly forbidden within the Monument.

Bayside trail

Area B-4: The Border Coast

Four square miles of marshes, tidal creeks, and chaparral-covered hillsides in and around the Tijuana River Estuary now enjoy federal protection as the Tijuana River National Estuarine Sanctuary. Included within this area is Border Field State Park, fronting the international border, and large tracts of land north and east adjacent to the communities of Imperial Beach and San Ysidro.

During the past several years, periodic sewage overflows from Tijuana, Mexico, have coursed through the Tijuana River and polluted parts of the estuary and beaches. Governments on both sides of the border are investigating solutions to this problem, which grows more serious every year as Tijuana's

population continues to explode. Hopefully, binational efforts will result in a manageable situation within a few years. In the meantime, the state park and the estuarine sanctuary are expected to remain open to the public.

Despite the bad publicity concerning the sewage problems, the Tijuana River Estuary remains one of southern California's most important wildlife habitats. A good way to become familiar with the ecosystem here is to attend one of the free guided walks cosponsored by California State Parks Department and the Southwest Wetlands Interpretive Association (see Appendix 3 for more information).

Trip 1: Border Field State Park

Distance	1 to 2 miles
Optional Map	USGS 7.5-min *Imperial Beach*
Best Times	All year
Difficulty	*

An old stone monument, placed here in 1851, commemorates the first point at which the boundary of the United States and Mexico was staked, following the 1848 Treaty of Guadalupe Hidalgo. The monument marks the extreme southwest corner of the conterminous United States, a place as significant from the standpoint of geographical trivia as Cape Flattery, Washington; Key Largo, Florida; and Madawaska, Maine.

South of the monument—and the steel-mesh fence—the goblet-shaped Bullring-by-the-Sea reaches skyward, and homes and businesses of Tijuana's "Playas" neighborhoods stretch for miles along the coast.

North of the monument, the landscape is mostly natural and unspoiled—except for the aforementioned occasional sewage flows out of Mexico. A wide strip of sand stretches about one mile to the mouth of the Tijuana River. Low dunes separate the beach from an interior salt marsh. Here, tidal creeks flow through thick mats of cordgrass, sea lavender, and pickleweed. In winter, these wetlands serve as an important source of food for many kinds of migratory birds. In summer, much of the marsh area turns bone dry, and the mud surface fragments into thousands of irregularly shaped polygons.

In the early 1970s, ownership of this area, which was used in the early 50s for

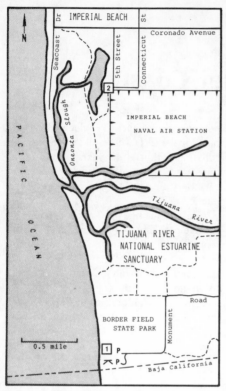

The Border Coast

protect nesting birds.) Roughly paralleling the border fence is a trail to another boundary monument and some World War II-era bunkers.

To reach the park, take the Coronado Avenue/Hollister Street offramp from southbound Interstate 5. Continue south on Hollister for two miles to Monument Road, then go two miles west to the entrance. Hours are 8:30 a.m. to sunset, seven days a week.

Egret, Tijuana River Estuary

airborne gunnery practice, was transferred from the federal government to the state. It was then opened to the public as Border Field State Park.

The lowest section of the border fence has been destroyed by the surf, allowing somewhat free movement along the beach between the two countries. On any given day, in fact, you're likely to see more Tijuana residents and Mexican tourists in the park than Americans. This free movement seems to be tolerated by the Border Patrol so long as these visitors don't move too far north.

The picnic and parking area next to the monument sits on a low coastal terrace and offers a superb view of the Coronado Islands, Point Loma, and the downtown San Diego skyline, which is bisected by the Coronado Bridge. Below, a network of informal horse and hiking trails radiates out into the marshlands and along the beach to the north. (Certain areas of beach may be closed to

Trip 2: Tijuana River Estuary

Distance	1 to 2 miles
Optional Map	USGS 7.5-min *Imperial Beach*
Best Times	All year
Difficulty	*

It may come as quite a surprise to some, but the natural wetlands in and around the Tijuana River Estuary just south of Imperial Beach are probably the county's richest habitat for birds. There is, of course, the problem of sewage flows into the river upstream; but the estuary, especially the north arms which are accessible from Imperial Beach, is flushed daily by tidal flows, and is seldom seriously contaminated. Birds congregate by the thousands here on a typical day. Over 240 bird species have been observed to date. You should see at least half these common ones: willet, marbled godwit, marsh hawk, redwing blackbird, brown pelican, California gull, American avocet, black-necked stilt, great blue heron, snowy egret, western sandpiper, killdeer, western meadowlark, American kestrel, pintail, common teal, and various ducks. Occasionally an osprey, a golden eagle, or a rare light-footed clapper rail will make an appearance.

Since the salt marsh surrounding the tidal creeks of the estuary receives both fresh water (from river flows and local runoff) and salt water (from tidal flows), plant life exists in tenuous balance. Plants must be able to survive in an environment that ranges from wet to dry, and from fresh to saline.

As you walk from higher elevations (a few feet above sea level), where nonnative grasses, cattails, and typical shrubs native to the coastal uplands flourish, toward lower areas along the tidal creeks, you'll notice a succession of plants tending toward greater salt tolerance: pickleweed, sea blite, sea lavender, and finally cordgrass. At the lowest levels, the soft sediment of the mudflats supports algal films, and houses worms, crabs, snails, and other small creatures which are food for the shorebirds.

To reach the estuary, take the Hollister Street/Coronado Avenue exit from Interstate 5. Drive 2.3 miles west on Coronado Avenue (this changes to Imperial Beach Boulevard) to 5th Street; then go 0.5 mile south on 5th to its terminus. Park along the street and walk west and south around the fence surrounding the naval air station. The area ahead is part of the national estuarine sanctuary. You can follow an old roadway toward the main Tijuana River channel or pick your way along the banks of one of the tidal creeks. Watch out for soft mud (wear an old pair of shoes), and take care to trample as little vegetation as possible.

Avocets, Tijuana River Estuary

Oak woodland along San Luis Rey River

THE COASTAL STRIP

Area C-1: Wilderness Gardens County Park

Wilderness Gardens Preserve is a new addition to the San Diego County Parks system. The park isn't a true wilderness, but rather the grounds of an old ranch—once the showplace of Manchester Boddy, owner of a Los Angeles newspaper and developer of the renowned Descanso Gardens in Pasadena—which have largely reverted back to nature. Down the middle of the park runs a wide strip of oak-woodland habitat fronting on the San Luis Rey River. Intermixed with the oaks and sycamores are remnants of exotic plants such as silver-dollar eucalyptus, camellias, roses, shiny-leaved holly, bottlebrush, pyracantha, and oleander. Surrounding hillsides are clothed with typical native chaparral and sage-scrub vegetation.

In addition to day hiking and exploring, the park offers overnight camping at several pleasant walk-in sites on the bank of the river. Hand carts are available to haul camping equipment from the parking area to the camping area. On many weekends, interpretive walks and nature-study classes are offered.

Wilderness Gardens is located 10 miles east of Interstate 15 on State Highway 76. The entrance is marked by an obscure sign (if you cross the bridge over Agua Tibia Creek, you've gone a bit too far east on the highway). The park may be closed during certain days or weeks in summer, so write to Wilderness Gardens or call County Parks (see Appendix 4) to check.

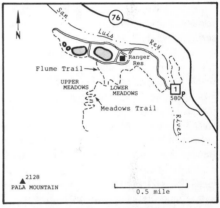

Wilderness Gardens

Trip 1: Wilderness Gardens Trails

	Distance	1 to 4 miles round trip
	Optional Map	USGS 7.5-min *Pala*
	Best times	November through May
	Difficulty	* to **

There are at least three distinct hikes you can make in Wilderness Gardens once you arrive at the parking area. Northwest of the parking area, a short trail loops around the sunny north bank of the San Luis Rey River, passing through a sparse cover of drought-resistant, desertlike vegetation.

By following the road toward the ranger residence and campground, you'll reach a series of five shallow ponds on the south bank of the river. These are fed partly by rainwater and partly by water pumped up from the water table, which lies just below the ground surface. The larger ponds are fringed by cattails and serve as a mecca for wildlife—over 140 species of birds have been seen here and in the surrounding area. Beyond the ponds is a loop road/trail through a canopy of oaks festooned with wild grape vines. Round trip to and from the parking lot and around the loop is about 2 miles.

The third hike is the Meadows Trail, a meandering path leading up the slope of Pala Mountain past two hillside meadows. After crossing the San Luis Rey River, bear left on the Meadows Trail. This follows a boulder-strewn former channel of the river for a while, then climbs a brush- and tree-covered slope overlooking a cluster of old buildings. Down below are the ranger's residence, an old barn remodeled as a conference center, a former chicken coop, and the remains of San Diego County's first grist mill, built in the 1880s. Sections of the trail follow the course of a flume to the old mill.

A little higher, you'll pass the lower meadow, a soft carpet of green dotted with wildflowers in late winter and early spring. After curving around the usually dry bed of an old reservoir, the trail dips and connects with a short trail to the ponds below. Bear left

and continue climbing to the upper meadow, smaller than the first. Skirting this meadow, you'll pick up the switchbacks of an old road, now reverted to a narrow trail. Sugar bush, toyon, mountain mahogany, ceanothus, chamise, manzanita, and buckwheat crowd close on both sides.

After about a mile of steady ascent on these switchbacks, the old roadbed begins to veer left and descend. You've now come about 2 miles. Consider this the end of the line unless, first, you've consulted with the ranger and obtained his permission to go on to the top of Pala Mountain, and second, you still have the inclination to tackle an arduous climb.

From this point, a path cleared in the thick brush continues for about one mile (1000' gain) and reaches the narrow summit ridge of Pala Mountain. Indian petroglyphs found on the crest are considered unusual, as they are quite west of other petroglyph sites.

Dudleya in Wilderness Gardens

Area C-2: Poway/Woodson Mountain

Much of the area east and northeast of Poway, extending to the outskirts of Ramona, has been earmarked as permanent open space. This includes Woodson Mountain, one of the county's most picturesque promontories, and a swath of land to the south of it.

The upper and middle slopes of Woodson Mountain were declared open space by the City of San Diego in 1978. In the area to the south, an administrative transfer of public domain land from the BLM to the City of Poway is making it possible for that city to initiate construction of a series of hiking and horse trails that will stretch from Lake Poway to Iron Mountain. This will eventually tie into a more intricate network of foot and horse paths being developed throughout the semirural neighborhoods of Poway.

Two of the major links of the Poway trail system are already in place: a nature trail encircling Lake Poway, and the Mount Woodson Trail from Lake Poway to High-

way 67. Both can be reached from the entrance to Lake Poway.

You can get to Lake Poway from Interstate 15 by taking the Rancho Bernardo Road exit: go east on Rancho Bernardo Road (and continue on its extension, Espola Road) four miles to the lake entrance. A nice complement of recreational facilities has been developed along the shoreline of the lake to serve the needs of the local residents (non-Poway-residents simply pay a $1 parking fee to get in). Visitors can picnic; play horseshoes, volleyball, or softball; rent boats to fish or cruise about on the 60-acre surface of the reservoir; camp at a primitive campground accessible only by foot or horseback; and, of course, hike or ride along the trails. The lake is open sunrise to sunset Wed.–Sun.

The only approach to the summit of Woodson Mountain is by way of an access road that begins along Highway 67. As yet, there is no trail connection between this road and the Poway trail system.

Poway/Woodson Mountain

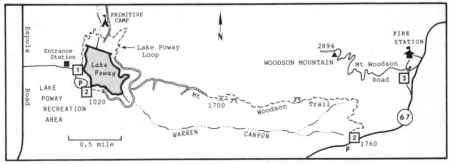

Trip 1: Lake Poway Loop

Distance	2.5 miles
Total Elevation Gain/Loss	400'/400'
Hiking Time	1½ hours
Optional Map	USGS 7.5-min *Escondido*
Best Times	All year
Difficulty	**

This loop trail around Lake Poway serves two purposes. It is an excellent exercise trail for runners and walkers, with a good mixture of flats, gentle hills, and a few fairly steep switchbacks. It is also an interpretive trail, with a leaflet (available at the lake entrance) keyed to numbered posts along way. In the course of the hike, you'll pass through or very near four distinct plant communities: sage scrub, chaparral, oak woodland, and riparian woodland.

Pick up the trail just beyond the lake entrance on the left (north) side of the developed area. The trail follows the west shore-line to a point beyond the dam, then drops well below the dirt-fill base of the dam to cross the creek. When you reach the dirt road below the dam, you can make a short side trip, if you wish, to visit the primitive campground. This is used mostly by horsemen, but backpackers are welcome too. Tables at vacant sites can be used for picnicking.

The loop trail resumes on the east side of the dirt road. Climbing via a long switchback, you gain the slope well above the lake and continue winding around the various coves of the lake until you reach the edge of the developed area.

Trip 2: Mount Woodson Trail

Distance	4.5 miles
Total Elevation Gain/Loss	1600'/850'
Hiking Time	3 hours
Recommended Map	Mount Woodson Trail topographic map (available at lake entrance)
Best Times	October through June
Difficulty	***

The Mount Woodson Trail starts at Lake Poway, traverses the rugged south slopes of Woodson Mountain, and ends on the shoulder of Highway 67. Hand tools and human labor alone were used to forge the eastern part of this trail. Huge boulders and a massive tangle of chaparral presented constant route-finding and construction difficulties. As a consequence, the pathway has turned out somewhat like a rabbit run through the brush. There are sudden turns, steep up and down stretches, and, in some places, a thick canopy of ground-hugging vegetation which blots out all views. It's a real adventure to walk this trail—but only if the following caveats are observed:

Pick a cool day. (My first experience on the trail coincided with a September sizzler, with air temperatures on the sunward slopes as high as 112°!) Allow plenty of hiking time, as suggested above, to negotiate the seemingly endless series of ups and downs. Although you'll be on trail tread all the way, wear shoes with studded or lug soles to ensure good traction.

One option is to start at Lake Poway and

hike up to (and back from) one of the two trailside rest areas. Each has a single picnic table set under the spreading limbs of an ancient oak, and each features a view of the boulder-strewn slopes of Woodson Mountain.

Another option is to be dropped off along Highway 67 and hike the trail one-way west toward Lake Poway. A third option, one-way west to east, is described here:

Begin at the parking and picnic area on the southwest edge of Lake Poway. For the first two miles, you'll be on well-graded dirt roads. After skirting the south shore of the lake for about 0.5 mile, the road dips to cross Warren Canyon and then rises to a junction. Take the road to the right (MT. WOODSON TRAIL) and climb east through a dense cover of chaparral. The white-flowering ceanothus, occurring here in almost continuous stands, comes into full bloom around March.

Pass two more road junctions (go left both times, trending east) and pass over a

summit. The road narrows to a footpath, drops slightly through sage-scrub vegetation, and climbs again. After passing over a second summit, with a view of Woodson Mountain, you begin a rollercoasterlike descent through brush and around huge boulders. For roughly two miles you travel east along the flank of Woodson Mountain; then you turn abruptly south. A final steep pitch takes you up to Highway 67. Wooden mileposts at half-mile intervals are some help in gauging your progress along the trail, but they seem to be somewhat inaccurately positioned. Trail's end is roughly mile 5 as marked by the mileposts.

There's no parking space as yet at the east end of the trail, but you can walk 100 yards southwest on the narrow shoulder of busy Highway 67 to reach a small turnout at Rock Haven Spring (mile 16.9). One hopes that future road widening will improve this somewhat dangerous situation.

Trip 3: Woodson Mountain

Distance	3.2 miles round trip
Total Elevation Gain/Loss	1200'/1200'
Hiking Time	2 hours round trip
Optional Map	USGS 7.5-min *San Pasqual*
Best Times	October through June
Difficulty	**

Indians called it "Mountain of Moonlit Rocks," an appropriate name for a landmark visible, even at night, over great distances. Early white settlers dubbed it "Cobbleback Peak," a name utterly descriptive of its rugged, boulder-strewn slopes. For the past 90 years, however, it has appeared on maps simply as "Woodson Mountain," in honor of a Dr. Woodson who homesteaded some property nearby well over a century ago.

The light-colored bedrock of Woodson Mountain and some of its neighboring peaks is a type local geologists call "Woodson Mountain granodiorite." When exposed at

the surface, it weathers into huge spherical or ellipsoidal boulders with smooth, almost polished surfaces. The largest boulders have a tendency to cleave apart along remarkably flat planes, forming "chimneys" from several inches to several feet wide. Sometimes, one half of a split boulder will roll away, leaving a vertical and almost seamless face behind. It's no wonder that local rock climbers consider Woodson Mountain (or "Mt. Woodson," as it is often called) to be the best place in the county for bouldering practice.

The mountain's upper and middle slopes are publicly owned open space managed by the City of San Diego. This open space surrounds a 15-acre parcel on the summit ridge reserved for communications antennae. The City does not consider Woodson Mountain to be park, and does not specifically encourage usage, but hikers and climbers have free access to the slopes via a paved road (closed to autos) serving the antenna site at the summit.

To reach the bottom end of the summit road, turn onto Mt. Woodson Road from intersections at mile 17.8 or mile 18.1 along Highway 67. At a point 0.2 mile from the south intersection, or 0.1 mile from the north intersection, you'll find space to park along the shoulder of Mt. Woodson Road. At this point the summit road going west is blocked by a gate. Squeeze around in the narrow space provided, and begin the climb, avoiding the road to the right, which leads to the Ramona Fire Station.

On a typical weekend, the sounds of nature will be accompanied by the sounds of clinking aluminum hardware, the shouts of "On belay!" and other phrases in climbers' parlance. Even if you don't see climbers, chalk marks (from gymnast's chalk) on boulders by the roadside mark their favorite routes. Near the top of the mountain, the road passes narrowly between immense, egg-shaped boulders and split-boulder faces 20–30 feet high—some, perhaps, unclimbable by "ethical" means.

When you reach the top of the mountain, you'll find a sturdy new fire lookout tower, a replacement for an older structure destroyed by wildfire in 1967. That fire, which eventually burned as far west as Highway 395 (now Interstate 15), leaped on raging Santa Ana winds from its point of origin in Ramona to the top of Woodson in just 90 minutes!

Immediately east of the fire tower is a cubical water tank with a peaked roof perched on a large boulder. On the surface of the boulder are bench marks indicating the highest (natural) point on the mountain.

You can stroll beyond the fire tower (go west on the narrow summit ridge) and reach a vantage point overlooking Poway, the North County coastal region, and the great blue expanse of the Pacific Ocean. Santa Catalina and San Clemente islands are visible on the clearest days.

Bouldering at Woodson Mountain

Area C-3: Penasquitos

Over half of San Diego's total share of acreage set aside as open space lies within the city's semi-developed northern sector. This area includes the fast-growing communities of Mira Mesa, Rancho Penasquitos, and North City West. Twenty or thirty years hence, when the urban fabric of San Diego and its northern suburbs joins together as a tightly woven tapestry, the wisdom of preserving these, and hopefully other, swatches of natural landscape will be readily appreciated.

One patch of this open space lies on the chaparral-clad slopes of Black Mountain, the dominant topographic feature in the Rancho Penasquitos area. Hike to the summit of this peak, and you'll experience a bird's-eye view of the city, the ocean, and the mountains to the east.

A much bigger patch of open space comprises the six-mile-long, 2400-acre Los Penasquitos Canyon Preserve, jointly owned by the City of San Diego and the county. Stretching from Interstate 5 to near Interstate 15, it includes both Los Penasquitos Canyon—a major east-west drainage—and Lopez Canyon, a tributary of the former. Riparian woodland, chaparral, and grassland habitats are superbly represented in both. Over 100 species of birds, 26 species of mammals, 22 species of amphibians and reptiles, and 90 species of flora have been identified in this area.

A look at our map reveals the "tuning fork" configuration of the Preserve's boundary, with most acreage along the canyon bottoms. Proposals to develop the long, narrow ridge between the two canyons for high-density housing have generated considerable controversy; it is believed that this action would severely disrupt the ecological integrity of the Preserve, and lead to the disappearance of predator species such as the bobcat and the mountain lion.

Today the Preserve is utilized as a passive, open-space park, with only minimal development on the east end. A parking/equestrian staging area off Black Mountain Road is the principal entry point. Nearby, the 125-year-old Johnson-Taylor adobe house and supporting buildings continue to be used as a working ranch. These also serve as headquarters for the Los Penasquitos Cultural and Natural Resource Center, an educational and interpretive facility (see Appendix 3). Guided hikes are offered on a regular basis.

On the west end of Los Penasquitos Canyon stand the crumbling remnants of the Ruiz adobe, one of the oldest structures in southern California. This was the home built by Captain Francisco Maria Ruiz, a commandant of the Presidio of San Diego, after he was given a land grant for cattle ranching in this valley in 1823. Even today a sizable herd of cattle roams the west end of the preserve, continuing the tradition carried on by Ruiz and succeeding owners of the land grant.

Most human activity within the preserve centers along the six-mile-long main dirt road through Los Penasquitos Canyon. A guard in a pickup truck makes regular forays to perform maintenance and assist visitors; otherwise this road and the one through Lopez Canyon are closed to motorized travel. Hiking, running, mountain biking, and horseback riding are the usual ways of getting around.

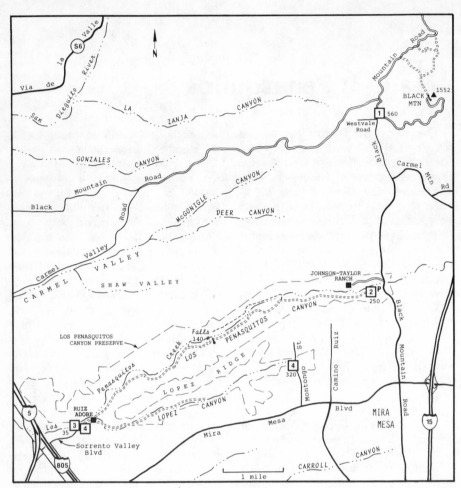

Penasquitos

Trip 1: Black Mountain

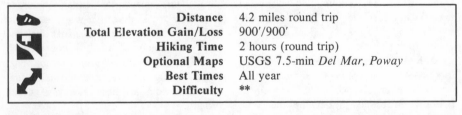

Distance	4.2 miles round trip
Total Elevation Gain/Loss	900'/900'
Hiking Time	2 hours (round trip)
Optional Maps	USGS 7.5-min *Del Mar, Poway*
Best Times	All year
Difficulty	**

Come up to Black Mountain in winter and catch a stupendous sunrise or sunset. Or stroll up on a summer's eve to watch Old Sol gradually sink and fade in the usual band of fog or haze. Just don't try this hike at noon on a warm day—there's no place to hide from the sun's direct rays.

The easiest approach is by way of a dirt access road to the telecommunications complex on the summit. The bottom end of this road intersects Black Mountain Road at a point opposite Westvale Road, 1.3 miles north of Carmel Mountain Road in Rancho Penasquitos. The access road is currently open to automobiles as well as hikers, and hang-gliding enthusiasts use it to drive up and launch their craft.

The scrubby vegetation on the slopes is mostly wild buckwheat, laurel sumac, and various sages. As you climb, there are good views to the south and west of the rapidly expanding community at the base of the mountain—Rancho Penasquitos. Farther south, overlain by seemingly endless housing and industrial developments, is a mesalike platform geographers call the Linda Vista Terrace. This is actually the middle level of three successive marine terraces in the San Diego area. A few remnants of the oldest and

highest terrace, the Poway Terrace, can be seen to the southeast and east.

Near the road's end, there is a heavy steel gate and "no trespassing" signs. You can stay below this and traverse left around the peak to the north and east. You'll get a good view of another booming community—Rancho Bernardo. A big swath of undeveloped rolling country and a small lake remain to the north, playing counterpoint to the scars of new construction.

After taking in the view, go back to the access road and return the way you came. (If you want to take a more difficult route back, you can follow the bulldozed track to the north. This forks, with branches going north and northwest back to Black Mountain Road. These routes involve very steep, rocky descents.)

Trip 2: Penasquitos Canyon—East Approach

Distance	6 miles round trip
Total Elevation Gain/Loss	300'/300'
Hiking Time	3 hours (round trip)
Optional Map	USGS 7.5-min *Del Mar*
Best Times	All year
Difficulty	**

Take along a picnic lunch and a blanket on this hike. There are many fine places— sunny meadows, oak-shaded flats, and the sycamore-fringed streamside—to stop for an hour's relaxation. A good turnaround point is a small set of waterfalls and pools in the canyon bottom. This is about three miles out, midway through the Preserve.

You begin at the parking and equestrian staging area on the west side of Black Mountain Road. This is just north of (and at the bottom of the hill from) Mira Mesa. On foot now, head west on the dirt road. In the first mile this hugs Los Penasquitos Canyon's south wall, a steep, chaparral-covered hillside (*Los Penasquitos* means "the little cliffs").

As you pass near the Johnson-Taylor ranch (screened from view by willows and

dense vegetation along the creek), you'll encounter many non-native plants—eucalyptus, fan palms, and fennel, for example— introduced into this area over the past century. Next you enter a long and beautiful canopy of intertwined live oaks, accompanied by a lush understory of mostly poison oak.

Small wooden mile posts along the roadside gauge your progress. At mile 2 the trail winds out of the dense cover of oaks and continues through grassland dotted with a few small elderberry trees. Wildflowers such as wild radish, mustard, California poppies, bush mallow, and violets put on quite a show here in March and April. Look, too, for the fuchsia-flowered gooseberry, quite unmistakable when in bloom.

Soon after mile 2, a road intersects and

goes north through the creekbed to connect with a parallel road on the north side. Consider this route as a possible way of returning from the falls ahead.

At the 3-mile marker the road goes through a gate with a turnstile, and then winds up onto the chaparral slope in order to detour a narrow, rocky section of the canyon. After the road goes down again, take one of the paths to the right (north) which lead to the canyon bottom. During the winter and early spring, a cascade of water tumbles through this constriction. Polished rock surfaces 10 feet up on either side testify to its sometimes violent flow. These outcroppings of greenish-grey rock are a type called the Santiago Peak volcanics; they're typical of the metavolcanic rock on Santiago Peak in the Santa Ana Mountains. Look for some slicks on the rock outcrops beside a shallow pool below the falls. These mark an area where Indians once milled and processed edible seeds.

Author jogging in Los Penasquitos Reserve in early morn

Trip 3: Penasquitos Canyon—West Approach

Distance	6 miles round trip
Total Elevation Gain/Loss	200'/200'
Hiking Time	3 hours (round trip)
Optional Map	USGS 7.5-min *Del Mar*
Best Times	All year
Difficulty	**

As in the previous trip, the destination of this hike is the waterfall at the midpoint of Los Penasquitos Canyon. This time you approach from the industrial complex at the east terminus of Sorrento Valley Boulevard.

Take the Sorrento Valley Road exit from either Interstate 5 or Interstate 805, then follow frontage roads to Sorrento Valley Boulevard. Parking may be somewhat limited during weekday working hours.

You'll enjoy the characteristic openness of this end of the canyon best if you come here on a cool day; the main dirt road is well away from the stream most of the time, and is fully exposed to the sun. Try this hike sometime on a summer evening: plan to reach the falls by sunset, then return by the light of the moon.

First stop is the Ruiz adobe ruins, now fenced and covered by a protective roof. These disintegrating adobe walls are at least a century and a half old. Just past the adobe, the road forks, the right branch swinging right (east) to enter Lopez Canyon (see Trip 4), and the left branch going straight into Los Penasquitos Canyon. In springtime especially, you should make a side trip to climb the nose of the ridge dividing the two canyons. In addition to the view of the emerald valley floor below, you'll come upon some fine displays of lupine and owl's clover which cannot be seen from the road.

After about one mile (near the 5-mile marker, measured from the east end of the canyon), you'll see some clumps of artichoke thistle, a Mediterranean plant which has become an invader of grasslands in many parts of California. By this time, the road has angled up to the creek, and it's tempting to cross and explore the far bank. Do this only if the foliage along the creek is leafed out, so that the poison oak, which flourishes here, can be observed and avoided.

Next, the road climbs a small hill and then descends to more grassland, dotted with small trees and shrubs such as elderberry, live oak, laurel sumac, toyon and gooseberry, and flanked on the creek side by large sycamores and cottonwoods. At a point about halfway between mile markers 4 and 3 (2.5 miles from your starting point), a disused road goes to the left and crosses the stream. Stay on the main road and continue about 0.5 mile as the road winds up through chaparral. At the bottom of the next dip take one of the several small pathways leading to the waterfall area in the canyon bottom.

Trip 4: Lopez Canyon

Distance	4 miles
Total Elevation Gain/Loss	0'/280'
Hiking Time	2 hours
Optional Map	USGS 7.5-min *Del Mar*
Best Times	All year
Difficulty	**

As "little brother" to Los Penasquitos Canyon, Lopez Canyon receives little use, yet it could stand alone on its merit as a canyon worth saving. If you want to see all of it, without retracing your steps, try this one-way trek from Mira Mesa to the west entrance of Los Penasquitos Canyon Preserve.

Start at the point where Montongo Street dips to cross the creek in Lopez Canyon, 0.8 mile north of Mira Mesa Boulevard. Parking is available along the dirt shoulder of Montongo Street.

Beyond the LOS PENASQUITOS CANYON PRESERVE sign, follow one of several paths through the cattails and reeds—and be prepared to get your feet wet. Within 100 yards, however, the vegetation and most of the water disappears. For the next mile or so, you'll be on mostly streambed cobbles, ranging in size from golf ball to football. A semblance of a road runs through here, occasionally appearing as wheel tracks on the bank of the creekbed. This section is, truthfully, not too scenic. New housing is filling the rim of the canyon, and the spoils from grading spill halfway down to the canyon floor.

After the first mile, the canyon deepens, the rim development recedes, and the vegetation patterns become more interesting. Dense chaparral intermixes with sage scrub on the slopes, and a line of sycamores appears by the creek. The road spends more time in smooth dirt than on cobbles, and in some places it edges close to the canyon wall where sandstone and conglomerate strata are clearly exposed.

After about two more miles, you'll pass under some enormous sycamores. One multitrunked specimen covers an area 100 feet across. Nearby are two gnarled and ancient apricot trees, still apparently healthy and bearing fruit.

Grasses and mustards replace the chaparral and sage as you approach Los Penasquitos Canyon. Near the Ruiz adobe, the creek feeds a fresh-water marsh covered by reeds and yerba mansa. Redwing blackbirds flit through here. In late winter wild radish, a variety of the cultivated radish which has escaped into the wild, sends up its flower stalks and paints the surrounding hillsides blue, yellow and white.

You're now in sight of the industrial buildings on Sorrento Valley Boulevard. Walk past the adobe and out the gate that marks the west end of the Preserve.

Sycamores in Lopez Canyon

Area C-4: Clairemont/University City

Aerial views of the Clairemont and University City neighborhoods of San Diego make one thing perfectly obvious: here is San Diego's "mesa and canyon" topography at its highest level of development. Geologists know this landform as an ancient marine terrace (the Linda Vista Terrace) incised by stream channels and their tributaries.

A strange kind of co-existence between unspoiled nature and full-speed-ahead development is apparent here: The mesa tops continue to fill up with a grid of housing developments and high-rise office buildings, while no more than a half mile away, a stream trickles through a canopy of oaks or a grove of sycamores in a canyon.

These once-ignored canyons, and their tributaries, or "finger canyons," have been the focus of many a fight between land developers and local homeowners. People have come to realize that canyons are valuable for their natural, educational, and recreational value. Thanks to the recent establishment of open space parks in the three largest major canyons of this area—Rose, San Clemente, and Tecolote—it looks as if the natural scenery will never be fully overwhelmed.

Clairemont/University City

While more complete recreational development is seen for the future, the canyons are already very popular among hikers, runners, and mountain bicyclists. If you live in Clairemont or University City, consider yourself lucky. If not, just hop on the freeway, or bicycle over on the surface streets, and you'll reach any of these canyons within minutes from most places around San Diego. Read on for more details.

Trip 1: Rose Canyon

	Distance	3 miles round trip
	Total Elevation Gain/Loss	50'/50'
	Hiking Time	80 minutes (round trip)
	Optional Map	USGS 7.5-min *La Jolla*
	Best Times	All year
	Difficulty	*

From its outlet at Fiesta Bay in Mission Bay, Rose Canyon extends north past the east brow of Soledad Mountain, then curves east toward the flat mesas of Miramar Naval Air Station. More than a hundred thousand people unwittingly follow part of its course every day: Interstate 5 parallels the lower canyon's stream channel for about three miles, and the Santa Fe tracks (the main railroad link to Los Angeles) stick with it for more than six miles.

The most beautiful section of Rose Canyon has just been declared an open space park by the City of San Diego. There are no facilities per se, but hiking is encouraged as long as you stay clear of the railroad tracks.

A convenient place to begin is along Genesee Avenue, across from University City High School. A large sign marks the beginning of a gravel road that goes along the south side of the canyon, well away from the tracks. Dense clumps of willows and syca-mores line the streambed and occasionally shade the road. Except for the passing of a train, 10 to 20 times a day, the canyon is remarkably quiet. But some of this silence will be sacrificed when the proposed Regents Road connection is completed around 1987.

After 1.5 miles, the road crosses the tracks and connects with La Jolla Colony Drive. This is a good turnaround point. For a longer hike, you can follow La Jolla Colony Drive and then the bike path paralleling Interstate 5 to the south. In this way you can reach the west end of San Clemente Canyon (see below).

Riparian woodland in San Clemente Canyon

Trip 2: San Clemente Canyon

Distance	1- to 4-mile hikes (out and back)
Optional Map	USGS 7.5-min *La Jolla,* or San Diego street map
Best Times	All year
Difficulty	* to **

Eastbound in the right lane of State Highway 52, the San Clemente Canyon Freeway, you can look down upon a long, slender, almost unbroken swath of natural vegetation: massive sycamores, stately live oaks, climbing vines, and tangled shrubs. This is one of San Diego County's best examples of riparian, or stream-loving, vegetation. (Recall that less than 0.2% of the county's land area consists of this type of vegetation.) The decision to divert the freeway well above the canyon bottom and spare the trees, at slightly added cost, was a happy one indeed.

Much of San Clemente Canyon and several of its steep finger canyons are now included within the boundaries of Marian Bear Park, an area set aside by the City of San Diego as natural open space. Some visitor facilities are here too: parking areas, picnic tables and rest rooms off Regents Road and Genesee Avenue, and benches elsewhere.

Missing, of course, is the important element of silence. If you come here early on a Sunday morning, however, noise from the adjacent freeway is not particularly objectionable.

The best hiking is along the old jeep road which runs through the canopy of trees along the canyon's seasonal stream. This road stretches about three miles, is almost flat, and crosses the stream bed four times. In summer these crossings simply mean walking across cobblestones, but in winter some wading may be necessary.

The east end of the canyon (between Genesee Avenue and Interstate 805) offers the prettiest vegetation, the densest shade, and the biggest infestations of poison oak—which lies mostly away from the road in great

Old live oak in San Clemente Canyon

tangled masses among the trees. Beginning about October, the leaves of the poison oak turn bright red in pleasing complement to the ever-green live oaks and the yellows and reds of the sycamores and willows. Beyond (east of) Interstate 805, the streambed of San Clemente Canyon passes through Miramar Naval Air Station, where hiking is officially not permitted.

There are several back entrances into Marian Bear Park. With the help of a city street map, you might incorportate these into a longer hike. For example:

From the west end of the jeep road in San Clemente Canyon, you can scramble over cobblestones in the creek to reach the bike path paralleling Interstate 5; you can then go north to connect with Rose Canyon (Trip 1 above) or south to connect with frontage roads along Interstate 5.

From a point between Regents Road and Genesee Avenue, an unmarked 0.5-mile-long trail goes north under Highway 52, follows a sage-scented ravine, zigzags through a hidden eucalyptus grove, and tops out at Standley Park in University City. From here you can take residential streets north to reach Rose Canyon.

On the south side of San Clemente Canyon, an obscure pathway/stairway goes up to Cobb Drive on the mesa above. Another path follows the high-voltage powerlines up to Kroc (formerly Einstein) Junior High School. These trails can be used in connection with residential streets in Clairemont to reach Tecolote Canyon Natural Park (see next trip).

Trip 3: Tecolote Canyon

Distance	6 miles
Total Elevation Gain/Loss	1000'/700'
Hiking Time	3½ hours
Recommended Map	San Diego street map
Optional Map	USGS 7.5-min *La Jolla*
Best Times	All year
Difficulty	***

Rustic signs along major streets now call attention to an area long known by insiders as one of the most valuable canyon habitats in San Diego's urban core: Tecolote Canyon Natural Park.

Tecolote Canyon does not yet have a developed trail system, but it's possible to poke into just about every nook and cranny. By day you're sure to spot a hawk soaring on the thermals or perching high on the crown of a dead oak tree. By night, perhaps, you might hear the yapping of a coyote or the plaintive hoot of an owl, the creature for which this canyon was named.

The title "Natural Park" refers to the native vegetation. The dominant plant communities are sage scrub (California sagebrush, white sage, black sage, lemonade berry, laurel sumac, monkey flower) and chaparral (chamise, toyon, scrub oak, holly-leafed cherry, redberry). Live oaks, willows, and sycamores grow along the stream channel in a few areas where water is most plentiful. Since Tecolote Canyon has been completely surrounded by an urbanized environment for more than 20 years, it is not surprising to find invading non-native plants here too. The worst "offenders" are tumbleweed, wild chrysanthemum, mustard, fennel, pampas grass, and ice plant.

For all but the most cursory examination of this canyon, you should wear a sturdy pair of hiking boots, or at least a pair of running shoes designed for off-road traction. Be forewarned that winter rains can turn clayey soils in the canyon into sticky mud. In summer, water flow in some parts of the canyon ceases and foul-smelling stagnant pools develop.

Take along a city street map to assist in general orientation and to aid your return to the starting point via city streets, if that is your wish. Most recent-edition maps show the park's boundary.

Begin at Tecolote Park and Recreation Center, opposite Interstate 5 from Mission Bay. The smooth, dirt roadway leading up the broad mouth of the canyon is suitable for casual walking, even jogging, at first. Once Tecolote Canyon Golf Course is reached, you'll have to struggle up and down some steep hillsides, since you must stay outside its perimeter. Follow the rough road along the perimeter fence, or go directly north along the bulldozed track accompanying the high-voltage powerlines.

Only the adventurous should continue now. Slip down a very steep section of bulldozed track to the bottom of the large eastward-heading tributary canyon (the trek up this oak-shaded side canyon to Genesee Avenue is worthwhile if you have the energy). Continue following the powerlines

upward to Via Bello, go left on Via Bello for one block, then use the shoulder of Mt. Acadia Boulevard to get back to the bottom of Tecolote Canyon. Someday, the construction of a trail skirting the golf course should make this awkward detour unnecessary.

Go up the canyon now on a narrow and sometimes obscure pathway along the east bank of Tecolote Creek. There are good picnic spots here and there among the oaks— but watch out for poison oak!

Balboa Avenue, next, presents some difficulty to further travel. You can cross underneath the roadway in the tunnel (if dry) that carries the floodwaters of the creek, or climb the embankment and attempt to scoot across the busy lanes and over the concrete center divider—a dangerous maneuver at best. On the safe side, you can walk up the south shoulder of Balboa Avenue, cross at the traffic light on Clairemont Drive, then walk back on the north shoulder.

North of Balboa Avenue you have two choices: go up the eastern tributary to Mt. Etna Park, or thread your way up the main canyon to Genesee Avenue or North Clairemont Park.

Lake Murray and Del Cerro from lower Cowles Mountain

Area C-5: Mission Trails Regional Park

Touted as the largest urban park in the country, Mission Trails Regional Park preserves some of the last remaining open space lying close to the heart of San Diego.

The concept of a new park on the east edge of San Diego was formalized in 1960, following the transfer of surplus former military reservation land to the jurisdiction of the City of San Diego. This park was to include Mission Gorge, the historic Old Mission Dam site along the San Diego River, and areas around Fortuna Mountain. By the late 70s, however, both the City and County of San Diego had cooperated in the purchase of 2000 acres on Cowles Mountain for preservation as open space, and a broader concept emerged—that of a 6200-acre regional park serving the diverse needs of residents throughout the entire county.

Efforts in recent years have focused on the acquisition of land to flesh out the far-flung boundaries of the park, and very few improvements (a notable exception being the small network of hiking paths on Cowles

Mountain) have as yet been made. Nevertheless, the park serves as a large reservoir of open space within an area rapidly filling in with suburban development.

The south end of the park encompasses Lake Murray, a city reservoir normally open to recreational uses such as picnicking and fishing, but closed over the past several years due to a stubborn infestation of hydrilla weed. As of this writing, the problem seems to have been solved. The paved road around the shoreline continues to be popular among joggers and strollers.

Cowles Mountain, centerpiece of the regional park, stands 1591 feet above sea level, the highest point within San Diego's city limits. It is this area of the park that hikers are, at present, most familiar with.

Anchoring the north end of the park are Mission Gorge and Fortuna Mountain, the nucleus of the original park proposed in 1960. Just east of the San Diego River in Mission Gorge are sheer rock outcrops that have long been popular with rock climbers.

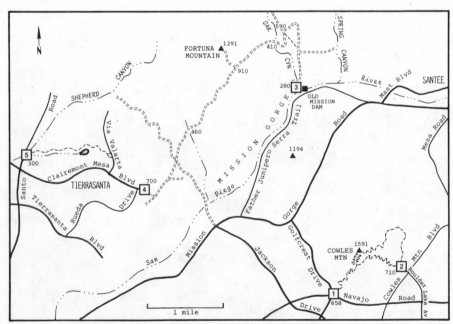

Mission Trails Regional Park

Fortuna Mountain is bordered by undeveloped land on Miramar Naval Air Station to the north, part of a virtually untouched expanse of land stretching as far north as Poway. Deer, coyotes, and even mountain lions prowl the hidden canyons and remote ridgelines of this seldom-visited area.

Illegal off-road vehicle activity and target shooting have been a problem in some areas of the park in recent years, though increased public awareness of its status as a regional park is now discouraging this.

The following descriptions are suggestions for five interesting trips in the Mission Trails Regional Park area. Aside from these routes, there are many other powerline service roads, firebreaks, and old jeep trails to wander along. New roads and housing projects along the park boundary are rapidly changing, and in some cases restricting, access to the park. We'll keep you posted of new developments in future editions of this book.

Trip 1: Cowles Mountain—South Approach

	Distance	3 miles round trip
	Total Elevation Gain/Loss	950'/950'
	Hiking Time	2 hours (round trip)
	Optional Maps	USGS 7.5-min *La Mesa;* San Diego street map
	Best Times	October through June
	Difficulty	**

Beginning at the corner of Navajo Road and Golfcrest Drive, this switchbacking trail ascends the sunny south slopes of Cowles Mountain, offering a vista stretching from the Pacific Ocean to Mexico. The predominant chaparral and sage scrub growth rarely exceeds shoulder height, so views are unobstructed from nearly every point on the trail.

Short spur trails branch from the main trail and lead to secluded overlooks—nice places to relax and enjoy the view, or have a picnic.

The main trail was cut on mostly decomposed granite, so it is quite susceptible to erosion. The tendency of many hikers to shortcut the switchbacks, of course, is an aggravating factor.

At a point 1.0 mile up, a trail goes right (east). Stay left and continue up the slope on the series of long switchbacks leading to the rocky summit of the mountain.

A blocky communications antenna facility obstructs the northward view somewhat, but otherwise the panorama is complete. Much time could be spent with binoculars and a street map identifying features on the

urban landscape. In the rift between the mesas to the west, for example, there's a good view of Mission Valley and the intricate tangle of freeways that pass over and through it. Southwest, the towers of downtown San Diego stand against Point Loma, Coronado, and the sparkling bay. Lake Murray shimmers to the south. The seven Santee Lakes contrast darkly with pale hills to the north. In all directions, scattered like a discontinuous carpet, are the abodes of a million people.

On clear winter days, the view expands to include most of the higher peaks of San Diego County. Southward into Baja, you can see the flat-topped "Table Mountain" behind Tijuana, and the Coronado Islands offshore. During absolutely crystalline weather, look for the profiles of Santa Catalina and San Clemente islands, to the northwest and west respectively.

Here's a suggestion for romantics and adventurers who don't mind descending the trail by flashlight: catch the sunset from Cowles' summit when the moon is full. After the sun slides into the Pacific, turn around and enjoy the moonrise over El Cajon Valley!

Trip 2: Cowles Mountain—East Approach

Distance	3 miles
Total Elevation Gain/Loss	1000'/1000'
Hiking Time	2 hours
Optional Maps	USGS 7.5-min *La Mesa;* San Diego street map
Best Times	October through June
Difficulty	**

Until the construction of foot trails on Cowles Mountain several years ago, the service road up the east side was the only access to the summit other than overgrown and eroded firebreaks. The road is still a popular, if somewhat steep, way to reach the summit. Public vehicular access is blocked at the bottom, ensuring a pleasant, quiet hike.

The service road begins near the western terminus of Boulder Lake Avenue, one block west of Cowles Mountain Boulevard. There are good views of suburban neighborhoods and the backdrop of mountains to the east. The chaparral here grows a bit denser and

higher than along the south-slope trail (Trip 1 above). Typical plants are chamise, ceanothus, black sage, laurel sumac and buckwheat. Two level stretches relieve the uphill grind, then six short, very steep switchback legs lead to the summit.

We suggest you make this a loop trip by starting your descent on the south slope trail. After 0.5 mile of long, lazy switchbacks, go left (east) on the trail that strikes a path northeast around the mountain. This trail soon descends abruptly on a series of tight switchbacks, and returns to the lower end of the service road.

Sunset from Cowles Mountain

Trip 3: Fortuna Mountain—East Approach

Distance	5 miles round trip
Total Elevation Gain/Loss	1400'/1400'
Hiking Time	3 hours (round trip)
Recommended Map	USGS 7.5-min *La Mesa*
Best Times	November through May
Difficulty	***

This hike begins at the historic Old Mission Dam (Padre Dam) on the San Diego River in the heart of Mission Gorge. The dam was built between 1807 and 1816 under the direction of the San Diego Mission, and was considered a major engineering feat of its day. A six-mile flume carried water from the dam to the mission located at the east end of Mission Valley. Today, the fully reconstructed mission and partially reconstructed dam are the two most important landscape features remaining from San Diego's Spanish era.

The parking lot near the dam site is located on the north side of Father Junipero Serra Trail, a paved road following the course of the San Diego River through Mission Gorge. (This lot is 0.8 mile west of Mission Gorge Road in Santee.) From here, you can't see the summit of Fortuna Mountain; it's hidden behind a ridge to the west.

Your first task is to cross the river. Steady releases of water from reservoirs upstream preclude a direct fording of the river, and the old dam itself acts as a spillway. Instead walk west about 200 yards and cross the river on a large steel pipe. Cut back east along the north bank of the river through willows and cottonwoods, avoiding patches of poison oak, and find the path that angles up the slope behind the bank. Look for traces of the old flume here.

The path climbs, descends to cross the bed of Oak Canyon, then climbs again to connect with a dirt road leading north across a grassy swale. After about 0.7 mile, the road curves left (west) and climbs toward some high-voltage transmission lines (it's possible to shortcut this wide bend by taking either of

two very steep bulldozer tracks). Some of the best spring wildflower displays in the area can be seen here: owl's clover, shooting star, California poppy, wild hyacinth, and Indian paintbrush.

Now go south, descend about 200 feet, and cross the bed of Oak Canyon for a second time. The canyon bottom is a delightful little riparian oasis, shaded by sycamores.

The road continues southwest up a steep ravine to a saddle southeast of Fortuna Mountain's summit. Just short of the saddle, the road becomes so steep it's difficult to keep from slipping in the dirt. Bear right at the intersection of roads on top, and proceed northwest up the steep, eroded firebreak to Fortuna's 1291-foot summit.

Unlike the view from Cowles Mountain, the view from Fortuna encompasses a good deal of undeveloped country. Low-sun illumination delineates the rolling, sensuous texture of the parallel ridges and shallow canyons to the northeast. Toward the southeast stretches a series of rounded promontories culminating in Cowles Mountain. It's easy to see why this range of mountains is called "Long Mountain" on century-old maps.

When you return to Oak Canyon at the base of Fortuna Mountain, you might consider a shortcut down along its bank. This involves some bushwhacking, and is probably worth the trouble only if the stream in Oak Canyon is flowing, usually December through April. At one point the water slides over a picturesque outcrop of rock and gathers in a natural pool.

Trip 4: Fortuna Mountain—West Approach

Distance	5 miles round trip
Total Elevation Gain/Loss	1400'/1400'
Hiking Time	3 hours (round trip)
Optional Map	USGS 7.5-min *La Mesa*
Best Times	November through May
Difficulty	***

This is an alternate, though no easier, way to reach the summit of Fortuna Mountain. A set of high-voltage powerlines parallels this route, simplifying navigation problems.

You begin at the east edge of Tierrasanta, a residential community within San Diego. The starting point is the (present) east terminus of Clairemont Mesa Boulevard, three miles east of Interstate 15. A proposed extension of this major road will someday connect with the future Jackson Drive along the west edge of the regional park.

From the dead end, pass under the powerlines and immediately swing south, descending steeply on a rutted path to cross a ravine. Follow a dirt path on the south side of this ravine as it climbs to join a wide dirt road going northeast along the hillside. Bypass the broad road cut on the right (the future path of Clairemont Mesa Boulevard) and continue straight along the left (west) slope of a chalky hill. The concrete cylindrical structures nearby are ventilators for the Second San Diego Aqueduct.

At the next intersection, continue straight, dropping sharply northeast toward the big-bowl-like valley west of Fortuna Mountain. This secluded valley is host to a small herd of mule deer, and is regularly patrolled by coyotes. Let the powerlines be your guide as you continue across the bottom of the valley and climb to the saddle southeast of the Fortuna Mountain summit. The last 300 yards are extremely steep. From the saddle, follow the ridgeline northwest for 0.4 mile to the summit.

If you're looking for a nice resting place or a picnic stop on the way back, here's a suggestion for a side trip: At the point where you cross the creekbed in the valley floor, simply walk downstream into the strip of oak woodland that extends from about 0.3 to 0.8 mile south of the powerlines. You'll reach a spot where the creek trickles over some large boulders, and oak limbs arch overhead in an intricate tangle. Some poison oak, naturally, is present in this area.

In Tecolote Canyon

Trip 5: Shepherd Canyon Hiking/Jogging Trail

Distance	2.6 miles round trip
Total Elevation Gain/Loss	250'/250'
Hiking Time	70 minutes (round trip)
Optional Map	USGS 7.5-min *La Mesa* (trail not shown on 1975 edition)
Best Times	All year
Difficulty	*

Though not a part of Mission Trails Regional Park, this hiking/jogging trail is an example of the creative use of canyon open space adjacent to the park. It is a part of a greenbelt park that includes most canyon bottoms in Tierrasanta.

The crushed gravel trail, marked by a prominent sign, begins along Santo Road 0.2 mile north of Clairemont Mesa Boulevard. It doesn't really follow the bed of Shepherd Canyon, but rather a southern tributary.

About 0.8 mile from Santo Road, the trail skirts a small reservoir to which birdlife and some larger animals—coyotes, for example—are attracted. The trail ends at Via Valarta, from which point it may be possible to go north on city streets toward the boundary of Mission Trails Regional Park. Ongoing construction of new subdivisions (with attendant fencing off of streets) may make this impractical, however.

Pond in Shepherd Canyon

Area C-6: Wildcat Canyon

Several years hence, no fewer than four parks and preserves, totalling several thousand acres, should be open to nature lovers and hikers in the Wildcat Canyon area northeast of Lakeside. Today, there are two: Stelzer County Park, with special facilities (including hiking trails) for the handicapped; and Silverwood Wildlife Sanctuary, an Audubon Society preserve and education center. Both lie on the east side of Wildcat Canyon Road.

Wildcat Canyon

Oak Oasis County Park, west of Wildcat Canyon Road, is awaiting future development as a picnic area with outlying trails. Also, under an agreement being worked out with the U.S. Bureau of Land Management, the County may soon develop a network of hiking/equestrian trails within a large parcel of BLM land stretching east from Wildcat Canyon Road to El Cajon Mountain.

Presently, at any rate, the Wildcat Canyon area offers the city-dwelling public a close-in opportunity to study and enjoy the chaparral and creekside vegetation that are rapidly disappearing on the county's urban fringes.

To reach Wildcat Canyon Road, take Highway 67 to Maple View Street in Lakeside, go east for 0.3 mile, then north on Ashwood Street. Ashwood becomes Wildcat Canyon Road after one mile.

Trip 1: Silverwood Wildlife Sanctuary

Distance	1- to 4 mile loops
Recommended Map	Silverwood trail map (available at director's house)
Optional Maps	USGS 7.5-min *San Vicente Reservoir, El Cajon Mountain* (trails not shown)
Best Times	October through June
Difficulty	* to ***

Silverwood: the name comes from the glittering effect of sunlight upon the leaves of the coast live oak. Scores of these trees, some of them 200-year-old giants scarred by fire, shade the canyon floor at the entrance to the Silverwood Wildlife Sanctuary and Nature Education Center. Owned and managed by the San Diego Audubon Society, the sanctuary preserves almost 600 acres of flora and fauna typically indigenous to the foothill region.

Silverwood is open to the public every Sunday (except in August) between 9 a.m. and 4 p.m. The entrance is at mile 4.8 on Wildcat Canyon Road. If this is your first visit, plan to attend the guided nature walk (at 10 and 1:30) to familiarize yourself with the area's natural history. Topics include plant identification, chaparral ecology, geology, bird watching, and identification of animal tracks and scats.

Several miles of hiking trails lace the area. A short and easy stroll from the parking lot to the director's house via the Creekside Trail will introduce you to a cool, moist environment in the shade of the spreading oaks. Half a dozen species of fungi will be found clinging to fallen limbs or pushing through the leaf litter. Just beyond the house is a small cienaga, or soggy meadow, adorned in spring with blue-eyed grass and paintbrush blossoms.

The outlying trails of Silverwood are narrow, rugged, easily overgrown, and not always maintained. Some of these climb, like spokes in a wheel, to Circuit Trail, a loop trail following the rugged, chaparral-clad ridgeline overlooking the oak-filled valley. A single eucalyptus tree, planted next to the director's house, stands head and shoulders above all else in the valley and marks the direction of return for lost hikers.

On the relatively short (two miles) but difficult hike around the Circuit Trail, the springtime blossoms of ceanothus, sage, coast spice bush, manzanita, and a dozen other flowering plants scent the air with sweet fragrances. There are two more-remote trips possible via the Circuit Trail—the Silverspring Trail (about three miles

round trip) and the Silverdome Trail (about four miles round trip)—both surprisingly arduous. These trips require the permission of the director; take lots of water and start at least four hours before closing time. Both traverse an area swept by fire in 1982.

The Silverdome Trail takes you to the top of a rounded granitic dome about 500 feet high, believed to be the largest granite monolith in San Diego County. Ecologists have done a study of the biological "successional islands" on the exposed, exfoliating surface of the dome. Lichens are the first colonizers; then come certain hardy mosses—but only in crevices and depressed areas where surface flows of rainwater are concentrated, yet not too erosive. If the mosses trap dust particles and debris to form a layer of soil, succulent live-forevers (specifically a type descriptively called "lady fingers") establish a foothold on the rock. The live-forevers act as a further trap for soil, which leads to colonization of many more species, including ferns, grasses and flowering plants. Some of the richer islands on the dome exhibit, in concentric zones, the full range of succession. In other places, succession has been halted, and only lichens and mosses survive, often in mazelike patterns on the rock.

Successional islands on rock are seen elsewhere in San Diego County, especially along parts of the San Luis Rey River (see Area M-4), and the upper San Diego River (Area M-7).

Granitic boulder in Silverwood

Trip 2: Stelzer County Park

Hiking Distances	1 to 2 miles
Optional Map	USGS 7.5-min *San Vicente Reservoir*
Best Times	October through May
Difficulty	* to **

Stelzer County Park, one of San Diego County's newest parks, features 314 acres of trails, campsites and picnic areas, and a small interpretive center. It is the only park in San Diego County designed to fully accommodate handicapped persons. Nonhandicapped visitors and hikers are welcome as well.

The park's well-marked entrance is on Wildcat Canyon Road, just two miles up from Maple View Street in Lakeside. Gates close at 5 p.m. for day users.

Of interest to hikers are two trails of quite different character. The Riparian Trail follows the bottom of Wildcat Canyon for about 0.5 mile, ending at a secluded picnic site. It is shaded throughout by a stream-hugging canopy of live oaks, some of which are draped with filigrees of wild grape and poison-oak vines.

The Stelzer Ridge Trail, on the other hand, switchbacks 0.6 mile toward the ridgeline south and east of Wildcat Canyon. This wide, gradually ascending dirt trail is soon to be upgraded to accommodate wheelchairs. It traverses slopes still recovering from a hot fire that swept through in 1982; pioneering vegetation includes various grasses, and hardy laurel sumac and toyon bushes.

At the top of the Stelzer Ridge Trail, there are two choices for those who wish a better view: you can go 0.3 mile southwest on a powerline access road to reach "Kumeyaay Promontory", or go 0.5 mile northeast up a steep ridge to "Stelzer Summit." Both points offer good views of the San Diego River valley and the cities of Lakeside and Santee to the south.

Sweetwater Reservoir from Sweetwater Trail

Area C-7: Lower Sweetwater River

From headwaters in the Cuyamaca
Mountains, the Sweetwater River flows
through foothills south of Descanso, pools up
in Loveland Reservoir near Alpine, flows
again through a broad valley and a rocky
canyon east and south of El Cajon, and
finally enters Sweetwater Reservoir—seven
miles inland from the river's mouth at San
Diego Bay. In recent years, water levels on
the Sweetwater Reservoir have been kept
fairly high.

Urban development has yet to catch up
with the rolling country south and east of
Sweetwater Reservoir. It's still a place where
wild oats and foxtails chafe in the afternoon
breeze, hawks glide overhead, and coyotes
and other small animals flourish.

Although the entire surface and shoreline
of the reservoir are closed to the public, a
horse and hiking trail—with a public easement—traverses the hills to the south and
east. This trail (described below) is not
marked by name, but it is part of the proposed
Sweetwater Trail, planned jointly by the San
Diego Trails Council, a horse rider's group,
and San Diego County. If the trail is completed as envisioned, it will be possible
someday to start at the mouth of the Sweetwater River in Chula Vista and hike or ride
well up into the Cuyamacas on a signed path
separate from highways and roads.

Lower Sweetwater River

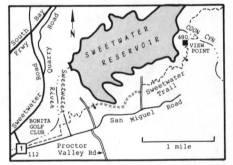

Trip 1: Sweetwater Trail

	Distance	7.5 miles round trip (to hilltop view spot)
	Total Elevation Gain/Loss	1100'/1100'
	Hiking Time	4 hours (round trip)
	Optional Maps	USGS 7.5-min *National City, Jamul Mountains* (trail not shown on 1975 editions)
	Best Times	October through June
	Difficulty	***

This segment of the Sweetwater Trail begins at the east end of Bonita Valley, east of National City and Chula Vista. Take the Bonita Road exit from Interstate 805 and drive four miles to the point where Bonita Road swings left to cross the Sweetwater River on a long, narrow bridge. Park off the pavement beside Bonita Road, or on a nearby residential street.

Pick up the narrow trail underneath the bridge and follow it east along the perimeter of the Bonita Golf Club course. After 0.7 mile the trail begins to zigzag up a grassy hillside. A view of Bonita Valley opens up, with a slice of the ocean in the distance. Passing over a small rise at 1.4 miles, you join a road and catch a first glimpse of the reservoir. The shoreline of the reservoir is strictly off limits to visitation, so be sure to stay on the trail.

The trail, following dirt roads now, meanders east, then north, then east again over rolling grassland, staying well back from the shoreline of the reservoir. Several newly bulldozed roads cross or diverge from the trail, making it hard to follow. Let the yellow-topped posts and the imprints of horseshoes be your guide. At 2.3 miles the route goes due north along a wide dirt road. Go 150 yards north through a dip in the road, then find the narrow path that heads east up a gentle hillside.

Now the narrow path descends sharply, goes up a set of switchbacks with wooden railings, drops again, and then climbs sharply to a hillside grove of pepper trees. It drops once more, passing a single tamarisk tree, contours across a grass- and scrub-covered hillside, and finally begins a switchbacking ascent of a prominent hill.

The top of this prominent hill offers the best view of the lake and surrounding mountains. To the east is 2565-foot San Miguel Mountain, its summit bewhiskered with television and radio antennae. Across the lake to the north and west is the somewhat unkempt suburban sprawl of Spring Valley. On the hilltop itself are many good examples of native coast cholla, and coast barrel and prickly pear cacti.

The hilltop is a good turnaround point. The trail ahead follows the Sweetwater River for an additional six miles to State Highway 94 near Jamacha Junction, but it's a difficult section to follow, with only orange plastic ribbons guiding the way at strategic places.

FOOTHILLS AND MOUNTAINS

Area M-1: Agua Tibia Wilderness

The 18,000-acre Agua Tibia Wilderness lies on the northwest slope of the Palomar Mountains, straddling the San Diego/Riverside county line in Cleveland National Forest. Until 1984, this was the only federal wilderness area in San Diego County. Now it is one of four in the Cleveland forest, including Pine Creek (Area M-13), Hauser (Area M-16), and San Mateo Canyon (not covered in this book).

Agua Tibia Mountain, one of the three distinct mountain blocks of the Palomar range, is the centerpiece of the wilderness. Forests of Coulter pine, big-cone Douglas-fir (also called big-cone spruce), incense cedar, and live and black oak cover the highest elevations, while the lower slopes are brushy and fluted by many steep canyons holding intermittent streams. The wilderness was named after one of these streams, Agua Tibia ("warm water") Creek.

Wild creatures are plentiful here, but covert in their appearances. Aside from the usual deer, squirrels, rabbits and common birds of chaparral and pine-oak forest habitats, the wildlife list includes bobcat, mountain lion, wild pig, prairie falcon, and bald and golden eagles.

There is only one easy access into the Agua Tibia Wilderness—Dripping Springs Campground, located 10 miles east of Interstate 15 on State Highway 79 in Riverside County. A new trail out the southeast corner of the wilderness, however, connects with an old jeep road called the Cutca Trail, which goes east toward Aguanga and Oak Grove below the northeast slopes of the Palomar range.

During a brief visit at Dripping Springs, you could try a short scramble up the bed of Arroyo Seco Creek. This normally bone-dry creekbed comes alive with the sound of rushing water in winter and early spring. Sycamores, cottonwoods and alders line the bank, contrasting with the somber green of the chaparral-clad hillsides. You can travel up the banks of the creek to a point 0.5 mile from the south end of Dripping Springs Campground; after this things get difficult due to steep canyon walls and poison oak. All other worthwhile trips in the wilderness involve long treks over primitive trails with no dependable water available. These trips are described below.

As in many national-forest wildernesses, permits are required for overnight *and* day use within the wilderness boundaries. They are available at the Dripping Springs Fire Station (open approximately April through November), and through any Cleveland National Forest office (see Appendix 4). It is best to call well in advance of your visit.

Due to the high potential for wildfire, open fires are never allowed in the Agua Tibia Wilderness. Backpack stoves may be used only in areas cleared of flammable material to a radius of 10 feet.

Agua Tibia Wilderness

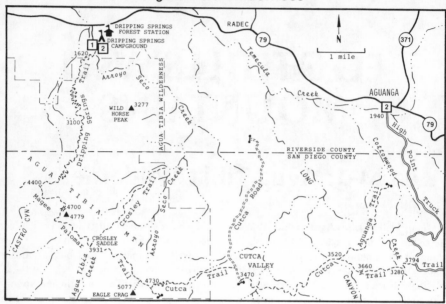

Trip 1: Dripping Springs Trail

	Distance	14 miles round trip (to head of Castro Canyon)
	Total Elevation Gain/Loss	2900'/2900'
	Hiking Time	8 hours (round trip)
	Recommended Map	Agua Tibia Wilderness map/brochure (available from Cleveland National Forest)
	Optional Map	USGS 7.5-min *Vail Lake* (trail not shown on 1982 edition)
	Best Times	November through May
	Difficulty	****

Make this an all-day hike to the summit ridge, or an overnight backpack, or set your sights on an intermediate destination. In any case, there is only one way up: the Dripping Springs Trail. Plan your water needs carefully; there is usually none available on the trail.

From the trailhead at the south end of Dripping Springs Campground, ford Arroyo Seco Creek and begin a switchbacking ascent through sage scrub and chaparral vegeta-

tion, liberally sprinkled with annual wildflowers in March and April. After about one mile, the trail gains the top of a nearly flat ridge and then continues south toward a series of 10 switchbacks that cross an old firebreak (stay on the trail—don't make short cuts). Vail Lake, in neighboring Rancho California, and southern California's highest mountains—Old Baldy, San Gorgonio and San Jacinto—are visible in the north. On a clear winter day, their snowy summits etched sharply against the blue sky are a memorable sight.

At about 3.5 miles (3100'), the trail crosses the head of a small creek, and the chamise- and ceanothus-dominated cover begins to yield to manzanita and ribbonwood (red shanks). The smooth, bronzed limbs and branches of the manzanita support dark green, leathery leaves which turn edge-on to the sun on hot days, thus conserving moisture. Ribbonwood, on the other hand, is characterized by perpetually peeling reddish bark and a graceful crown of feathery foliage. Starting in about February, the manzanita sports myriads of tiny white or pinkish blossoms shaped like hanging lanterns. Later in the year, red berries (*manzanita* is Spanish for "little apple") appear. When ripe, these edible berries taste like a pippin apple.

At about 4 miles (3300') truly giant specimens of manzanita and ribbonwood appear, up to 20 feet in height. Parts of the wilderness have gone unburnt for well over a century, and these specimens represent the equivalent of a "climax forest" consisting wholly of chaparral species. The first live oaks on your hike appear shortly beyond this point.

At about 4.5 miles, the trail descends a little across an area of poor soil and thin vegetation, and a view opens up to the southeast. The white dome of the Hale Telescope at Palomar Observatory gleams on Palomar Mountain, nine miles away. You cross the heads of two ravines, with some pools of water present after major storms, then resume rather steep climbing up a series of switchbacks. Passing through areas shaded by live oaks and a few Coulter pines, and across sunny patches of low-growing manzanita, you finally arrive (approx. 6.8 miles) at the Magee-Palomar Trail (formerly Palomar Mountain Truck Trail) on the crest of Agua Tibia Mountain. This former maintained fire road has been allowed to revert to a foot path, and is overgrown in places. Coulter pine, live oak and black oak, intermixed with thick brush, grow here.

At the very least, you should walk about

0.2 mile south along the Magee-Palomar Trail to a point overlooking Castro Canyon. On most winter days, a clear panorama of north San Diego County is spread before you, including a conspicuous linear feature—Interstate 15. On the far horizon to the west and south are the Pacific Ocean and the mountains of Baja California.

Several campsites free of vegetation are along (or actually in the old roadbed of) the Magee-Palomar Trail, including a very large one about a mile south of the junction of the Dripping Springs Trail. An interesting side trip to Agua Tibia Mountain's summit (bench mark at 4779') may be made, as well as exploratory forays into the upper reaches of Castro Canyon. The very difficult descent into Castro Canyon is best made via the west extension of the Magee-Palomar Trail—the old Magee pack trail—now thickly overgrown. Drop down one of the steep, brushy ravines into Castro Canyon, and you'll find a seasonal creek and waterfalls deeply shaded by towering oaks and big-cone Douglas-fir. You'll need topo map and compass for these kinds of explorations.

Manzanita trunks in rain

Trip 2: Dripping Springs to Aguanga

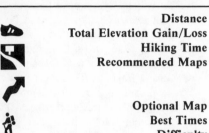

Distance	25 miles
Total Elevation Gain/Loss	5600'/5300'
Hiking Time	14 hours
Recommended Maps	USGS 7.5-min *Vail Lake, Aguanga* (Dripping Springs Trail not shown on 1982 edition of *Vail Lake*)
Optional Map	Cleveland Natl. Forest recreation map
Best Times	November through May
Difficulty	*****

At least two groups of runners have completed this trip in less than ten hours, but it is more commonly done as a two- or three-day backpack. The route traverses some very lonely country, in fact, some of the most remote territory found anywhere in the coastal mountains of southern California. Water is available part of the year at lower elevations, but check with the Forest Service first. You'll also need a remote camping permit (as well as a wilderness permit for passing through Agua Tibia) if you camp outside the wilderness boundary. Leave one car at Dripping Springs and another at Aguanga, unless you arrange to be picked up at the end of the trip.

Refer to Trip 1 above for the description via the Dripping Springs Trail to the Magee-Palomar Trail (6.8 miles). From this point, follow the Magee-Palomar Trail as it winds generally southeast past the summit of Agua Tibia Mountain and down to Crosley Saddle. Fast-growing shrubs tend to smother this section of trail as fast as Forest Service workers can clear it, but the old roadbed is always obvious. In early spring, thousands of ticks lie in wait on the yerba santa along the trail, ready to pounce on any wild animal or hiker passing by; so check your legs frequently.

The Crosley Trail, another old overgrown roadbed, goes northeast from Crosley Saddle to a tributary of Arroyo Seco Creek, then passes into private property. Stay right (east) on the Magee-Palomar Trail and begin a long, gradual climb through beautiful oak and pine woods to the shoulder of Eagle

Crag, the highest point in the wilderness. As a side trip, a rugged bushwhack up the northeast slope (500 feet gain in 0.3 mile) brings you to the brink of a rock pile affording probably the best view in the Palomar

Eagle Crag

Mountains. According to the register nearby, only a few parties reach this peak each year.

At a point just beyond Eagle Crag (11.8 miles from the trailhead and 5.0 miles from the upper end of the Dripping Springs Trail), leave the old roadbed and go left (east) on the Cutca Trail. This narrow, seldom used, and in places hard-to-follow trail descends sharply on switchbacks through brush and Coulter pines to a small canyon shaded by incense-cedar and big-cone Douglas-fir. Compared to the high and dry country above, this area seems like a piece of the Pacific Northwest, complete with trickling stream and sword ferns.

Passing out of the wilderness, you emerge at Cutca Valley, and intersect Cutca Road (14.1 miles). Walk 0.4 mile south on the road, then resume eastward travel on the Cutca Trail. Continue over rolling terrain, through chaparral and oaks, crossing two major tributaries of Long Canyon. Seasonal flows here and in Cottonwood Creek ahead are your best opportunities to fill up canteens during the trip. Filter or purify the water, of course. At 17.4 miles, the Aguanga Trail splits off to the northeast. This short cut to Aguanga is blocked by private property, so you must stay right on the Cutca Trail. Climb to a saddle at 18.1 miles, descend to cross the shady depths of Cottonwood Creek, then climb sharply to the High Point Truck Trail (19.4 miles).

All that remains now, unless you can be reached by 4-wheel-drive vehicle at this point, is a tedious but downhill walk down the road to Aguanga.

Boulders and Coulter pines

Area M-2: Palomar Mountain

Without a doubt, the rolling high country of Palomar Mountain contains San Diego County's most picture-perfect mountain scenery. Palomar's uplands, covered with thick forests of pine, oak, fir and cedar, and its gentle valleys, laced with sparkling streams, bring to mind landscapes more commonly seen in mountain ranges far to the north. With an average annual precipitation of more than 40 inches, snowfalls of up to three feet in winter, and vibrant spring and fall color, this is San Diego County's best answer to those who might complain about the lack of four seasons in southern California.

Palomar Mountain is the middle of three distinctively named promontories forming the 25-mile-long range popularly known as the Palomar Mountains. Agua Tibia Mountain anchors the range to the northwest, while Aguanga Mountain stretches to the southeast. Several faults pass through the area, including the Elsinore Fault, which lies along a stretch of the San Luis Rey River south of Palomar Mountain.

The amount of public acreage open to hikers on Palomar Mountain is not large. The trails that do exist, however, provide easy access to the some of the most beautiful places. All seven trips below are in a roughly four-square-mile block of land including Palomar Mountain State Park and a part of the Cleveland National Forest. Surrounding this is a patchwork of private lands and small, often detached parcels of national forest. The east side of Palomar Mountain is dominated by Palomar Observatory lands (closed to hiking) and national forest areas around High Point, a 6140-foot summit accessible to the public only from the east (see Area M-3).

Public campgrounds are located in Palomar Mountain State Park (open year-round), Palomar Mountain County Park (open year-round) and national-forest land (open seasonally) along the road to Palomar Observatory. Backpacking is not permitted in Palomar Mountain State Park, and not normally allowed on the national forest between the observatory and the state park. Backpacking and remote camping is allowed—and encouraged—in other areas of the Palomars, such as Agua Tibia and Barker Valley (Areas M-1 and M-3).

Palomar Mountain is served by two major highways that climb up from State Highway 76. South Grade Road (County Highway S-6) is steep and winding; while East Grade Road (County Highway S-7) offers a longer, more gradual ascent. Both offer spectacular roadside scenery. At the junction of South Grade and East Grade roads on the Palomar Mountain crest, you can turn west toward Palomar Mountain State Park (Trips 1–4 below), or north toward the national-forest campgrounds (Trips 5–7 below) and Palomar Observatory.

The famous 200-inch Hale Telescope at Palomar Observatory, still the largest in the country, is a "must see." The observatory gates are open 9 a.m. to 4:45 p.m.

Palomar Mountain

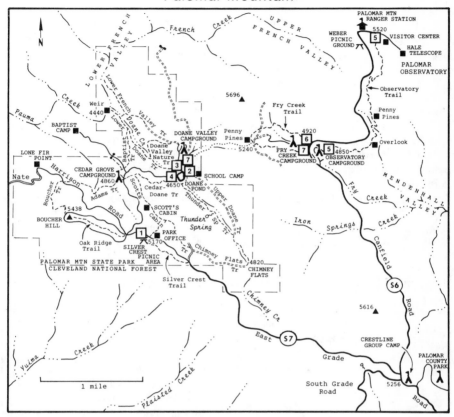

Trip 1: Scott's Cabin/Boucher Hill Loop

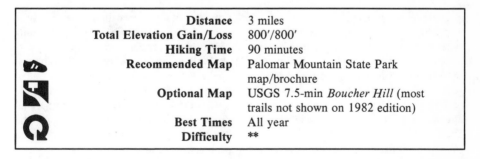

Distance	3 miles
Total Elevation Gain/Loss	800'/800'
Hiking Time	90 minutes
Recommended Map	Palomar Mountain State Park map/brochure
Optional Map	USGS 7.5-min *Boucher Hill* (most trails not shown on 1982 edition)
Best Times	All year
Difficulty	**

Like most hikes on Palomar Mountain, this one is at its very best during spring and fall, especially April–May and October–November. The route begins along an open ridge dotted with black oaks, and these trees undergo rapid color changes in both seasons.

Park at the Silver Crest Picnic Area, just beyond the state park's entrance. Walk back to the paved road and go west toward a junction of five roads. Now continue west up the ridgeline between the two roads to the left (these roads are a one-way loop around the summit of Boucher Hill), following a narrow, unmarked trail through the grass and bracken ferns. Black oaks crown the ridgeline, their gnarled limbs bare in winter, but alive with fluttering leaves during the remainder of the year. A few white firs appear as you near the fire tower and microwave structure on Boucher Hill. From the parking area at Boucher Hill, there's a good view west down to Pauma Valley, but it's often too hazy to spot the Pacific Ocean.

Now find the Boucher Trail, which descends on a stretch of old fire road to the north. Beyond more black oaks, bracken ferns, and a meadow dotted with baby-blue-eyes, the trail swings right to traverse a north slope, entering a dense, almost gloomy forest of white fir. Upon reaching Nate Harrison Road, cross and pick up the Adams Trail on the other side. You're in mixed forest now, with a few big-cone Douglas-fir trees whose wandlike limbs tower head and shoulders above all else. Winding around a sunlight-flooded ravine, you'll see beautiful specimens of dogwood and ceanothus, in bloom during April and May. In early summer, tiger lilies brighten the shady areas.

When you arrive at Cedar Grove Campground, walk out to the entrance, where you can pick up the trail to Scott's Cabin. A steep climb through mostly white fir forest takes you to the modest remains of the cabin, built by an early homesteader. Complete the circle by bearing right at the next junction, taking the trail that ends up opposite the Silver Crest Picnic Area.

Trip 2: Thunder Spring/Chimney Flats Loop

Distance	4 miles
Total Elevation Gain/Loss	900'/900'
Hiking Time	2 hours
Optional Map	Palomar Mountain State Park map/brochure (some trails not shown); USGS 7.5-min *Boucher Hill* (trails not shown on 1982 edition)
Best Times	All year
Difficulty	**

This loop has a little of everything—a walk along a stream-edged meadow; a passage through a canopy of western azaleas (relatively rare in San Diego County); a stroll through a century-old apple orchard; a visit to an old grave; the best views in the entire park; and a visit (once more, if you've already taken Trip 1) to the old ruins of Scott's Cabin.

The parking lot at Doane Pond—the lowest elevation on this hike—is a good place to begin. Tiny Doane Pond is stocked with trout and is very popular, especially with youngsters. The buildings east of here are San Diego City and County's Palomar school camp. This camp, along with Camp Cuyamaca in Cuyamaca Rancho State Park, provides fifth-graders with an opportunity to experience a week of adventure and learning in lieu of regular class attendance.

Walk around the lake, then go southeast up the Thunder Spring Trail (or, if it's one of those frosty days of winter, you can gravitate toward the Upper Doane Trail, the parallel dirt road on the sunny side of the valley). The Thunder Spring Trail skirts a patch of skunk cabbage, then plunges into a dark forest of oaks and conifers. Alder-fringed Doane Creek on the left appears luminescent in the sunlight. A side path on the right leads to Thunder Spring, framed by four-foot-long fronds of chain fern in a shady ravine.

At the end of the valley, commence a steep climb up the east slope of the canyon containing Chimney Creek (this section is to be replaced by a more gradual trail on the west slope in the future). Azalea grows thickly along the trail, displaying hundreds of white blossoms about mid-May. Azalea may also be seen along the Azalea Glen Trail in the Cuyamaca Mountains (Area M-9, Trip 6).

Next you reach Chimney Flats, an oak-fringed, bracken-filled meadow. Bear right (west) on the Chimney Flats Trail, an old fire road. Climb through the forest to another flat, this one filled with the remains of a century-old apple orchard believed to have been tended by the man who built Scott's Cabin. At the entrance to this flat, turn left on the service road from the reservoir, cross East Grade Road, and pick up the unsigned Silver Crest Trail. On the left is "Big Willy's grave," the resting place of William Pearson, an early settler, killed by a falling tree.

According to the inscription, Willy was "aged 66 Y's 1 Mo. 16 D's." The Silver Crest Trail meanders along the edge of a steep ridge affording spectacular wintertime views of the San Luis Rey River valley and the distant Pacific Ocean. Up ahead is Silver Crest Picnic Area, where water is available.

From the picnic area head east across the road and pick up the Scott's Cabin Trail. Follow this past the cabin, down through the white-fir forest, then go right (east) on the Cedar-Doane Trail—formerly known as the "Slide Trail" because of its steepness. This passes through mixed forest and emerges at the shoreline of Doane Pond, your starting point. There is much poison oak along this narrow trail, especially in association with oak forest. Avoid brushing against any leafless twigs in winter and early spring; poison-oak twigs contain the same toxic oil as the leaves.

Trip 3: Doane Valley Nature Trail

	Distance	1 mile
	Total Elevation Gain/Loss	150'/150'
	Hiking Time	30 minutes
	Optional Map	USGS 7.5-min *Boucher Hill* (trail not shown on latest edition)
	Best Times	All year
	Difficulty	*

This is a trail for inspiration. Here is the Palomar forest at its best, complete with a trickling stream straight from the land of sky-blue waters.

The brochure available at the trailhead is excellent in its descriptions and sketches of trees and shrubs seen along the route. Among the more interesting species: box elder (a tree rare in San Diego County), creek dogwood, wild strawberry, mountain currant, and Sierra gooseberry. At one point, the brochure calls attention to a massive incense-cedar that towers 150 feet and mimics the giant sequoia of the Sierra Nevada.

You'll find the trailhead at the Doane Pond parking lot. The trail goes downhill along Doane Creek for about 0.3 mile, then curves and climbs around a hill to connect with Doane Valley Campground. Walk through the campground and down the road toward Doane Pond to close the loop.

Trip 4: Lower Doane Valley/Lower French Valley

Distance	2.5 miles round trip
Total Elevation Gain/Loss	300'/300'
Hiking Time	90 minutes
Recommended Map	Palomar Mountain State Park map/brochure
Optional Map	USGS 7.5-min *Boucher Hill* (Lower Doane Trail not shown on 1982 edition)
Best Times	All year
Difficulty	**

Unquestionably, the best time of day to make this hike is during the first two hours of daylight. At midday the landscape is bathed in a harsh, flat light. In the late afternoon haze from the lowlands has usually blown in, diluting the purity of the light. In the early morning, however, magic is wrought. Long shadows from the treetops stab across the pillowy surfaces of the meadows, then recede quickly as the sun gains altitude. Delicate colors come alive in the foliage as light from the blue sky intermixes with the pure white glow of sunlight. Silver dewdrops glisten on the blades of grass.

Again a good place to start is the Doane Pond parking lot. Follow the Doane Valley Nature Trail, as above in Trip 3, but bear left at the trail fork in 0.3 mile. This is the Lower Doane Trail, taking you along the bank of Doane Creek through stately groves of white fir and incense-cedar. Walk all the way down to the weir at the end of the trail, and admire the stone-and-mortar structure above it. This dam and gauging station were used in the late 1920s to test the hydroelectric potential of the stream. The tests proved there was not enough flow to justify construction of a power plant. There is enough water, though, to soak your feet in on a warm day.

Fishermen and hikers alike know about the spectacular and very rugged stretch of Pauma Creek below the weir. At present, however, it is legal to scramble down the creek only to the park boundary, just 0.2 mile away. Beyond this point access is strictly forbidden. The creek flows through the Pala Indian Reservation and eventually joins the San Luis Rey River in Pauma Valley. During high water, even the short 0.2-mile stretch within the park can be quite treacherous.

From the weir, backtrack 0.2 mile and take the short connecting trail across Lower Doane Valley to the Lower French Valley Trail. Go left (north), passing into Lower French Valley. The setting is idyllic: rolling grasslands dotted with statuesque ponderosa pines, surrounded by hillsides clothed in oaks and conifers.

Several of the ponderosa pines are riddled with holes, some being filled with acorns. This is the handiwork of the acorn woodpecker, who uses the holes to store acorns filled with larvae. The birds retrieve these grubs in leaner times. Listen for the repetitive, guttural call of this bird, and observe the distinctive red patch on its head and the white wing patch when in flight.

You can hike up as far as the bank of French Creek, then return along the same trail, staying left to finish the hike on the Lower French Valley Trail.

Trip 5: Observatory Trail

Distance	2.2 miles
Total Elevation Gain/Loss	100'/750'
Hiking Time	1 hour
Optional Maps	Cleveland National Forest recreation map; USGS 7.5-min *Palomar Observatory, Boucher Hill*
Best Times	All year
Difficulty	*

The Observatory Trail has won kudos as one of only four National Recreation trails in San Diego County. Winding along a hillside below Palomar Observatory, it parallels a section of Canfield Road (Highway S-6), and thus is easily adaptable to a car shuttle (or a drop-off and pick-up, if you have friends) between starting and end points.

Since you have your druthers on this one, you may as well start at the upper end of the trail and walk down. You begin just west of the entrance gate to Palomar Observatory, along the south shoulder of Canfield Road. Drop down through pine, oak, cedar, and mixed chaparral, and through meadows fringed with bracken fern. The road runs quite close to the trail—but it's out of sight mostly, if not out of sound.

About halfway down, a delightful ravine

is bridged, alive with the sound of a trickling spring in the early part of the year. Soon there's a wooden platform with benches overlooking Mendenhall Valley, one of several idyllic valleys tucked into Palomar's rolling flanks. Mendenhall Valley and the slopes around it are a part of the headwaters of the San Luis Rey River's West Fork. The water flows east through Barker Valley (see Area M-3), makes a semicircle around the southeastern tip of the Palomar Mountains, passing through Lake Henshaw, and finally rushes down along the base of the Palomar Mountains toward the ocean (see Areas M-4 and C-1 for trips along the lower San Luis Rey River).

The Observatory Trail comes to an end at a point opposite sites 19 and 20 in Observatory Campground.

Mendenhall Valley overlook

Trip 6: Fry Creek Trail

	Distance	1.5 miles
	Total Elevation Gain/Loss	300'/300'
	Hiking Time	1 hour
	Optional Maps	Cleveland National Forest recreation map; USGS 7.5-min *Boucher Hill* (trail not shown on 1982 edition)
	Best Times	All year
	Difficulty	*

This beautiful trail circles the head of Fry Creek and returns to Fry Creek Campground. You'll find the trailhead just inside the entrance to the campground, two miles below Palomar Observatory and 2.7 miles north of the South Grade/East Grade road junction.

The trail winds up along the slope north of the creek, passing through live and black oaks, pines (mostly Coulter pines), and scattered underbrush. This mix of vegetation is well adapted to the sunny, somewhat dry south-facing slopes. October and November are the most glorious months: the black oak in full autumn color delights the eye, and the sporadic pitter-patter of falling acorns pleases the ear (if not the top of the head).

In late April and early May there's a curious kind of psuedo-autumn color in these forests. When the black oak leaves first emerge from buds, they're reddish in color. They gradually acquire the normal light green shade as they unfold. A stand of oaks in an area of varying elevation and sun exposure will, at the right time of year, exhibit colors ranging from red or reddish brown to light or dark green, since the trees leaf out at different times and rates. This effect is best seen near the Penny Pines Plantation at the top of the trail, where springtime pseudo-autumn color contrasts with the gray-green of white firs, and the somber green of live oaks and young planted Coulter pines.

Common birds seen and heard in this area include Steller's jays, chicadees, and acorn woodpeckers. I have seen mule deer here, and once at twilight, a striped skunk.

Cross the dirt road just past the Penny Pines, and follow the continuation of the Fry Creek Trail (a narrow footpath) down the steep slope south of Fry Creek to the campground. The trail winds through closely spaced incense-cedar, white fir, and live oak; with few black oaks and no Coulter pines present. Little underbrush is present either, since only late spring and early summer sunlight can reach these slopes.

Trip 7: Fry Creek to Doane Valley

	Distance	1.5 miles
	Total Elevation Gain/Loss	300'/550'
	Hiking Time	80 minutes
	Optional Maps	Cleveland Natl. Forest recreation map; USGS 7.5-min *Boucher Hill* (Fry Creek Trail not shown on 1982 edition)
	Best Times	All year
	Difficulty	**

This short, cross-country route serves as the only convenient connection (for hikers) between the Fry Creek/Observatory campground area in Cleveland National Forest, and Palomar Mountain State Park. The distance from start to end point via roads is almost seven miles.

From the entrance to Fry Creek Campground, walk up either branch of the Fry Creek Trail (see Trip 6) to the Penny Pines Plantation. Several roads and trails diverge here. Find the informal path that goes west down a narrow ravine. All other paths go up,

or back down toward Fry Creek.

Toward the bottom of the ravine, you'll be boulder-hopping over outcrops of gray metasedimentary rock. Back along Fry Creek, the rock is granitic. You're on one of several wedges of pre-Cretaceous metasedimentary rock that alternate with younger granitic rock exposures along the summit of Palomar Mountain.

At the bottom you come out behind the buildings of the Palomar School Camp. The parking lot at Doane Pond lies a short distance away.

Doane Pond at dawn

Area M-3: Oak Grove/Barker Valley

Here, on the drier eastern slopes of Palomar Mountain and Aguanga Mountain, the elfin forest of chaparral is king. This is hotter country than the highlands of Agua Tibia Mountain and the west end of Palomar Mountain, but ridgetop views are panoramic and unobstructed. Barker Valley is an oak-filled grassy swale tucked between chaparral-clad slopes and caressed by the gentle flow of the San Luis Rey River's West Fork.

Cleveland National Forest covers most of this area, with a few private inholdings. You'll need a remote camping permit to stay overnight on forest lands—other than the Forest Service campground in Oak Grove. Permits are available at the Oak Grove Fire Station (open about April through November) or at any Forest Service office. There is no restriction on day hiking.

Both trips below are accessible via State Highway 79 northwest of Warner Springs. North County residents can reach Highway 79 via Highway 76 and Lake Henshaw. South County residents should take Highway 67 to Ramona, Highway 78 to Santa Ysabel, and Highway 79 north from there.

Oak Grove/Barker Valley

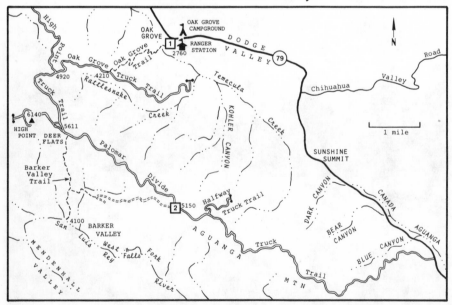

Trip 1: Oak Grove to High Point

Distance	14 miles (round trip)
Total Elevation Gain/Loss	3600'/3600'
Hiking Time	8 hours (round trip)
Recommended Map	Cleveland Natl. Forest recreation map
Optional Maps	USGS 7.5-min *Aguanga, Palomar Observatory*
Best Times	October through May
Difficulty	****

How's this for a climb of Palomar Mountain from bottom to top? Start at Oak Grove, along the base of the mountain, and climb steadily up seven miles of foot trail and fire road, gaining 3,400 feet, to reach High Point—highest summit within a radius of 14 miles. Of course, with the right kind of vehicle it is possible to drive to High Point, but you'd miss all the exercise. There's no water along this route, so plan accordingly.

Oak Grove is 14 miles north of Warner Springs via Highway 79. You begin at the fire station at mile 49.1 on Highway 79. Follow the "Oak Grove Trail" signs directing you over dirt roads and footpaths behind the station. After crossing a small stream just behind the station and passing through a gate, the trail meanders up to a ridgeline and begins cutting back and forth across an old firebreak.

You're now in the usual chaparral community of the mid-elevation mountains, where chamise, ribbonwood, scrub oak, and manzanita are common. A few conifers cluster below in the ravines on either side of the ridge. Sunny exposures along the trail support a fair springtime growth of annual wildflowers, including wild canterbury bells, chia, monkey flower and aster. A view opens to the north toward the summits of San Gorgonio Mountain and San Jacinto Peak.

At about 1.8 miles you come upon the roadbed of the Oak Grove Truck Trail, closed to public travel below this point. Go uphill (west) on the truck trail, and come to the High Point Truck Trail at 3.9 miles. Turn left and continue uphill through chaparral and oak forest to the Palomar Divide Truck Trail at 5.7 miles. Go right and head west around the north flank of High Point through a cool, shady forest of oaks and pines. At 6.7 miles you veer left on the steep road to the summit.

The 67-foot-high fire tower at the summit has been out of commission for some time, but it is still possible to climb up the first few flights of steps for a better view of the surroundings. The list of peaks visible— including the one you're on—reads like a roster of the highest points in southern California. Combs Peak, whose summit is right about eye level if you stand on the tower, is the nearest rival, 14 miles to the east. Parts of the Santa Rosa, San Ysidro, and Vallecito mountains in the Anza-Borrego Desert are visible, along with the Laguna and Cuyamaca Mountains farther to the southeast. In the north are the real giants—Old Baldy, San Gorgonio, and San Jacinto. On very clear days, several of the Channel Islands are visible far out in the Pacific. A lookout here once reported a fire burning in Santa Barbara County, almost two hundred miles away.

As an alternative to the long climb up, you could have someone drop you off at the top (High Point is accessible to sturdy vehicles via the Palomar Divide Truck Trail from the south, and the High Point Truck Trail from the north), and do this hike one-way downhill to Oak Grove. But then you'd miss the fun of coming up. Right?

Trip 2: Barker Valley

Distance	6.5 miles round trip
Total Elevation Gain/Loss	1000'/1000'
Hiking Time	4 hours round trip
Recommended Map	Cleveland Natl. Forest recreation map
Optional Map	USGS 7.5-min *Palomar Observatory* (no trails shown on 1982 edition)
Best Times	October through July
Difficulty	**

A cool current caressed my feet, erasing the memory of several long, hot miles on the trail. Sunlight scattered among a thousand fluttering leaves, and a tiny sliver of new moon glowed softly in a blue wedge of sky overhead. Water skaters flitted nervously on the rippled surface of the pool, casting fleeting shadows on a trio of small fish feeding on the bottom. Even in the warm month of July, it seemed, with the creek ebbing, Barker Valley could still be delightful.

Barker Valley perches squarely in one of the more remote corners of the Palomar Mountains, about three miles by dusty foot trail and about 8 miles by bone-shaking truck trail from the nearest paved road, Highway 79. At the least, you'll need a sturdy, high-clearance passenger car or truck to reach the trailhead. Turn west from Highway 79 at a point 6.5 miles northwest of Warner Springs (mile 41.9) and continue up the Palomar Divide Truck Trail for 7.7 miles to the gated, abandoned jeep road on the left (west) side.

Park off the main roadway and head down the old road. Older maps call this the Barker Valley Spur; it has been erased on the latest USGS *Palomar Observatory* quad. On the way down, keep an eye out for bald eagles in the sky. A number of these raptors roost in old snags on the shore of nearby Lake Henshaw during the winter.

Hike for 1.8 miles on a gradual descent until the road switches back sharply. At that point, continue straight (west) down the nose of a steep ridgeline on an informal trail. The Forest Service plans to rework this slippery

section of trail soon. At the bottom, cross a creek and curve left toward a trail junction at 2.3 miles. The right branch climbs north through chaparral to join the Palomar Divide Truck Trail in the vicinity of Deer Flats. We go left (south) and wind through chaparral and oaks to reach the gently sloping, oak-rimmed meadows of Barker Valley. Campsites are abundant along a stretch several hundred yards long. Just beyond is West Fork San Luis Rey River, framed by dense growths of willow, sycamore, and cottonwood trees.

Barker Valley is notorious for cold air drainage at night. I had the interesting experience of sweating out an 85° July day, then awakening next morning to find frost along the stream.

A rugged set of falls and pools awaits the adventurous hiker a few hundred yards downstream from Barker Valley. It is reported that native trout live in some of the pools below the first falls. This can be a somewhat hazardous area for those not familiar with hiking on water-polished rock, so use extreme caution if you go here.

Area M-4: La Jolla Indian Reservation

The La Jolla Indian Reservation welcomes campers to its busy campground along the San Luis Rey River, and hikers (even backpackers) are welcome to explore certain areas along the river banks.

"Tubing" down the river is a popular pastime here starting about May and continuing through summer. A new water slide near the campground is also popular during the warmer months. If it's peace and quiet you're looking for, you'll find this area a lot quieter for hiking during late fall through early spring.

The campground is located at mile 41.7 on State Highway 76, about 25 miles east of Interstate 15. The day or overnight fee levied at the entrance booth entitles you to a

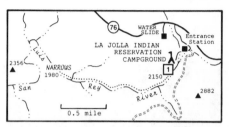

LaJolla Indian Reservation

"trespass permit" for hiking or backpacking on the reservation. Be sure to discuss with a reservation official plans for any ambitious hike. Read on for a description of one (rather moderate) hike down the San Luis Rey River.

Trip 1: San Luis Rey River

Distance	3 miles round trip (to narrows)
Total Elevation Gain/Loss	150'/150'
Hiking Time	3 hours (round trip)
Optional Maps	USGS 7.5-min *Palomar Observatory, Boucher Hill*
Best Times	All year
Difficulty	**

Steady releases of water from Lake Henshaw have kept the San Luis Rey River flowing year round during the past decade or so. Below Lake Henshaw the river follows a V-shaped canyon at the base of Palomar Mountain. At the La Jolla Reservation campground, the canyon widens somewhat, and is graced with a dense riparian strip of willows, sycamores, cottonwoods and live oaks.

The best hiking is downstream from the campground. Drive to the farthest camping

area on the downstream side, and begin hiking along the right (northwest) bank of the river. You'll be on a fairly well-defined trail beaten down by tubing enthusiasts who have to cart their tubes upriver after floating down. Poison oak appears here and there. In places you may have to scramble over rock outcrops if you don't want to get your feet wet.

Shady camp spots are available back from the bank. You probably won't want to drink the river water, even after purification. Runoff from cattle ranges and agricultural

areas upstream gives the water a murky
tint.

At about 1.5 miles down the river, the
canyon walls abruptly narrow. This is a good
spot for the average person to turn back. The
more adventuresome can continue by making a long traverse over steep rock slabs on
the right bank, or by staggering right through
the water, usually about mid-thigh depth.
Using the latter method invites a fall, as the

bottom contour is often invisible through the
semi-opaque water.

Over the next two miles, the canyon
swings around a gooseneck and tumbles over
several waterfalls two to four feet high.
Beyond this stretch, a diversion dam takes
virtually all the water and sends it through a
canal to Lake Wohlford, leaving a bone-dry
creekbed below.

San Luis Rey River

Area M-5: Warner Springs/Caliente Wilderness

This area encompasses Cleveland National Forest's Caliente Wilderness Study Area near Warner Springs. The Caliente Wilderness Study Area is one of two national forest WSA's in San Diego County not made official wilderness in the California Wilderness Bill enacted in 1984. The other is the Sill Hill WSA adjoining Cuyamaca Rancho State Park (see Area M-9, Trip 3). As of this writing, the two WSA's are still eligible for possible future inclusion in the National Wilderness Preservation System.

Caliente WSA is characterized by untouched stands of chaparral and small groves of Coulter pines. Some of the larger canyon bottoms and ravines are lined with a pleasant mixture of live oak, black oak, sycamore, cottonwood and Coulter pine trees. While these botanical arrays are by no means unique in southern California, the undisturbed nature and the remoteness of the Caliente WSA make it especially attractive for hiking and backpacking. A new section of the Pacific Crest Trail, one of the last to be completed in San Diego County, passes right through the area.

Both trips below utilize a part of the PCT. Camping space along or near the trail isn't easy to find; you'll have to make do with small sites. Since the Caliente WSA is in the national forest but not administered as wilderness, you need no permit for day hiking—but a remote camping permit is needed for overnight visits. Open fires are not permitted except at Indian Flats Campground, west of the WSA boundary.

The resort area of Warner Springs, gateway to the Caliente wilderness, is a few miles north of Lake Henshaw. The lake is reached by way of Highway 76 from Oceanside or Highways 78 and 79 from most locations in the south half of the county.

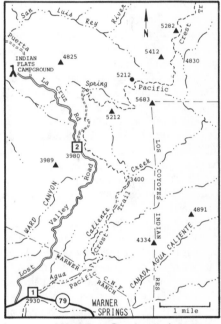

*Warner Springs/
Caliente Wilderness*

Trip 1: Agua Caliente Creek

Distance	8.0 miles round trip (to point where PCT leaves Agua Caliente Creek)
Total Elevation Gain/Loss	900'/900'
Hiking Time	4 hours (round trip)
Recommended Map	Cleveland Natl. Forest recreation map
Optional Maps	USGS 7.5-min *Warner Springs, Hot Springs Mtn.*
Best Times	November through May
Difficulty	***

Until a few years ago, these middle reaches of Agua Caliente Creek seldom saw the intrusion of humans. Now that a section of the Pacific Crest Trail has been routed through, it's become a favored stopping place for hikers headed north or south. This is one of only four places in San Diego County where the PCT dips to cross a fairly dependable stream, and the only area where the trail closely follows water for some distance.

The creek drains the Lost Valley area abutting the Caliente Wilderness Study Area, and the north slope of Hot Springs Mountain on the Los Coyotes Indian Reservation. The flow of water, if not year-round, is dependable from the first rains of fall into early summer.

Begin at the Agua Caliente Creek bridge at mile 36.6 on Highway 79. There is a large turnout for parking just west of here. Drop into the normally dry, sandy bed of the creek and proceed upstream on the sunny path that tracks above the highest level of flood waters. In this first mile, the trail goes through an easement across the Warner Ranch resort property. Near the Cleveland National Forest boundary (camping allowed past this point), the creek exits from a canyon mouth. The trail swings away east to detour around this canyon and begins a moderate ascent into ribbonwood-clothed hills. Almost two miles of somewhat tedious twisting and turning in the chaparral follow, and then you drop abruptly back into Agua Caliente Creek canyon at the 3200-foot contour.

Now the gorgeous scenery begins. In the next mile the trail crosses the stream several times and passes a number of appealing small campsites well up on the bank. Live oaks, sycamores, willows, and alders line the creek. The canyon walls soar several hundred feet on either side—clad in dense chaparral on the southeast side, dotted with sage and yucca on the northwest.

After a final crossing of the creek, the trail doubles back and begins a switchbacking ascent toward Lost Valley Road. This is a good turnaround point.

Further options for exploration include scrambling up the alder-choked bed of Agua Caliente Creek as far as the boundary of the Los Coyotes Indian Reservation (don't enter the reservation without prior permission), about one-half mile away. It's also possible to make a rugged trek down a tributary of Agua Caliente Creek by starting from the northeast slope of Hot Springs Mountain (see Area M-6, Trip 1) and exiting on the PCT. This trip would involve several detours around small waterfalls and the possibility of wading or swimming through at least one pool.

Trip 2: Upper Caliente

Distance	12 miles round trip (to a tributary of Agua Caliente Creek)
Total Elevation Gain/Loss	1700'/1700'
Hiking Time	7 hours (round trip)
Recommended Map	Cleveland Natl. Forest recreation map
Optional Maps	USGS 7.5-min *Warner Springs, Hot Springs Mtn.*
Best Times	November through May
Difficulty	***

This section of the Pacific Crest Trail through the Caliente wilderness winds along boulder-strewn ridges dotted with Coulter pine, and through small ravines shaded by mini-groves of live oak. In the upper reaches, there's no noise other than the wind, and no signs of man other than the trail itself. Even the skies are quiet; the area seems to be removed from the flight paths of airliners.

To reach the starting point, drive north on graded Lost Valley Road from mile 37.0 on Highway 79. After 4.6 miles of winding road, you'll come to a road summit and the intersection of a gated, abandoned dirt road. (Indian Flats, the developed national forest campground, is three more miles up the main road.) Park in the limited space provided, and walk up this abandoned road 0.5 mile to the point where the PCT joins from the right. Continue uphill on the old roadbed, somewhat monotonously, a mile farther to the point where the PCT tread diverges right, and follow it. (The roadbed itself sharply descends to a seasonal spring.)

The scenery improves with every step now. You wind up through scattered Coulter pines and picturesque granitic outcrops, with nice views of Lake Henshaw and the grasslands of Valle de San Jose surrounding it. You then lose the view as you pass north of Peak 5212 and contour around the head of a ravine. The ravine contains a smooth bed of sand, making it suitable as a small campsite.

The trail continues to climb moderately and winds around another ravine, this just south of a knob also labelled 5212 feet. It then descends slightly to cross a saddle and resumes climbing on the south side of a hill. From this hill there's a wonderful vista into Agua Caliente Creek and across to the north slope of Hot Springs Mountain. From nearly every vantage point but this, Hot Springs Mountain looks like a diminutive bump on the ridgeline, but from here it looks decidedly massive. Black oaks cluster along the small drainages along its flank, flashing gold in the fall season.

Next the trail bends north and contours, with small ups and downs, along the east side of the ridge containing Peak 5412. In late April and early May, these slopes are tinted pink with the blossoms of manzanita, and blue and white with blooming ceanothus. A dozen exotic fragrances scent the air. The Coulter pines are joined by live oaks and an occasional black oak.

At a point east of Peak 5412, you'll see below and to the east a grassy flat, filled with Coulter pines and black oaks, along an upper tributary of Agua Caliente Creek. This is a perfect place for a midday picnic, and even better for an overnight stay. Leave the trail at any point where the brush thins, and descend cross-country about 0.2 mile, losing 150 feet, to the seasonal creek. Water trickles through here until about June after a normal wet season.

Farther north, the Pacific Crest Trail winds over a stretch of less interesting chaparral country. This hidden glade, then, is a good turnaround point.

Area M-6: Los Coyotes Indian Reservation

Hikers and backpackers are in on a little secret when they find out about the Los Coyotes Indian Reservation. This is the largest (25,000 acres) of the 17 reservations in San Diego County, yet one of the least populated. Developed camping facilities are

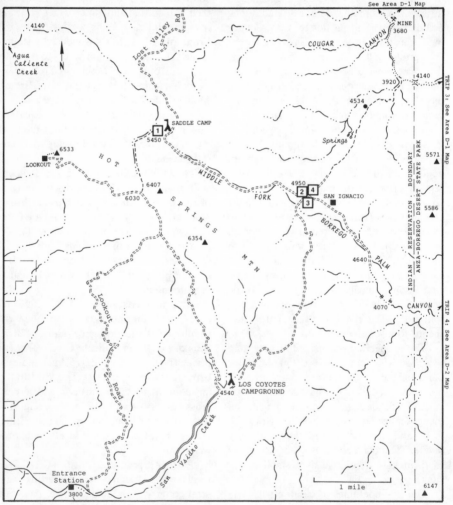

Los Coyotes Indian Reservation

provided for visitors, along with almost un-limited opportunities to explore the undeveloped backcountry afoot.

A network of graded dirt roads and jeep trails penetrates the flatter parts of the reservation, giving access to 4-wheel-drive vehicles and hikers alike. Motorcycles are prohibited and vehicle traffic is usually very light. This, coupled with a general prohibition on hunting and shooting, practically ensures peace and quiet. A number of primitive campsites with fire rings are located along some of the roads.

Hot Springs Mountain (6533'), known locally as "Warner's Peak" or "The Lookout," is San Diego County's highest mountain, topping better-known Cuyamaca Peak by just 17 feet. It is accessible from the south by poor roads from the reservation's entrance and main campground areas, and from the northeast via an abandoned jeep road (Trip 1 below). These and other roads in the north part of the reservation serve as superb

cross-country ski routes on the dozen or so days every winter when enough snow is on the ground. The eastern parts of the reservation serve as excellent jumping-off points for rugged trips into the remote reaches of Anza-Borrego Desert State Park (Trips 2–4 below).

To reach Los Coyotes, turn east on Camino San Ignacio from State Highway 79 (mile 35.0) at Warner Springs. After 0.6 mile, bear right on Los Tules Road and continue 4.5 miles to the entrance gate. Here you obtain your entrance permit, a sketch map of roads in the reservation, and a list of regulations. The main campground (last water available) lies another 2.7 miles on via paved and dirt road. Starting points for the trips below are still farther on.

Los Coyotes is open year-round, weather and road conditions permitting. You should call first, especially if planning a weekday trip (see Appendix 4).

Trip 1: Hot Springs Mountain

Distance	5.5 miles round trip
Total Elevation Gain/Loss	1250'/1250'
Hiking Time	3½ hours (round trip)
Recommended Map	USGS 7.5-min *Hot Springs Mtn.*
Best Times	All year (snow may block access in winter)
Difficulty	**

In the mist, the ghostly, abandoned fire lookout finally appears. We climb the steps and reach the observation deck. Suddenly there's a radiant heat around us and a flood of light from above. The cloud is passing on. A residue of tiny water droplets floats amid a blue sky, and a dozen mountain peaks pop out along the horizon. We spot the glistening summits of San Jacinto and San Gorgonio in the north, the somber Santa Rosas to the east, the dark Lagunas and Cuyamacas southward. In the chasm of Agua Caliente Creek to the northwest, a tenuous rainbow rides a billowing cloud.

That's what it's often like in winter—uncertain weather, but spectacularly clear if and when the clouds part. Summer days, on the other hand, are more dependably sunny and warm, but somewhat hazy. Like the Palomar and Cuyamaca mountain areas, Hot Springs Mountain exhibits the full range of seasonal change in spring and fall too.

Drive up Los Coyotes' main road, past the developed campground, to an intersection of roads in the valley at the head of Middle Fork Borrego Palm Canyon (6.1 miles past the entrance gate). Turn left (west) and drive up the valley on a sandy road to reach a saddle at the head of the valley, 2.2 miles farther. Just beyond this saddle, on the left (west) side of the road, is a primitive camping area (we'll call it "Saddle Camp") nestled in a shallow bowl shaded by live oak, pine and cedar. Picnic tables, fire rings and privies are here.

Park, and begin hiking southwest up a small tributary stream that flows north and west into Agua Caliente Creek. Follow traces of an abandoned jeep trail up this drainage, gaining more than 500 feet in 1.1 mile, and come up to the old road leading toward the lookout tower on Hot Springs Mountain. Then turn west and go another 1.6 miles along the ridgeline to the tower. You'll pass through dense forests of black oak, Coulter pine and white fir, and across sunny meadows dotted in late spring and early summer with many wildflowers.

The tower, dilapidated and seemingly on its last legs, sits on the west shoulder of the mountain. You can go higher by following a faint trail through thick brush and around boulders to the true summit. A flat concrete platform, the foundation of an old radio antenna, caps the summit block.

Several other trips may be done in this area of the reservation. Starting from Saddle Camp, you can go north and east to explore the uppermost reaches of Cougar Canyon. Or you can go north and west down the tributary of Agua Caliente Creek, reaching some pleasant campsites about one mile away. A rugged, one-way hike is possible down Agua Caliente Creek, with an exit on the Pacific Crest Trail near Warner Springs (see Area M-5, Trip 1).

Trip 2: Upper Cougar Canyon

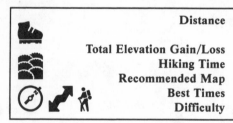

Distance	6 miles round trip (to mining area in Cougar Canyon)
Total Elevation Gain/Loss	1400'/1400'
Hiking Time	4 hours (round trip)
Recommended Map	USGS 7.5-min *Hot Springs Mtn.*
Best Times	October through May
Difficulty	***

Several interesting mountain-to-desert routes will become apparent if you spend much time exploring the northeastern corner of the Los Coyotes Reservation. One such route, dropping into Indian Canyon, is described in Trip 3. Others, noted below, depart from an upper level of Cougar Canyon. The canyon itself is pleasant enough to visit on a day hike, and its seclusion makes it attractive as a destination for a backpack trip.

Drive to the intersection of roads in the valley at the head of Middle Fork Borrego Palm Canyon, 6.1 miles past the entrance gate. Find a parking spot nearby off the road. Begin by hiking northeast 0.3 mile over a low saddle, where a view opens up of the northern

Santa Rosa Mountains and San Jacinto Peak. Descend, moderately now, on eroded jeep tracks, past some springs at 4650 feet, to a 4534-foot knob, 1.5 miles from the start, then continue sharply downhill to the bed of a usually wet south tributary of Cougar Canyon. Here you'll find a strip of live oaks, sycamores, and alders.

The road peters out; but continue north down this tributary, pushing through willow and alder thickets. Occasionally there's a snippet of road above the washed-out bank. When you reach the confluence of Cougar Canyon, you'll find a delightful grove of tall live oaks flanked by bracken and chain ferns. You can make camp on any of several flat beds of grass and oak leaves (be sure to find a fire-safe place to operate your camp stove).

Downstream about 300 yards, near a few more live oaks and two Coulter pines, are the remains of some mining equipment including a sluice box. Beyond this the bottom of Cougar Canyon gets quite rugged, so this is a good place to turn back.

The mine area can be the starting point for at least two very rugged trips down to the desert floor (you'll have to have some way of getting picked up in Collins Valley or in Coyote Canyon below Lower Willows):

The first is by way of lower Cougar Canyon. From the mine area, go down along Cougar's south wall, detouring around a rocky section with small waterfalls, until you can drop back to the streambed at 3400 feet. An easy section follows, with some possibilities for camping along the way. Below the 3080-foot contour, the canyon becomes impassable without technical climbing equipment. Here you must climb south out of the canyon and make a long traverse over a rocky ridge. See Area D-1, Trip 5 for further details.

The second is by way of an old jeep trail from the mine area to a 4490-foot peak (unlabelled on the topo map) north of the reservation boundary. The jeep trail is completely overgrown in a few spots, and covered in other places (during spring) with a profuse growth of wildflowers: goldenbush, paintbrush, blue-and-white ceanothus, and lupine.

Pinyon-dotted Peak 4490 offers a nearly panoramic view, cut off only by a slightly higher summit in the north—Peak 4649 ("Square Top")—between the two forks of Sheep Canyon. Like some other vantage points in the area, Peak 4490 has within visual range perhaps a hundred square miles of mountains and desert, and no visible signs of the works of man, save a microwave tower on distant Toro Peak.

Superb (if dry) wind-sheltered campsites can be made on the roadbed itself along the east shoulder of Peak 4490. From here it's possible to drop down the slope into South Fork Sheep Canyon. See Area D-1, Trip 4, for more details about that canyon.

Cougar Canyon below mine

Trip 3: Los Coyotes to Indian Canyon

Distance	6.0 miles (to roadend south of Sheep Canyon Primitive Camp)
Total Elevation Gain/Loss	300'/3650'
Hiking Time	5 hours
Recommended Maps	USGS 7.5-min *Hot Springs Mtn., Borrego Palm Canyon*
Best Times	November through April
Difficulty	***

For this spectacular descent into the Anza-Borrego Desert, we assume someone with a vehicle can pick you up at the end near Sheep Canyon Primitive Camp; you certainly won't want to climb back up this route. See Area D-1 for details about the road system on the desert floor. If a 4-wheel drive is unavailable, you'll have to walk out an additional four or five miles through Collins Valley and past Lower Willows, and rendezvous along a stretch of road suitable for conventional automobiles.

Begin as above in Trip 2. At about 2.0 miles (3920'), after joining the wet south tributary of Cougar Canyon, look to your right (east) and you'll see a saddle about 200 feet higher. The most recent USGS maps show a trail across this saddle, though it long ago succumbed to the elements. This was in fact a well-used Indian route connecting settlements at Santa Catarina Spring in Coyote Canyon with the village of San Ignacio in the valley at the head of Borrego Palm Canyon. West of San Ignacio, this trail continued to the hot springs at what we now call Warner Springs. East of Santa Catarina Spring, a branch of the trail continued through Box Canyon to another village at Hidden Spring (see Area D-3, Trip 6).

Scramble up through the decomposed granite soil and gain the saddle. Before you is a magnificent panorama of the Santa Rosa and San Jacinto mountains, Collins Valley and Coyote Canyon. Now descend sharply, staying right (south) of the ravine ahead— this is the route of the ancient trail into Indian Canyon. Though easy at first, thick chaparral at lower levels makes for slow going later. Near the bottom you can pick up a trace of the old trail through the brush. In his 1919 book *California Desert Trails* desert writer Joseph Smeaton Chase colorfully describes a single day's 20-mile journey, traveling with burro but mostly dismounted, up this trail and over to Indian settlements beyond San Ignacio.

Continue down the vegetation-choked bed of Indian Canyon for about one mile, then pick up the horse trail that leads north past the mouth of Cougar Canyon to the Indian Canyon road end. This is just around the corner from Sheep Canyon Primitive Camp.

Trip 4: Borrego Palm Canyon to Desert Floor

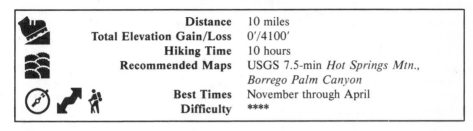

Distance	10 miles
Total Elevation Gain/Loss	0'/4100'
Hiking Time	10 hours
Recommended Maps	USGS 7.5-min *Hot Springs Mtn.,* *Borrego Palm Canyon*
Best Times	November through April
Difficulty	****

What dyed-in-the-wool local hiker has hiked lower Borrego Palm Canyon and hasn't wondered what it would be like to explore the canyon in its entirety? Well, here's your chance. We'll tell you about Palm Canyon's main (middle) fork from top to bottom. But be forewarned: mile after mile of slippery rock, small waterfalls, and thickets of brush and alder will necessitate a very slow, painstaking, and difficult descent. Needless to say, this is for expert hikers only. Long pants and sturdy boots are essential. Also take along a 30-foot piece of cord to use for lowering your pack down one or more of the falls. Middle Fork is a perennial stream with fair-to-good water quality, depending upon the amount of grazing upstream on the reservation.

Park in the valley at the head of Middle Fork, as in Trips 2 and 3 above. Walk southeast on a dirt road past some old buildings and a cemetery at San Ignacio (Don't linger here, or around any other structures or homes on the reservation.) The pastoral valley on the right, lined with 100-foot-tall cottonwoods, is used for cattle grazing. Continue down the road under a canopy of live oaks, until you reach the point (1.3 miles) where the road swings south—away from the creek. You have two choices: leave the road to follow the creekbed to a confluence at 4070 feet, or stay on the road south about 0.2 mile, then drop southeast into a western tributary of Middle Fork and go down it to the confluence. The two alternatives are of equal length, and both involve some serious bushwhacking and awkward detours around waterfalls. Either

way, this is the most difficult and hazardous stretch of the trip.

Below the confluence of the western tributary (2.0 miles, 4050') you enter a botanical transition zone of high-desert-mountain vegetation. The slopes are covered with ribbonwood, scrub oak, mountain mahogany, manzanita, chamise, ceanothus, and sugar bush. A few pinyons dot the north-facing slopes, wherever moisture is conserved in the soil for long periods of time. In a narrow band along the stream, willows and cottonwoods thrive, along with small water- or shade-loving shrubs and herbs such as wild rose, nettles, miner's lettuce, cattails, and wild peony.

The creek meanders on a gentle gradient for a mile below the confluence, with grassy campsites along the inner banks. You're now passing from a zone containing the common Cretaceous granitic rocks that make up the core of the Peninsular ranges, to an area with older (pre-Cretaceous) granitic and metamorphic rocks exposed. Colorful outcrops of orange-banded gneiss and other metamorphic rocks will be seen in the next six miles or so.

At 3.0 miles (3650'), the water shoots over a 15-foot vertical fall. Below this the creek drops steeply through a narrow gorge. Alder trees appear, and they conspire with the willows to impede your progress. It's easiest to walk right down the middle of the creek most of the time, underneath the tangle of tree limbs. Cottonwoods appear at about 3.8 miles (3300').

At 5.3 miles (2900'), just above the first palm tree, an easy traverse north over a ridge into the North Fork is possible. From here to the confluence of North Fork (5.7 miles, 2700'), both the creek and banks in Middle Fork are overgrown by a junglelike growth of vines that act like trip wires.

Below the confluence, the canyon becomes more open and less thickly vegetated. Slippery, water-polished rock is now the biggest difficulty. At about 6.2 miles (2450') you'll traverse around two sets of falls.

By the time you reach the confluence of South Fork (6.7 miles, 2200'), the sparser vegetation of the low desert has begun to

appear on the canyon walls, and palms line the canyon in greater numbers. The going gets progressively easier now (see Area D-2, Trips 1-3 for more details).

At 8.5 miles (1300') you come upon the lowest grove of palms; here you pick up the Borrego Palm Canyon Nature Trail, leading to Borrego Palm Canyon Campground. Curiosity satisfied, you can saunter down this "tourist trail," smug in the knowledge that you, unlike the untold thousands who only glimpse the beauty of the canyon, have truly seen it all.

Upper Middle Fork, Borrego Palm Canyon

Borrego Palm Canyon just below South Fork confluence

Area M-7: Upper San Diego River and Tributaries

The San Diego River and its upper tributaries begin life in the pastoral valleys and forested hillsides around the old gold mining town of Julian, and along the steep western slopes of the Cuyamaca Mountains. The water flows southwest in V-shaped canyons cut deeply into chaparral-covered foothills, and eventually reaches El Capitan Reservoir. Quite frequently the water encounters resistant layers in the underlying igneous and metamorphic rocks, where it tumbles over cataracts up to a hundred feet high. The grinding of stones trapped in pockets below these falls has in some cases created deep pools, known locally as "punchbowls."

The area is not well known among hikers, even though it lies just 10–20 air miles east of the edge of suburbia as defined by the communities of El Cajon, Santee, Lakeside, and Poway. One reason is that most of the area is served only by winding dirt roads not quickly reached from the coast. Another reason is that legal access—public access—to many of the most interesting streams and waterfalls is problematical. The ragged boundaries of the Cleveland National Forest encompass much of the area, but a maze of private inholdings and roads with locked gates make travel either by car or afoot awkward.

The trip descriptions below include the Inaja Trail, a roadside nature trail overlooking the headwaters of the San Diego River, and three rugged and sometimes devious hiking routes to several of the most spectacular waterfalls in all of San Diego County.

As in most parts of the Cleveland National Forest, car camping and backpacking are permitted on forest land in this area if you have a remote camping permit. Contact any Forest Service office to obtain a permit (see Appendix 4). No permit is required for day hiking.

Trip 1: Inaja Trail

	Distance	0.5 mile
	Total Elevation Gain/Loss	100'/100'
	Hiking Time	20 minutes
	Optional Map	USGS 7.5-min *Santa Ysabel* (trail not shown on 1960 edition)
	Best Times	All year
	Difficulty	*

The Inaja Trail, one of four trails in San Diego County to have earned the appellation "National Recreation Trail," begins at the Inaja Picnic Area along State Highway 78/79, one mile east of Santa Ysabel and six miles west of Julian. The picnic area memorializes 11 firefighters who lost their lives in the San Diego River canyon while battling the 60,000-acre Inaja Fire in 1956.

An excellent trail brochure, available at the trailhead, gives information about the typical live-oak-chaparral vegetation seen

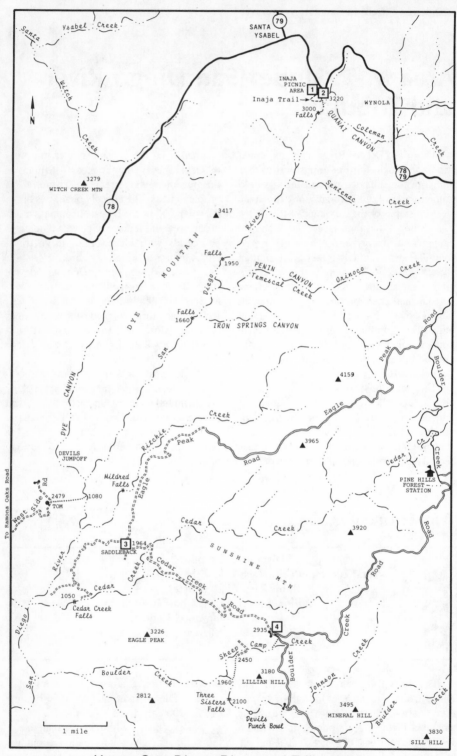

Upper San Diego River and Tributaries

here and elsewhere in the upper foothills of San Diego County. An overlook at midpoint in the trail gives a good view down the linear canyon of the San Diego River. At 3440 feet elevation, this overlook is often just above a temperature inversion layer that traps cooler, moist air below. On some mornings, you'll find the canyon hidden by a cottony blanket of fog, while neighboring peaks and ridges stand like islands in clear air.

Out along the north side of the trail is a view of the fertile Santa Ysabel Valley, the rolling hills of Mesa Grande, and the dark, brooding Volcan Mountains.

San Diego River Canyon

Trip 2: San Diego River

Distance	10.5 miles
Total Elevation Gain/Loss	1400'/3000'
Hiking Time	11 hours
Required Maps	USGS 7.5-min *Santa Ysabel, Ramona*
Best Times	November through May
Difficulty	****

A trip down this canyon in early spring is really an eye opener. Runoff from winter storms fills the bed of the river with a silvery band of water. New leaves and gaily colored wildflowers brighten the banks as well as the slopes. The stream drops abruptly several times over precipices up to a hundred feet high.

Bedrock morteros and metates along the river, especially near groves of oaks, attest to frequent use of the canyon by our Indian predecessors. Contemporary human usage pales by comparison; only an occasional hiker, backpacker or hunter penetrates these canyon depths today.

Sturdy boots and a patient, cautious attitude are essential for this trip. Long pants are recommended, as are small clippers to prune back the branches of poison oak in a few tight spots. If you're traveling with a heavy or awkward pack, bring a 30-foot length of cord to assist in lowering it over rock faces as you detour around the waterfalls. Avoid the canyon after intense storms, when high water levels may make stream crossings difficult or hazardous. Before the winter rains come, on the other hand, there may be no water at all.

The hike begins at Inaja Picnic Area (see Trip 1 above) and ends at the east terminus of Ramona Oaks Road in San Diego Country Estates. To reach the latter from Ramona, take San Vicente Road south and east about seven miles to Ramona Oaks Road; turn left and go three miles east to the roadend at the edge of Cleveland National Forest. If you're setting up a car shuttle, the following devious short cut through San Diego Country Estates will allow you to drive from the ending to the

starting point in less than 30 minutes: go back (west) on Ramona Oaks Road 2.5 miles; turn right (northwest) on Watt Road and go 1.0 mile; turn right (northeast) on Gunn Stage Road and go 0.7 mile; turn left (west) on Arena Way and go 0.2 mile; turn right (north) on Baba Drive and go 100 yards; turn right (east) on Gymkhana Road and go 50 yards; turn left (north) on Sargeant Road and go 0.3 mile; turn left (northwest) on Vista Ramona Road and go 1.9 miles; turn right (north) on Old Julian Highway and follow it 6.1 miles to Highway 78; and finally turn right (east) and continue 7.0 miles to Inaja Picnic Area.

From Inaja Picnic Area, drop into the oak-shaded canyon on one of the obscure paths through the brush below the restrooms near the Inaja Trail head. In just 0.5 mile you come to the first falls, a set of two, each about 50 feet high. Make a difficult traverse through brush and over tilted rock slabs on the right (west) side.

The riverbed ahead is choked with small willows and a variety of water-loving plants including wild berry vines. Live oaks and sycamores are rooted to the banks. Much time is spent dodging vegetation and stepping over water-worn boulders, mostly dark gray- and black-colored gabbro. At 1.5 miles, a usually wet tributary, Sentenac Creek, comes in from the east. Here you can pick up some eroded bulldozer tracks, first on the east bank, then the west, for about 0.4 mile. Another usually wet tributary comes in from the east at 2.2 miles (2190').

You continue on a fairly gradual descent, boulder-hopping much of the way, until you reach the abrupt lip of a 100-foot fall at 3.2 miles (1950'). The water tumbles into an open grotto fashioned of granite and gneiss, and collects in a shallow pool perhaps 60 feet across. Traverse on the left (south) side of the canyon, over club moss and through shrubbery, taking care not to approach the brink of the grotto too closely.

At a wide bend in the river at 3.7 miles (1760′), excellent campsites can be found among spreading oaks on the bank—but watch out for clumps of poison oak (in winter, these will be leafless and hard to identify). At 4.4 miles (1660′), you come upon another beautiful fall, 30 feet high with a deep pool below about 70 feet across. This is probably your best opportunity for a refreshing dip if the weather and water temperature allow.

The vegetation thins now, and walking becomes easier over alternating stretches of sand and rocks on the banks, and exposures of bedrock—with pools—in the canyon bottom. Cottonwoods appear and increase in number as the canyon gradually widens.

Watch carefully for the major tributary entering from the north at 7.6 miles. This usually dry canyon comes down from a steep rock face (on private property) known as the Devil's Jumpoff. From this point, continue south down the canyon, pass a gully on the right in 0.2 mile, and then go straight up the steep ridge that climbs westward to survey point "Tom," nearly 1400 feet above on West Side Road. This steep, brushy climb is best done in the late afternoon, when the sun is hidden from view. Make your way up

100-foot waterfall on San Diego River

through an obstacle course of mostly waist-high chamise and buckwheat, relieved on occasion by bare patches filled with spring wildflowers such as lupine and baby-blue-eyes. Then pick up West Side Road and follow it 1.8 miles down to Ramona Oaks Road.

An alternative to this last part is to continue down the San Diego River canyon, turn up Ritchie Creek and climb up to Eagle Peak Road (see Trip 3). Transportation arrangements are more difficult this way.

Trip 3: Cedar Creek Falls

Distance	4.5 miles round trip
Total Elevation Gain/Loss	1200'/1200'
Hiking Time	2½ hours (round trip)
Recommended Maps	USGS 7.5-min *Santa Ysabel, Tule Springs*
Best Times	November through June
Difficulty	**

Here is one of San Diego County's hidden treasures, tucked back in a tributary of the upper San Diego River, and accessible (legally) only by a circuitous ride down a long dirt road and a hike on an abandoned road. Before the construction of El Capitan Dam in the early 30s, the falls were a popular destination for Sunday outings, and could be reached relatively easily by way of the San Diego River bed from Lakeside.

Helix Water District controls land below the 995-foot contour in the San Diego River drainage north of El Capitan Reservoir, including the lower reaches of Cedar Creek. The area is well posted with NO TRESPASSING signs. Curiously, the boundary of this withdrawal within the national forest was to have coincided with the level of El Capitan Reservoir at maximum storage. The original plans for the dam were scaled down, and today the maximum level stands at only 750 feet. Since the 995-foot contour passes just below the deep pool at Cedar Creek Falls, the only legal access to the pool and falls is from above.

To reach Cedar Creek Falls from the coast, drive east through Ramona toward Santa Ysabel and Julian. Six miles east of Santa Ysabel and one mile short of (west of) Julian, turn south on Pine Hills Road. After 1.5 miles, bear right on Eagle Peak Road. After 1.4 more miles, veer right on Eagle Peak Road (Boulder Creek Road goes left). Now you face 8.2 miles of progressively poorer dirt road (may be impassable when wet). At 7.7 miles, you come to a eucalyptus grove and a cattle grate. Proceed downhill another 0.5 mile to "Saddleback," a four-way junction of roads on national forest land.

Park here and begin walking.

Go west on the road that leads along the edge of the canyon containing Ritchie Creek. Mildred Falls, beautifully visible up the canyon, is arguably San Diego County's highest, at more than 100 feet. Unfortunately, it's often little more than a dark stain on an orange-tinted cliff. Several small reservoirs upstream squelch the flow to a trickle most of the time. In flood, however, it is truly an awesome sight.

The road winds farther west, offering a splendid view of the upper San Diego River canyon, then turns south on a long descent to the river bed. At 1.0 mile a severe washout, which has gone unrepaired for several years, blocks vehicle traffic. At 1.4 miles (1270'), take the spur road that goes left (southeast) over a low saddle into the Cedar Creek drainage. Descend to the bank of the creek and follow it to the road's end. A few flat spots provide possible camping areas.

The brink of the falls lies just below. Be extremely cautious, and don't peer over the top from the slippery rock in the creekbed. Long-time San Diego hiker Uel Fisk remembers quite vividly watching one of his classmates fall to her death from this brink in 1926. You can work your way with some difficulty over the north wall of the canyon and drop down to the bottom of the falls. A large, flat-topped rock outcrop along the way gives a dizzying view of the 90-foot-high cascade of water, the deep pool, and the cottonwoods below.

The punchbowl at the bottom is perhaps 50 feet across and 20 feet deep. Have a nice swim, but don't dive too deep—you won't want to trespass below the 995' contour!

Cedar Creek Falls

Trip 4: Three Sisters Waterfalls

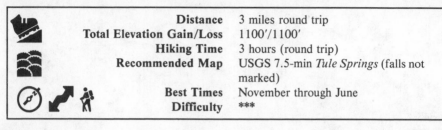

Distance	3 miles round trip
Total Elevation Gain/Loss	1100'/1100'
Hiking Time	3 hours (round trip)
Recommended Map	USGS 7.5-min *Tule Springs* (falls not marked)
Best Times	November through June
Difficulty	***

This triple set of waterfalls in Boulder Creek, dubbed the "Three Sisters" by local ranchers, is located in a patch of national forest heavily incised by private inholdings. Dirt roads to the north give easier access to the falls, but these cross unoccupied private land whose owner specifically denies access to both vehicles and hikers. Another road leads toward the falls from above (east), but this too passes through a private ranch. Follow carefully the hiking directions below to avoid trespassing.

The starting point is reached most easily via Pine Hills Road and Boulder Creek Road near Julian (see Trip 3 above). At the point where Boulder Creek Road and Eagle Peak Road diverge, go south on Boulder Creek Road 8.4 miles (pavement ends in 3.2 miles) to a four-way intersection of roads, including Cedar Creek Road (Forest Road 13S11). Park here, taking care not to block any of the roads. This point may also be reached by driving 13.0 miles north on Boulder Creek Road (less than half paved) from Oak Grove Drive in Descanso.

From the intersection, walk precisely 200 yards southeast on Boulder Creek Road; then bushwhack straight down the chamise-covered ridge on your right (southwest), dropping into Sheep Camp Creek. For the next 0.5 mile follow down this creek, dodging overhanging shrubbery and clumps of poison oak (clippers may come in handy). Bedrock comes to the surface in places, along with water, so be careful of slippery rock.

When you come upon an old jeep trail, follow it along the south bank, once again dodging encroaching growths of poison oak, for about 0.3 mile; then turn south over a low

saddle. From the saddle you can both see and hear (in late fall through spring) the falls below. Make camp here if you don't want to carry your heavy pack down the slope.

Now drop very steeply cross-country down the slope, losing 500 feet in 0.2 mile. On the way down, enjoy the superb display of April wildflowers, which includes paintbrush, California poppy, deerweed, morning glory, phacelia, monkeyflower, scarlet bugler, wild hyacinth, baby-blue-eyes, woolly blue curls, wild pea, owl's clover, and peony.

Camp may be made at the bottom along a flat overlooking Boulder Creek. Ahead to the south lies about 0.3 mile of tricky rock hopping. Great masses of poison oak, intermixed with wild grape vines, lie along the banks, forcing you to zigzag across the bouldered bed of the creek or negotiate a path directly down the middle of it. Be very cautious of slippery rocks.

Finally you reach the base of the waterfalls—and all the previous trouble is suddenly worth it. The "middle sister" is the most impressive, with water sliding 50 feet down a smooth channel worn in the bedrock into a kidney shaped pool about 80 feet long and at least 10 feet deep.

Since much of the upstream drainage of Boulder Creek comes from Cuyamaca Reservoir, water releases there affect the flow of water over the falls. During my visit in April, there was plenty. Upstream from the falls is a circular feature worn in the bed of Boulder Creek called the Devils Punch Bowl. An attempt to mine placer gold here a number of years ago was unsuccessful. The punchbowl lies on private property, and is not open to hikers.

Area M-8: Julian

The town of Julian enjoys a reputation far wider than its diminutive size would seem to call for. Tourists come in droves to this gold-mining-boom-town-turned-apple-growing-center to tour its quaint museums, buy an apple pie, bend an elbow at the soda fountain, and, of course, to walk in the pine-scented woods. What seasoned hikers know, and many first-time tourists don't, however, is that there's precious little woods-walking available close to town. Beyond the little grid of streets, east of town, one might find the path leading to the site of the old Washington Mine; otherwise it's all private land, fenced and posted. The highways and paved back roads, of course, may be walked, but cycling them is better.

Hiking opportunities multiply if you drive some distance out of town. Cuyamaca Rancho State Park and the Laguna Mountain Recreation Area (Areas M-9 and M-11), 10 or more miles south of Julian, offer almost unlimited trail hiking. Somewhat closer to Julian is William Heise County Park, with its small network of trails in a superb forested setting; and the Banner Toll Road, a historic wagon road through a parcel of BLM land. These two areas are profiled below in Trips 1 and 2.

To reach Julian, you can take either of two routes, each about 60 miles long as measured from San Diego. The first is by way of Interstate 8, then Highway 79 through Cuyamaca Rancho State Park; the other—which is shorter from North County areas—is by way of Highway 78 via Ramona and Santa Ysabel.

Trip 1: William Heise County Park

Hiking Distance	1 to 3 miles
Recommended Map	William Heise County Park map/brochure
Optional Map	USGS 7.5-min *Julian* (trails not marked on 1982 edition)
Best Times	All year
Difficulty	* to **

At Heise Park you can find your quintessential walk in the pine woods. The park is located in one of the most beautiful and unspoiled pockets of undeveloped land around Julian, and is large enough to contain a significant network of footpaths.

About 10 percent of the park is devoted to meticulously maintained camping and picnic areas. These lie along the thickly wooded bottomlands of Cedar Creek and its upper tributaries. The surrounding area is a virtual wilderness laced with about seven miles of loop trails. Heise Park is also the northern terminus of the outstanding new Kelly Ditch Trail, which leads into Cuyamaca Rancho State Park (see Area M-9, Trip 1 for a full description).

The Cedar Trail and the self-guiding Nature Trail, each a mile in length, stay beneath a shady canopy of oaks, pines and cedars.

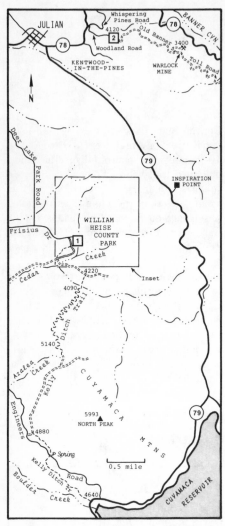

Julian

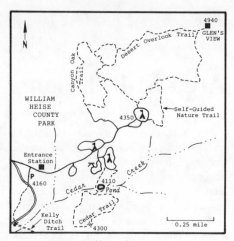

Julian inset

of timbered hills toward the summits of the Cuyamaca and the Laguna mountains. Eastward, the Anza-Borrego Desert and the Salton Sea shimmer in the distance. On late summer afternoons, when conditions are propitious, you can watch massive thunderheads roil in as moist air flowing across the desert from the Gulf of California rises over the mountains.

The well-marked turnoff to Heise Park is one mile west of Julian on Highway 78/79. Signs direct you south on Pine Hills Road to Frisius Drive, then east on Frisius to the park entrance.

Oak-shaded trail in Heise Park

The Manzanita and Canyon Oak trails, on the other hand, climb up along steep slopes clothed with dense chaparral; in some places, the manzanita grows to 10 feet or more in height, enclosing the trails in a tangled tunnel.

Glen's View lies on a windswept ridgeline in the northeast corner of the park. The view here is similar to, but more inclusive than, that enjoyed by motorists at Inspiration Point, a half mile below on Highway 79. To the south you can look over a rolling expanse

Trip 2: Old Banner Toll Road

	Distance	2.5 miles round trip
	Total Elevation Gain/Loss	700'/700'
	Hiking Time	90 minutes (round trip)
	Optional Map	USGS 7.5-min *Julian*
	Best Times	October through June
	Difficulty	**

Honeycombed hillsides and bits and pieces of rusted equipment—that is the legacy left behind by Julian's gold-mining heyday over a century ago. Although a few mines continue to be worked sporadically even today, most have long been abandoned. For a look at one of the first mines to be discovered (1870), and one of the last to be extensively worked, try this short hike down the Old Banner Toll Road.

Drive one mile east of Julian on State Highway 78, then turn right at Whispering Pines Road. Immediately after, make a sharp right, then a left to connect with Woodland Road. After 0.4 mile on Woodland Road, go left at a fork (the right fork leads to a locked gate) and proceed another 0.1 mile to the end of the pavement. Park here, well off the roadway.

On foot now, take the rough dirt road that curves steeply downward to the left (generally east). This is one of the two roads down Banner Canyon from Julian to Banner shown on a circa-1910 topographic map of the area. Nature has not been kind to this old road in recent years. Violent storms over the past several winters have caused deep washouts across its bed. As tracks show, only foot travelers, horses, coyotes, and a few intrepid motorcyclists come this way today.

Below you is the modern road through Banner Canyon—Highway 78. It appears only slightly less twisting than the road you're on, but offers a more gradual—if longer—descent to the town of Banner. Below Highway 78, near the very bottom of the canyon, there once existed even earlier routes of travel between Julian and Banner. The earliest was a "skid road" so steep that a driver descending it would have to drag an uprooted tree behind his wagon to provide enough braking power.

The linear shape of Banner Canyon is due to repeated ruptures along the Elsinore Fault. This splinter fault of the San Andreas is the most extensive fault system in San Diego County, and is believed capable of causing a major earthquake.

Abandoned mine shafts pierce the earth on the steep slopes above and below you, but nearly all are concealed by a heavy growth of chaparral. You'll see one obvious opening, however, on the right about 0.5 mile down the road. At about one mile, the Warlock Mine, with its processing mill, comes into view. The mine suspended operations in 1957 and now lies in a state of advanced dilapidation.

It's worth a look around though. You'll find the relatively intact ball mill perched on the hillside, the superintendent's formerly cozy cottage with its fine view, and other buildings in a state of collapse. In 1962 the mine's shafts were declared a radioactive fallout shelter for 222 people by the Civil Defense Commission and stocked accordingly with emergency provisions. A cave-in two years later ended its usefulness in that regard. (Safety reminder: tread carefully among the ruins, and don't enter the mine openings.)

The BLM plans to establish an interpretive station in this area to introduce visitors to the history of gold mining in the Julian District, and to explain the fascinating geology of Banner Canyon.

Beyond the Warlock Mine, Old Banner Toll Road runs into private property, so it's best to turn back after visiting the mine.

Area M-9: Cuyamaca Mountains

Who among those unfamiliar with the real southern California would believe that such beautiful forests could exist just an hour's drive from downtown San Diego? Who would believe the intensity of the fall and spring color? Who would believe that snow can blanket the Cuyamacas, while at the same time the coastal area bakes in subtropical sunshine?

This knowledge is not lost among San Diego hikers. The Cuyamaca Mountains are probably the most popular place to hike in San Diego County. There are three reasons for this: first, the area's easy access by freeways and highways from the abodes of two million residents in San Diego's urban and suburban areas; second, the fact that most of this beautiful mountain area is preserved as public land in the form of Cuyamaca Rancho State Park, one of California's largest state parks; and third, the opportunity to explore 100-plus miles of old roads and newer hiking trails within the park.

Indians summered in the Cuyamacas for at least 7000 years before the coming of the Spanish. Then, as now, game and certain basic vegetable foodstuffs, such as acorns, were plentiful. The Indians called the area *Ah-ha-Kwe-ah-mac,* variously translated as "the place where it rains," and "rain yonder," in reference to the relatively wet climate at higher elevations—about 35 inches of precipitation a year. Dozens of rich archeological sites exist throughout these mountains; bedrock morteros are a common feature along trails and around springs and resting areas.

In 1845 the area became a Mexican land grant, Rancho Cuyamaca. The promise of harvesting timber from the rancho was never fulfilled, and it was not until 1855 that the first non-Indian, James Lassator, settled here.

Gold was discovered in the hills around Julian and along the north edge of the Cuyamacas in the 1860s, and within a few years the influx of prospectors and miners had displaced the remaining native people. A prospect near the shoreline of today's Cuyamaca Reservoir eventually became southern California's most productive gold mine, the Stonewall Mine.

After the gold boom, the old rancho property changed hands several times until it was purchased by the state in 1933 for use as a park. Today's park, with inclusions beyond the old rancho boundary, totals nearly 30,000 acres. Of this, some 13,000 acres have been set aside as state wilderness.

The dominant topographic feature of the park, and the area surrounding it, is the chain of forested peaks—North, Middle, and Cuyamaca peaks—that form the main massif of the Cuyamaca Mountains. Most of North Peak is in private ownership, while Middle Peak and Cuyamaca Peak anchor the park's west side. Lower, drier, chaparral-covered peaks, such as Stonewall and Oakzanita peaks, lie along the park's eastern edge, not far from the Laguna Mountains to the east.

The highest ridges of the Cuyamaca Mountains are crowned with forests of live and black oak, incense-cedar, white fir, and four varieties of pine—Coulter, sugar, ponderosa, and Jeffrey. Below these are broad, treeless mesas and valley bottoms, awash in tall grasses. Sycamore, alder, and willow cling to the major watercourses. Still lower are rugged foothills densely covered with chaparral broken by rock outcrops. Only one other mountainous area in San Diego County offers a similarly rich diversity of habitats: Palomar Mountain.

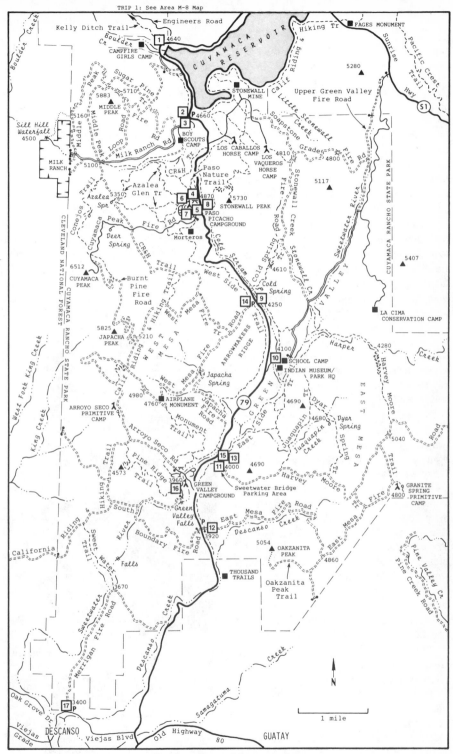

Cuyamaca Mountains

For better and for worse, the park is split asunder by a rather heavily trafficked (on weekends, at least) road—State Highway 79. This route allows easy access from Interstate 8 on the south and from the Julian area on the north, but unavoidably dispels some of the area's tranquillity. Since many of the trails depart from the highway and head into the backcountry in a very direct fashion, however, it isn't too difficult for hikers to get away from traffic noise—and most other people too—fairly quickly.

Most visitor activity in the park centers on campgrounds and points of interest located near the highway. Green Valley and Paso Picacho campgrounds are popular for family camping, while Los Caballos and Los Vaqueros cater to horsemen. There are interpretive displays outside Paso Picacho Campground and at the Indian Museum next to park headquarters. On display at the Stonewall Mine site are a few old relics of the mining days. Ranger-led walks, and lectures on the geology, wildlife, and history of the area are offered on most weekends.

Backpacking within the park is rewarding, but somewhat limited. There are only two designated trail camping areas, shared by hikers and horsemen: Arroyo Seco and Granite Spring primitive camps. Both are in the southern part of the park. These sites are available on a first-come-first-served basis by pre-registration at park headquarters, Green Valley Campground, or Paso Picacho Campground. "Environmental" (walk-in) sites are available near Paso Picacho Campground. See Appendix 4 for more information. Potable water is available at several locations in the park—the campgrounds, the park headquarters area, and all developed trailside springs (shown on our area map).

There are no restrictions on day hiking, except for parking regulations (usually no overnight parking) at certain trailheads. The trips described below include many of the older, more popular trails in the state park, as well as some new routes in areas recently added to the park. Trips 1 and 3 include areas on the boundary of the park. (See Area M-11, Trip 15 for a one-way route from the

Laguna Mountains into the park.) One trip intentionally not described in this book is a visit to a grove of one of the rarest trees in the world—the Cuyamaca cypress. This relative of the Tecate cypress is now confined to an area of less than one square mile along the west boundary of the park. The rangers at park headquarters should be able to help you find these trees if you express an interest in seeing them.

The Cuyamaca Mountains offer special opportunities for two other modes of travel: mountain bicycling and cross-country skiing. Mountain biking is by law confined to dirt roads not included in state wilderness areas, while skiing is limited in a practical sense to the dozen or so days every year when enough snow lies on the ground. Favorite skiing routes include roads and trails on Middle and Cuyamaca peaks.

On the Doane Valley Nature Trail

Trip 1: Kelly Ditch Trail

Distance	5.5 miles (Cuyamaca Reservoir to Heise Park)
Total Elevation Gain/Loss	1000'/1600'
Hiking Time	4 hours
Optional Maps	USGS 7.5-min *Cuyamaca Peak, Julian* (trail not marked on 1982 editions)
Best Times	All year
Difficulty	***

One of the most beautiful forested areas in San Diego County, heretofore inaccessible to the public, is now open to hikers and horsemen. Recent purchases of property on the north end of Cuyamaca Rancho State Park and on the south end of William Heise County Park have made feasible the construction of a trail linking the two parks. Dedicated in 1985, the trail follows, in part, the so-called Kelly Ditch, a century-old diversion channel; and an old "skid road" once used to slide timber down from a steep ridge.

A remarkable aspect of this trail is its apparent isolation. A look at the most recent topo maps reveals a network of new roads and many structures—second homes—just outside park boundaries and not far from the trail. But these are seldom seen from the trail itself because of the screen of trees.

The preferred direction on the trail is south to north—Cuyamaca Reservoir to Heise Park. Aside from this being a mostly downhill hike, you can take advantage of maximum shade by going this way, provided you start early in the morning. Leave one car near the entrance kiosk at Heise Park (see Area M-8, Trip 1) and drive the other car south from Julian about 8.3 miles to the intersection of Engineers Road and Highway 79. Parking space is available nearby along the highway shoulder.

Pick up the trail 0.1 mile west of Engineers Road, just north of where the highway crosses the low dam of Cuyamaca Reservoir. The eroded and overgrown ditch to the right (north) of the trail is Kelly Ditch.

Built by Russian and Chinese laborers with pick and shovel about a century ago, its purpose was to divert runoff from the south slopes of North Peak into the then new Cuyamaca Reservoir. Ordinarily this water would flow directly into Boulder Creek downstream from the dam.

In the first mile, the trail strikes a path sometimes parallel to the old channel and sometimes directly in it. A tunnel-like canopy of live oaks and tall shrubs keeps the sun off you. The earthen berms of the ditch and some of the stonework are still relatively undisturbed, except in places where flooding in ravines has breached the walls. Watch for poison oak here and there at the trailside.

After about one mile the trail climbs abruptly out of the ditch, veers north through a sunny patch of chaparral, and crosses Engineers Road. We pass a spring-fed horse trough, then continue along a yucca-dotted slope to join an old road that curves up and around the west slope of North Peak. Past a couple of ancient sugar pines, this road enters a delightful, parklike meadow, dotted with black oaks and carpeted with bracken ferns. On the clear, crisp days of late October and early November, the tawny yellows and browns of leaves, ferns and dry grasses contrast sharply with the deep blue of the sky, and the hazier blues of distant ridges to the west. On the most transparent days, another distinct shade of blue is visible along the horizon—the ocean.

At the next fork in the road (about mile 2.5) bear left and continue north across a sunny bowl at the head of Azalea Creek. The road peters out, but our way continues as a trail into a thickly forested zone of live and black oaks, ponderosa and Coulter pines, incense-cedar and white fir. Passing over a summit, we now begin a long set of switch-backs leading to a tributary of Cedar Creek—a loss of more than 1000 feet in somewhat less than two miles. A glade of ferns, wild berries, and a delightful trickling stream awaits us at the bottom.

Beyond the creek, the trail goes up a steep ravine evidently cut deeply by some agent other than running water. This is a remnant of a skid road hacked out in the days when timber from these mountains served the needs of the nearby gold mines and the boom towns of Julian and Cuyamaca.

After a gain of about 120 feet, the trail tops out on a saddle and joins a dirt road. Turning left, we drop down about 200 feet, cross the main Cedar Creek, continue across a meadow, and finally pick up the last link of trail leading directly toward the parking lot near the entrance kiosk of Heise Park.

Oak forest along Kelly Ditch Trail

Trip 2: Middle Peak

Distance	5.7 miles
Total Elevation Gain/Loss	1100'/1100'
Hiking Time	3 hours
Recommended Map	Cuyamaca Rancho State Park map/brochure
Optional Map	USGS 7.5-min *Cuyamaca Peak*
Best Times	All year
Difficulty	**

If you like big trees, Middle Peak is the place to go. Middle Peak's cone-shaped bulk is crowned with the largest conifers in the Cuyamaca Mountains—and possibly in all of San Diego County.

The fire trails that encircle Middle Peak have long been popular hiking routes. This trip description, however, introduces a varia-tion: along with one of the older loop trails, it includes the new Sugar Pine Trail, which goes through an area recently added to the park.

Please note: During the warmer months, especially in late spring, you may not want to take your picnic lunch along. The gnats, flies and harvester ants out at this time can make any but brief stops frustrating.

Begin at the parking area just south of Cuyamaca Reservoir, mile 10.7 on Highway 79. Walk across the highway and pick up the path going north along the roadside. At about 0.7 mile, the trail pulls away from the highway, turns westward behind several cabins, and joins a dirt road. Continue 0.2

mile on this dirt road, then go left on the marked Sugar Pine Trail (an old roadbed) toward Middle Peak.

You climb moderately through dense forests of black oak, white fir and incense-cedar, reversing direction twice. After the second switchback (hairpin turn), ponderosa pines appear along with patches of bracken fern. A little higher, you come upon the first sugar pines; notice the long, narrow cones on the tips of the drooping branches. Some of the sugar pines on Middle Peak have diameters over six feet. Both sugar-pine and ponderosa-pine trunks exhibit "puzzle patterns" in their bark, but ponderosas are distinguished by smaller cones and shorter branches.

At 2.5 miles the road passes the foundation of an old cabin and then curves southwest to join Middle Peak Fire Road. Keep left at the intersection, go 50 yards, and then turn left, staying on Middle Peak Fire Road.

The summit of Middle Peak now lies south and about 200 feet above you. (You can make the trailless scramble to the top easily enough as a side trip, but views in all directions are screened by brush and trees.) Continue east, then south around the upper flank of Middle Peak, keeping straight on Middle Peak Loop Road (if you prefer to stay with our trip description) as Middle Peak Fire Road veers left and begins a sharp switchbacking descent toward the starting point.

In another mile you'll come to a six-way intersection of roads and trails on the saddle between Middle and Cuyamaca peaks. Double back (left, east) on Milk Ranch Road to complete the hike. As you walk along Milk Ranch Road, you'll be treated to some superb parklike vistas of broad, rolling meadows and distant, thickly forested slopes. When the leaves of the black oaks flush a bright yellow around late October and early November, these vistas are strongly reminiscent of Appalachian landscapes.

Trip 3: Sill Hill Waterfall

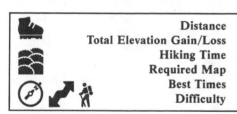

Distance	6.5 miles round trip
Total Elevation Gain/Loss	1400'/1400'
Hiking Time	4½ hours (round trip)
Required Map	USGS 7.5-min *Cuyamaca Peak*
Best Times	November through June
Difficulty	***

This hidden grotto and 30-foot-high waterfall lie within Cleveland National Forest, just outside the west boundary of Cuyamaca Rancho State Park. It is a part of the Sill Hill Wilderness Study Area, one of two National Forest WSA's in San Diego County that failed to win official wilderness designation with the passage of the 1984 California Wilderness Act.

Finding the waterfall and grotto is a puzzle—a real challenge for those who don't mind being slightly lost part of the time. The last quarter mile or so involves some fairly difficult rock hopping and bushwhacking. In addition, you must take care not to enter an

island of private land between the national forest and the state park.

Begin at the parking area (day use only) at mile 10.7 on Highway 79. (Overnighters can inquire about parking at the resort area near Cuyamaca Dam or at Paso Picacho Campground). From the parking area, cross the highway and go up Milk Ranch Road. After climbing gradually around the southeast flank of Middle Peak, you come to a saddle and a six-way intersection of fire roads and trails. Continue straight (west) for 0.4 mile, then bear right (north) on the Middle Peak Fire Road (labelled "Middle Peak Loop Fire Road" on the topo map).

Climb for 0.7 mile through oak and pine forest until you come abreast of a barbed-wire fence on the left (west) side of the trail, precisely at the 5160-foot contour. Step over the fence, entering Cleveland National Forest, and descend west and northwest along a faint path through the oak forest.

You'll soon come upon a beautiful hillside meadow, with views stretching to the coastline. The south-pointing finger of Point Loma is visible along with much of the suburban sprawl of the coastal strip and inland valleys. This meadow is one of several conspicuous bald spots on Middle Peak that can be clearly seen from San Diego on exceptionally clear days.

Since the meadow is on national-forest land outside the state park, an overnight stay (with remote camping permit from the Forest Service) is permitted. Both the meadow and the surrounding forest are completely covered by flammable dry grass and duff most of the year, so practice minimum impact camping in this case and leave your camp stove at home (open fires, of course, are never allowed outside of campgrounds in the national forest).

From the southwest edge of the meadow, work your way south-southwest along the oak- and brush-covered slopes, skirting the corner of the fenceline that defines the island of private land. Try to lose elevation grad-ually, while carefully dodging thickets of poison oak. Within 0.3 mile of the meadow, you'll hear the sound of falling water—if you're lucky. The waterfall is located at about 4500 feet elevation along the perennial stream that arises from La Puerta Springs near the aforementioned six-way intersection of roads and trails.

The water makes a quite spectacular leap over a bluff of dark gabbroic rock into a grotto shaded by oak and alder trees. For reasons having to do with light, shade and sun angle, it is difficult to take a photograph that will do these falls justice.

The surrounding area isn't suitable for camping, but the rocks at the base of the falls are fine for lounging or having lunch. (Safety reminder: resist the temptation to approach the lip of the falls; fallen leaves conceal a slippery rock surface.) With extreme caution, you can explore downstream and come upon more falls sculpted into the bed of the canyon.

Probably the biggest navigational difficulty on this trip is finding your way back to the meadow. Despite your best efforts to retrace your path, there's a distinct possibility of getting temporarily lost in the brush and trees. Careful work with your compass, both going there and coming back, should pay off.

Ranger-led bird walk in Cuyamaca Rancho State Park

Trip 4: Paso Nature Trail

Distance	0.4 mile
Total Elevation Gain/Loss	50'/50'
Hiking Time	15 minutes
Optional Map	Cuyamaca Rancho State Park map/brochure
Best Times	All year
Difficulty	*

This short, self-guiding nature trail highlights some of the native trees and shrubs of the Cuyamaca Mountains. Look for it at the north end of the picnic area at Paso Picacho Campground. There are 12 stations along the trail, keyed to a leaflet available at the entrance station. If you aren't, as yet, very familiar with the local flora and fauna, visit the small interpretive center (just outside the entrance to the campground) as well.

Trip 5: West Side Trail (to Morteros)

Distance	0.7 mile round trip
Total Elevation Gain/Loss	50'/50'
Hiking Time	20 minutes (round trip)
Recommended Map	Cuyamaca Rancho State Park map/brochure
Optional Map	USGS 7.5-min *Cuyamaca Peak*
Best Times	All year
Difficulty	*

At least a dozen major Indian villages existed in the Cuyamaca Mountains prior to about 130 years ago. These were the "mountain villages" or "summer camps" of the Kumeyaay Indians, who divided their time between the mountains and the desert. Many of these sites are today occupied by modern campgrounds, as the presence of bedrock morteros confirms. Other old encampment sites have remained more isolated, reachable only by trail. One such place, marked by a large cluster of morteros on a granite slab, lies a short distance from Paso Picacho Campground by way of the West Side Trail.

The easiest way to reach the West Side Trail is by way of the paved Cuyamaca Peak Fire Road beginning in back of the fire station just outside the campground entrance. Just beyond the gate that blocks vehicle traffic on the fire road, a sign marks the beginning of the West Side Trail—a trail that parallels Highway 79 all the way to Green Valley Campground.

After about 0.2 mile on the West Side Trail, you emerge from the forest cover and skirt the north edge of a meadow. Look for a complex of about 30 morteros near the trail. You'll find even more nearby if you search around a bit.

With a modest leap of imagination, it's not too difficult to picture a typical scene on a summer's day two hundred years ago: Indian women grinding acorn meal, children squalling nearby, the men off hunting small game, or perhaps fashioning stone tools or arrowheads. Collectors have long ago carried off the arrowheads and the tools, but the well-worn pits in the granite remain as reminders of an age not far removed from our own.

Trip 6: Azalea Glen Trail

Distance	3.0 miles
Total Elevation Gain/Loss	550'/550'
Hiking Time	90 minutes
Recommended Map	Cuyamaca Rancho State Park map/brochure
Optional Map	USGS 7.5-min *Cuyamaca Peak* (trail not shown on 1982 edition
Best Times	All year
Difficulty	**

Of all the trails in Cuyamaca Rancho State Park, this one is surely the finest. There are dense forests, a sunny meadow, a trickling brook, Indian morteros, and a refreshing spring—all in one delightful three-mile loop hike.

You begin across from the picnic area at Paso Picacho Campground, just past the entrance kiosk. After following the trail about 0.2 mile west you'll come to a split. Take the right fork to hike the trail counterclockwise, as we describe it.

Contour through the mixed forest of oaks, pines, firs, and cedars, crossing three small ravines. At 0.6 mile from the split, you emerge from the shade into a cheerful, bracken-fringed meadow. It's hard to miss the fine collection of bedrock morteros on the flat granite slabs here. Leaving the meadow, you plunge into the dark forest again, and descend to the bank of a small brook, informally called Azalea Creek. Here, western azalea, thimbleberry, and other mois-

ture- and shade-loving plants form a delicate understory of greenery under dense stands of white fir and incense-cedar. Come in late April or early May to see the azaleas in bloom.

Our route joins the California Riding and Hiking Trail and turns steeply uphill through white fir forest, then through thickets of manzanita and other brush forms. After about half a mile, the trail tops out, joining Azalea Spring Fire Road in a clearing. Dependable Azalea Spring is nearby, serving as a popular resting place and water stop for hikers and horses. A giant sugar pine, with a trunk perhaps six feet in diameter, stands on the slope just south of the spring.

From Azalea Spring, it's back into the forest again as you descend moderately on the last leg of the Azalea Glen Trail. Let gravity pay its debt, but don't rush through: watch and listen for gray squirrels, chipmunks, chickadees, acorn woodpeckers, and the ubiquitous Steller's jays.

Riding in Green Valley

Trip 7: Cuyamaca Peak

Distance	5.5 miles round trip
Total Elevation Gain/Loss	1650'/1650'
Hiking Time	3 hours (round trip)
Recommended Map	Cuyamaca Rancho State Park map/brochure
Optional Map	USGS 7.5-min *Cuyamaca Peak*
Best Times	All year
Difficulty	***

Cuyamaca Peak, San Diego County's second highest summit, lies only a few miles from the county's geographical center. Its unique position and height make it the best land-based vantage point for studying the topography of our county. The view from ground level on the peak is somewhat less than a continuous 360 degrees due to the presence of a fire tower, antenna structures, and a few trees; but you can still take in the complete panorama in increments by simply moving around a bit.

The one-lane, paved Cuyamaca Peak Fire Road ("Lookout Road" on the USGS topo map), is closed to public vehicles, but provides a very straightforward passage to the top of the peak for self-propelled travelers—be they hikers, runners, bicyclists, or cross-country skiers. Deer Spring, a dependable and delicious source of water located fortuitously near the midpoint of the road, is an added delight.

You can pick up the road at its intersection with Highway 79 just south of the Interpretive Center, or you can wend your way through Paso Picacho Campground and pick it up just beyond the southernmost campsites. It's an uphill grind all the way, moderate at first, then steep beyond the intersection of the California Riding and Hiking Trail. Forests of oak, pine, fir, and cedar once covered the entire east slope of Cuyamaca Peak, but destructive wildfires in 1950 and 1970 were quite effective in eliminating big timber at the higher elevations. The lower slopes are delightfully wooded, however.

After 1.5 miles the road grade becomes flat for a short stretch; this is a helpful clue for finding Deer Spring, on the left (south) side of the road. The water flows briskly from a pipe, and is refreshing in any season.

Views improve as you continue beyond the spring into an area still recovering from the fires. A few large snags remain, serving as perches for a variety of birds. Photographers can use these as foreground elements for pictures of the distant landscape, which now includes Cuyamaca Reservoir and desert ranges to the northeast.

In the final steep stretch, you go through a small surviving grove of mature timber and suddenly arrive at the flat, somewhat cluttered summit of the peak.

During a Santa Ana condition in fall or winter, and after major winter storm fronts, Cuyamaca Peak becomes a grandstand seat for views stretching into at least five counties and one foreign state. To name some of the features visible within San Diego County: the Palomar Mountains (look for the tiny white speck on the summit ridge—the Hale Telescope dome) northwest more than 30 miles away; Hot Springs Mountain, 26 miles almost due north over the summit of nearby Middle Peak; Granite Mountain, 11 miles to the northeast; the south end of the Santa Rosa Mountains, 40 miles northeast; and Whale Peak and the Vallecito Mountains, 18 miles east-northeast.

Close in, just 10 or so miles to the southeast, are the conifer-covered Laguna Mountains. South and southwest along the international border are Tecate Peak and

Otay Mountain, 25–30 miles away. The Pacific Ocean gleams in the west, with Point Loma, the Silver Strand, San Diego Bay, and Mission Bay visible from a distance of about 40 miles. Nearly every peak described in this book within the coastal strip and foothill areas can be seen too—Black Mountain, Fortuna Mountain, Cowles Mountain, Lyons Peak, Corte Madera Mountain and Viejas Mountain—along with other significant landmarks such as El Cajon Mountain, San Miguel Mountain, Mount Helix, and Soledad Mountain.

Obviously, you'll enhance the pleasure of your stay on the peak if you bring along a good county map and binoculars.

Trip 8: Stonewall Peak

Distance	4.5 miles round trip
Total Elevation Gain/Loss	850'/850'
Hiking Time	2½ hours (round trip)
Recommended Map	Cuyamaca Rancho State Park map/brochure
Optional Map	USGS 7.5-min *Cuyamaca Peak*
Best Times	All year
Difficulty	**

Stonewall Peak's distinctive cap of bright granitic rocks is a conspicuous landmark throughout Cuyamaca Rancho State Park. A hiker on Stonewall's angular summit can see more of the park's territory than from any other vantage point. It's no wonder the trail to the top—judging by the steady foot traffic on weekends—is probably the most popular of all the park's hiking routes.

Beginning across the highway from the entrance to Paso Picacho Campground, the trail climbs steadily and moderately on a set of well-engineered switchbacks up the west slope of Stonewall Peak. Thick groves of live and black oaks, pines, and incense-cedars cluster along the lower reaches of the trail, creating a sun-dappled effect.

About halfway up the trail, a view opens to the north and east. Cuyamaca Reservoir lies to the north, its level and its extent variable according to the season and the year's precipitation. When it is full, its surface covers nearly 1000 acres.

When you reach the top of the switchbacks, turn right (south) toward the summit of the peak. (The trail to the left descends sharply to Los Caballos Camp; if you prefer, this can be used as an alternate, but substantially longer, return route.) Follow the trail through chaparral and scattered trees to the base of the exposed granite cap. A series of steps and a guardrail are provided in the last hundred feet or so.

Distant views to the west are cut off by the main Cuyamaca Mountains massif, but the foreground panorama of the park's rolling topography is impressive enough. The patches of meadow along the streamcourses and the bald grassland areas on East Mesa and West Mesa change color with the seasons: green in spring, yellow in summer, brown or gray in fall, and occasionally white with fallen snow in winter. In the forested areas, the seasonal change of color in the crowns of black oaks plays counterpoint to the fairly constant dark hue of pines, firs, cedars, and live oaks.

Several direction-finder plaques on the summit assist in the identification of major peaks in the middle and far distance. Occasionally a bald eagle can be seen soaring overhead; these birds, along with egrets, herons, and ospreys, sometimes congregate along the shoreline of nearby Cuyamaca Reservoir during the cooler months of the year.

Trip 9: Stonewall Creek/Soapstone Grade Loop

Distance	8.2 miles
Total Elevation Gain/Loss	1050'/1050'
Hiking Time	4 hours
Recommended Map	Cuyamaca Rancho State Park map/brochure
Optional Map	USGS 7.5-min *Cuyamaca Peak*
Best Times	September through June
Difficulty	***

This is probably the flattest of any of the longer hikes possible within Cuyamaca Rancho State Park. Instead of climbing a mountain or a mesa, the route follows, for the most part, the gentle valleys of Stonewall Creek and the upper Sweetwater River. Most elevation gain takes place in the first three miles.

Begin at the parking turnout on the east side of Highway 79 at mile 7.3. Cross the creek (Cold Stream), and go east about 100 feet to join the Cold Stream Trail. Go left (north) and continue about 200 yards to Cold Spring, the only potable source of water directly along this route.

From the spring, bear right on the Cold Spring Trail and follow it northeast 1.2 miles, up and over a chaparral- and oak-covered ridge. On the far side of the ridge you'll cross Stonewall Creek, whose flow becomes sluggish after the rainy season, but pools up in shallow bedrock basins until about June. Turn left (north) at the next intersection— Stonewall Creek Fire Road.

Stonewall Creek Fire Road meanders along the east bank of Stonewall Creek, passing through chaparral, oaks, and pines, and finally across grassland, to a low saddle just east of the two equestrian campgrounds (a side trip to piped water sources is possible at this point). This stretch is coincident with the routes of the Pedro Fages expedition and the Jackass Mail, both of which followed a major prehistoric Indian pathway between lower Green Valley and the desert below Oriflamme Canyon (see Area M-10 for more details).

Just beyond the low saddle is Soapstone Grade Fire Road. Turn right (east) and skirt the edge of the broad, open valley containing Cuyamaca Reservoir. Trees stood in this valley in fair abundance before discovery of the nearby Stonewall Mine—afterward, the sudden demand for lumber caused a brief logging bonanza. The road is named for the soapstone, a talclike rock used commercially as a base for bath powders, exposed in the area.

After contouring for about one mile, the road turns sharply downhill along a scrubby hillside; in less than one more mile, it meets the Upper Green Valley Fire Road amid a fine canopy of spreading oaks. Now it's simply a matter of following the Sweetwater River downstream on the adjacent road. Your accompaniment is a riparian strip of oaks, pines, and willows, providing welcome shade on warm days, and shelter from the wind on blustery days. Stay with the Upper Green Valley Fire Road for 2.3 miles, pass the lower end of the Stonewall Creek Fire Road, and continue another 0.4 mile to a cutoff on the right. Go west on this cutoff trail for 0.4 mile, passing over a low ridge. Then merge into northbound Cold Stream Trail, and in just 0.6 mile you'll be back at your starting point.

Trip 10: Harper Creek

Distance	2.5 miles round trip
Total Elevation Gain/Loss	200'/200'
Hiking Time	90 minutes (round trip)
Recommended Map	Cuyamaca Rancho State Park map/brochure
Optional Map	USGS 7.5-min *Cuyamaca Peak*
Best Times	October through June
Difficulty	**

If you visit Harper Creek's jewel-like pools during a winter cold snap, you might be surprised to find some of them icebound. Come on a warm day in May or June, on the other hand, and you may feel like sliding into one of the pools for a bracing splash. In the heat of late summer, though, you may find only dry, sun-blasted slabs of water-polished rock here.

The parking area next to the Indian Museum and park headquarters (entrance at mile 6.2 on Highway 79) is a good point to start this hike, but parking is limited to two hours. You can park for an unlimited time (during the daylight hours) in any of several nearby turnouts along Highway 79; the most convenient of these is right at the intersection of Highway 79 and the Indian Museum entrance road.

From the Indian Museum walk east around the buildings of Camp Cuyamaca, a San Diego city and county school camp, and drop down to the sandy bank of the Sweetwater River. Find one of several crossings over the shallow river, and pick up the East Side Trail on the far side.

Follow the East Side Trail northeast across a grassy bluff overlooking the river. In about 0.9 mile, the trail turns east, continues briefly along Harper Creek, and then crosses the creek. At this crossing, leave the trail and simply scramble up along the bank or the creekbed. Be careful of your footing, especially in winter, when the dark, "wet" streaks on the rock may actually be ice.

The stream water flows over bedrock slabs, often streaked with mineral deposits, and collects in small pools, two to four feet

deep, fed by mini-waterfalls. The exposed rock above the creek is almost completely covered by a gray-green mantle of lichens. High on the slopes on either side are belts of chaparral, chiefly mountain mahogany, punctuated by the flower stalks of Our Lord's Candle yucca. The best pools are about 0.1 mile up from the point where you leave the trail; but the creekbed remains interesting for another 0.2 mile.

Retrace your steps to return. Alternately, you can continue up the creekbed and pick up the Harvey Moore Trail, which parallels Harper Creek on the north. Go west on this trail and you'll be led back to the East Side Trail.

On Harper Creek

Trip 11: Dyar Spring/Juaquapin Loop

Distance	5.8 miles
Total Elevation Gain/Loss	800'/800'
Hiking Time	3 hours
Recommended Map	Cuyamaca Rancho State Park map/brochure
Optional Map	USGS 7.5-min *Cuyamaca Peak* (most trails not shown on 1982 edition)
Best Times	All year
Difficulty	**

If water is an element essential to your hiking pleasure, you won't want to miss this hike. Dyar Spring, midway along the route, gurgles from a pipe at head-high level, offering the possibility of a cool shower as well as providing some of the best tasting water in the Cuyamacas. Downstream, along Juaquapin Creek, you can sit in the shade and listen to the most peaceful of sounds—the gentle flow of water over stones.

The starting point is the large parking area at the Sweetwater River bridge, between mile 4.8 and 4.9 on Highway 79. From here, take the Harvey Moore Trail south and east across a hillside, passing first through a belt of oaks and pines, then later through chaparral.

After 2.4 miles, turn left (north) on the Dyar Spring Trail and enter the domain of East Mesa, an open, grassy expanse studded with oaks. Several shallow ravines, tributaries of Juaquapin Creek, indent the surface of the mesa. Most are outlined by clumps of wild rose, squaw bush, and (in the wettest areas) nettles. At a point about 0.8 mile north of the Harvey Moore Trail, a small sign directs you left (northwest) toward Dyar Spring. You'll find the spring somewhat hidden on the edge of a meadow among elderberry, willow, live oak, and black oak trees.

The East Mesa area is excellent for spotting mule deer and coyotes. Station yourself on one of the knolls above Dyar Spring, enjoy a picnic, and watch the parade of wildlife below.

Back on the trail again, go northwest over a small rise and drop steeply down a slope densely covered by chaparral. Arriving at an oak-shaded saddle, turn left (south) on the Juaquapin Trail and continue downhill along a grassy draw that leads toward the west bank of Juaquapin Creek. Good displays of wildflowers are seen here in spring: forget-me-not, lupine, wallflower, checker, wild onion, and more.

The Juaquapin Trail stays on a bench above the creek, and finally turns northwest around the brow of a ridge. Look for several bedrock morteros in a clump of oak trees just south of the junction of the trail to Juaquapin Crossing. (This trail is a short cut to the Harvey Moore Trail.)

Dyar Spring cool-off

Upon reaching the next junction, turn left (the right fork goes toward the Indian Museum and park headquarters). Drop into a narrow, shady ravine; cross it, and then follow the bank of Juaquapin Creek; then come to the East Side Trail. Now simply follow the East Side Trail—and the Sweetwater River—downstream to the bridge.

Trip 12: Oakzanita Peak

Distance	8.2 miles round trip
Total Elevation Gain/Loss	1300'/1300'
Hiking Time	4 hours (round trip)
Recommended Map	Cuyamaca Rancho State Park map/brochure
Optional Map	USGS 7.5-min *Cuyamaca Peak*
Best Times	October through May
Difficulty	***

Oakzanita Peak is one of only a handful of named peaks in the Cuyamaca Mountains, yet its humble appearance—at least on approach—would not inspire most hikers to climb it. In reality, the view from its rocky summit is quite impressive on a clear day, and well worth the long hike—if done during cool weather. The name, of course, is a contraction of "oak" and "manzanita," two plant species that complement each other in the foothills of the Cuyamacas.

Begin at the parking turnout at mile 3.7 along Highway 79. The long march up East Mesa Fire Road begins along a chaparral slope, but is quite pleasant once you reach the shade of oaks along Descanso Creek.

After 2.8 miles turn right on the Oakzanita Peak Trail. You now cross a beautiful spread of grassland, and swing west toward the terminus of the trail—a point just south of the summit of Oakzanita Peak. A brief scramble through scattered brush is necessary to reach the jumbled pile of metamorphic rocks on the summit. The view includes most of the Cuyamacas' southern reaches: Pine, Airplane, and Arrowmakers ridges to the northwest, and the meadows of East Mesa to the northeast. In the distance lie the dark, wave-shaped form of Cuyamaca Peak and the pointed, alabaster summit of Stonewall Peak.

Live oak tree above Descanso Creek

Trip 13: East Mesa Loop

	Distance	10.5 miles
	Total Elevation Gain/Loss	1300'/1300'
	Hiking Time	5½ hours
	Recommended Map	Cuyamaca Rancho State Park map/brochure
	Optional Map	USGS 7.5-min *Cuyamaca Peak* (some trails not shown on 1982 edition)
	Best Times	October through May
	Difficulty	***

This is what we might call the "grand tour" of the East Mesa area—and the state wilderness that encompasses it. Describing a rough circle, we follow the route of the Harvey Moore Trail up and over the rolling meadows of East Mesa and down the canyon of Harper Creek, then we use the East Side Trail along the Sweetwater River to close the loop. There's enough scenic variety on this trip, as well as elevation change, to keep things interesting.

A good starting point is the Sweetwater River bridge parking area at mile 4.8–4.9 on Highway 79. (If you plan to stay overnight at Granite Spring, you must park at nearby Green Valley Campground.) Follow the Harvey Moore Trail south and east across a hillside, passing first through a band of oaks and pines, then through chaparral. After about two miles, oaks and pines appear again. At the junction of the Dyar Spring Trail (2.4 miles), you'll have gained almost 800 feet, already the majority of the total elevation gain during the entire trip. East Mesa now lies ahead.

East Mesa isn't a mesa in the usual desert sense, but rather a gently inclined bench of broad grasslands interrupted by tree- and brush-covered promontories. The diversity of habitats in this area supports the largest deer herd in the Cuyamaca Mountains.

Go right at the next junction (0.6 mile after the Dyar Spring Trail), and climb southeast 0.4 mile over a low saddle. Just beyond this saddle, turn left and continue 0.6 mile to Granite Spring Primitive Camp. Of the two trail camps in the park designated for hikers and equestrians, this one is more remote from trailheads and therefore less popular. A hand pump dispenses potable, but somewhat unpleasant-tasting, iron-rich water.

From Granite Spring Primitive Camp, continue north on the Harvey Moore Trail 0.6 mile to a junction. Turn right and go 0.4 mile (passing over the high point on this trip—5040 feet) to the next trail junction. Swing left here and follow the Harvey Moore Trail north toward the canyon containing Harper Creek. The descent is gradual at first, then quite steep on a set of short switchbacks. A lush growth of oaks, pines, manzanita, and other head-high brush forms provides plenty of shade. After a loss of 700 feet, you reach Harper Creek.

The trail turns west and follows Harper Creek downstream; after three crossings, it climbs abruptly up the brushy north slope to a position about 100 feet above the creek to avoid the rocky gorge below. It then contours for about 0.4 mile and then drops sharply to the bank of the creek just below the gorge. (An alternate route straight down the bed of the gorge is more interesting, but involves some scrambling over slippery rock—see Trip 10.) Leave the Harvey Moore Trail at this point, cross the creek, and pick up the East Side Trail. This will take you directly back to the Sweetwater River bridge, about three miles away.

Trip 14: West Mesa Loop

	Distance	7.2 miles
	Total Elevation Gain/Loss	1100'/1100'
	Hiking Time	3½ hours
	Recommended Map	Cuyamaca Rancho State Park map/brochure
	Optional Map	USGS 7.5-min *Cuyamaca Peak*
	Best Times	All year
	Difficulty	**

The forest: you're never far from it on this hike. The fluttering of oak leaves, the soughing of pine needles in the breeze, the scurrying of gray squirrels, the pungent sweetness in the air—these you can enjoy any time of year. The best sights, sounds, and smells in this forest, however, are reserved for two special times of year—spring and fall.

The route is entirely on well-graded fire roads along the massive, but rather gently sloping, southeast flank of Cuyamaca Peak. There's more shade than sunshine along the way, and, if you're not unlucky, you'll see more deer than humans. Unfortunately, there's no dependable source of potable water.

Begin at the day-use parking area at mile 7.3 on Highway 79. Head west around a gate and continue up West Mesa Fire Road through a forest of mostly oaks and pines. After 0.5 mile you come to a junction from where West Mesa Fire Road continues southwest and the West Mesa Fire Trail branches right (northwest). (Here's a possible side trip from this intersection: You can go cross-country 0.3 mile southeast to a flat area on Arrowmakers Ridge to see one of the largest ancient Indian sites in the Cuyamacas. Dozens of morteros are worn into the exposed slabs of bedrock here.)

Either direction you choose at the intersection is fine since this is a loop hike, but we'll assume you're going counterclockwise. Head northwest on the West Mesa Fire Trail, and ascend through stands of ponderosa and Coulter pine. Keeping left at the next two trail junctions, you level off at about the 5200-foot contour and continue around several small ravines. These are carpeted with bracken fern and other shade-loving greenery. Elsewhere, ceanothus, ablaze with white blossoms in May, complements the various shades of arboreal foliage: these run the gamut from the light green of black oaks, to the dark green of incense cedars, to the curious dull reds and browns of flowering live oaks.

The Burnt Pine Fire Trail, intersecting from the right, can be used to reach Cuyamaca Peak, but it's a long and tedious haul. Beyond this intersection, the West Mesa Fire Trail starts a gentle descent across a bald spot on the mountain slope. From here a beautiful panorama of swaying grasses, rolling hills, and distant ridges is seen.

The descent quickens and you soon come to West Mesa Fire Road. Turn left and continue through Coulter pines and oaks on a route that sticks very close to the top of Airplane Ridge; after 0.9 mile, round the hairpin turn (Monument Trail junction on the right) and look for a side trail on the left leading to the Airplane Monument (see Trip 15).

Continue descending, into and around the shady canyon of Japacha Creek, and in 1.2 miles from the hairpin turn come to the junction of Japacha Fire Road. Japacha Spring is nearby, accessible via a short spur trail (see Trip 15).

Continue northeast along the edge of the broad meadow at the foot of Arrowmakers Ridge, and after 0.8 mile more pick up the last segment of road that leads back to your starting point.

Trip 15: Arroyo Seco/Monument Loop

	Distance	7.2 miles
	Total Elevation Gain/Loss	1200'/1200'
	Hiking Time	4 hours
	Recommended Map	Cuyamaca Rancho State Park map/brochure
	Optional Map	USGS 7.5-min *Cuyamaca Peak*
	Best Times	September through May
	Difficulty	***

"In Memory of Col. F. C. Marshall and 1st Lt. C. L. Webber who fell at this spot Dec. 7, 1922." Without this inscription, the presence of an old 12-cylinder engine permanently mounted in stone atop remote Airplane Ridge wouldn't make much sense to a hiker passing by. The Airplane Monument is just one of several interesting sights along this loop hike.

One option is to carry your overnight gear along this route and stay at Arroyo Seco Primitive Camp; if so you must park your car overnight at Green Valley Campground. Day hikers can start from the Sweetwater River bridge parking area (mile 4.8–4.9 on Highway 79) and avoid the day-use fee at the campground.

From the bridge parking area, walk north over the Sweetwater River bridge and immediately turn left on a short spur trail that connects with the West Side Trail. Continue north about 0.4 mile, paralleling the highway, then bear left on Japacha Fire Road. You now wind uphill, following the south wall of the canyon containing Japacha Creek, and after about 0.8 mile cross the creek. Bracken fern, sword fern, thimbleberry and wild strawberry thrive in the shade of oaks and sycamores along the creek bottom. Turning northeast to follow a shady draw, you soon come to a marked spur trail to Japacha Spring. The water merely dribbles from cracks in the bedrock, but there are some flat rocks to rest upon in a shady spot nearby.

Go back down to Japacha Fire Road and follow it north to West Mesa Fire Road, where you turn left (southwest). Climb gradually through a magnificent conifer and oak forest, and cross Japacha Creek once again. Now watch carefully for the small footpath—on the right about 0.2 mile past the creek crossing—that leads to the Airplane Monument. Here again is a nice place for relaxation. You can sit in the shade on the stone bench, while the breeze fans across you, and look out through the trees toward Arrowmakers Ridge and Stonewall Peak.

Returning to West Mesa Fire Road, you continue around a hairpin turn, doubling back to the northwest to follow the top of Airplane Ridge. (The Monument Trail branches south from the hairpin turn, providing a shortcut to Green Valley Campground for those who wish to bail out of this trip early.) Continue for one mile along the ridgetop, staying left at the next road junction, then leave the road by turning left on a narrow, poorly maintained segment of the California Riding and Hiking Trail. The trail descends quite rapidly on a series of long switchbacks through a dense forest of oaks (watch for poison oak here), passes an intermittent spring marked by an old water trough, and then favors a straight course through tall chaparral. Turn left at the bottom of the trail and continue downhill into Arroyo Seco Primitive Camp.

The camp lies at the south end of a wide meadow frequented by mule deer and other wildlife. To return to your starting point, go downhill 1.5 miles to Green Valley Campground and then follow the well-beaten trail northeast along the bank of the Sweetwater River. A cutoff trail north of the campground can be used to bypass it.

Trip 16: Pine Ridge Trail

	Distance	3.3 miles
	Total Elevation Gain/Loss	600'/600'
	Hiking Time	2 hours
	Recommended Map	Cuyamaca Rancho State Park map/brochure
	Optional Map	USGS 7.5-min *Cuyamaca Peak*
	Best Times	All year
	Difficulty	**

This hike is especially worthwhile during the winter months, when melting snow or soggy ground at higher elevations in the Cuyamacas can make hiking in those areas difficult. A good part of the route is open to the winter sun's southern rays, and the added warmth can be quite welcome and invigorating at that time. The hike is also short enough to be suitable for a sunrise or a sunset stroll, even during the hottest months of late spring and early summer.

Park in one of the day-use lots at Green Valley Campground, then head for campsite 38 at the southwest edge of the campground. The Pine Ridge Trail goes straight up the chaparral-covered ridge behind this site, and soon gains a foothold on a steep, south-facing slope overlooking the Sweetwater River canyon. Green Valley Falls lie below, unseen but often heard. Higher still, the trail swings to the north side of Pine Ridge and offers a spectacular view of West Mesa, Cuyamaca

Peak, and the length of Green Valley. In the valley just below you can trace your return route, Arroyo Seco Road.

In the first mile, the trail has passed through only thick chaparral—mostly manzanita, chamise and ceanothus. But some timber appears as you approach the topmost knoll of Pine Ridge. These trees—Coulter pines and black oaks—cling to the north slopes of the ridge, where less sunshine permits a greater retention of ground moisture.

Past the topmost knoll, the trail drops sharply to the California Riding and Hiking Trail in ½ mile of switchbacks. Turn right (east), go 0.1 mile, and turn right again on Arroyo Seco Road. An easy return to Green Valley Campground follows. Mule deer, apparently accustomed to the human activity around the nearby campground, are often seen grazing in and around the meadow areas along this road.

Sweetwater River

Trip 17: Lower Sweetwater River

Distance	4.0 miles round trip (to Sweet Water Trail junction)
Total Elevation Gain/Loss	450'/450'
Hiking Time	2 hours (round trip)
Recommended Map	Cuyamaca Rancho State Park map/brochure
Optional Maps	USGS 7.5-min *Descanso, Cuyamaca Peak*
Best Times	All year
Difficulty	**

South of Green Valley Campground and Green Valley Falls, the Sweetwater River flows through a picturesque gorge, shaded by oaks, sycamores, willows, and alders. Beaver were introduced along this stretch years ago, and they thrived until floods in the late 70s apparently obliterated them. As late as 1980 beaver dams constructed of young willow saplings and mud could still be seen at several places along the river channel.

The recent purchase of a key parcel of land at the southern tip of the state park, the establishment of a new southern trailhead, and the opening of an old road to hiking and equestrian use have now made possible the exploration of this heretofore seldom visited stretch of river.

The trailhead is located on Viejas Boulevard, 0.6 mile east of the crossroads marking the center of Descanso, and 1.1 miles west of Highway 79. A small dirt lot is provided for day-use parking only.

From the lot walk north past some park-employee residences, and through a gate. Continue across a broad meadow and up onto a chaparral-clad slope. Soon the road passes over a saddle, and then descends a little to follow a course parallel to, but well above, the Sweetwater River. Blue ceanothus paints the brushy hillsides in April through early May. Mountain mahogany is conspicuous in late summer, sporting thousands of hairy seed tufts that resemble twisted pipe cleaners.

Just beyond the saddle, the first of two spur trails branches left toward the river and

its accompanying strip of riparian vegetation. The second spur trail, 0.4 mile farther, leads to a silted-in diversion dam on the river.

About 1.5 miles from the trailhead, we enter a magnificent grove of canyon live oaks. Through a screen of willows and alders, we can see the sparkling river surface dancing over a bed of gravel. Soon after, the road descends slightly, enters a riverbank clearing dotted with oaks and a few pines, and bends abruptly to the east—up and over a saddle toward Highway 79.

This bend marks the end of the line for casual exploration. But after lunch and a foot-soak in the river, you might want to go farther. Here are a couple of options:

You can cross the river and pick up the new Sweet Water Trail. This strikes a course northwest, first along a sandy bench, then along a shady ravine, toward the California Riding and Hiking Trail.

Or you can continue upstream along the river itself, walking mostly in the water to avoid willow thickets and poison oak along the banks. As the canyon walls close in, the river flows over exposed, polished bedrock and collects in a series of shallow pools. After 0.4 mile a waterfall blocks easy progress.

A loop trip via the river, the South Boundary Fire Road, the California Riding and Hiking Trail, and the Sweet Water Trail is possible, but only for those willing to tackle a short, difficult stretch of the Sweetwater River in the area of the aforementioned waterfall.

Area M-10: Oriflamme Canyon

North of the Laguna Mountains and east of Cuyamaca Reservoir is a gash in the mountain escarpment—a natural passage leading to the brown floor of the desert. Although modern travelers know little of it, this passage through what is now known as Oriflamme Canyon played an important role in Southern California's early American, Mexican, Spanish, and pre-Spanish periods.

Over many centuries, a well-beaten pathway through Oriflamme Canyon allowed local Indians to migrate easily between winter homes in the desert and summer encampments in the valleys of the Cuyamaca Mountains. This pathway was also a part of the Yuma Trail, a main travelway between Indian settlements along the Colorado River and fishing villages at San Diego Bay.

In 1772 Pedro Fages, the Spanish military commander of California, led a detachment of three soldiers down Oriflamme Canyon in search of army deserters who had reportedly fled inland from San Diego. This was the first recorded passage by Europeans into California's interior desert. Fages and his men traveled as far east as the present-day shoreline of the Salton Sea, then turned northwest into Coyote Canyon—preceding the first of the famous Anza expeditions by two years. In succeeding weeks the Fages party found and entered Cajon Pass, traversed a corner of the Mojave Desert, dropped down into the San Joaquin Valley, and reached San Luis Obispo near the coast, thus completing one of early California's most remarkable explorations. In later campaigns, Fages traveled through Oriflamme Canyon three more times, dubbing it *"el camino de San Diego."*

In 1826, soon after the beginning of California's Mexican period, a survey party recommended *el camino de San Diego* as the best possible route for a mail link between Sonora, Mexico, and San Diego. The Oriflamme Canyon "road," according to the report, was superior to any other desert road north or south of it.

Only with the opening of the American period, however, did this route—now called the San Diego Trail—begin to fulfill its promise. Pioneer mail carriers Joseph Swycaffer and Samuel Warnock transported U.S. Army mail over the trail on horseback and muleback between 1854 and 1857. In 1857 it became part of the San Antonio and San Diego Mail Line—the famed Jackass Mail. The route of the Jackass Mail was not negotiable by stagecoaches, and hence was used only as a cutoff route by mule riders to speed mail delivery to San Diego. Passengers had to go by the much longer but more gradual emigrant road up through Box Canyon and Warner's Ranch (traced by today's County Highway S-2).

In 1857 James Lassator, a rancher who had settled at Green Valley, hired 40 Indian laborers to build a new road parallel to the old mule path in Oriflamme Canyon, which was to make coach travel possible over the shorter route to San Diego. Because of untimely circumstances—the takeover of the mail line by the Butterfield Company, and the Civil War—Lassator's new road was never used for this purpose. Later, Lassator was able to use it to transport supplies of hay, grown at his Green Valley homestead, to the desert stations of the Butterfield Stage.

After Lassator's death in 1865, the hay road was abandoned, and the once-vital Oriflamme Canyon mountain-desert transportation corridor sank into permanent obscurity. In the 1930s, an unpaved roadway was constructed on the north slope of the canyon by the Civilian Conservation Corps. Now known as the Mason Valley Truck Trail, it is currently closed to through auto traffic.

It is both ironic and fortunate that Oriflamme Canyon, the equivalent of today's "Interstate 8" from the point of view of early Indians and settlers, has been ignored as a transportation corridor in modern times. As a consequence, this is one of the few significant historic pathways in San Diego County where the weight of history seems almost tangible, undiluted by the noise of traffic or the sight of extensive disturbances to the landscape.

There are several ways for hikers to traverse the Oriflamme Canyon corridor. Because of the roughly 2,500-foot difference in elevation between the mountains and the desert, point-to-point trips in the downhill direction are preferred. We suggest three different routes below, with starting points along Sunrise Highway. Each hike ends near the Box Canyon historical site along Highway S-2. Why not persuade your compatriots to drop you off at one of the starting points? Then, while you hike, they can enjoy a few hours of sightseeing in the mountains before the rendezvous at Box Canyon.

Overnight trips are possible too; there are some nice camping spots along Oriflamme Canyon. Both BLM and Anza-Borrego State Park lands are included in the area. No permit is required for camping, though fire restrictions apply.

Oriflamme Canyon

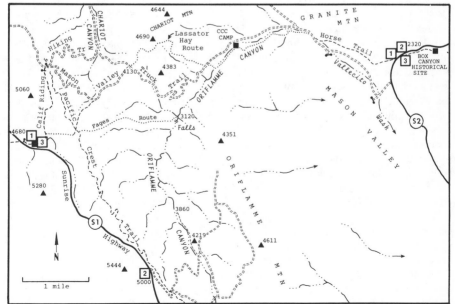

Trip 1: Mason Valley Truck Trail

Distance	8.5 miles
Total Elevation Gain/Loss	200'/2400'
Hiking Time	4 hours
Recommended Maps	USGS 7.5-min *Cuyamaca Peak, Julian, Earthquake Valley*
Best Times	October through May
Difficulty	***

This is the easy way down the rugged confines of Oriflamme Canyon—on a section of the old California Riding and Hiking Trail, downhill almost the entire way. Start at the Pedro Fages monument (mile 36.0 on Sunrise Highway—1.7 miles southeast of Highway 79), where a large turnout is available for overnight parking if needed. Walk 300 yards west along the highway to a cattle grate and find, on the north side, an unlocked gate in the barbed-wire fence. Pass through the gate (please close) and follow the faint horse trail that leads east and north into the broad, treeless valley extending north from the monument. A carpet of tidy tips and other flowers fills the bottom of this valley in late April and early May.

At the north end of the valley, pass through a second gate, turn right (east) when you reach the Mason Valley Truck Trail, and proceed through a third gate. An old water tank is on the right, in a pleasant grove of planted pines. Springtime displays of blue ceanothus, bush poppies and goldfields, and the white exclamation points of blooming Lord's Candle yucca brighten the otherwise drab slopes.

Now choose between two alternate routes: Our recommended route to the right (stay on the Mason Valley Truck Trail) descends gradually to a broad saddle between Oriflamme and Chariot canyons. The road on the left is more rugged and dips sharply into the upper reaches of Chariot Canyon; you'd have to climb about 300 vertical feet back up to reach the broad saddle.

At about 3.5 miles, just past the saddle, the Mason Valley Truck Trail begins a sudden plunge down the north wall of Oriflamme Canyon on a short series of tight turns. The furnace breath of the desert is upon you now, but from down below comes the sound of rushing water. Continue down the road another mile or two and you'll be able to reach the stream without difficulty. Tree-shaded campsites—and good picnic spots—are found in fair abundance on the far side of the stream.

Back on the road again, you'll bypass the scanty remains of a CCC camp used during construction of the truck trail. After that, you emerge onto a broad alluvial fan leading out to Mason Valley. Rodriguez Canyon's jeep trail joins from the left, and the road veers gently right (southeast) to skirt the base of massive Granite Mountain. Cacti of many species are represented here, including a peculiar hybrid resembling both the buckhorn cactus and teddy-bear cholla cactus.

About 0.6 mile past the Rodriguez Canyon junction, the main road is blocked by a gate (private property), but a lesser road continues east and southeast around this parcel and eventually joins Highway S-2 at mile 26.8. A more direct way to reach Highway S-2 is via a remnant of the seldom maintained California Riding & Hiking Trail. It continues east along the base of Granite Mountain and reaches Highway S-2 at mile 26.5— a good pick-up point. This point is 0.8 mile west of the Box Canyon historical site.

Trip 2: Oriflamme Canyon

Distance	8 miles
Total Elevation Gain/Loss	100'/2600'
Hiking Time	5 hours
Recommended Maps	USGS 7.5-min *Cuyamaca Peak, Julian, Earthquake Valley*
Best Times	November through May
Difficulty	***

Roadbound tourists will never be a party to the hidden beauty of Oriflamme Canyon. Look down from Sunrise Highway and you'll see nothing but dry hillsides and the distant, shimmering desert. But know that somewhere down there in those unpromising folds is a delightful little stream—a stream that you can walk along, and even camp next to.

The water flows from a source high on the east slope of the Laguna Mountains. It gurgles over polished granite and schist, tumbles over small waterfalls, and nourishes a canopy of shade-providing oaks, sycamores, willows and cottonwoods. Its momentum spent after six or seven miles, it seeps into the dry sands of the desert floor.

An old cow path, once used to move cattle back and forth between the Lagunas and the desert, threads the narrow parts of the canyon. Technically, the passage is not too difficult except in a few tight spots where brush and poison oak encroach. This journey, then, calls for long pants, and perhaps small clippers, to do battle with the poison oak.

The intersection of roads at mile 33.3 along Sunrise Highway is a good place to begin. (If you park at the entrance to the Lucky 5 Ranch on the west side of the highway, take care not to block traffic.) From the east side of the highway, descend the graded dirt road to the southeast. After 0.5 mile you reach an upper tributary of Oriflamme Canyon. After another 100 yards, there's a five-way intersection of roads and a trail—the Pacific Crest Trail. This segment of the PCT twists and turns in an effort to maintain a gentle gradient, striking a path just east of, and below, Sunrise Highway. Most

hikers find it quite tedious. Our route, however, continues north (downhill) on the graded roadway.

Western redbud brightens these slopes in late spring with masses of magenta-colored blossoms. Except for this outlying colony (several specimens of redbud may be seen along Sunrise Highway), western redbud normally grows only north of the Tehachapi Mountains.

At 1.5 miles, after a loss of 800 feet, the road enters a sandy flat along a usually dry upper section of Oriflamme Canyon. Follow the canyon bed downstream for 0.4 mile to a marshy area (just west of Peak 4219) where the stream usually begins. Past this point an old cowpath continues down along the bank, but soon rises to a bench on the east slope to avoid a narrow section of canyon with a waterfall. On the bench you'll pass a "lone giant" live oak tree, perhaps 130 feet tall, its side branches conspicuously absent.

After descending again to pass some mining ruins shaded by a tangle of oaks (2.5 miles, 3860'), you once again join the now-very-narrow canyon bottom. Expect to do battle with poison oak and stinging nettles as you cross and recross the stream several times. The aromatic California bay tree (see Area D-12, Trip 7) makes a rare appearance here.

A second waterfall is detoured (3.2 miles, 3560') opposite a tributary canyon entering from the west. After 200 yards, another tributary comes in from the west, with a sandy bench suitable for camping at its mouth. Springtime flowers in this open area include paintbrush, mariposa lily, wild pea, wallflower, wild rose, chia, goldfields, wild hyacinth, phacelia, and scarlet bugler. The creamy-white flower stalks of the ubiquitous yucca punctuate the brushy slopes.

At 4.1 miles (3160′), the path bypasses yet another waterfall—a sublime, almost hidden 15-foot-high cataract—and shallow pool, framed by the twisted trunks of sycamores. Just below this (4.2 miles, 3120′), another major tributary enters from the west, and the main canyon turns decidedly northeast toward the desert floor at Mason Valley. This junction seems to be the point at which the original Yuma Trail of the Indians (a.k.a. Fages Trail, San Diego Trail, etc.) departed Oriflamme Canyon and wound steeply up the ridge to the west toward present-day Cuyamaca Lake. West from this point in Oriflamme Canyon, the old route closely follows for about one mile the northern edge of the *Cuyamaca Peak* 7.5-minute map, then swings west-southwest toward the Fages monument on Sunrise Highway. When hiking this route (which requires hours of tedious bushwhacking through almost impenetrable growths of ceanothus, manzanita, sugarbush, scrub oak, and chamise), I discovered a potsherd and an old bottle—good indicators of use during the Indian and the early American periods. Although the ancient trail is almost impassable today, it is important to realize that, in earlier days,

frequent fires swept these slopes, helping to keep the trail open.

Below the junction at 4.2 miles, the canyon widens, and the cowpath that continues along the stream bank is essentially coincident with the ancient trail. Old sources say that a natural roadway led down this part of the canyon until 1916, when a great flood washed it out. No artifacts or traces of the original trail, then, are found along the stream today—but several bedrock morteros are in evidence.

At about 5.0 miles (2850′), the path diverges from the creek and climbs toward Mason Valley Truck Trail and the old CCC camp. Pick up the truck trail at any convenient point and follow it out to Highway S-2 near Box Canyon (see Trip 1 above).

It is possible to combine this route through Oriflamme Canyon with others in the Laguna Mountains for a lengthy traverse from, say, Pine Valley to Box Canyon. Consider, for example, a two- or three-day trip by way of the Noble Canyon Trail, the Indian Creek Trail, the PCT north of Pioneer Mail Picnic Ground (refer to Area M-11, Trips 1, 4, and 14), and finally Oriflamme Canyon. Such a trip would offer much more variety and interesting scenery than one of equal length done solely on the PCT.

Waterfall in Oriflamme Canyon

Trip 3: Lassator Hay Road

Distance	7 miles
Total Elevation Gain/Loss	600'/2800'
Hiking Time	6 hours
Required Maps	USGS 7.5-min *Cuyamaca Peak, Julian, Earthquake Valley*
Best Times	November through April
Difficulty	***

The "new" road up the north slope of Oriflamme Canyon that was to serve the coaches of the San Antonio and San Diego Mail Line after 1857 never did fulfill its purpose. It was, however, used successfully by James Lassator and others to haul supplies of hay grown in the Cuyamacas to the Vallecito station of the Butterfield Overland Stage in Vallecito Valley. In view of the extreme steepness of this road, it is difficult to see how it could have served its original purpose anyway. Lassator's hay was transported by wagon to the brink of the hay road; there the wheels had to be removed and the wagon bed sledded down the mountain to the Butterfield Stage road. Reportedly, some passengers did travel on muleback up the hay road to lodgings at Lassator's ranch in Green Valley, but there seems to be no record of any passenger-bearing stagecoach making the journey.

In recent years, several interested persons have attempted to track the course of this road, abandoned for well over a century. Anza-Borrego ranger Paul Remeika, who has mapped this and other historic routes in the Anza-Borrego area in precise detail, kindly provided me with information I needed to find and follow the route myself.

Trying to follow the Lassator "hay road" is both fascinating and frustrating. Its trace can be clearly seen from afar under the right illumination by sunlight, but the road seems to disappear when you are upon it, much like a desert mirage. Most of the roadbed is completely eroded out, and heavy brush can throw you off course, as well as tax your patience. In the context of today's road building, the route seems illogical, unless you

realize that the road had to be built by human labor and primitive tools alone. That is why it had to be somewhat awkwardly routed well above the steep, rocky gullies that characterize the Oriflamme Canyon drainage.

It's convenient to begin this hike, as in Trip 1 above, by following the old California Riding and Hiking Trail east and north from Sunrise Highway near the Fages monument. Veer off to the east, however, into the southernmost tip of Section 35, as shown on the *Cuyamaca Peak* 7.5-minute quadrangle. Pass northeast through a saddle (crossing the PCT), and continue north and northeast down an eroded jeep track. This track is essentially coincident with the hay road and it leads very sharply downhill to the Mason Valley Truck Trail.

On the way down, look for the trace of the hay road on the southwest slope of Chariot Mountain, one mile ahead. At the bottom of the grade, pick up the Mason Valley Truck Trail and follow it northeast across the broad saddle (1130') between Chariot and Oriflamme canyons. Your path is still coincident with the hay road.

When you reach the T-intersection on the far side of the saddle, continue northeast through thick brush, trying as best you can to hold the thread of the old road. After a steep climb of 450 feet and some difficult thrashing, you reach a point on the shoulder of Chariot Mountain just south of Peak 4690. This is a major summit along the road. Now the hay road drops sharply about 200 feet northeast, and traverses a steep gully at a point free of large rocks. Below this point the gully offers no practical crossing points. With this major obstacle breached, the route contours east for about 100 yards and then begins a steady and steep decline—east for about 0.1 mile, south for about 0.2 mile, then generally east-southeast for about 0.7 mile— through mostly low and scattered shrubs like sage and yucca. The best trace of the road is seen near the middle of Section 30, where the original crude stonework is in evidence.

The hay road crosses the Mason Valley Truck Trail just above the 3000-foot contour, and continues east to cross the creek in Oriflamme Canyon. Past the CCC camp, traces of the road hug the north side of Oriflamme Mountain, cross the Mason Valley Truck Trail, and then hug the base of Granite Mountain, parallel to the California Riding and Hiking Trail. Faint traces continue on to Highway S-2 at the mouth of Box Canyon. This is the point where the hay road joined the Butterfield Overland Stage Route—the route closely followed by Highway S-2.

Fages Monument on Sunrise Highway

Area M-11: Laguna Mountains

East of the Cuyamaca Mountains—the first great moisture-wringing barrier to Pacific storms—lies a second and slightly drier range, the Laguna Mountains. Here the storm clouds yield enough precipitation to support a patchwork forest of Jeffrey pines and black oaks. Farther east still, the land falls away abruptly. Below this escarpment lies the desert.

The human history of the Laguna Mountains closely parallels that of other mountain and foothill regions in southern California. The first peoples to arrive were bands of Kumeyaay Indians, who summered here to escape from the heat of the lowlands and gain sustenance from the natural resources of the forest. Bedrock morteros, commonly seen along the trails, are a reminder of this era.

The 1800s brought livestock ranching to the Lagunas, then mining for gold and other minerals. Mining activity peaked in the late 1800s, but it continues on a small scale even today. Grazing continues on both private and Forest Service lands.

After the turn of the century, recreation played an increasingly dominant role. The Laguna Mountains were included within the boundaries of the Cleveland National Forest in 1893, and one of the first ranger stations in California, El Prado Ranger Cabin, was constructed here in 1911. Summer homes were erected on private land within the National Forest, and on certain parcels of forest land by lease arrangement. In recent years, the emphasis has been on serving the public-at-large.

For most San Diegans today, the Laguna Mountains are the place to go to enjoy some snowplay after a big winter storm, or cool off a bit during the worst midsummer heat waves. The Laguna crest, after all, includes the highest elevations (about 6000 feet) in the county normally accessible by automobile.

Ironically, relatively few people bother to come up during the seasons that are really most beautiful—spring and fall. Daytime temperatures are pleasant then, and the colors of the trees and foliage are bold and vibrant.

The highest elevations of the Laguna Mountains have been placed administratively within a zone called the Laguna Mountain Recreation Area. The Forest Service is managing it as a heavy-use area, with campgrounds, picnic areas, and nature trails throughout. On summer weekends, interpretive walks, evening campfire programs, and guided visits to San Diego State University's Mount Laguna Observatory are given.

About 50 miles of hiking trails lace the Laguna Mountains. The biggest share of this mileage is in the form of the Pacific Crest Trail, which passes north–south over the Laguna crest. For several miles the PCT edges close to the spectacular eastern escarpment—the "sunrise" side—of the Lagunas. Nowhere else in San Diego County can the interface between mountain and desert be experienced so dramatically.

For information about camping and forest regulations, you should contact the Descanso District Office of Cleveland National Forest (see Appendix 4). In general, remote camping, including trail camping, is allowed in all areas of the Laguna Mountains within Cleveland National Forest jurisdiction, except in the Laguna Mountain Recreation Area south of Sage Road. Outside of the developed campgrounds, a free camping permit from the Forest Service is required.

Getting to the Laguna Mountains by car is easy and direct—at least from the city of San Diego. Take Interstate 8 east to Sunrise

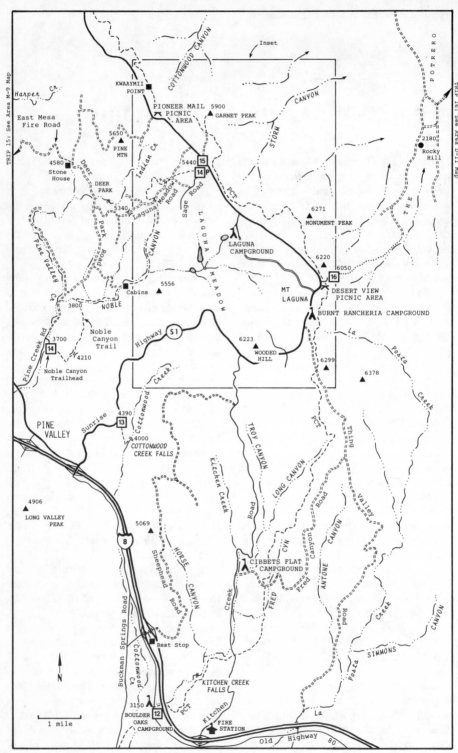

Laguna Mountains

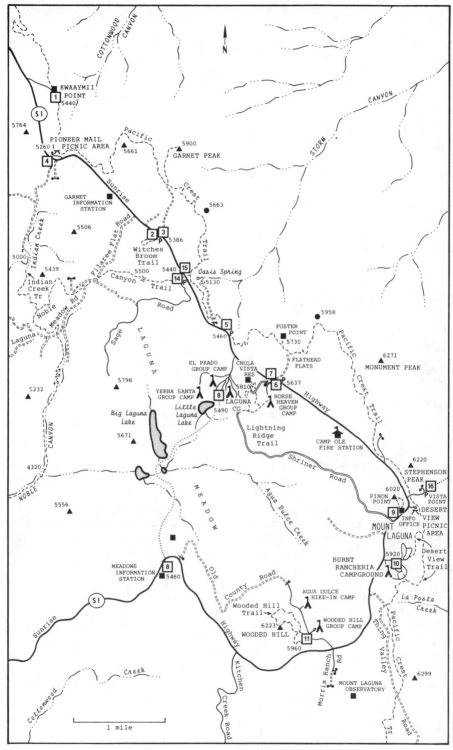

Laguna Mountains inset

Highway, then go north on Sunrise to the Laguna crest. A stop at the Meadows Information Station (mile 19.1 on Sunrise Highway) is worthwhile, especially if this is your first visit.

From North County areas, it's better to take Highway 76 or 78 to Julian, then Highway 79 to Cuyamaca Reservoir, then the north leg of Sunrise Highway toward the Laguna crest. If you approach from this direction, you can stop in at the Garnet Information Station (mile 28.5 on Sunrise Highway).

At the rustic village of Mount Laguna, on the summit of Sunrise Highway, you'll find a Forest Service Information Office (mile 23.5), staffed on summer weekends; and private facilities including a store, restaurant, and rental cabins.

Trips 1 through 11 below are mostly within the Laguna Mountain Recreation Area (see inset map). Each of these originates on or near Sunrise Highway. Trips 12 through 14 generally lie outside the Recreation Area (still within the National Forest) in the lower, drier, chaparral zone. Trip 15 takes you west into Cuyamaca Rancho State Park, and Trip 16 is a spectacular descent of the Laguna escarpment, ending at Agua Caliente County Park.

Trip 1: Kwaaymii Point

Distance	1 mile round trip
Total Elevation Gain/Loss	150'/150'
Hiking Time	30 minutes (round trip)
Optional Map	USGS 7.5-min *Monument Peak*
Best Times	All year
Difficulty	*

If you have no more time to spare than a half-hour during a cruise through the Laguna Mountains, at least stop at Kwaaymii Point and take this brief stroll along the eastern escarpment. Here, in the abbreviated transition zone between mountain and desert, you can peer down into the depths of the desert, almost 4000 feet below, and at the same time catch sight of cool forests on the Laguna rim.

You'll be walking on a segment of the Pacific Crest Trail incorporating an old roadbed literally chiseled into a cliff. A decade ago, this was the most hair-raising part of Sunrise Highway; but it is now bypassed by a newer, less spectacular, safer stretch of road to the west.

The starting point can be either Kwaaymii Point (turnoff at mile 30.3 on Sunrise Highway) or Pioneer Mail Picnic Ground (mile 29.3). Parking may be unavailable at Pioneer Mail when it's closed for the winter season. The old roadbed between these two points skirts the lip of Cottonwood Canyon, a forbidding-looking abyss with just a hint of lushness in its deepest creases. An ancient and now probably defunct Indian trail through this canyon once provided a steep but very direct passage from the desert to Laguna's meadows. Springs and seasonal flows of water in the canyon undoubtedly served its travelers well. For a time this trail was mistakenly believed to be the route of the Jackass Mail—hence the naming of Pioneer Mail Picnic Ground. Later research showed the true route to be Oriflamme Canyon (see Area M-10).

In an attempt to return the old roadbed to some semblance of naturalness, trail builders removed its macadam surface. The outer retaining walls seem to be holding, but tons of rock, exposed during construction of the old road, have fallen onto the trail from above.

Trip 2: Witches Broom Trail

Distance	0.5 mile
Total Elevation Gain/Loss	Flat
Hiking Time	20 minutes
Optional Map	USGS 7.5-min *Monument Peak*
Best Times	All year
Difficulty	*

This interpretive trail (trailhead at mile 27.9 on Sunrise Highway) tells the story of dwarf mistletoe, a common parasite of the Jeffrey pine. The trail leads to a fenced Jeffrey pine tree with a huge, deformed limb supporting a witches broom—a cluster of closely spaced branches. This broom is considered by some to be the world's largest.

Unlike the green varieties of mistletoe, which photosynthesize and draw only water from their hosts, the tiny yellow dwarf mistletoe steals both water and nutrients from its host, the Jeffrey pine. The prolific branching is caused by the killing of terminal buds and the stimulation of dormant lateral buds by the presence of the parasite.

Trip 3: Garnet Peak

Distance	2.4 miles round trip
Total Elevation Gain/Loss	550'/500'
Hiking Time	90 minutes (round trip)
Optional Maps	Cleveland National Forest recreation map; USGS 7.5-min *Monument Peak*
Best Times	All year
Difficulty	**

Although Garnet Peak isn't the highest peaklet along the edge of the spectacular eastern escarpment of the Lagunas, its exposed position makes it a good place to view both the pine-clad plateau and the raw desert below. Especially rewarding is a predawn pilgrimage to observe the sunrise from its summit. Around the time of the winter solstice, the sun's flattened disk peeps up over the desert wastes of northwestern Sonora, Mexico, some 150 miles away. On the clearest mornings at this time of year, you might observe the famed "green flash," an event occasionally seen at sunset from San Diego's coast, but seldom seen anywhere in San Diego County at sunrise.

The easiest way to approach the peak is by way of Garnet Peak Road, a rutted track

unsuitable for most standard cars. If you plan to walk this road, you can park nearby at the entrance to the Witches Broom Nature Trail, mile 27.9 on Sunrise Highway. From here, walk 0.1 mile southeast on the highway to the point where Garnet Peak Road intersects. Follow the road about 0.5 mile north through Jeffrey pine forest, then out into open chaparral country. Cross the Pacific Crest Trail and continue north on the unmarked rocky path leading sharply upward toward the peak. Poking through the low ceanothus and manzanita brush along the trail are the tall flower stalks of the Lord's Candle yucca.

The summit is crowned by a jagged cluster of layered, tan-colored metasedimentary rock, the type seen along much of the Laguna escarpment. The peak falls away abruptly, revealing a vertiginous panorama of Storm Canyon and its distant alluvial fan. Along the horizon lie the Salton Sea and Baja's Laguna Salada, two landlocked desert sinks. To the south and west, the Laguna crest, dusky with oak and pine forests inter-mixed with patches of chaparral, seems to roll like a frozen wave to the edge of the escarpment.

Watch your step as you move around on the summit, and hang on to your hat. This must be one of the windiest places in the county.

Trip 4: Indian Creek Loop

Distance	8 miles
Total Elevation Gain/Loss	1000'/1000'
Hiking Time	5 hours
Recommended Maps	Cleveland National Forest recreation map; USGS 7.5-min *Monument Peak*
Best Times	March through June
Difficulty	***

Here's a nice way to incorporate a scenic portion of the Pacific Crest Trail into a circle hike. You'll sample a variety of appealing environments—shady woodland, spice-scented chaparral, sage-dotted meadow, and open scrubland featuring bird's-eye views of the desert.

A good place to start this loop hike is along Sunrise Highway, at the intersection of Sage Road (mile 27.3), where parking is available. A Penny Pines plantation lies east of the highway here, and beyond it, the main hub of the Lagunas' trail system—the junction of the Pacific Crest and Noble Canyon trails.

Begin by following the Noble Canyon Trail west through the Jeffrey-pine forest. (For more on the Noble Canyon Trail, see Trip 13.) Take care not to become misled by the maze of intersecting jeep roads. After gaining the north slope of a hill, dropping to cross dirt roads three times, and ascending once again to circle around the north end of a ridge, you'll come to a sign (about 2.2 miles from your starting point) which states "Indian Creek Trail, Dead End ½." (The Forest Service hopes to build an extension of this trail west into Cuyamaca Rancho State Park someday.) Take this trail anyway. It will lead you gradually downhill through black oaks and chaparral to the sage-dotted flats above Indian Creek. After 0.5 mile, you will pass into the corner of a private inholding (not fenced or posted), where the trail becomes merely an informal footpath (no camping allowed here). At any convenient place, cross shallow Indian Creek and pick up the jeep road on the far (west) side.

Continue north on the jeep road until you reach Sunrise Highway at Pioneer Mail Picnic Ground. The sinking of a well here (estimated completion 1986) should provide a reliable source of water.

Next, pick up the Pacific Crest Trail, passing downslope of the picnic tables, and head east. After paralleling Sunrise Highway for about 0.5 mile, the PCT rises on oak- and pine-shaded hillsides dotted with wallflowers, lupine, and paintbrush to gain a saddle overlooking Cottonwood Canyon. After contouring around a lilac-scented, north-facing slope, it circles back south, intersects the trail to Garnet Peak, and strikes a course just west of the edge of the steep eastern escarpment facing the desert. The scrubby ceanothus, manzanita, and mountain mahogany along these western slopes seem to cower in the almost incessant wind. You can work your way across this brush at several points along the trail to reach the very brink of the escarpment, or wait until you reach the point where a view opens up from the trail itself into the depths of Storm Canyon.

Leaving this viewpoint, you descend gently through oak and pine-forest to the Penny Pines, and reach your starting point along Sunrise Highway.

Trip 5: Oasis Spring

Distance	2.0 miles round trip
Total Elevation Gain/Loss	300'/300'
Hiking Time	1 hour (round trip)
Optional Maps	Cleveland National Forest recreation map; USGS 7.5-min *Monument Peak*
Best Times	All year
Difficulty	*

A more restful place could scarcely be imagined. A warm breeze from the desert below wafts up the shady canyon, bringing with it the scent of sage and California bay. A lone bigleaf maple tree shimmers in the sunlight. A sparkling stream gushes out of the ground and begins a headlong rush toward the dry desert sands a half mile below. "Oasis" is a perfectly apt description of this idyllic spot.

Oasis Spring lies only 200 yards from Sunrise Highway, but about 300 feet lower in elevation. The best way to reach it is by way of a gradually descending dirt road from the south. This gated road intersects Sunrise Highway at mile 26.7, but parking is very limited here. An east-side turnout at mile 26.5 offers more room. Just below this turnout, you may pick up the Pacific Crest

Trail and follow it north. After about 300 yards, the PCT dips into a shallow ravine and briefly joins the road to Oasis Spring. Stay on the road and continue descending through an elfin forest of mostly mountain mahogany.

Curving left, the road leaves the ravine and briefly traverses the abrupt face of the Laguna escarpment. From the lip of the road there's a dramatic view of Storm Canyon and the distant alluvial fans and barren peaks of the desert.

From the road's end, a trail descends on tight switchbacks through a thick growth of live oak and bay to reach an old pumphouse. Nearby is the aforementioned bigleaf maple tree. The normal range of the bigleaf maple is from the San Bernardino Mountains to western Canada; this particular thriving specimen was planted here some years ago.

Hoarfrost on oak in Laguna Mountains

Trip 6: Lightning Ridge Trail

Distance	1.5 miles
Total Elevation Gain/Loss	250'/250'
Hiking Time	1 hour
Optional Maps	Cleveland National Forest recreation map; USGS 7.5-min *Monument Peak*
Best Times	All year
Difficulty	*

You can reach this trail from either the amphitheater at Laguna Campground or the access road to Horse Heaven Group Camp intersecting Sunrise Highway at mile 25.7. We'll start from the latter.

Park in the turnout on the north side of the highway. Cross the highway, and head west down the road to Horse Heaven Group Camp. After 100 yards you'll come to a fork. Take the dirt road to the right. This goes to Chula Vista Reservoir, a water tank on top of the forested hill ahead of you. After another 0.2 mile, go right on the unmarked footpath—the Lightning Ridge Trail. This will lead you to the top of the hill in a leisurely fashion.

The spectacular, tree-framed view from the reservoir includes Little Laguna Lake

and a long stretch of Laguna Meadow. The water level in the lake rises and falls. In spring, the brimming surface is like a mirror, reflecting the greens and blues of the surrounding forest and sky. In the southwest, ridge after forested ridge leads the eye out to the distant, haze-shrouded coastal foothills.

The Lightning Ridge Trail continues downslope toward Laguna Campground. You can follow it as it switchbacks through a confusing maze of false trails and short cuts to the bottom of the hill, then continue around the south side of the hill to reach Horse Heaven Group Camp; or you can drop only halfway down the hill and cut back to reach the reservoir access road at the point where you first left it.

View of Laguna Lakes from Lightning Ridge Trail

Trip 7: Foster Point

Distance	1.4 miles round trip
Total Elevation Gain/Loss	100'/100'
Hiking Time	1 hour (round trip)
Optional Maps	Cleveland National Forest recreation map; USGS 7.5-min *Monument Peak*
Best Times	All year
Difficulty	*

Come to Foster Point not only for the great view, but also for a chance to identify many of southern California's highest mountains. A direction finder, constructed by the Sierra Club, shows 17 peaks, including the Southland's highest, San Gorgonio Mountain.

Park opposite the entrance to Horse Heaven Group Camp at mile 25.7 on Sunrise Highway. Walk up the old jeep road going east into a gently sloping forested area known as Flathead Flats. After 0.2 mile the road bends north and then soon parallels the narrow but well-defined tread of the Pacific Crest Trail. Switch over to the PCT (remember where you do so, so you don't get lost on your return) and continue north through oaks and pines another 0.2 mile.

At this point the forest cover abruptly ends, and dense chaparral begins. Walk 50 yards past the last of the small Jeffrey-pine trees, and you'll find a small trail to the right, marked by a FOSTER POINT sign. This trail leads about 100 yards through waist-high manzanita, ceanothus, and chamise to the top of a rounded knob where you'll find the direction finder.

Monument Peak and its supporting ridgeline cuts off the distant view to the east and the south, but the panorama from north to northeast is excellent. Try coming for a nocturnal view sometime, especially when the moon is between first-quarter and full phases.

Trip 8: Laguna Lakes

Distance	2.3 miles
Total Elevation Gain/Loss	200'/150'
Hiking Time	90 minutes
Recommended Maps	Cleveland National Forest recreation map; or USGS 7.5-min *Mount Laguna, Monument Peak*
Best Times	January through May
Difficulty	*

With a car shuttle or a drop-off-and-pick-up arrangement, you can do this pleasant walk in a one-way direction down Laguna Meadow and visit every one of the ephemeral Laguna Lakes along the way. Interestingly, this hike covers a bit more than two miles of flat, easy terrain, while the auto route via Sunrise Highway measures a hilly eight miles.

Since "laguna" means "lake" or "lagoon" in Spanish, the name "Laguna Lakes" is quite redundant. Actually the lakes' formal name comes from the name of the mountains, which were themselves so named because there were lakes (lagunas) on them.

In an average rainy season, the lakes begin to fill with water or snow by December or January. Carpets of wildflowers—tidy tips, buttercups, goldfields, dandelions, wild onions, and western irises—appear on the meadows surrounding the lakes in April and May. By June, the hot sun causes water levels in the lakes to decline rapidly.

If winter snowfalls are heavy enough, the Laguna Meadow area becomes San Diego County's best playground for cross-country skiing. As the terrain here is mostly flat to gently sloping, there is probably no better area in San Diego County for easy skiing.

Late winter and early spring usually mean soggy terrain and wet feet—prepare accordingly. If you venture out during the warm summer months, expect to spend a lot of time afterward picking out foxtails and dry seeds from your shoes and socks. Mid-spring seems to be trouble-free on most accounts, though.

Start at the Meadows Information Station at mile 19.1 on Sunrise Highway, where abundant parking is available. (You will end at Laguna Campground, entrance at mile 26.2 on Sunrise Highway.) Walk 0.1 mile north along the highway, then strike a course due north as the highway curves east. After passing over a low oak-studded saddle just west of Laguna Ranch, you'll emerge at the south arm of Laguna Meadow. This was for many decades a private ranch; but most of the meadow was transferred into public ownership about 10 years ago. Local ranchers still retain grazing rights, however, and large herds of cattle roam the meadow during the warmer months. Barbed-wire fences are up, and you'll end up passing over, around or through two or three of them.

Stay on the left (west) edge of the meadow, and you'll come to the southern-most and lowest lake. The outflow from this lake tumbles down a steep and densely overgrown ravine to reach Noble Canyon. The water then flows to Pine Valley Creek, Barrett Reservoir, Cottonwood Creek, Rio Tijuana in Mexico, and finally the Tijuana River Estuary just north of the border. Much of the Laguna Mountain crest sheds water which, if not intercepted by aqueducts, flows through Mexico—a little-known fact.

Next, swing northeast past the shore of Big Laguna Lake and into the northeast arm of Laguna Meadow. Stay well to the right (east) of the soggy shoreline of Little Laguna Lake. Laguna Campground lies just beyond.

Little Laguna Lake

Trip 9: Kwaaymii Trail

Distance	0.5 mile
Total Elevation Gain/Loss	100'/100'
Hiking Time	20 minutes
Optional Map	USGS 7.5-min *Mount Laguna*
Best Times	All year
Difficulty	*

This walk begins at the Visitor Information Office (mile 23.5 on Sunrise Highway) and loops over a small hill called Pinon Point. The leaflet for this trail describes Indian uses of native plants for food, shelter, clothing, and medicine. Bedrock morteros (deep holes) and metates (shallow depressions) used for grinding acorns may be seen along the trail. The Kwaaymii, the most recent native American inhabitants of the Laguna Mountains, were a subtribe of the Kumeyaay Indians.

The large pinyon pine on Pinon Point is a Sierra Juarez pinyon, with needles in clusters of five. Nearby is another smaller pinyon of the four-leaved variety. Pinyon pines with one, four, and five needles are distributed throughout the desert-facing slopes of San Diego and Riverside counties and the Sierra Juarez range of Baja California, but they are relatively rare here in the Lagunas.

Near the large pinyon on Pinon Point are a patch of prickly pear cactus and several holly-leaved cherry bushes. October brings a bountiful harvest of native fruit—a bit less than sweet to our pampered palates and full of seeds, but no doubt a fitting dessert after a meal of acorn and seed porridge.

Trip 10: Desert View Trail

Distance	1.2 miles
Total Elevation Gain/Loss	100'/100'
Hiking Time	50 minutes
Optional Map	USGS 7.5-min *Mount Laguna*
Best Times	All year
Difficulty	*

This self-guiding nature trail starts at a day-use parking area within Burnt Rancheria Campground (entrance at mile 23.0 on Sunrise Highway) and winds up through the vanilla-scented Jeffrey-pine forest to a chaparral-covered ridge. There are two fine viewpoints: the first overlooks the La Posta Creek canyon on the Cuyapaipe Indian Reservation, and the second gives a glimpse of the desert floor and the distant blue arc of the Salton Sea. Part of this trail is coincident with a stretch of the Pacific Crest Trail.

An interpretive leaflet for this trail is available at the trailhead.

Trip 11: Wooded Hill Trail

	Distance	1.5 miles
	Total Elevation Gain/Loss	300'/300'
	Hiking Time	1 hour
	Optional Map	USGS 7.5-min *Mount Laguna*
	Best Times	All year
	Difficulty	*

The Wooded Hill Trail will take you to the highest wooded summit in the Laguna Mountains. Three slightly higher summits lie north and east of Wooded Hill, but these are entirely brush-covered. From the top of the trail, in spite of the tree cover, you can view a 270° panorama, including San Diego, Point Loma, and (on exceptionally clear days) Santa Catalina Island, San Clemente Island, and Mexico's Islas de Los Coronados.

To reach the trailhead, turn north from Sunrise Highway (mile 21.7) onto Old County Road. Go 0.3 mile to the parking area on the left. Self-guiding booklets should be found in the box at the base of the trail.

As you wind up the hill, you'll catch sight of white domes on a nearby ridge to the southeast. This is Mount Laguna Observatory, home of four telescopes ranging in aperture from 16 to 40 inches. A fifth telescope, at least 90 inches in aperture, is planned for the future. This site is recognized as one of the best in the United States for astronomical research.

There's a somewhat broader variety of trees and shrubs on Wooded Hill than elsewhere in the Lagunas. The booklet is keyed to stops at specimens of Jeffrey pine, black oak, incense-cedar, scrub live oak, mountain mahogany, manzanita, squaw bush, coffeeberry, serviceberry, ceanothus, and chokecherry. It also describes a host of other interpretive features along the trail.

Trip 12: Kitchen Creek Falls

	Distance	4.5 miles round trip
	Total Elevation Gain/Loss	900'/900'
	Hiking Time	2½ hours (round trip)
	Recommended Map	USGS 7.5-min *Cameron Corners*
	Best Times	December through May
	Difficulty	**

For the most part, San Diego County's section of the Pacific Crest Trail sticks to high and dry ridgelines and slopes, avoiding most canyon bottoms and streamcourses. On the southern slopes of the Laguna Mountains, however, the PCT passes just 200 yards above a hidden series of waterfalls on Kitchen Creek. Here, water from about 20 square miles of drainage flows through a narrow constriction in the bedrock, and tumbles about 150 vertical feet over water-polished slabs.

During brief periods following major storms, the sound of the falling water gives away the location of the falls; at other times, finding them may be a bit difficult. A short stretch of moderate scrambling is required to reach them.

A convenient starting point is Boulder Oaks, a major access point on the PCT. Take the Buckman Springs Road turnoff from Interstate 8 and go south on the frontage road—Old Highway 80—two miles to the Boulder Oaks store and campground.

Across the old highway from Boulder Oaks is a broad pathway marked by a PCT post. Follow this as it meanders along an oak-shaded bench overlooking Kitchen Creek, and under the twin bridges of Interstate 8. Immediately past the second bridge, find the marked PCT, which abruptly ascends to the right. After a steep climb on tight switchbacks confined between two fencelines, you'll begin a gradual and winding ascent of the brushy slopes above Kitchen Creek.

As the noise from the freeway recedes, you can concentrate on the pervading hum of countless bees and other insects drawn by the sweet fragrances of blue- and white-flowered ceanothus, manzanita, and many kinds of annual wildflowers. From mid-April through mid-May is the most intense blooming period.

At a point just over two miles from Boulder Oaks, the PCT pulls close to the deeply creased canyon containing Kitchen Creek. Look for an obscure path through the low brush to the north of the trail. This path wanders north past a couple of very small campsites, then drops suddenly about 200 feet to the falls area, located (but not marked) on the topo map between the 3440-foot and 3600-foot contours.

The dry, water-polished granitic rock on either side of the flowing water provides fair traction, but beware of wet streaks from seeps on the slopes.

Trip 13: Cottonwood Creek Falls

Distance	1.8 miles round trip
Total Elevation Gain/Loss	500'/500'
Hiking Time	1 hour (round trip)
Optional Map	USGS 7.5-min *Mount Laguna*
Best Times	December through June
Difficulty	**

Yet another set of falls south of the Laguna Mountain crest invites your exploration. Although these falls on Cottonwood Creek are somewhat less spectacular than those on Kitchen Creek (see description above), they do have the added attraction of swimmable pools.

Public access to the Cottonwood Creek falls is by way of a brushy draw which drains south from Sunrise Highway. There is direct vehicle access to the falls, too, via a road that passes through a private ranch in the valley downstream. This road appears to be little used. In short, the falls and pools are seldom visited and are normally very private.

Park in either of the two large turnouts between mile 15.3 and mile 15.4 on Sunrise Highway. The highway runs across a broad hogback at this point. Walk north on the east shoulder of the highway until you come to the top of the draw leading south toward Cottonwood Creek, 400 feet below. Here you'll find a narrow, partly overgrown trail going down along the bottom of the draw to a barbed-wire gate (please keep closed). On the far side of the gate, an old road, following powerlines overhead, will take you down to a dirt road paralleling Cottonwood Creek. Along the way you'll find good floral displays of white ceanothus (April), and beard tongue and woolly blue curls (May).

Head north, now, and discover the falls— a set of three—at the point where Cottonwood Creek emerges from a narrow canyon. The biggest one, about 10 feet high, features at its base a rock grotto with a crystalline pool about eight feet deep. The water warms to comfortable temperatures by June, though by this time the flow in the creek may be fairly sluggish.

The creekbed above the falls is choked with a dense growth of grasses, shrubs and trees, making further exploration upstream unrewarding. Just above the highest fall, however, are some flat, smooth rocks in the shade of oak trees—a good place to meditate and contemplate the water sliding by.

The broad banks of the creek just below the falls provide some nice camping space— if you don't mind packing overnight gear and hauling it on such a short journey.

Cottonwood Creek Falls

Trip 14: Noble Canyon Trail

	Distance	10 miles
	Total Elevation Gain/Loss	650'/2400'
	Hiking Time	5 hours
	Recommended Maps	USGS 7.5-min *Monument Peak, Mount Laguna, Descanso*
	Optional Map	Cleveland Natl. Forest recreation map
	Best Times	October through May
	Difficulty	***

Beautiful Noble Canyon is the rightful recipient of a new federally designated scenic trail—the Noble Canyon National Recreation Trail. Actually, this is an extension and reworking of an older trail built in the 1930s by the Civilian Conservation Corps. Since its completion in 1982, the trail has proven very popular among both hikers and equestrians. Fortunately for those who appreciate quiet and solitude, automobile access to the midsection of the canyon, formerly possible via a spur road, is now blocked by a locked gate.

With transportation arrangements set up in advance, you can travel one-way along this trail in the relatively easy downhill direction. You'll find the top end of the trail at Sunrise Highway, near the intersection of Sage Road (mile 27.3), where parking space is plentiful. The bottom end is the developed Noble Canyon trailhead near Pine Valley; to reach it, drive 1.2 miles northwest from Pine Valley on Old Highway 80, then 1.6 miles north on Pine Creek Road to the trailhead entrance. A 0.2-mile spur road leads to parking spaces and a horse staging area. Potable water is not available at either trailhead, so plan for your water needs in advance.

Good campsites are fairly abundant along the trail, particularly on shady benches along the midportion of Noble Canyon. Water flows in the canyon bottom year-round, though it slows to a trickle before the first rains of autumn. Purification is necessary if you intend to rely on it for your drinking or cooking needs.

From the Penny Pines plantation adjacent to the parking area on Sunrise Highway, cross the highway and head west along the marked Noble Canyon Trail. Threading a maze of old roads through a parklike setting of Jeffrey pines, you soon gain the north slope of a steep hill. Here, the tree-framed view extends to the distant summits of San Jacinto Peak and San Gorgonio Mountain. Next, you descend to cross dirt roads three times, then climb and circle around the chaparral-clad north end of a north–south trending ridge. This seemingly out-of-the-way excursion avoids private inholdings in the National Forest, but also opens up interesting vistas to the north and west. Three varieties of blooming ceanothus brighten the view in late April and early May.

Descending on a long switchback into the upper reaches of Noble Canyon, the trail passes across a grassy hillside alive with the springtime blooms of blue-purple beard tongue, scarlet bugler, woolly blue curls, yellow monkey flower, Indian paintbrush, wallflower, white forget-me-nots, wild hyacinth, yellow violets, phacelia, golden yarrow, checker, lupine, and blue flax.

The trail sidles up next to the creek at about 3.0 miles, then stays beside it for the next four miles. Past a canopy of live oaks, black oaks, and Jeffrey pines, you emerge into an steep, sunlit section of canyon. The trail cuts through thick brush on the east wall, while on the west wall only a few hardy, drought-tolerant plants cling to the exposed schist.

Back in the shade of oaks again, you soon cross a major tributary creek from the east. This drains the Laguna Lakes and Laguna Meadow. Pause for a while in this shady glen, where the water flows over somber, grayish granitic rock and gathers in languid pools bedecked by sword and bracken fern. Look for tiger lilies in the late spring or early summer.

The riparian woodland area continues downstream. Mixed in with the oaks, you'll discover dozens of fine California bay trees and a few scattered incense-cedars. The creek itself lies mostly hidden by willows, sycamores, and dense thickets of poison oak, squaw bush, wild rose, wild strawberries, and other types of water-loving vegetation. The line of trees is narrow enough that light from the sky and the sunny chaparral-covered slopes above is freely admitted. Greens and browns—and in fall, yellows and reds—glow intensely.

You'll pass some mining debris—the remains of a flume and the stones of a disassembled "arrastra" (a horse- or mule-drawn machine for crushing ore). This dates from gold mining activity in the late 1800s. Next you'll come upon the foundations of two cabins, then two more cabins in disrepair. Someone long ago planted what is now a huge cypress tree in front of the larger cabin.

Crossing to the west side of the creek, you break out of the trees and into an open area with sage scrub and chaparral vegetation. The trail contours to a point about 100 feet above the creek, then maintains this position as it bends around several small tributaries.

Midday temperatures, even in spring, can be quite warm along this stretch. Yucca, prickly-pear cactus, and even hedgehog cactus—normally a denizen of the desert slopes—make appearances here. There are also excellent vernal displays of beard tongue, scarlet bugler, paintbrush, peony, wild pea, milkweed, wild onion, chia, and larkspur.

At about 7 miles, the trail switches back, crosses the Noble Canyon creek for the last time, and veers up a tributary canyon to the south. (The purpose of this maneuver, once again, is to avoid a private inholding.) The trail joins the bed of an old jeep road, reaches a saddle after about two miles from Noble Canyon, then diverges from the road, going right (west) over another saddle. It then descends directly to the developed trailhead facility along Pine Creek Road.

Trip 15: Laguna to Cuyamaca

Distance	11 miles (shortest route between upper Noble Canyon trailhead and Sweetwater River bridge)
Total Elevation Gain/Loss	1150'/2600'
Hiking Time	6 hours
Required Maps	USGS 7.5-min *Monument Peak, Cuyamaca Peak*
Best Times	October through May
Difficulty	***

This route, following mostly dirt roads and fire trails, provides a fairly direct and convenient connection between the Laguna Mountain Recreation Area and Cuyamaca Rancho State Park. Only a small part of the route is shaded, so plan accordingly if the day is warm. The crossing of Indian Creek, near the 4-mile point, offers the only opportunity for replenishment of water supplies directly on route. This water must be purified.

A car shuttle can be set up between the upper Noble Canyon trailhead (mile 27.3 on Sunrise Highway) in the Laguna Mountains, and the Sweetwater River bridge parking area (mile 4.8–4.9 on Highway 79) in Cuyamaca Rancho State Park.

If you plan to backpack, note this: The Sweetwater bridge parking area is reserved for day use only, but you can leave a car overnight at nearby Green Valley Campground for a small fee. Along this route you can camp anywhere on nonprivate land in the national forest (with a remote camping permit from the Forest Service). Within the state park, however, trail camping is allowed only at two primitive camps (see Area M-9); one of these, Granite Spring Trail Camp, is just off our route.

The hike begins pleasantly with a scenic stretch of upper Noble Canyon Trail (see start of Trip 14). After about one mile, the trail dips and crosses dirt roads three times. At the third crossing, leave the trail and continue south on Laguna Meadow Road through a small, nonposted private inholding—this saves about one mile of travel over the longer Noble Canyon Trail route, which swings north around the nose of a ridge. After 0.5 mile, bear right at the fork (the road on the left drops into Noble Canyon), and climb southwest to a wide saddle, passing a private dirt road south. Continue 0.2 mile west through scattered trees to the next intersection, then bear left (south), staying on Laguna Meadow Road.

Over the next 0.8 mile the road undulates through a low cover of scrub oak and chaparral, staying close to the ridgeline overlooking the canyon containing Indian Creek. Bear right at the next jeep trail—this is a sharply descending shortcut road that joins Laguna Meadow Road again. On the way down, you can enjoy fine views of the oak-dotted Indian Creek drainage to the north, and the far-off meadows of East Mesa to the west.

Back on the main road again, continue west, cross a low saddle just south of Indian Creek, and traverse down a southwest-facing slope to the intersection of Deer Park Road. You have now walked about four miles. Turn right (north) on Deer Park Road and descend about 150 vertical feet to Indian Creek. The creek merely trickles in summer and fall. In the wetter seasons, though, a side trip 0.3 mile upstream is worthwhile: at the bottom of a narrow section of canyon, you'll find a series of small waterfalls and shallow pools.

Continue north on Deer Park Road about 0.8 mile to a grove of oaks and pines. On the left you'll find the remains of an arrastra, a circular ore-milling machine powered by horses or mules. Several mine shafts are located nearby, indicated on your topo map. These features date from the mining boom of the late 1800s.

Just beyond the arrastra, the road crosses a shady tributary of Pine Valley Creek, then

curves around a hill to follow Pine Valley Creek. Note the stone house on the left; this is a critical landmark. Just 200 feet beyond this, cross the bed of the creek and pick up a disused, eroded, and unmarked section of East Mesa Fire Road; this leads straight into Cuyamaca Rancho State Park. After passing through a wire gate at the park boundary, a long climb begins up a sun-blasted, chaparral-covered slope. Near the top of the grade, some large black oak trees provide welcome shade and a good excuse to catch your breath.

East Mesa Fire Road tops out at about 5000 feet, then begins a long and gradual descent across an open meadow. On clear days, beyond the rolling and wind-rippled expanses of grass, Point Loma and the ocean horizon may be seen. The Harvey Moore equestrian trail joins from the right (north), then soon departs to the left (south) toward Granite Spring Primitive Camp. To proceed to the Sweetwater River bridge in the most direct fashion, stay on East Mesa Fire Road until the Harvey Moore Trail joins once again from the left. Keep right here; the remaining three miles to the Sweetwater bridge are entirely downhill.

Trip 16: Mount Laguna to Agua Caliente Springs

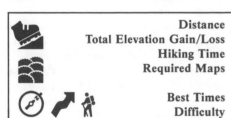

Distance	11 miles
Total Elevation Gain/Loss	300'/5100'
Hiking Time	8 hours
Required Maps	USGS 7.5-min *Mount Laguna, Monument Peak, Agua Caliente Springs*
Best Times	November through May
Difficulty	****

Get set for an incredible journey. Botanically and climatically, this is the equivalent of traveling from Canada to Mexico. From the edge of cool pine forest, you descend to a land desiccated by the hot sun and inhabited by austere-looking plants. Depending on the time of day, the temperature increases by perhaps 50°F and air you breathe becomes noticeably both drier and denser.

This route offers the only relatively easy way to drop from the top of the Lagunas to the desert floor without trespassing on private property. You'll cross National Forest land, a big swath of BLM land, a strip of Anza-Borrego Desert State Park, and finally Agua Caliente County Park. The BLM land is part of the federal 35,000-acre Sawtooth Wilderness Study Area. The area is seldom visited, rugged in its upper reaches, and extremely remote from the usual pathways of travel.

This hike is strictly a one-way downhill affair, unless for some reason you have the desire (and stamina) to scramble up 3000 feet of loose rock and scree. Backpacking is an option, but day-hiking with light but sufficient gear is probably more rewarding and trouble-free. Plan your water needs carefully, as there is no guarantee of availability.

Hitchhiking is unreliable, and a car shuttle a bit too time-consuming, so have someone (preferably with a good long book to read) take you to the starting point, and pick you up later at Agua Caliente Springs. The starting point is reached by taking the "Vista Point" turnoff from Sunrise Highway at mile 23.8. (This turnoff is distinct from the turnoff to Desert View Picnic Area, 0.1 mile to the south.) Drive up the Vista Point road exactly 0.25 mile to the first parking area overlooking the desert. The continuation of this road leads to the abandoned Air Force radar station on Stephenson Peak. For directions to Agua Caliente Springs, see Area D-11.

At the Vista Point, you'll be able to see most of the route ahead. The green patch in the distance is the *cienaga* at Vallecito Valley. You will turn to the right before reaching Vallecito Valley, go over a divide and drop into Agua Caliente Springs, hidden from this vantage point by the Sawtooth Mountains.

The key to an easy descent on this cross-country route is to avoid going straight down. Instead, angle down and to the left (northeast) through low chaparral until you reach a ledge occupied by a gnarled pinyon pine rooted tenuously to the bare rock. Step behind this tree, keep angling down along the ledge, and cross a ravine. You should now be able to pick up one of several deer trails lacing this mountainside in order to avoid the worst of the brush.

Resist the temptation to drop too fast. Stay generally about 300 or 400 feet lower than (south of) the ridgeline that is directly east of Stephenson Peak. You'll traverse fairly open slopes, dotted with mountain mahogany, scrub oak, and ceanothus shrubs,

and occasional colorful patches of lupine.

After a total of about 1.5 miles, you'll have reached a point where it seems best to drop into the canyon below. If you're here in April and May, you'll be able to see, even from a great distance, some spindly yellow-flowered shrubs in the canyon bottom. This is a colony of fremontia, or flannel bush, one of the showiest of California native plants. Some of these specimens are 15 feet high and bear thousands of waxy one- to two-inch-diameter flowers.

A small stream flows through the canyon at this point, flanked by dense clusters of California bay, willow and scrub oak. Follow the water where convenient, or push through the vegetation on the banks. This vegetation includes white sage and desert apricot, typical inhabitants of the higher desert. At the 3160-foot contour, the canyon widens, and you'll pass under a broken plastic pipe suspended over the canyon by a barbed-wire strand. Follow this pipe north to a dry watering trough, and pick up a disused jeep road leading north into "The Potrero," the large scrub-covered alluvial basin that abuts against both the Laguna and Sawtooth mountains. The Potrero is also called Treasure Canyon, after a story about a cattle rustler and bandit who robbed miners from the rich California gold fields and reportedly hid the loot here.

You now face a long and somewhat tedious march down the length of The Potrero. The disused road merges with a better road, and this road continues about two miles toward a prominent rocky hill. At 0.4 mile past the hill, bear right, and go about 0.3 mile to pick up a well-traveled dirt road aligned due north. After 0.5 mile, veer right at the fork and continue northeast about 1.5 miles to the point where the road swings abruptly left (northwest).

In the course of this walk down The Potrero, the dominant vegetation goes from prickly-pear cactus, agave, catclaw, jojoba and various grasses, to creosote bush, indigo bush and ocotillo.

Where the road swings abruptly northwest, leave it and head cross-country east-northeast over an easy saddle into a tributary of Squaw Canyon. (Take care not to blunder into one of the drainages that go north into Vallecito Creek.) In Squaw Canyon you will pick up the Squaw Pond Trail, leading to the camping area at Agua Caliente County Park.

In the last mile of this hike, there may be only one thing driving you on: the thought of a dip in Agua Caliente's cold "Indian Pool," then a long soak in the famous hot springs!

See Area D-11 for more information.

The edge of the Carrizo Badlands, which includes some of the rawest desert anywhere, lies an easy three or four miles beyond Agua Caliente Springs. This fact opens up the possibility of experiencing, in a single day's walk, environments ranging from cool pine forests to hot, barren badlands. There are few places in the world where such a trip is possible.

Lookout on Lyons Peak

Area M-12: Alpine

The area around Alpine includes parts of the Cleveland National Forest reachable in as little as half an hour from the homes of many San Diegans. A look at a National Forest map, however, reveals a maze of private inholdings here. Some of these inholdings, as well as the non-Forest areas surrounding Alpine, are now under rapid development. Private communities surrounded by fences and five-to-ten-acre "ranchettes" are replacing the chaparral that once spread almost unbroken from El Cajon Valley to the pine-crested Cuyamaca and Laguna mountains.

The old California Riding and Hiking Trail once crossed this area on a succession of footpaths and dirt roads. But now it has been cut to pieces by private developments and by property owners who have rescinded public access across their lands. One small piece of the CR & H Trail near Loveland Reservoir (southeast of Alpine) is still maintained by the Forest Service; so too is another piece that runs southwest out of Cuyamaca Rancho State Park toward Descanso. Within the state park itself (see Area M-9), the CR & H Trail is maintained for the benefit of park users.

We're left with only one hiking route in the Alpine area worth describing: the trail to the summit of Viejas Mountain.

Trip 1: Viejas Mountain

Distance	3.5 miles round trip
Total Elevation Gain/Loss	1600'/1600'
Hiking Time	2½ hours (round trip)
Optional Map	USGS 7.5-min *Viejas Mountain*
Best Times	October through May
Difficulty	***

Undistinguished by either its moderate height or its rather squat shape, Viejas Mountain is nonetheless a fairly prominent topographic feature. Standing aloof from nearby peaks, it can be seen from many parts of metropolitan San Diego as a dusky, obtusely triangular feature along the eastern horizon. An obscure trail up the west slope offers the only straightforward passage to the summit, a trek that is well worth the effort as long as it is not done under a hot sun. You'll need a remote camping permit from the Forest Service if you intend to stay overnight on the summit.

Most San Diegans can drive to the trailhead in as little as 40 minutes. Exit Interstate 8 at Tavern Road, go south 0.1 mile, then go east on Alpine Boulevard through the town of Alpine. After 1.5 miles, turn left (north) on East Victoria Drive, passing under the lanes of Interstate 8. Proceed 1.1 miles north to Anderson Road, turn right and continue northeast 0.5 mile to a large green water tank and gate—the boundary of Cleveland National Forest. Park here and continue on foot 0.3 mile uphill to a point just short of where the road starts to level off before descending. To your right (east) look for the unmarked beginning of the informal trail up the brushy slope of Viejas Mountain.

The ascent is straight up the mountain at first, then slightly winding as you near the summit, through waist-to-shoulder-high chaparral all the while. The occasional passage of hikers and coyotes is apparently all that keeps this rocky path open. Scattered among the tangled web of chamise, scrub oak, manzanita, ceanothus and yucca are a few open areas with fair displays of spring wildflowers—woolly blue curls, prickly phlox, wild onion, and cow parsnip.

Not long ago there existed on the summit of Viejas Mountain an arrangement of stones interpreted by local anthropologists to be a winter-solstice marker once used for ceremonial purposes by the Indians. The marker consisted of a T-shaped array of stones that pointed precisely to a small peak on the southeastern horizon about 16 miles away. At winter solstice (December 21) the sun comes up directly behind this peak. On topo maps, this peak is identified as "Buckman" peak, elevation 4641 feet, located south of Pine Valley. Unfortunately the marker was thoughtlessly destroyed by campers in the mid-1970s. In its place now is a wall of stones evidently built as a windbreak.

The view from the Viejas summit is wide-ranging enough—but you never really get the feeling of being "away from it all." Interstate 8 and the burgeoning outskirts of Alpine are simply too close. This is no cause for complaint, though, if you can manage to get here on an exceptionally clear day: the view then stretches from Mexico to Orange County, and the blue ocean lies seemingly a stone's throw away.

Alpine

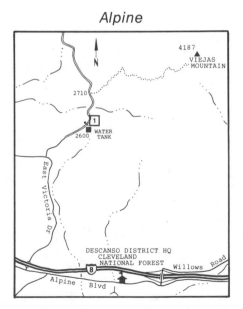

Area M-13: Pine Creek Wilderness/ Corte Madera Mountain

The newly created Pine Creek Wilderness encompasses 13,000 acres of chaparral-covered slopes and riparian woodlands southwest of Pine Valley and the Laguna Mountains. A 15-mile stretch of Pine Valley Creek meanders through the heart of the wilderness, flanked by walls up to 1000 feet high. Motorists eastbound on Interstate 8 can catch a fleeting glimpse of this impressive gorge when crossing the Pine Valley Bridge, the highest bridge in the Interstate Highway System.

During the next several years, new trails will be added to the Pine Creek Wilderness, including one that will follow the entire length of the gorge. For now, access by foot is mostly by way of the Espinosa Trail, beginning near Lyons Valley Road, and the Horsethief Trail from Horsethief Ridge. No formal paths as yet follow Pine Valley Creek

and its tributaries, but boulder hopping along these routes is popular.

The Pine Creek Wilderness is among the most accessible wilderness areas in California, just 45 minutes east of downtown San Diego via Highway 94 through Jamul, and one hour or less via Interstate 8 through Alpine. A wilderness permit from the Forest Service is required for entry, whether day or overnight. See Appendix 4 for details.

In this section, we've also included a hike to Corte Madera Mountain, a prominent landmark south and east of the wilderness. This is most easily approached by way of the eastern end of the Espinosa Trail, accessible by dirt road from the Morena Reservoir area. A wilderness permit is not required for this hike, since it lies outside the wilderness boundary. A camping permit, however, is needed if you plan to stay overnight.

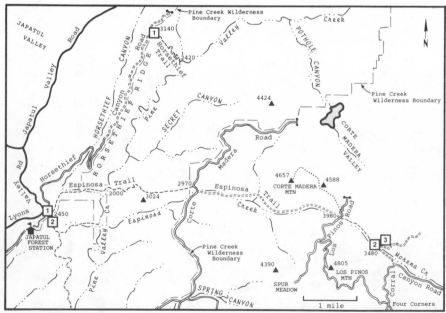

Pine Creek Wilderness/Corte Madera Mountain

Trip 1: Pine Valley Creek

Distance	6.3 miles
Total Elevation Gain/Loss	500'/1150'
Hiking Time	5 hours
Recommended Map	Cleveland Natl. Forest recreation map
Optional Map	USGS 7.5-min *Viejas Mountain*
Best Times	October through June
Difficulty	***

Boulder-hopping trips along Pine Valley Creek can range from moderately easy, if the water level is low, to hazardous, after major storms. In any case, you should expect to get your feet wet. In winter the water can be achingly cold, for the creek carries snowmelt from the Laguna Mountains. In warmer weather, though, you'll find yourself looking for excuses to wade right through the deepest pools. It's tempting to wear old running shoes or tennis shoes instead of sturdy hiking boots on this trip, but doing so might increase the risk of an ankle sprain. And this type of shoe could delaminate when soaked. Jungle boots or hybrid running-hiking shoes might be your best bet.

Suggested here is a one-way route through the most scenic section of the gorge. Normally you will want to start at the Horsethief Trail, make your way downstream, and exit at the Espinosa Trail. If the water level is high, this route may be inadvisable, since the most difficult passage along the creek comes near the end, just above the Espinosa Trail. A reconnaissance down the Espinosa Trail to check the water level might be appropriate if it seems the water may be high

A car shuttle works well for this hike, so take two cars. To get to the starting point from San Diego, follow Highway 94 east to Jamul; then turn north at the sign for Lyons Valley. The new high-speed road ahead, Skyline Truck Trail, takes you over the mountains quickly. After nine miles, turn left on Lyons Valley Road, and proceed about five miles to the intersection of the road leading to Japutul Forest Station (mile 16.4 on Lyons Valley Road). Leave one car in the dirt parking area

here, and drive the sturdier vehicle 6 miles up Horsethief Canyon Road (this road becomes more and more rutted and pebble-strewn, but remains passable for all but low-slung cars). A large turnout is on the right, with the Horsethief trailhead at the back of it.

You waste no time in descending the chaparral-covered slopes, and soon reach a large meadow, favored by cattle, on the west side of the creek. (Grazing of livestock is still allowed in many of the newer wilderness areas where it was allowed at the time these areas were designated as wilderness.) Here begins almost four miles of boulder hopping and wading. Keep track of your progress on the topo map as you swing around the many horseshoe bends. The creek flows over polished bedrock slabs and tumbles over several small waterfalls, accompanied most of the while by scattered willows, cottonwoods, and sycamores. Oak-dotted benches here and there offer shade for a lunch stop, and the two biggest—one just north of the junction of Secret Canyon and the other at the junction of Horsethief Canyon—make fine campsites for large groups.

The biggest hazards along the creek are likely to be rattlesnakes, poison oak, and slick, wet rocks. A slow, deliberate and observant style of hiking should be adequate precaution for all three. The poison oak exists mostly as widely spaced small plants and shrubs; from November to mid-March, however, the stems may be barren of leaves and difficult to identify—so wear long pants!

Below Secret Canyon, Pine Valley Creek squeezes between steep canyon walls, and tumbles through a somewhat spectacular obstacle course of eroded outcrops and car-sized boulders. This is the aforementioned difficult spot during times of high water.

Past this narrow section, the canyon opens broadly, and the Espinosa Trail crosses the creek just below a wide, shallow

pool. Follow the Espinosa Trail west along the bottom of oak-shaded Horsethief Canyon for one mile. Don't miss the turn to the left (south) that takes you out of the canyon and up to Horsethief Canyon Road.

Pine Valley Creek

Trip 2: Espinosa Trail

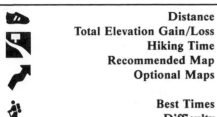

Distance	7.3 miles
Total Elevation Gain/Loss	1100'/2100'
Hiking Time	3½ hours
Recommended Map	Cleveland Natl. Forest recreation map
Optional Maps	USGS 7.5-min *Morena Reservoir, Descanso, Viejas Mountain*
Best Times	November through May
Difficulty	**

If you can arrange to be dropped off at the east end of this route and picked up later at the west end, this can be an enjoyable and rather easy trip across the mountains. Do it in the early spring if possible, when the chaparral blooms and water bubbles down even the most insignificant ravines.

The east trailhead is approached by way of Interstate 8 and Buckman Springs Road. At mile 6.6 on Buckman Springs Road (three miles south of I-8), turn west on Corral Canyon Road, then proceed 3.8 miles past the shores of Morena Reservoir to the turnoff to Four Corners and the National Forest's Corral Canyon Off-Road Vehicle Area. Stop at this juncture if your car is a low-slung model; otherwise stay right (northwest) and continue another 0.5 mile to a hairpin turn and a small parking area/turnaround. This is the east end of the Espinosa Trail. Your friends can drive around to the west terminus via I-8, Japatul Valley Road, and Lyons Valley Road; or they can take the more scenic southern route via Highway 94 and Honey Springs Road. Arrange to be picked up at mile 16.4 on Lyons Valley Road.

After one mile of climbing, you top a saddle and cross Los Pinos Road. Continue straight ahead (west) and begin a sharp descent toward Espinosa Creek. The next three miles of the Espinosa Trail are an official "green sticker" route, open to off-road vehicles, but not heavily used by them. In the wet season, Espinosa Creek trickles under a canopy of live oaks and splashes over at least one waterfall hidden in the brush. To the right, framed by twisted oaks, the sheer face of Corte Madera Mountain thrusts skyward.

When you reach Corte Madera Road, jog north for 0.2 mile on it, then go west again on the continuation of the Espinosa Trail, now free of ORV's. This section of trail cuts across a chaparral-covered flat, then descends viewfully into the Pine Valley Creek gorge.

The creek is forded just above its junction with Horsethief Canyon. True to its name, this corral-like canyon was used in the 1870s and 80s by horse thieves to conceal stolen horses in preparation for their passage across the international border.

Continue up along the oak-shaded bottom of Horsethief Canyon for one mile, then bend sharply left (south) to follow a steep, eroded jeep trail up to Horsethief Canyon Road. Go left here and walk the final 300 yards out to the parking area along Lyons Valley Road.

Trip 3: Corte Madera Mountain

Distance	5.5 miles round trip
Total Elevation Gain/Loss	1600'/1600'
Hiking Time	4 hours (round trip)
Recommended Maps	USGS 7.5-min *Morena Reservoir, Descanso*
Optional Map	Cleveland Natl. Forest recreation map
Best Times	November through May
Difficulty	***

Here is one of San Diego County's prime view spots, affording a panorama that sometimes stretches from Santa Catalina and San Clemente islands to the Sierra Juarez plateau in Baja California. Corte Madera Mountain's sheer south face is noticeable as an abrupt drop in the mountain profile as seen from many parts of metropolitan San Diego; at one point there is a near-vertical dropoff of about 300 feet.

A bit of scrambling and some tough bushwhacking are required to reach the summit. Begin at the east terminus of the Espinosa Trail—see Trip 2 above for directions. Upon reaching Los Pinos Road, on the saddle one mile up the trail, turn right and continue 0.3 mile to another saddle, this one a half mile southeast of Peak 4588. You should now leave the road and work your way cross-country through chamise and other brush forms waist-to-shoulder-high toward another saddle, just northwest of Peak 4588. The summit of Peak 4588 itself, dotted with angular boulders and tall Coulter pines, is worth a visit. Among the pines are a few marginal campsites—but if you camp, watch out for falling pine cones. Coulter pines have the most massive cones of any pine in California.

On the saddle northwest of Peak 4588, you will pick up a narrow path that meanders northwest along the crest toward the undistinguished summit plateau of Corte Madera Mountain. This path was worn in by Forest Service workers during an insect-spraying program several years ago. The view north from the crest includes a fabulous vista, available nowhere else on public land,

of the privately owned Corte Madera Valley. A big beautiful lake and oak-studded meadows fill the valley. The name "Corte Madera" (Spanish for "woodyard") apparently refers to the use of this area as a source of timber during the building of the San Diego area missions.

Corte Madera Mountain's summit plateau is covered by large sheets of granitic rock, with some patches of chaparral. From the southernmost point on the plateau you can peer over the abrupt face into the canyon drained by Espinosa Creek. To the southeast is Los Pinos Mountain, topped by a fire lookout, one of the few remaining in San Diego County used on a regular basis.

Rock formation below Lyons Peak

Area M-14: Lyons Valley

Like the two previous areas in this book, the southwest corner of the Cleveland National Forest near Lyons Valley is just minutes away from San Diego. Some Forest Service-approved off-road vehicle routes cross the area, but there are no trails. Nonetheless, some hiking is possible, as the following two trip descriptions attest.

Although recreation does not play a major role here as yet, let us be thankful that this block of land serves today as a barrier to the eastward creep of roads and houses from the fringes of El Cajon and San Diego.

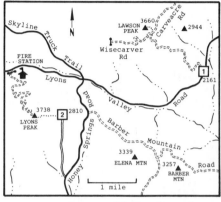

Lyons Valley

Trip 1: Lawson Peak

Distance	4.5 miles round trip (from Lyons Valley Road)
Total Elevation Gain/Loss	1600'/1600'
Hiking Time	3 hours (round trip)
Optional Maps	Cleveland National Forest recreation map; USGS 7.5-min *Barrett Lake*
Best Times	November through May
Difficulty	***

Those with access to a sturdy 4-wheel drive vehicle may be able to shorten this peak climb to a not-so-trivial half mile. Others should start at Lyons Valley Road, and hoof it two miles up an unpaved road to the base of the peak.

To get to the starting point quickly from San Diego, follow Highway 94 east to Jamul. Turn north at the sign for Lyons Valley; this road becomes the Skyline Truck Trail. After nine miles, turn left on Lyons Valley Road and proceed about three miles to mile marker 13.0. Two small turnouts for parking are available.

Rising steeply from the west side of Lyons Valley Road is unsigned Carveacre Road, a challenge for off-road drivers, easy for hikers. The road crests in two miles, then descends to join Wisecarver Road. Lawson Peak lies straight ahead, a massive heap of granite slabs.

The fun begins now as we plunge ahead through low brush and boulders east and north of the summit block. Close to the summit on the west side is a near-vertical fissure with abundant hand- and foot-holds. At the top of this is a narrow rock cave. By groping 15 feet or so into the darkness in back of the cave, we find an opening above. Mantling up onto a ledge, we come to a broad shelf (a nice picnic spot) with a view to the east. Nearby is an easy route to the topmost boulders on the peak.

The panorama is superb. To the northwest is Lawson Valley, cut with new roads and dotted with ranches. In most other directions, the view is simply mile upon mile of sun-dappled chaparral and gleaming rock. Lyons Peak and Tecate Peak are prominent on the southwest and south horizons, while Barrett Lake nestles below an almost unbroken rim of mountains to the east. To the west, a slice of the ocean is often seen.

Lawson Peak summit

Trip 2: Lyons Peak

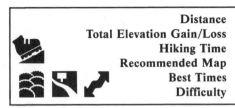

Distance	1.4 miles round trip
Total Elevation Gain/Loss	1000'/1000'
Hiking Time	3 hours (round trip)
Recommended Map	USGS 7.5-min *Dulzura*
Best Times	November through May
Difficulty	****

Lyons Peak is one of the most conspicuous promontories visible from San Diego on clear days. Its rocky summit is crowned by one of the few remaining active fire-lookout towers in southern California.

The peak lies near the center of a small (one-quarter-mile square) parcel of Cleveland National Forest detached from the main body of forest land to the east. Mostly private land surrounds it. Although a road leads to the summit via the north slope, this route is posted against all public entry, hikers included. Fortunately for those with a burning desire to reach the summit, and to do it without trespassing, there is a legal access to the forest land on the summit—a small parcel of public-domain (BLM) land adjoining to the east. A dirt road open to public travel runs along the east edge of this parcel.

For those who are motivated, and willing to fight through brush thickets and scramble over some rather intimidating boulders, this hike-climb can turn out to be a rewarding adventure. If you stay on an easy route, you'll encounter no more difficult climbing than Class 3; nevertheless, a short rope may prove handy.

To reach the starting point, follow Highway 94 past Jamul, turn left (east) on Honey Springs Road, and continue to mile marker 18.0: turn left here on the dirt road indicated by the sign CIRCLE J RANCH. Drive 1.2 miles north on this dirt road to the point where a gate blocks further progress. A survey marker nearby indicates the corner of sections 10, 11, 14, and 15. Seek out a place to park without blocking any gates.

The summit of Lyons Peak now lies due west, just over a half mile away, but nearly 1000 feet higher. There is no trail; just make

a beeline for the peak. After about 100 yards of easy passage through scattered chamise and deerweed, you'll encounter the first of the denser and more scratchy thickets of scrub oak, manzanita, and ceanothus. Stay with the more pliable chamise and deerweed cover if you can!

As the slope steepens, head directly for the bouldered east ridge of the peak. Just before reaching its base, you'll have to crawl through (or under) a band of 10-foot-high shrubs. In the moist, shady micro-environment under these shrubs, you'll find a profusion of ferns and mosses. Some poison oak also appears here.

While the rocky ridge may be relatively free of brush, the immensity of the boulders themselves introduces a new kind of challenge. Work around the left (south) side of the ridge first. About 200 vertical feet up, move to the right (north) side. Climb an additional 50 feet, then gain the top of the ridge. At this point you'll catch sight of boulders just below the summit. While climbing with hands and feet, remember that rattlesnakes frequent this kind of territory. Look first before grasping handholds.

The fire lookout is normally occupied from mid-May to November, the usual fire season. Even if it is not, you can still climb about halfway up the stairs to get a wider view of your surroundings. The latest edition of the USGS 7.5-min *Dulzura* map (1972, photorevised 1982) shows in purple tint the startling increase in rural development (roads, structures) which has taken place in the area during the last 10 years. The next decade or two will likely see a kind of low-density suburbanization of the entire region.

Area M-15: Otay Mountain/ Tecate Peak

Most admirers of San Diego's beautiful setting of mountain and sea are somewhat familiar with the long, pillowy range of mountains on the city's southeastern horizon. These are officially called the San Ysidro Mountains (not to be confused with another range of the same name near Borrego Springs—see Area D-2). More commonly, however, they're referred to simply by the name given to their highest summit—Otay Mountain.

Otay Mountain is one of San Diego's spectacular but unrecognized resources. Its western slopes offer unexcelled views of San Diego, San Diego Bay, Point Loma, the Silver Strand, Tijuana, and Mexico's Coronado Islands. Seen on a clear winter morning, this wide-ranging panorama is almost aerial in perspective, and must be seen to be believed.

The slopes are host to 14 "sensitive" plants, many of which are locally common, but found nowhere else in the world. A recent Bureau of Land Management report states that "the number of unusual, unique, or otherwise 'listed' plant species make the Otay Mountains (sic) a botanical study area unequalled in California." The most important rare plant species found here is the Tecate cypress, which grows in dense stands on north slopes.

On a sober note, the report also considers Otay Mountain the most "explosive and dangerous fire hazard zone in California." This is due in part to the heavy buildup of chaparral as a consequence of long-term fire suppression, and in part to the occasional use of this area by undocumented aliens careless with open fires.

The bulk of Otay Mountain is in the public domain, currently administered by the BLM as a National Cooperative Wildlife Management Area. These lands and some other BLM parcels adjacent to Cleveland National Forest may soon be administratively transferred to the Forest Service as part of a nationwide land swap between federal agencies.

Otay Mountain is penetrated by three graded dirt roads that join together at Doghouse Junction on the summit ridge. These roads serve communications installations on the mountain crest and provide access for fire-fighting equipment when needed. For many years, the public lands on Otay Mountain were in a state of "legal lockout," all public access being barred by surrounding private lands. Now, however, the east approach by way of Marron Valley Road and the Otay Mountain Truck Trail is open to foot travelers. As of this writing the BLM is undertaking negotiations that should eliminate private inholdings within the Wildlife Management Area and help consolidate its western boundary. A provision to allow public access on the road from Otay Mesa on the west is included. The third road, through Thousand Trails Resort on Otay Lakes Road, is definitely off limits to hikers and is expected to remain so. Contact the BLM (see Appendix 4) for the latest update on access.

To the east of Otay Mountain, also along the border, is Tecate Peak. Some of the uncommon flora on Otay Mountain are found here also, including the Tecate cypress (on the north slopes) and southern mountain misery. A locked gate on the road to the summit of Tecate Peak blocks access to vehicles, but hikers are allowed.

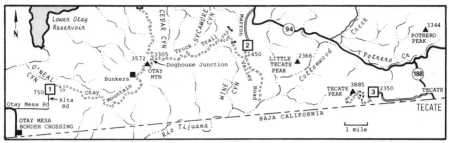

Otay Mountain/Tecate Peak

Trip 1: Otay Mountain—West Approach

Distance	14 miles round trip
Total Elevation Gain/Loss	3100'/3100'
Hiking Time	7 hours (round trip)
Recommended Maps	USGS 7.5-min *Otay Mesa, Otay Mountain*
Best Times	October through May
Difficulty	***

Good timing can make this hike a memorable experience, rather than simply a long day's slog. Try to pick a crystal-clear morning following the passage of one of the bigger winter storms. On the clearest mornings the view from the summit of Otay Mountain stretches all the way to the snow-capped summits of Mount San Antonio (Old Baldy), San Gorgonio Mountain, and San Jacinto Peak—each more than a hundred miles to the north.

To reach the starting point for this hike, drive south on Interstate 5 or 805 to Highway 117, then east toward the Otay Mesa border crossing on the new high-speed, four-lane Otay Mesa Road. Just before the border crossing, turn left (continue east) on the old Otay Mesa Road. After 1.5 miles, turn north on Alta Road and continue 1.1 miles to a cluster of farm houses and a gate. Here begins Otay Mountain Truck Trail—check with the BLM beforehand to see if this route is open to hikers.

The first couple of miles are uninspiring, but soon the first Tecate cypresses appear.

The young cypresses are quite slender, while the more mature specimens, some more than 20 feet tall, assume a bushy form. A recently burned area is next, with the spindly skeletons of hundreds of cypress trees lining both sides of the road.

After about four miles, the road traverses a north slope thickly grown with an almost pure stand of cypress. This is at a level (approximately 2500') where coastal low clouds collect quite frequently and give up some of their moisture. Tecate cypress, it seems, prefers the coastal influence. Groves in the Santa Ana Mountains in Orange County are situated at similar elevations and distances from the coast.

The road continues up along the crest, swinging back and forth across a swath denuded of trees and large shrubs—the International Fuelbreak. This was created some years ago as a containment barrier for wildfires, particularly those sweeping north. At six miles you come upon an old concrete structure and other remains nearby. During World War II, massive gun emplacements, ammunition batteries, and lookouts were established here to defend against an anticipated Japanese naval assault.

Finally, after about seven miles, a paved spur road swings up the slope to the left, leading to an unsightly clutter of antennas on the summit ridge. Near the summit are some nice outcrops of grayish-green metavolcanic rock. A band of this metavolcanic rock stretches northwest from Otay Mountain to San Miguel Mountain and beyond. It is a remnant of the island-arc volcanoes that predated the rise of the Southern California batholith and the formation of the Peninsular Ranges.

Trip 2: Otay Mountain—East Approach

Distance	15 miles round trip
Total Elevation Gain/Loss	2500'/2500'
Hiking Time	7 hours (round trip)
Recommended Map	USGS 7.5-min *Otay Mountain*
Best Times	October through May
Difficulty	***

One of the most spectacular wildflower displays I have ever witnessed was found one mid-April day along the northeast flank of Otay Mountain. The road to the summit was lined with a changing palette of blooming plants: yellow and red monkey flower, morning glory, yerba santa, chaparral pea, wild pea, clematis, nightshade, mountain misery, and wild hyacinth. On one slope recently swept by wildfire, there were tens of thousands of bush poppy plants, each bearing hundreds of big, delicate, four-petaled flowers—millions of flowers in all, swaying in the breeze.

The eastern approach to the summit of Otay Mountain is a little longer than the western approach, but it involves slightly less elevation gain and loss. To reach the starting point from San Diego, drive east on Highway 94 about 28 miles (1.5 miles past Dulzura), to mile 29.8. Turn south on Marron Valley Road, and proceed 2.1 miles south on a graded surface to a locked gate just beyond the South Bay Rod and Gun Club shooting range. Park here and begin the long trek.

Hike for 0.6 mile south of the gate, descending about 200 feet, then turn right (west) on Otay Mountain Truck Trail. At about 1.6 miles, pass through a wire gate (please keep closed). Bear left (west, uphill)

at the next intersection. In the next 4.5 miles, you ascend along mostly north-facing slopes, partly in shadow during the cooler months. The Tecate cypress prefers these north slopes; few large ones are seen, but vast numbers of seedlings are naturally regenerating wherever fires have swept through. Scattered scrub oak and a few large manzanitas intermix with the bigger cypress trees.

At Doghouse Junction (6.7 miles), bear left (south). The road traverses a steep, sunny slope providing views south into sparsely populated areas of Baja California between Tijuana and Tecate. After another 0.6 mile, turn right (north) on the road to the summit.

Southern mountain misery

Trip 3: Tecate Peak

Distance	9 miles round trip (via the road)
Total Elevation Gain/Loss	1600'/1600'
Hiking Time	5 hours (round trip)
Optional Map	USGS 7.5-min *Tecate*
Best Times	November through May
Difficulty	***

Tecate Peak straddles the U.S./Mexico border, overlooking the twin towns of Tecate, California and Tecate, Baja California. Kumeyaay Indians called this peak "Kuchumaa," and believed that a holy power, for healing or harm, emanated from the mountain's granitic boulders. According to oral historical accounts, medicine men from tribes involved in disputes would meet at the summit for peace conferences. Recent archeological evidence suggests that the mountain was also used for fertility ceremonies. Even today, descendants of the Kumeyaay, who have been granted vehicle access to the upper slopes of the mountain, make periodic journeys to its summit.

Most of Tecate Peak is in the public domain, administered by the BLM and the California Division of Forestry. In 1958 a dirt road was constructed on the eastern slope to serve a communications installation on the summit. A locked gate along this road bars unauthorized vehicles, but not hikers, so you can enjoy a pleasant and usually traffic-free hike to the top.

This is a good late afternoon/early evening trip. Since the road approaches from the east, you can avoid most of the hot sunshine by being in the afternoon shadow of the mountain. You can take in a spectacular sunset at the top, then watch the twinkling lights of Tecate, Mexico, as you make your descent. If you time your visit to coincide with the moon's phase from first-quarter to full, you probably won't need to use your flashlight.

To reach the starting point from San Diego, drive 35 miles east on Highway 94, then turn south on Highway 188 toward the Tecate border crossing. When you reach the sign reading INTERNATIONAL BORDER 1500 FEET, turn west on an unnamed dirt road. The road quickly swings south, then turns west again to follow the border fence for about 1.5 miles. It then turns northwest to climb the lower slopes of Tecate Peak. The road surface ahead may be rutty. The locked gate is 3.4 miles from Tecate; there are two or three small parking areas along the road shoulder just below it.

Common vegetation seen along the first part of the hike includes chamise, ceanothus, laurel sumac, and yerba santa. Higher up, you'll find thickets of low-growing manzanita and a curious shrub called southern mountain misery. The sticky, fernlike foliage of the mountain misery exudes an aroma similar to wintergreen or witch hazel; clusters of white flowers, resembling strawberry blossoms, appear on it in early spring.

At a point 0.5 mile above the gate, you have the option of cutting off about 0.4 mile of tedious road walking by following the top edge of a huge, tilted granite slab bordering a ravine to the right. After about 100 yards of climbing, you can rejoin an upper level of the roadway. This is the most worthwhile of several possible short cuts on the way to the summit.

The commanding view from the summit includes most of San Diego County and vast stretches of northern Baja California. To the east is an almost aerial view of the twin border towns. There is a striking delineation between Tecate, California (population 88), and Tecate, Mexico, with a rapidly expanding population of more than 70,000. The landmark Tecate brewery is visible near the center of town.

Area M-16: Hauser Canyon

Across the south end of Cleveland National Forest lies a parched landscape of steep, chaparral-covered slopes, and ridgetops crowned by eroded rock formations. In the midst of this is Hauser Canyon, a narrow, V-shaped gorge complemented by a parklike growth of oak woodland and riparian vegetation.

Just north of Hauser Canyon is the Hauser Wilderness, one of four wilderness areas within the Cleveland National Forest. Curiously, the wilderness does not take in the riparian strip at the bottom of Hauser Canyon—only the brushy slopes and ridgetops on the canyon's north wall. The Pacific Crest Trail misses it too, passing east of the boundary.

A new section of the PCT is being constructed over BLM land on Hauser Mountain, south of Hauser Canyon, to provide a link between the international border at Campo and an existing stretch of the PCT north of Hauser Canyon. This is the last uncompleted link of the PCT in San Diego County—indeed one of the last gaps in the

entire 2600-mile, Mexico-to-Canada trail. Under an agreement being worked out between the Forest Service and the BLM, Cleveland National Forest's boundary may soon expand to include Hauser Mountain.

Public access to Hauser Canyon is by way of a rambling section of the PCT south from Morena Reservoir. No wilderness permit is needed since neither the PCT nor the bottom of Hauser Canyon is included in the Hauser Wilderness. Backpackers must, however, obtain a remote camping permit from the Forest Service.

Hauser Canyon

Oak canopy, Hauser Creek

Trip 1: Hauser Creek/Cottonwood Creek

Distance	13.5 miles round trip (to Marine Memorial)
Total Elevation Gain/Loss	2400'/2400'
Hiking Time	6½ hours (round trip)
Recommended Map	USGS 7.5-min *Morena Reservoir*
Best Times	October through May
Difficulty	***

A lovely stroll down Hauser Canyon will be your reward for putting up with a long, somewhat uneventful approach on the Pacific Crest Trail. Years ago the public could drive into the canyon via a dirt road from Lake Morena Drive; upstream there was a developed campground. Today, the lower end of the road is blocked by a locked gate. The upper end is washed out and visited only by hikers and, unfortunately, increasing numbers of undocumented aliens. Some unpleasant confrontations have been reported recently; don't travel alone, and don't leave gear unattended. It's worth noting that the vast majority of these illegals are simply looking for work and wish only to slip through this area undetected.

The starting point for this hike is Lake Morena County Park, 12 miles south of Pine Valley via Interstate 8, Buckman Springs Road, and Morena Village. The PCT passes within a few feet of the county park campground gate. You begin by hiking west on the PCT up a long incline along the slope south of Morena Reservoir. Fine views of the reservoir are had for a while, but then the trail swings away, generally south over and around several hilltops. Good displays of blooming ceanothus liven things up in April; otherwise the scenery is quite drab. At about 2.0 miles, you begin a steady, winding descent into Hauser Canyon. A few battered live oaks cling tenaciously to the south-facing slopes.

When you reach the road at the bottom (3.3 miles), turn right (down-canyon), pass an old cattle pond, and proceed down along the slope north of Hauser Creek. The road meanders next to, or right through a shady canopy of oaks and sycamores. In recent years, Hauser Creek has been flowing nearly year-round.

At 5.8 miles Cottonwood Creek comes in from the north. Its flow depends almost solely upon releases at Morena Dam, less than two miles upstream. A small waterfall and pool, set amid smooth granitic rock slabs, are just above the confluence. Nearby is a pint-size rock cave sometimes used by undocumented aliens.

High water in recent years has all but destroyed the road beyond the confluence and stimulated the growth of a tangle of riparian vegetation. Just pick your way along the bank, or splash along through the shallow water. The site of the old "Hauser Creek" campground is an oak-shaded bench along a bend in the creek at 6.3 miles. No facilities remain. Nearby is a concrete dam and pond that once harbored bass (and perhaps still does). After another 0.4 mile, you'll come upon the Marine Memorial—a memorial to nine Marine Corps fire fighters who perished here during a 1943 fire.

Beyond the memorial, the waters of Cottonwood Creek enter a long, narrow valley and trickle down to Barrett Lake, a county reservoir closed to public use.

Borrego Valley

THE DESERT

Area D-1: Coyote Canyon

Coyote Canyon is the biggest rift between two major mountain complexes in the Peninsular Ranges—the San Ysidro Mountains and the Santa Rosa Mountains. The canyon is underlain by the San Jacinto Fault Zone, a splinter of the San Andreas Fault Zone. Being a natural passage through the mountains, it was for a time an important route of travel.

Pedro Fages was the first white man to pass through; his 1772 trip in pursuit of deserters from the presidio at San Diego took him as far north as the San Joaquin Valley. In 1774, and again in 1775, Juan Bautista de Anza led parties of soldiers and settlers up the canyon while enroute from Sonora, Mexico, to settlements in northern California.

Although many proposals for a paved highway through Coyote Canyon have been advanced, steadfast opposition has kept it free of pavement. A primitive jeep road down the canyon from Terwilliger Valley (near Anza in Riverside County) to the north edge of Borrego Valley remains the only vehicle access route. This road was built in the 1930s, and has not been maintained in the last two decades. This state of affairs has won the approval of most users, who prefer that Coyote Canyon remain a place difficult, but not impossible, to get to.

Because of its beauty and semi-isolation, Coyote Canyon has become one of the more popular destinations in Anza-Borrego Desert State Park. Coyote Creek's year-round flow supports three dense riparian areas: Upper Willows, Middle Willows, and Lower Willows. All three attract off-road enthusiasts (ORV's must stay on designated roads), car campers, and horsemen. Hikers and backpackers usually try to avoid these areas during busy times.

Between Lower and Middle Willows, extending west to the base of the San Ysidro Mountains, is a broad alluvial basin called Collins Valley. A network of jeep roads and horse trails crosses the valley floor, providing direct access to the major tributary canyons on the west side: Salvador Canyon, Sheep Canyon, South Fork of Sheep Canyon, Cougar Canyon, and Indian Canyon. These canyons, along with several more to the south (see Area D-2) are part of a vast roadless (and nearly trail-less) area designated as state wilderness. Here, the intrepid hiker will find solitude, adventure, and rugged beauty.

For the purposes of this book, I've chosen hiking routes in the five tributary canyons mentioned above. More information about the Coyote Canyon area, especially the upper tributaries of Coyote Canyon within Riverside County, will be found in Lowell and Diana Lindsay's guidebook, *The Anza-Borrego Desert Region.*

Coyote Canyon's "road"—at times little more than the creekbed itself—is infamous. Protruding rocks, soft sand, and stream crossings have conspired to render inoperative many an automobile driven too far. (Let it be noted that most towing insurance policies do not cover extrication of vehicles in situations like these.)

Only sturdy, high-clearance, 4-wheel-drive vehicles are appropriate for travel beyond the first or second road crossing of

Coyote Creek. In the trip descriptions to follow, it is assumed that you will start your hike at certain roadends accessible by 4-wheel drive. If you approach Coyote Canyon with a conventional auto, you can park in the canyon's lower reaches and backpack (or possibly hitchhike) to and from these starting points.

The sprawling desert town of Borrego Springs is the gateway to Coyote Canyon and most other areas in the northern half of Anza-Borrego Desert State Park; the town itself is reached in less than two hours from most parts of coastal San Diego County by way of Montezuma Highway (County Highway S-22) from the Lake Henshaw/Warner Springs area. A somewhat longer, but equally scenic approach is through Julian on Highway 78, and then on Yaqui Pass Road (County Highway S-3).

To reach Coyote Canyon from Christmas Circle in the middle of Borrego Springs, go east 0.5 mile on Palm Canyon Drive, then north on DiGiorgio Road 4.8 miles to the end of the pavement. Now set your odometer at 0.0. The dirt road ahead is normally suitable for any car if driven slowly. It crosses the usually dry bed of Coyote Creek west to east, then continues up-canyon close to the base of Coyote Mountain. At 3.2 miles there is a parking area for Desert Gardens, a picnic spot in the midst of typical low-desert flora. At 3.6 miles you'll come to the first (wet) crossing of Coyote Creek. Parking space on the hard-packed sand is abundant just before this crossing, and many choose to drive no farther than this. (On the west side of the first crossing, a dirt road branches south. This road is used by some as a shortcut to or from Borrego Springs, but it goes through a notorious patch of soft sand.) Second crossing is at 4.9 miles—the limit for conventional autos. Thereafter, the road dips into the creek with increasing frequency until it literally runs right through the water in Lower Willows. Above Lower Willows, the road leaves Coyote Creek and continues across Collins Valley; spur roads branch and lead to a primitive campground at the mouth of Sheep Canyon and toward Salvador Canyon.

From the first or second crossing, hikers can follow either the jeep route through Lower Willows or a horse trail that leads west up a small canyon just south of Lower Willows in order to reach Collins Valley and the starting points for trips 2 through 5 below. See Trip 1 for details.

No permit is required for day or overnight use of the Coyote Canyon area or, for that matter, any other area, wilderness or otherwise, within Anza-Borrego Desert State Park. Do, of course, become familiar with the park regulations first. Aside from common-sense camping practices, these include a prohibition of ground fires (camp stoves and barbecues are OK).

Coyote Canyon and its tributaries are closed to *all* entry between June 16 and September 16 to protect the watering rights of bighorn sheep. No other area in the park is subject to this restriction.

Waterfall and pool, Cougar Canyon

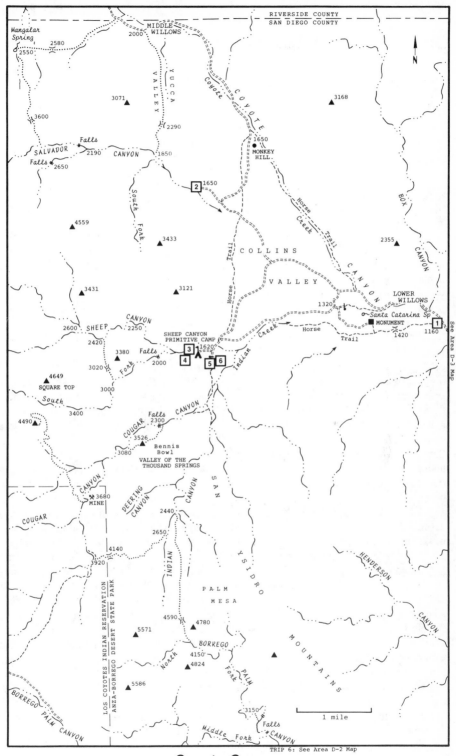

Coyote Canyon

Trip 1: Lower Willows Loop

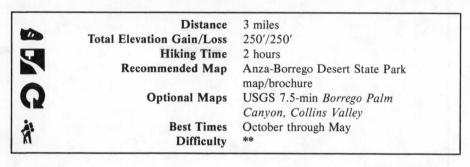

	Distance	3 miles
	Total Elevation Gain/Loss	250'/250'
	Hiking Time	2 hours
	Recommended Map	Anza-Borrego Desert State Park map/brochure
	Optional Maps	USGS 7.5-min *Borrego Palm Canyon, Collins Valley*
	Best Times	October through May
	Difficulty	**

This loop trip will introduce you to the Santa Catarina Spring/Lower Willows area of Coyote Canyon, one of the richest riparian habitats in the Colorado Desert. Don't forget your binoculars—the birding is excellent. Be prepared to get your feet wet and muddy, especially in the second half.

The Lower Willows area has been open to 4-wheel-drive and motorcycle traffic for decades; but this may change in late 1986 if a proposal is implemented to close the Willows area to motorized traffic. Vehicle access to Collins Valley would thereafter be by way of a new jeep trail up a small tributary canyon west of Coyote Canyon to the bluff south of Santa Catarina Spring. Since a riding and hiking trail already traverses this path, a new trail would be blazed parallel to the road in order to keep vehicles separate from horses and hikers. For the purposes of the hike described here, the rerouting of the road would mean little except that the willows area would become free of traffic and its associated noise.

From the end of the pavement at DiGiorgio Road, the starting point for this hike is 5.6 miles northwest up the main Coyote Canyon jeep road. This point is 0.3 mile southeast (down-canyon) from the mouth of Box Canyon—a major northern tributary. (You may have to leave your car at some point below.) Look for signs indicating the horse/hiking route through the shallow, dry canyon to the west.

After gaining about 250 feet of elevation, the trail tops out, then descends slightly across a barren flat incised with many small, shallow gullies. At the next trail junction, take the path to the right (north) toward a stone monument at the edge of a low bluff overlooking Santa Catarina Spring. The monument commemorates the passage of the Anza party during Christmas of 1774. The view here encompasses the gently sloping expanse of Collins Valley and the rugged mountains surrounding it.

Next, pick up the jeep road heading west down to the spring. Turn right at the next intersection, and go east to a vehicle dead-end. The horse trail ahead leads to Santa Catarina Spring, comprising several oozing acres. This is one of the biggest water producers in San Diego County, and a major source of Coyote Creek's dependable flow. Plow ahead through the sucking mud: this is probably the closest you can get to a real "jungle experience" in California. Willow and tamarisk trees and wild grape vines form a tunnel around you, transforming the sunlight into dappled shades of light green and yellow. The air is heavy with humid odors, and colorful insects—grasshoppers, beetles, katydids, preying mantises—seem to be everywhere.

The horse trail gains firm ground within a few hundred feet, and joins the Coyote Canyon jeep road; the road continues through Lower Willows, crossing and re-crossing the stream several times, and finally emerges into the open. Your starting point is just ahead.

Trip 2: Salvador Canyon/Yucca Valley Loop

Distance	9 miles
Total Elevation Gain/Loss	2400'/2400'
Hiking Time	6 hours
Required Maps	USGS 7.5-min *Collins Valley, Bucksnort Mtn.*
Best Times	November through April
Difficulty	****

Salvador Canyon was "opened up" (in a sense) to hiking in 1980, after an Anza-Borrego summer bighorn sheep count volunteer accidentally touched off a wildfire. The fire charred most of Salvador Canyon and its tributaries, along with part of neighboring Sheep Canyon, but it removed thorny brush that had been steadily accumulating for several decades. Although recent heavy rains have promoted a vigorous regrowth, these shrubs have not, as yet, knitted themselves together again.

A good starting point for this rambling trip is the end of the half-mile-long spur road up the alluvial fan of Salvador Canyon in the northwest corner of Collins Valley. From the road end, go up the wide mouth of the canyon. Follow either the main course of the dry wash, or stick to the bench on the right (north) side.

You'll notice that the granitic boulders embedded on the bench and up on the slopes of the canyon exhibit dark, coppery shades, while the boulders in the wash bottom are grey or white—the normal color of granitic rock. The dark coating is called desert varnish. One theory explains it as a thin patina that develops when microscopic amounts of manganese and iron are deposited by water moving through a fine clay film on the surface of the rock. It takes thousands or tens of thousands of years for a really dark desert varnish to form, but only minutes for its removal on a rock scoured by sand particles during a flash flood. Desert varnish is commonly seen throughout the Anza-Borrego Desert.

After about one mile, the South Fork of Salvador Canyon becomes visible as a large canyon to the left. Opposite South Fork is a small canyon to the north; along its east wall, about 50 feet above the bottom, you'll find a faint, ducked trail. Follow this trail, gaining about 200 feet, cross the canyon bottom, and continue climbing due north toward a low saddle. From the top of this saddle, you can look south and see a trio of palm groves in South Fork.

We then go north over the saddle, and down into Yucca Valley—well named for the hundreds of large Mojave yucca plants here. These plants send up waxy, white flower clusters every year; in March and April the valley is awash in blossoms as far as the eye can see. Jackrabbits provide entertainment as they bolt unexpectedly from clumps of Mormon tea or creosote bush.

Pass left (west) of the rocky hill at the bottom of the valley to avoid a dense growth of thorny mesquite along the margins of Middle Willows. Next, pick up the Coyote Canyon jeep road and follow it west about 0.5 mile to the San Diego/Riverside county line. Leave the road now, and turn left (southwest) into a broad valley bearing a close resemblance to Yucca Valley. Work your way to the upper reaches of this valley, and pass over an outcrop of granitic slabs. Continue due west to a saddle, and west 0.5 mile more to Mangalar Spring—you'll find it at the base of a ravine just beyond a rocky ridgeline.

At the spring you'll discover mesquite, catclaw, desert apricot, and many old mangalar (the Indian name for sugarbush, a type of sumac) shrubs—grown to heights of up to 20 feet. The area is somewhat muddy and trampled by cattle. Old troughs and broken pipes lie scattered about. Good water, however, flows from a pipe hidden below the tallest mangalar on the west side of the ravine. Its temperature is about 80°F.

After visiting the spring, go up the ravine south of it. In 100 yards you'll pick up a trail to the left, leading to a ridgeline east of the ravine. Now you're in the zone burned by the 1980 fire. Scattered manzanita, desert apricot, desert plum, and mangalar are resprouting from the unburned root crowns. Fire-blackened potsherds can be seen along the trail.

Stay with the ridgeline (going south) and gain about 1000 feet. Within 50 feet of the top—the north wall of Salvador Canyon—you may find a large fire pit. This shallow depression at least ten feet in diameter has a ring of large rocks removed from its center and ashen soil within. Perhaps it was used by the Indians to roast agave, which grows on the nearby slopes.

Now step over the top and enjoy the panoramic view of Salvador Canyon. A line of scattered palms, sycamores, and cottonwoods traces the bottom. Then pick out a feasible route of descent: the next 1000 feet of elevation loss comes in just 0.5 mile of map distance. The footing is quite stable at first, but the loose metamorphic rock on the lower slopes is tricky. Turn left (east) when you reach the bottom.

An earlier name for Salvador Canyon was Thousand Palms Canyon. This seems an exaggeration, since the canyon and all its tributaries have never (in historical times) contained more than a few hundred mature palm trees. Today, the palm trunks are black as coal from the 1980 fire, but nearly every one sports a new crown of bright green fronds. Salvador Canyon normally carries water only for a few weeks after each major storm.

As you make your way down-canyon, detour around the first waterfall by climbing around a knob on the left (north) side. Continue in the canyon bottom past newly established mesquite and catclaw thickets. Detour around a second 30-foot-high fall by climbing the slope to the right. Below this fall is the confluence of an unnamed but major south fork of Salvador Canyon containing a year-round spring and several clusters of palms. (Just above the highest palms in this tributary is a sheer 100-foot-high waterfall, usually dry. A good overview of both Salvador Canyon and this tributary is possible from the narrow ridge dividing the two.)

All that remains now are a few more palm groves to pass, two or three thickets of mesquite to fastidiously avoid, and a couple of miles over sand and rocks in the wash bottom. Don't bypass your starting point—the road's end on the bench to the north.

Mojave Yucca in Yucca Valley

Trip 3: Sheep Canyon

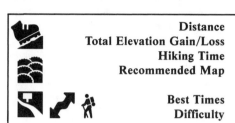

Distance	4 miles round trip
Total Elevation Gain/Loss	1200'/1200'
Hiking Time	4 hours (round trip)
Recommended Map	USGS 7.5-min *Borrego Palm Canyon, Hot Springs Mtn.*
Best Times	November through April
Difficulty	***

Each of Coyote Canyon's major tributaries has its own unique character, and Sheep Canyon is no exception. Palms are scarce here, but sycamores and cottonwoods thrive. Your footsteps will play counterpoint to the gurgle and spatter of water over polished boulders. Shady grottos provide coolness and shade at frequent intervals along the way. For many years Sheep Canyon was an intermittent stream, drying up completely (save for small, isolated springs) by the summer. Since 1976–77, the beginning of the current wet cycle, contributions from both winter and summer rainfall have kept it running year-round. Springtime flows in Sheep Canyon are greater than in Salvador Canyon to the north, but less than in Cougar Canyon to the south.

Though parts of Sheep Canyon are rugged and overgrown with lush vegetation, foot traffic in the lower end has hewn out a followable, if primitive, footpath. From Sheep Canyon Primitive Camp it is only two miles—and a net gain of 900 feet—to a point where you enter a broad, bowl-shaped valley. This valley is a good destination for backpackers (there are plenty of campsites around), and also a good base camp for further exploration of points all around the compass. I will mention several possible side trips in the following paragraphs.

From the primitive camp go upstream along the banks of the wash (or stream as the case may be). Take care to bear right at the major canyon fork at 0.3 mile, staying in the main canyon. As the bed of the canyon twists and turns, you'll cross the shallow stream several times and climb up and over the rocky canyon walls in order to detour around several waterfalls up to 15 feet in height. Most of these detours are usually much easier on one side of the canyon than the other, so look carefully for footprints or the rudiments of a trail to determine the best route.

At 1.2 miles (2250'), a tributary canyon leads north to a saddle; on its far side is the South Fork of Salvador Canyon. Cottonwoods have begun to appear, and they will gradually replace the sycamores as you continue to climb. There is little evidence of a trail now; you simply negotiate the easiest route across great slabs of fractured granitic rock.

Next, the canyon floor widens slightly, and you make your way directly through the streambed, or across grass- and shrub-covered flats to either side. At 1.5 miles the canyon turns abruptly to the right (west).

At 1.6 miles (2420'), a steep ravine climbs sharply south to a saddle between the two forks of Sheep Canyon. South of this saddle lies a broad valley at elevation 3000 feet in South Fork Sheep Canyon (see Trip 4). From the top of the saddle, two peak climbs are possible: The first is a boulder-strewn 3380-foot summit overlooking both forks, easily within reach to the northeast. The second is to the west—the massive, flat-topped 4649-foot promontory I will call "Square Top," a conspicuous landmark seen from Collins Valley and points east. Square Top may be climbed from the east and possibly the south sides; attempts on the north and west sides will be doomed to failure by a combination of huge boulders and dense chaparral just below the summit.

At 1.9 miles, Sheep Canyon emerges into

a broad bowl where two major and several minor tributaries come together. This is the area where campsites for backpackers are abundant. For day hikers, it's a good place to enjoy the view of rugged peaks in every direction before turning around. The bowl was swept by the 1980 Salvador Canyon fire, so only snags remain of most of the large trees. Around the margins of the bowl, seasonal springs lie in several of the small tributaries.

The presence of surface or subsurface water is indicated by clusters of young cottonwood trees and other riparian vegetation. Much time could be spent exploring these and other features of the bowl.

Further travel in the main Sheep Canyon, and along routes into Salvador and Alder canyons, is described in Lowell and Diana Lindsay's guidebook, *The Anza-Borrego Desert Region.*

Trip 4: South Fork Sheep Canyon

Distance	3 miles round trip (to valley at 3000')
Total Elevation Gain/Loss	1500'/1500'
Hiking Time	4 hours (round trip)
Required Map	USGS 7.5-min *Borrego Palm Canyon, Hot Springs Mtn.*
Best Times	November through April
Difficulty	****

The terrain covered on this hike is more technically difficult than that on any other trip described in this book. Skilled scramblers need not use ropes, but certain precautions must be observed.

Careful route finding is the key to safe passage through this canyon. Some routes (especially going downhill) may look promising, but lead to steep rock exposures so that much time can be wasted in backtracking. Other routes can lead to deadends in the canyon bottom where it is difficult (or impossible) to climb out in the absence of outside help, so don't jump or slide down rocks if you can't determine the feasibility of the route ahead. Because of these difficulties, it is recommended that you don't backpack through this canyon without first having traveled it with a light day pack.

The rewards are a close-up view of an idyllic waterfall, glimpses of a half-dozen more, and the pleasure of exploring a hidden valley seldom visited by humans. Less water flows through the South Fork than the main fork of Sheep Canyon. Try to arrive here soon after a major storm, when the stream bubbles with vigor and crashes over the falls.

Begin as in Trip 3, but stay to the left at 0.3 mile, entering South Fork. A well-beaten trail goes up along the bank, but peters out rapidly as boulders and underbrush become a hindrance. Find a way through the brush and climb over rounded granite slabs, passing two palm groves, until you reach (at 0.6 mile, 2000') the base of a sublime 30-foot waterfall. This is arguably the most beautiful waterfall in Anza-Borrego. Framed by full-skirted palms both top and bottom, and a lush carpet of grass below, this is a point of interest well worth reaching even if you don't intend to continue farther up-canyon.

From a point just below the base of the waterfall, climb the steep, rocky slope to the right (north side of the canyon). Climb sharply upward until you can traverse at an easier gradient, staying parallel to and about 200 feet above the canyon bottom. The slope is infested with cactus, agave, and sharp rocks, but if you stay at the right level, the footing is relatively stable. You can hear the splashing of water in several virtually inaccessible grottos below.

Continue along the north wall of the canyon for about 0.3 mile, then contour into the canyon bottom at the 2600-foot level. Now thread your way around immense boulder complexes, staying generally close to the north wall. Note your route carefully so that you can retrace it when you return.

Turning south, you enter a valley at 3000 feet with many possible campsites scattered about on several flat, sandy areas on the west side. This is a worthy enough destination for a day hike; there are good views of distant peaks and ridges, and small pools in the stream to soak the feet in. Backpackers can reach this valley by way of a longer and less problematic route through the main Sheep Canyon and over a saddle between the two forks (see Trip 3 above). (It may be tempting to make a circle trip clockwise around the two forks by going up Sheep Canyon, across the saddle, and then down South Fork—but don't do this unless you've had prior experience in the South Fork. Counterclockwise around this loop is OK.)

Further exploration up South Fork is equally challenging and equally rewarding. Here are some highlights:

The canyon turns west at 3120 feet. Typical high-desert vegetation now appears on the slopes—ribbonwood, scrub oak, and yucca—while palms, sycamores, cottonwoods, and alders shade the stream. At 3250 feet, there is a narrow, grassy bench providing the last marginal campsites in this canyon. Amazingly, an incense-cedar grows here, miles away from its normal habitat high up in the mountains. Scattered palms extend several hundred feet upstream. This is truly an extraordinary overlap of mountain and desert flora.

Above 3400 feet there's a series of small falls, then huge boulder mazes and heavy brush. (Refer to Area M-6, Trip 2, for a route into this area from the Los Coyotes Indian Reservation.) From these upper reaches of South Fork, a very difficult, brushy traverse can be made into Sheep Canyon via the saddle west of "Square Top."

Lower fall, South Fork Sheep Canyon

Trip 5: Cougar Canyon

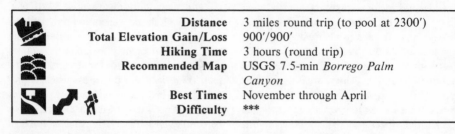

Distance	3 miles round trip (to pool at 2300′)
Total Elevation Gain/Loss	900′/900′
Hiking Time	3 hours (round trip)
Recommended Map	USGS 7.5-min *Borrego Palm Canyon*
Best Times	November through April
Difficulty	***

Cougar Canyon is a place where new worlds open up at every turn. There are more beautiful sights to see along a half-mile of this canyon than in a full day's hiking in many other parts of Anza-Borrego.

Cahuilla Indians were using seasonal camps in the area around the mouth of the canyon as recently as about 150 years ago, and the evidence left behind in the form of bedrock morteros and ceremonial caves gives another interesting dimension to a hike here.

Cougar Canyon is, however, one of the more heavily used areas of Anza-Borrego. If you plan to stay overnight, the flat, open areas just below the mouth of the canyon make spacious and convenient campsites. A few marginal camping areas do exist in the canyon proper, but these have been overused and are really too close to the canyon stream to be considered appropriate places to set up camp.

Mileages in this description start from the road closure on the spur road (the old Indian Canyon jeep road) going south from the mouth of Sheep Canyon. Begin by walking south on this eroded and partly overgrown jeep trail. After crossing Cougar Canyon's streambed three times, you'll reach a point a little beyond the mouth of Cougar Canyon (0.7 mile). Find the informal path which goes right (west) up Cougar's alluvial fan along its south edge. A little northwest of this point, on a bench overlooking the stream, is a rock cave reputed to have been used as an Indian temescal, or sweat-house. Some modern embellishments have been added to it.

Follow the path west past the aforementioned flat campsites, and cross the stream

once more (0.9 mile). Now on the north bank, the path climbs to about 50 feet above the stream as the canyon walls close in rather tightly. You'll pass another rock cave with a wide opening, to the south; in the back of this is a faded, dusky pictograph of an "anthropomorph," or humanlike figure, several inches high.

Staying on the path well above the stream, it seems almost a shame to miss the beautiful scenery down below along the sycamore-shaded creek. But soon, steep walls of granite and gneiss force you to descend anyway. Go up the cobbled bed of the stream to the beginning of a palm grove, then climb up to a sandy, shaded bench on the left bank (1.3 miles). On a rock facing the bench is a huge psychedelic "eye,"—rock art, circa 1970. Just beyond the eye, upstream, is a deep, shaded pool fed by a silvery waterfall.

The path, now obscure, continues up the south wall of the canyon to avoid a narrow section just beyond the eye. After climbing over a series of rock buttresses, you'll come to a point overlooking a feathery cascade of water flowing down a slab of banded rock in the canyon bottom. Just beyond this you can descend to the streambed again, and work your way up-canyon to a large cottonwood tree nestled beside a sculpted granite wall. Using the limbs of this tree to hoist yourself up and over, you'll come upon the most beautiful spot of all—a clear, deep pool surrounded by sheer, polished granite walls, fed by a 20-foot waterfall.

This pool and waterfall (1.5 miles, 2300′) mark the end of progress in Cougar Canyon proper without resorting to technical climbing aids. A long detour is necessary to bypass the next 0.6 mile. If you're interested, here's the way:

Back up to the point overlooking the feathery cascade. Now go straight up the south wall, dodging brush and boulders, until you reach a point on the ridgeline east of Peak 3526. Here you have a bird's-eye view of palm groves in Bennis Bowl and Valley of the Thousand Springs, and a view of some

nearly inaccessible palms in Cougar Canyon. Follow this jagged ridgeline west, pass over Peak 3526, and traverse just south of two smaller peaklets. Then drop 250 feet northwest through a gully to reach the bed of Cougar Canyon at the 3080-foot contour. From here it's possible to continue up the stream banks for some distance. For more on this, see Area M-6, Trip 2.

Rock cave at mouth of Cougar Canyon

Trip 6: Indian Canyon/Borrego Palm Canyon Traverse

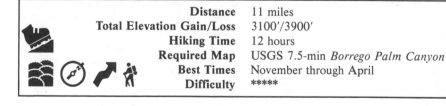

Distance	11 miles
Total Elevation Gain/Loss	3100'/3900'
Hiking Time	12 hours
Required Map	USGS 7.5-min *Borrego Palm Canyon*
Best Times	November through April
Difficulty	*****

This is a grand tour of one of Anza-Borrego's most remote, rugged, and beautiful areas. In the midsection of this trip, you'll pass through a pristine wilderness where the tracks of a mountain lion are far more common than the impressions of a lug-soled boot.

The trip is best done as an ambitious (strenuous) two-day backpack. Lightly loaded internal-frame packs are recommended for ease of movement. A light rope will come in handy for lowering packs in a few places. Water may be scarce; plan on the possibility of a dry camp.

Transportation logistics are a bit problematical. The drive between the starting and end points is 15 miles, mostly on the rugged jeep road through Coyote Canyon. If your vehicle won't make it past Lower Willows, you'll have to walk at least four extra miles across Collins Valley.

Mileages in this description start from the closure on the old jeep road into Indian Canyon, as in Trip 5 above. Follow the jeep road (now a horse and hiking path) south past Cougar Canyon, and into the wide mouth of Indian Canyon. At 1.3 miles the canyon bends right (southwest) and narrows. Pass a palm-studded tributary on the west side—the so-called Valley of the Thousand Springs—and an old tin mine near the mouth of Deering Canyon (2.0 miles).

By now the path has faded almost to insignificance. Follow the brush-choked streambed as it curves around in a gooseneck, and continue south to the point where two tributaries join from the southeast. Fill your water bottles here for a possible long, dry stretch ahead.

Climb steeply south up the ridge dividing the upper of the two tributaries from the main Indian Canyon. This ridge continues steadily uphill for 2000 vertical feet, with only moderate brush to contend with and good footing all the way. As you climb, hidden palms become visible in the tributary below, and the distant view expands to encompass Collins Valley and most of Coyote Canyon.

When the ridge tops out, traverse south, then climb slightly to a saddle (4.0 miles) just northwest of Peak 4780. The remaining seven miles are all downhill, but rather more difficult than the four miles you've just covered.

Continue going south: descend obliquely down a brushy slope, and drop into the North Fork of Borrego Palm Canyon. The floor of the canyon is delightfully shaded by dense growths of ribbonwood and scrub oak, in places forming a canopy over the narrow, rocky bed.

After 0.3 mile in the canyon, you'll come to the top of a set of waterfalls (4150'). On the left (north) side, look for morteros and metates on several orange-colored metamorphic rock slabs. There are at least 45 of these, including two that are worn completely through the thinnest slab. This must be one of the most extensive milling sites in San Diego County—also one of the most difficult to reach. Its presence is perhaps explained by the intermittent springs in the canyon below and the abundance of scrub-oak acorns nearby. Access into this area was by way of a trail, now completely overgrown and almost washed away, west to San Ignacio on the Los Coyotes Indian Reservation. Part of this trail is shown on the *Borrego Palm Canyon* topographic map.

Bypass the waterfalls on their left, and continue down the gravel-and-bedrock floor of the canyon. After passing a major fork leading north toward Palm Mesa (no palms here!), the canyon trends south. Several small dry falls must be descended, but the intervening canyon bed is relatively flat. Patches of sand become more abundant—but wait till you reach a wide, flat patch of sand at about 3400 feet if you're looking for a good campsite.

At the 3150-foot elevation, you must leave the canyon bottom and climb south up and over a low saddle. From the top of the saddle you descend 200 feet over a brush- and agave-strewn slope to return to the canyon bottom. This maneuver bypasses a gooseneck containing a 50-foot dry fall.

For the next 0.3 mile, the canyon floor is mostly bedrock, with potholes that may contain water. Just before the confluence of the Middle Fork of Borrego Palm Canyon, there is another set of dry falls—the "crux" of this challenging trip. Negotiate a route over the loose metamorphic slabs on the nose between the two forks. (Your only other alternative is to backtrack about 0.1 mile, climb up and over the ridge to the west, and drop into Middle Fork at a point 0.5 mile above the confluence.)

The Middle Fork carries a good supply of water year-round. For a description of the remaining 4.3 miles to Borrego Palm Canyon Campground, see Area M-6, Trip 4.

Area D-2: San Ysidro Mountains

West of Borrego Springs, the fluted walls of the San Ysidro Mountains rise to a height of over one vertical mile. Slashing back from the edge of this escarpment are a number of beautiful canyon systems containing palms, sycamores, cottonwoods and other riparian vegetation. Best-known of these is Borrego Palm Canyon, first set aside as a park in the early 1930s. This was the small nucleus that eventually grew to encompass 600,000 acres—the Anza-Borrego Desert State Park. Today, tens of thousands of people every year hike up Borrego Palm Canyon to view the palms.

Borrego Palm Canyon may be the largest and most beautiful, but the other, less popular canyons nearby are worth visiting too—especially if crowds are a turn-off to you. Most of the hikes below start from either the state park Visitor Center or Borrego Palm Canyon Campground; the others begin along Montezuma Highway, no more than a few miles away.

A stop at the Visitor Center is highly recommended. Aside from the excellent interpretive displays, you can view a multi-image slide show that will surely whet your appetite for exploring the Anza-Borrego Desert region.

No permit is needed for entry into any part of the San Ysidro Mountains within Anza-Borrego Desert State Park, though it is classed as state wilderness. Nor is there any restriction on overnight wilderness camping, except for a prohibition against ground fires. If you plan to use the developed Borrego Palm Canyon Campground as base camp, know that reservations are required weeks in advance during the busy winter and early spring seasons.

Trip 1: Borrego Palm Canyon Nature Trail

	Distance	3 miles
	Total Elevation Gain/Loss	450'/450'
	Hiking Time	90 minutes
	Optional Maps	Anza-Borrego Desert State Park map/brochure; USGS 7.5-min *Borrego Palm Canyon*
	Best Times	October through May
	Difficulty	*

In the first mile, there's nothing but sun-blasted vegetation, either thorny or low and prostrate. As you round a bend, you suddenly catch sight of a patch of iridescent green cradled in the yawning mouth of the canyon ahead. Hundreds of noble palms stand here, each holding high a crown of feathery, fan-shaped fronds. Water splashes over boulders and gathers in pools, delighting all the senses. It's enough to make anyone as yet unimpressed with the desert an instant convert to the ranks of "desert rats"!

You can learn more about the Colorado Desert flora on this trail than anywhere else in the park. Be sure to pick up the interpretive leaflet at the Visitor Center, or upon

San Ysidro Mountains

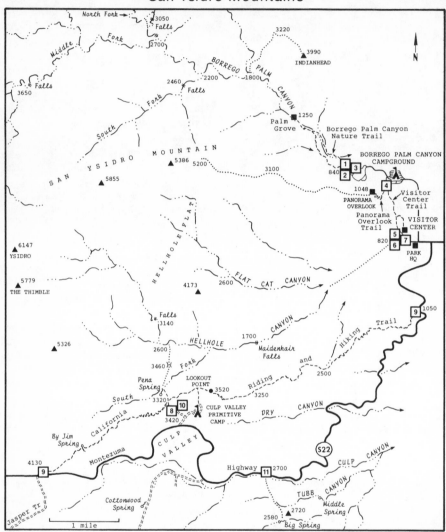

entering Borrego Palm Canyon Campground.

You begin hiking at the west end of the campground, where a special parking area/trailhead has been established. A pond holding transplanted desert pupfish is nearby. The trail crosses the seasonal stream, and starts winding up the rocky alluvial fan toward the canyon's mouth. Along the lower part of the trail are various cacti, mesquite and catclaw (with the parasitic desert mistletoe), indigo bush, desert lavender, creosote bush, brittlebush, ocotillo, desert-willow, chuparosa and sage. These may look drab most the the year, but they can really light up in a rainbow of colors by March or April of a wet year.

Soon after the palms first become visible, the trail enters the portals of the canyon. Desert-varnished rock walls soar 3000 feet up on both sides. After a second stream crossing, the trail goes up a series of steps hewn in the rock, passes a gauging station and a waterfall, crosses the stream once again, and enters the shade of the palms.

The palms are of one variety, *Washingtonia filifera,* the only palm indigenous to California. Although they are generally well-adapted to wildfire, several blackened and headless trunks in this grove show that some simply have failed to survive periodic fires. A few alders and sycamores struggle for light among the massive, straight trunks of the palms.

Part of the grove is fenced off to prevent root compaction by hikers' feet. Please respect this barrier—there are plenty of other places to rest or picnic.

The trail terminates at a point just below a small waterfall and pool at the upper end of the palm grove, 1.5 miles from the trailhead. Further travel up-canyon is by boulder hopping (see Trips 2 and 3 below). See Area M-6, Trip 4, and Area D-1, Trip 6, for complete descriptions of the canyon's uppermost reaches.

On the return leg, try the alternate trail that winds along the upper edge of the alluvial fan. Here you can study how certain plants are stratified according to habitat. Here less water is absorbed by the soil, so the drought-tolerant ocotillo dominates.

Trip 2: Indianhead Mountain

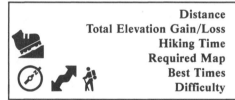

Distance	7 miles round trip
Total Elevation Gain/Loss	3200'/3200'
Hiking Time	7 hours (round trip)
Required Map	USGS 7.5-min *Borrego Palm Canyon*
Best Times	November through April
Difficulty	****

The north wall of Borrego Palm Canyon culminates in a spectacular, jagged promontory known as Indianhead. This is a conspicuous landmark seen and admired from most locations in Borrego Valley, and one of the few named summits in the San Ysidro Mountains. Mapmakers, it seems, haven't bothered to measure or estimate its height—

Ocotillo blossoms on Borrego Palm Canyon Trail

its elevation is not recorded on topographic maps.

There are many ways to climb Indianhead, nearly all involving very steep ascents from the desert floor. My favorite route (detailed here) is somewhat longer, but safer. This can be a challenging day hike, or involve a night's stay in Borrego Palm Canyon. With a base camp established well up in the canyon, you'll have the opportunity to do the climb in the early morning, when the air is clearest and the temperature moderate.

Begin as in Trip 1 above. Beyond the first grove (1.5 miles), but before the first major bend in the canyon (to the north), you'll scramble over some large, light-colored granitic boulders, soon picking up a fair trail on the south side of the creek. Mesquite, catclaw, willow, and desert-willow crowd in along the banks. Palm trees resume as you round the second bend (1.8 miles), and are present intermittently—mostly in dense clusters—for the next two miles. An illegal campfire sparked a blaze here in 1985 that charred 100 acres, including several dozen palms in the so-called third and fourth groves. (Reminder: ground fires are prohibited throughout the state park.)

Almost coincident with the return of the palms is a change in the nature of the rock in the canyon bed. The granitic rock is abruptly replaced by tan- and orange-tinted schist and gneiss. In several places, the creek flows over colorful slabs of this rock and collects in small pools shaded by palms both young and old. Small campsites are fairly abundant in the wider parts of the canyon, especially on its north side.

The turnoff point for Indianhead is reached at 2.5 miles (1800'), where a tributary canyon comes in from the north. Climb northeast straight up the ridge just east of this tributary. After about 0.7 mile, you'll reach a 3220-foot saddle northwest of Indianhead. From here make your way southeast around huge boulders and over slab rock to reach the highest point on Indianhead's flat summit.

Now the entire sweep of the San Ysidro Mountains lies before you. In the north, beyond lesser ranges, the snow-capped San Jacinto Mountains float like a mirage. To obtain the best view of the bottom of Borrego Palm Canyon, scramble about 0.1 mile south of the high point, and work your way out to a jagged outcrop. You can sit here, legs dangling, and look almost straight down upon the crowns of hundreds of palms.

Trip 3: South Fork Borrego Palm Canyon

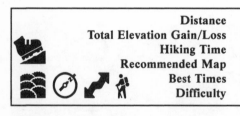

Distance	7.5 miles round trip
Total Elevation Gain/Loss	1700'/1700'
Hiking Time	6 hours (round trip)
Recommended Map	USGS 7.5-min *Borrego Palm Canyon*
Best Times	November through April
Difficulty	****

To some, that which seems almost impossible *is* impossible. To others, it is challenging—and intriguing. Take one look at the bed of Borrego Palm Canyon's South Fork, and you'll be either energized or enervated. The reward for your trouble is a hidden set of waterfalls, very seldom visited. Water flow in the canyon is greatest from January through March; at other times there may be only a trickle over the falls.

Even if you decide not to enter the South Fork, long pants are still recommended for the brushy sections of Borrego Palm Canyon below the South Fork. In the South Fork, heavy boots are especially useful—the better to bash the brush with.

Refer to Trips 1 and 2 for the description up to 2.5 miles. Near 3.0 miles (2040'), you'll come upon several possible campsites on benches above the creek. Just beyond, a large cottonwood tree stands at a major southward bend in the canyon. Poison oak appears in isolated clumps from this point on.

At 3.3 miles, the South Fork branches obviously to the southwest, away from the Middle Fork. The Middle Fork contributes perhaps 75% of the water, the South Fork 25%. Stay well up on the north side of the South Fork gorge, taking care to bypass a mesquite thicket along its upper rather than its lower edge. After 0.2 mile steep walls on both sides will force you into the canyon bottom. Squish through the water, and

flounder through almost impenetrable growths of horsetail, willow, yerba santa, and cattails, avoiding occasional poison-oak clumps. For a short distance you can traverse again along the north wall, and then you cross to the south side and continue 100 yards to the base of a beautiful, 30-foot stairstep waterfall (3.7 miles). Bare rock exposures on either side make good places to lie in the sun or have lunch.

Above this fall is an upper tier—a 15-foot stairstep fall—not visible from below. About 200 yards past this is a sheer 80-foot fall (normally dry) in a tributary canyon.

Trip 4: Panorama Overlook Trail

Distance	1 mile round trip
Total Elevation Gain/Loss	300'/300'
Hiking Time	40 minutes (round trip)
Optional Maps	Anza-Borrego Desert State Park map/brochure; USGS 7.5-min *Borrego Palm Canyon*
Best Times	All year
Difficulty	*

Starting near campsite 71 in Borrego Palm Canyon Campground, this well-used trail climbs sharply up one of the ridge spurs of San Ysidro Mountain, offering a superb vista of Borrego Valley and its spectacular backdrop of mountains. The flat area at the top of the trail is called Panorama Overlook (or Panorama Outlook on some maps). Any good map of the Anza-Borrego region will help you identify the major topographical features visible along the horizon from northeast through the south: Coyote Mountain and the distant Santa Rosa Mountains; Fonts Point and the Borrego Badlands; Pinyon Ridge and a slice of the Vallecito Mountains. Facing west, you must crane your neck to follow the continuation of the rocky ridge you're standing upon. This culminates about 4000 feet higher, on the crest of San Ysidro Mountain (see Trip 5 if you intend to climb higher than Panorama Overlook).

Panorama Overlook is an excellent spot to witness the sunrise on the crisp mornings of fall and winter. Late afternoons are nice too; you can watch the mountain shadows slowly stretch across Borrego Valley as the sun sinks unseen.

This trail is one of the few in Anza-Borrego short enough for summer hiking. Summer afternoon thundershowers over the desert floor can be interesting to watch from here, but only if they're far enough away.

Trip 5: San Ysidro Mountain

Distance	7 miles round trip
Total Elevation Gain/Loss	4400'/4400'
Hiking Time	8 hours (round trip)
Recommended Map	USGS 7.5-min *Borrego Palm Canyon*
Best Times	November through April
Difficulty	****

The eastern brow of San Ysidro Mountain overlooks Borrego Valley from an elevation of nearly one mile. Here, in the cool pinyon-pine-and-juniper belt, you can experience a startling pseudo-aerial perspective of Anza-Borrego quite unlike that seen from any other land-based vantage point.

On this hike horizontal distance is trivial and vertical gain is everything. It's a taxing but immensely satisfying journey. Every step upward takes you closer to the heavens, and farther from the civilized world. The roads, dwellings, and windbreak-bordered fields etched on the floor of Borrego Valley always remain visible through the clear desert air, but they become more and more toylike and abstract—as if viewed from space—as you climb.

This is a tough hike, no matter how you do it. The gradient at times approaches 3000 feet of gain per mile of horizontal distance, often over a rugged landscape of weathered granitic boulders. No water is available anywhere along the route. Dayhikers should allow a full dawn-to-dusk day for the round trip; backpackers need almost this much time for the ascent alone—especially in view of the amount of water that must be carried. Navigation is easy in the uphill direction, but a topo map and compass are useful for reference during the return leg, because it's possible to stray off the main ridge.

A convenient place to begin this trip, especially if you are backpacking, is the Visitor Center, where free parking is available. From the parking lot you can clearly see the route ahead. The transparent desert air compresses distance and height, and an illusion of perspective makes it appear as if the

truck-sized boulders high on the ridge are really much smaller. The effort required to reach the top seems—well—trivial.

Head directly across the desert floor toward the spur ridge to the northeast, 0.5 mile away (or use the Visitor Center Trail to angle over in that direction). Pick up the switchbacks of the Panorama Overlook Trail, then continue beyond the overlook using the faint trail up the ridge. This trail peters out fairly quickly.

A full range of desert slope vegetation is observed as you climb; first, the creosote bush/brittlebush/ocotillo/cactus community typical of the lower desert alluvial fans and slopes; then agave and shrubby but widely scattered plants such as sugarbush, scrub oak, and juniper; and finally pinyon pine.

Beyond Panorama Overlook, you're on granitic rock or decomposed granite (sandy soil) throughout. Above a small flat on the ridge at 3100 feet, the slope becomes distinctly steeper. Large monoliths and stiff vegetation impede progress.

Topping out at 5200 feet, you'll find abundant flat, sandy campsites nearby. It was here that I had a memorable experience: watching an orange-tinted full moon rise over the Salton Sea, awash in the purple glow of evening twilight.

Further exploration along the undulating ridgeline of San Ysidro Mountain is possible, but very difficult due to brush and boulders. The easiest way back to Borrego Valley is by retracing your steps; alternate return routes by way of Hellhole Flat and Flat Cat or Hellhole canyon, for example, involve even more rugged terrain.

Trip 6: Flat Cat Canyon

Distance	5.5 miles round trip (to palms at 2600')
Total Elevation Gain/Loss	1800'/1800'
Hiking Time	5 hours (round trip)
Recommended Maps	USGS 7.5-min *Borrego Palm Canyon, Tubb Canyon*
Best Times	December through March
Difficulty	***

Flat Cat Canyon is the curious name given to a rugged gorge just north of lower Hellhole Canyon. Anza-Borrego rangers found a dead bobcat (presumably *very* dead) in this canyon, and followed the honorable Western tradition of assigning colorful names to "colorful" places. As viewed from the alluvial fan below, Flat Cat Canyon looks like a boulder-choked ravine, seemingly unpromising. But its upper reaches hold a surprise or two.

Wear long pants and sturdy shoes; the canyon presents some serious bushwhacking and scrambling challenges. Begin at the Anza-Borrego Desert State Park Visitor Center, where parking (day and overnight) is available. Note the tall flagpole here. The Visitor Center is largely underground, and a sighting of this flagpole will be the best way to find your car on the return leg of the hike.

From the Visitor Center parking lot, head straight for the mouth of Hellhole Canyon, the big canyon to the southwest. Don't enter Hellhole Canyon. Instead, at 1.4 miles from the Visitor Center, bear right (west) and ascend Flat Cat Canyon.

Climb for about one mile, gaining about 1000 feet. The sandy wash at the bottom of the canyon provides smooth going except when choked with vegetation—notably thorny desert apricot and catclaw bushes. Marginal trails of animals and occasional hikers thread the canyon walls, providing serviceable alternate routes. Flat Cat Canyon is hewn from granitic rock: note the contrast between the dark, desert-varnished rock high on the canyon walls, and the whitish, flood-scoured boulders on the lower slopes.

At 2100 feet elevation (in a moderately wet year, at least) your ears will discover a most welcome sound—the trickle of water. A little above this, you come upon a place where the water slides over a 20-foot precipice. Two hundred feet higher, you top a small rise and discover—palms!

Below the first group of palms is a flat bench suitable as a campsite for four or five people. Just above these palms, on the north side of the canyon, be sure to look for a spectacular example of exfoliation. Temperature changes and the prying action of freezing and melting water have carved the rock on the canyon wall into concentric layers, resembling those of an onion. Higher still, where the canyon evenly divides (2600'), is the biggest grove—about two dozen palms.

Horned lizard

Trip 7: Lower Hellhole Canyon

Distance	6 miles round trip (to Maidenhair Falls)
Total Elevation Gain/Loss	900'/900'
Hiking Time	4 hours (round trip)
Optional Maps	Anza-Borrego Desert State Park map/brochure; USGS 7.5-min *Borrego Palm Canyon, Tubb Canyon*
Best Times	December through April
Difficulty	***

In the midst of what is regarded as one of America's hottest and driest deserts, it seems a bit surprising to find a place where mosses, ferns, sycamores, and cottonwoods flourish around a sparkling waterfall. Maidenhair Falls is such a place, and it lies just three miles (only two hours away by foot) from the Anza-Borrego Desert State Park Visitor Center.

Both day and overnight parking are allowed at the Visitor Center parking lot. From the lot head straight across the alluvial fan toward the mouth of the big canyon to the southwest—Hellhole Canyon. The sandy surface of the fan supports a variety of vegetation, stratified according to elevation. Indigo bush (dormant and dead-looking until about March), chuparosa, cheesebush, bur-roweed, creosote bush, desert lavender, and buckhorn cholla are the common plant species of the lower fan. These are largely replaced by jojoba, brittlebush, ocotillo, and teddy-bear cholla on the upper fan. Everywhere, jackrabbits flit among the bushes, startled by your approach.

In a dry year water is first encountered at the canyon's mouth; in a wet year, the flow may extend a half mile or more down the fan. Recent floods have gouged out a small chasm (5–10' deep) in the sandy floor of the canyon. Stay generally left of this until the south slope pinches in so tightly that you have to move to the right (north) side of the canyon. In the next half mile or so you'll want to stay away from the boulder-filled and vegetation-choked canyon bottom. Hikers have beaten down paths along both banks, but passage

still is not easy. There are difficult scrambles over large boulders and fallen trees, and unexpected encounters with wicked catclaw thorns. The dead snags and fallen trees in your path are a result of a 1975 wildfire that burned the entire Hellhole Canyon drainage. Young sycamores and cottonwoods are now pushing through the wreckage of the older giants.

Palms, too, are present in the canyon bottom, but sparsely distributed. About 200 yards past the densest cluster of palms, the canyon walls pinch tightest. Here you'll find the grotto containing Maidenhair Falls. The falls plunge 25 feet into a shallow pool. Tiers of maidenhair fern adorn the grotto, and sopping wet mosses cover the places the ferns don't.

Farther travel up-canyon from Maidenhair Falls involves considerable bushwhacking—extremely slow going with a backpack. As the vegetation continues to recover from the fire, passage through this part of the canyon will become even more challenging. See Trip 10 below for more on upper Hellhole Canyon.

Trip 8: Culp Valley Lookout/Pena Spring Loop

Distance	1.7 miles
Total Elevation Gain/Loss	300'/300'
Hiking Time	1 hour
Optional Maps	Anza-Borrego Desert State Park map/brochure; USGS 7.5-min *Tubb Canyon*
Best Times	September through June
Difficulty	*

While the low desert swelters, the temperature hovers in a more moderate register at Culp Valley, 3000 feet higher. This is the only designated camping area in the Anza-Borrego Desert where the heat on the cooler days of June and September is quite bearable. July and August daytime temperatures are probably too warm for most people's tastes—typically in the 90's and 100's.

Grayish-colored granitic boulders are piled up all around the floor of Culp Valley, sharply etching the horizon. The west wind blows capriciously, often whistling eerily through the rocks. Nearby, out of sight from the valley, is a hillside spring surrounded by an oasis of green grass and small trees. It is this kind of contrast that makes this hike immediately rewarding.

To reach the starting point, drive to mile 9.2 on Montezuma Highway (2.8 miles east of the highway summit near Ranchita; 9.4 miles west of Borrego Springs) and turn north on the unpaved entrance road to Culp Valley Primitive Camp. The campground is truly "no frills"—just a few nooks and crannies where you can park your car overnight—but it makes a fine base camp for exploring the entire Culp Valley/Hellhole Canyon region. We'll begin our description, however, from the parking area (vehicle closure) on the road toward Pena Spring, southwest of the campground.

Several years ago, auto traffic was barred from the last 0.3 mile of road to the spring in deference to the water needs of the local wildlife. Walk down this stretch until you reach the grove of large sugarbush shrubs at road's end, then go west through a thicket of yerba santa and wildflowers to the hidden hillside meadow containing the spring. Yerba mansa flowers poke up through the grass blades where the ground is saturated. A wooden barrel stores water emerging from a buried pipe, and the overflow feeds an open pond for the wildlife. Rabbits and coyotes seem to be the most frequent users. On the margins of the wash that lies just below the spring (the bed of South Fork Hellhole Canyon) is evidence of Indian occupation. Under the desert-willow, mesquite, and catclaw, you might chance upon some pieces of pottery.

After visiting the spring, backtrack up the road 0.2 mile to the intersection of the California Riding & Hiking Trail, marked by a small wooden post. Go east on this, climbing up, then along, a rather flat-topped ridgeline offering good views of Culp Valley, Pinyon Ridge and San Ysidro Mountain, and tantalizing glimpses of the big gorge to the north—Hellhole Canyon. Here you'll find typical high-desert vegetation mixed with types that grow also in the chaparral and sage-scrub zones on the west side of the mountains: juniper, catclaw, desert apricot, various cacti, sugarbush, buckwheat, Mojave and Lord's candle yucca, and white sage.

After 0.5 mile on the C R & H Trail, you'll come to the intersection of a road that goes down to the campground, 0.3 mile south. About 100 feet north of this point are some rock outcrops offering the best views of the Hellhole Canyon gorge, Borrego Valley, and the great wall of mountains beyond the valley. The pinyon-fringed, flattish summit of Rabbit Peak is conspicuous as the highest point visible on the long crest of the Santa Rosa Mountains.

East another 0.2 mile on the C R & H Trail is the marked Vista Point (or "Lookout Point" on most park maps) offering a more panoramic but somewhat less spectacular view than seen earlier. Northwest down the slope from the Lookout Point is a huge, weathered boulder split cleanly down the middle; it's fun to squeeze through the slot, or "chimney" up to the top.

Lastly, backtrack a little and take the road toward the campground and your parked car.

Ocotillo on alluvial fan

Trip 9: California Riding & Hiking Trail

Distance	7.5 miles
Total Elevation Gain/Loss	500'/3600'
Hiking Time	4 hours
Recommended Map	USGS 7.5-min *Tubb Canyon* (trail not shown on 1959 edition)
Best Times	October through May
Difficulty	***

This delightful one-way (preferably downhill) route has a long and varied history. Originally a well-beaten Indian trail, it was used for many decades by cattlemen moving herds from the Mesa Grande area near Lake Henshaw to winter and spring grazing grounds at the mouths of Hellhole Canyon and Borrego Palm Canyon—then known simply as "Pam Canyon" or "Palm Canyon." After World War II the trail became a branch of the California Riding & Hiking Trail. Today, while the statewide C R & H Trail has largely fallen into disuse, this one desert segment continues to be maintained. Curiously, the trail almost never has the imprint of horseshoes; hikers and mountain bicyclists use it almost exclusively.

Car shuttling is easy for this trip, as both ends of the trail intersect the same road—Montezuma Highway. The top of the trail is at mile 6.8, across the highway from the junction of the signed Jasper Trail. This is just 0.2 mile east of the highway summit east of Ranchita. The bottom end is at mile 16.0, about one mile from the edge of Borrego Valley. The road shoulder is narrow here, precluding parking, but there is a turnout 0.2 mile north (mile 16.2) big enough for parking.

Topside, pick up the trail, marked by faded, yellow-topped posts, and follow it northeast over a low saddle. The vegetation here is mostly common chaparral—mountain mahogany, chamise, and scrub oak—but there are some high-desert plants too, such as juniper, sugarbush, desert apricot, buckhorn cholla cactus, and beavertail cactus. After descending slightly to By Jim Spring, you'll find a trickle of water (in winter and spring) and the ruins of pipes and a tank. The trail continues on or close to a ridgeline for the next mile.

At about 2.0 miles the trail passes just below peak 4068, and a spectacular view of Culp Valley and the distant Borrego Valley opens up. From this point, the trail descends sharply, crosses the road to Pena Spring (the only dependable water source near this route), and climbs toward Lookout Point (3.5 miles) as described in Trip 8 above.

From here, the trail sticks mostly to the top of the ridge between Hellhole Canyon and Dry Canyon. Some flat, sandy areas at 4.2 miles (3250') would make good campsites. Beyond this, the trail descends sharply again, tending to the left (north) side of the ridge, with good views across Hellhole Canyon to the mountain slopes rising from Borrego Valley. At 5.5 miles (2500') the trail

skirts a ravine where you can see the greatest variety of shrubs and spring wildflowers on the route. To name a few: juniper, jojoba, brittlebush, deerweed, cholla and beavertail cacti, agave, yucca, buckwheat, white sage, chuparosa, apricot mallow, goldenbush, scarlet bugler, and lupine.

Near the bottom of the trail, the vegetation is dominated by ocotillo, creosote bush and brittlebush—the latter creating great swaths of yellow color across the stony slopes when in full bloom during March or April.

Trip 10: Upper Hellhole Canyon

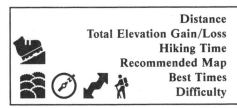

Distance	3 miles round trip (to 30' waterfall)
Total Elevation Gain/Loss	1600'/1600'
Hiking Time	4 hours (round trip)
Recommended Map	USGS 7.5-min *Tubb Canyon*
Best Times	December through April
Difficulty	***

The easiest entry into the upper reaches of Hellhole Canyon is not by simply going up from the mouth of the canyon past Maidenhair Falls. Nor is it by descending the South Fork below Pena Spring, though this is an interesting and challenging hike in its own right. Rather, it is by dropping down the ridge to the north of Pena Spring. This is a steep and at times slippery descent, but one accomplished in a fraction of the time required on the other routes. In this description, I will describe the way to a 30-foot-high waterfall in a northern tributary of Hellhole Canyon.

Begin this hike at the dead end on the road to Pena Spring, as in Trip 8 above. Hike down to the spring first, then go north cross-country 0.4 mile, gaining almost 200 feet, to reach a flat part of the ridgeline overlooking Hellhole Canyon. Now head straight down (north) toward the large cottonwood tree in the canyon bottom ahead. In just over 0.2 mile of horizontal distance on the map, you lose 800 feet. If you choose your route carefully, the footing is quite stable on dirt and sparse grass, and over boulders. Be aware of

the possibility of dislodging rocks, especially if traveling with others. Proceed very carefully if carrying a heavy backpack.

In recent years Hellhole Canyon, like most other major canyons in the desert, has enjoyed a year-round supply of running water. A more "normal" climate trend in the future, if it happens, may cause the flow to cease during the nonrainy months.

Travel along the Hellhole Canyon bottom is very difficult due to vines, boulders, and fallen trees. About 100 yards downstream from the cottonwood tree, the canyon bends and widens, offering good camping possibilities. The tributary with the waterfall, however, lies upstream about 100 yards.

Go up the bottom of the tributary about 150 yards, passing several mini-waterfalls, until forced by dense vegetation to gain the slope on the right (east) side. Traverse for about 300 yards on the rocky slope until you can drop again into the canyon bottom at a point close to a multilevel cascade. Then make your way over large boulders and slabs to a grotto containing the 30-foot fall. The water shoots over in a thin stream, perfect for a shower on a warm day—but be careful of the slippery rocks.

Further exploration beyond this fall is problematical if you remain in the canyon, but relatively easy if you gain the slopes and ridgelines. Hellhole Flat is one possible destination. So too are The Thimble (5779') and the highest summit on San Ysidro Mountain (6147').

A herd of feral cattle has flourished in the upper reaches of Hellhole Canyon and its northern tributary (above the 30-foot fall) for at least 20 years. Because these cattle tend to displace bighorn sheep and other wildlife, there have been some attempts to drive them out—all unsuccessful. This gives a modern dimension to the same predicament faced by the old-time cattlemen around the turn of the century: so many stray cattle wandered into this canyon that it became known as a "hellish" place from which to extricate a cow—hence the name "Hellhole."

Trip 11: Tubb Canyon

Distance	1.5 miles round trip
Total Elevation Gain/Loss	200'/200'
Hiking Time	1 hour (round trip)
Recommended Map	USGS 7.5-min *Tubb Canyon*
Best Times	October through May
Difficulty	*

Big Spring in a tributary of Tubb Canyon ("Tub" Canyon on some maps) is one of the most reliable water producers in the Anza-Borrego Desert. As such, it is an important watering hole for local wildlife. Tracks on the sandy pathways leading to the spring show evidence of visits by coyotes, mountain lions, and bighorn sheep.

Unmarked on the state park map, and unknown to most park visitors, this isolated spring is actually very easy to reach on foot. The best place to begin is the small parking turnout on the north side of Montezuma Grade (Highway S-22) at mile 11.2. Walk due south across 400 yards of flat terrain, and cross over a gentle saddle. At this point you'll pick up a faint wildlife trail that descends into a sandy wash—the head of Tubb Canyon. After about 200 yards downstream the trail leaves this wash and passes over a low saddle to the south. Big Spring lies beyond, in the bottom of Tubb Canyon's south branch.

At the spring, the water gushes through tall thickets of seepwillow and thorny tangles of catclaw and mesquite—so it's hard to reach the water with one's hide intact. A few small willows and cottonwoods raise their crowns above it all. Enhancing the scene is the massive presence of Pinyon Ridge, rising to the south.

Before going back to the highway, climb the small hill (2720') east of the saddle you just passed over. This is one of the panoramic viewing sites used every summer by volunteers in the Anza-Borrego Desert bighorn-sheep-count program.

Young antelope ground squirrel

Area D-3: Coyote Mountain/Rockhouse Canyon

The Anza-Borrego Desert State Park extends over such a large area that duplication of place names is common. For example, the Rockhouse Canyon and Coyote Mountain in the north sector of the park are distinct from the Rockhouse Canyon (near Bow Willow) and the Coyote Mountains (near Ocotillo) that lie in the south sector.

The northern Coyote Mountain is a barren-looking, brownish ridge separating lower Coyote Canyon from Clark Valley and Clark (dry) Lake. Geologically, it is a spur of the Santa Rosa Mountains which has drifted away from the main crest by fault action. Coyote Mountain and its extension of lower hills to the northwest form a wedge between the San Jacinto Fault in Clark Valley and the Coyote Creek Fault in Coyote Canyon.

Rockhouse Canyon drains a large alluvial basin at the foot of the Santa Rosa Mountains. It meanders southwest between precipitous walls, then strikes a course southeast along the San Jacinto Fault. Below it lies Clark Valley.

Trips 2, 4 and 5 below start along the only vehicle route penetrating Rockhouse Canyon. Standard passenger cars, if driven carefully, can usually maneuver up about nine miles of this progressively more primitive unpaved road. To get to the starting points of these three trips, refer to the following directions:

At mile 26.7 on Borrego-Salton Seaway (Highway S-22), just east of Pegleg Monument, turn north on Clark's Well Road. Pavement soon ends. Bear right, avoiding the spur road on the left to a highway-maintenance gravel pit. After 1.5 miles (from S-22), the road divides again. Take the left fork (right fork leads to the Clark Lake Radio Observatory complex on the bed of the dry lake). The left fork (Rockhouse Truck Trail on topo maps) skirts the west edge of Clark Dry Lake (starting point for Trip 2), swings around a spur of Coyote Mountain, and continues toward the mouth of Rockhouse Canyon. At 9.2 miles from S-22, you come to the junction of jeep roads into Butler and Rockhouse canyons (starting point for Trips 4 and 5). Travel beyond this point by vehicle is for tough 4-wheel-drive rigs and motorcycles only.

Most of Coyote Mountain and the lower end of Rockhouse Canyon are classed as state wilderness. The upper end of Rockhouse Canyon and the valley above it are under the jurisdiction of the BLM and the California Department of Fish and Game; in these areas some state park regulations, such as the prohibition of ground fires, don't apply. No permits are required for day or overnight use.

Clark Valley from Coyote Mountain

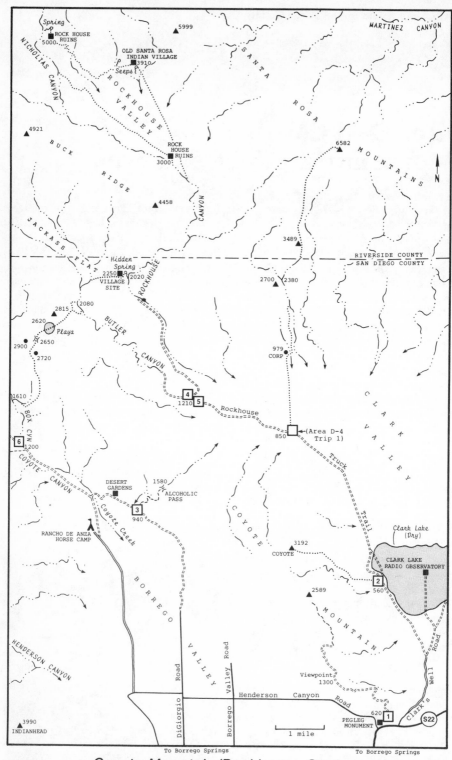

Coyote Mountain/Rockhouse Canyon

Trip 1: Coyote Mountain—South Spur

Distance	4 miles round trip (to view point)
Total Elevation Gain/Loss	750'/750'
Hiking Time	2 hours (round trip)
Optional Map	USGS 7.5-min *Clark Lake*
Best Times	November through April
Difficulty	**

A spectacular view of upper Borrego Valley—with its patchwork of tamarisk windbreaks, fields, citrus orchards, and palm nurseries—is the highlight of this hike. You begin at Pegleg Monument, nestled against the south spur of Coyote Mountain, and climb steadily on an old jeep road for two miles until you reach a point on the steep southwest escarpment offering the best view.

The Monument, seven miles northeast of Borrego Springs on Highway S-22, commemorates Pegleg Smith, a prospector and spinner of tall tales, and his famous lost gold. Adding stones to the big rock pile here, it is said, brings luck to the treasure hunter.

Vegetation seen along the jeep road is sparse—mostly ocotillo, creosote bush, and brittlebush. At higher elevations, however, the brittlebush is dense enough to create splashes of yellow color on the hillsides and in the ravines when it blooms in March.

Beyond the viewpoint at 2.0 miles, the road continues winding up along ridges and through hidden valleys for another 2.5 miles until it fades out completely near peak 2589. The summit of Coyote Mountain (3192') lies about one mile farther north. This summit is more easily reached by climbing from the west edge of Clark Lake (see Trip 2 below).

Trip 2: Coyote Mountain—East Approach

Distance	4 miles round trip (to summit)
Total Elevation Gain/Loss	2600'/2600'
Hiking Time	5 hours (round trip)
Recommended Map	USGS 7.5-min *Clark Lake*
Best Times	November through April
Difficulty	***

According to the informal register at the top of Coyote Mountain, only about three parties per year bother to make the summit—or at least sign the notebook. A variety of routes have been used, but most people climb from Clark Lake, on the east.

This is basically a walk-up ascent, though quite steep. Outcrops of solid, desert-varnished rock provide mostly good footing on the lower slopes; higher up, however, a veneer of small stones underfoot makes walking a little difficult.

To reach the starting point, drive 3.5 miles north of Highway S-22 (on Clark's Well Road and the Rockhouse Truck Trail) and stop at the "yellow hopper," a conspicuous yellow-painted steel structure at the west end of Clark Lake's dry bed.

From the hopper simply go straight up the steep slope to the west. Scattered shrubs and succulents—like brittlebush, cholla cactus, agave, and creosote bush—cling tenaciously to soil pockets amid the rocks.

As you climb, a pattern of lines becomes

visible on the dry lake bed below, not unlike the famous intaglios of the Nazca Plain in Peru. These include the outlines of the sprawling T-shaped antenna array of the Clark Lake Radio Observatory, and a nearby landing field. Beyond the dry lake, the panorama of the west escarpment of the Santa Rosa Mountains, its rugged ravines, and classic (from a geologist's view point) alluvial fans, is almost stupefying.

The broad, rounded summit at 3192 feet is topped by red and white flags placed here by a party of San Diego County surveyors who arrived by helicopter in January 1985. The view is, of course, panoramic, but doesn't include much of the valleys below. You must step well away from the summit in order to look down. Some small, probably windswept campsites can be found 0.2 mile southwest of the summit.

Trip 3: Alcoholic Pass

Distance	2 miles round trip (to pass)
Total Elevation Gain/Loss	650'/650'
Hiking Time	1½ hours (round trip)
Optional Map	USGS 7.5-min *Borrego Palm Canyon*
Best Times	November through April
Difficulty	**

For centuries Indians used Alcoholic Pass as a convenient short cut between Coyote Canyon and Clark Valley. In time, a well-beaten trail was worn across the precipitous slopes west of the pass. Around the turn of the century, the Clark brothers, early cattlemen who homesteaded in Coyote Canyon, used this trail to transport some primitive well-drilling equipment to the site now known as Clarks Well in Clark Valley. Near the top of the pass, the old Indian trail squeezed between two boulders so closely spaced that the burros had to be unpacked before going through. Today, you can still follow the obvious trace of this historic pathway.

The starting point for this hike is along the main Coyote Canyon jeep road, 2.8 miles north of the end of the pavement at DiGiorgio Road. There is a small roadside turnout here, suitable for one or two cars. East of this turnout is a steep ravine leading up toward the pass. The old Indian trail does not ascend this ravine directly, but instead rises on the ridge immediately south of it. You'll find the base of the trail about 150 yards to the right (south) of the mouth of the ravine.

You climb on a somewhat rough and rocky path, gaining altitude quickly. In a few places, foot travel and erosion have worn the bed of the trail to a depth of two feet. Looking behind you to gauge your progress as you climb, you'll be inspired by the ever-widening, almost aerial, view of Coyote Canyon and the surrounding mountains.

In the upper reaches of the pass, the trail levels somewhat and is difficult to follow. Just head for the pile of boulders at the top of the pass. Here you'll catch sight of the massive wall of the Santa Rosa Mountains, topped by the dusky, pinyon-covered summit of Rabbit Peak.

The remainder of the old Alcoholic Pass route goes east along the sandy bed of a wide wash and eventually reaches the desolate floor of Clark Valley. The Rockhouse Truck Trail is three miles northeast of the pass; you could arrange for someone to meet you there on the truck trail if you wanted to hike one-way from Coyote Canyon to Clark Valley.

Trip 4: Jackass Flat/Butler Canyon

Distance	10 miles
Total Elevation Gain/Loss	1000'/1000'
Hiking Time	6 hours
Recommended Maps	Anza-Borrego Desert State Park map/brochure; or USGS 7.5-min *Clark Lake NE, Collins Valley*
Best Times	November through April
Difficulty	***

A visit to an ancient Cahuilla Indian village is the highlight on this long loop hike over mostly gentle terrain. Hidden Spring, about halfway around the loop, nearly always has some surface water, but cannot be considered a good source for drinking needs.

From Highway S-22 drive 9.2 miles up Clark's Well Road and the Rockhouse Truck Trail to the junction of roads into Rockhouse and Butler canyons. On foot follow the Rockhouse road northward across a low bank and into the broad wash of Rockhouse Canyon. The next four miles are somewhat uneventful, though the canyon deepens impressively. The San Jacinto Fault parallels this section of canyon. At about three miles, there is a road closure sign. Continue another mile to Hidden Spring, well-identified by a prominent sign. A small catch basin holds about two or three gallons of insect-infested water.

From the catch basin walk 150 feet back down along the canyon wall to a grove of mesquite trees. A path through the mesquite will guide you to a very deeply worn, eroded

trail that angles south and upward across a 200-foot-high bluff. At the top, on the eastern brink of Jackass Flat, are the remains of a Cahuilla Indian village occupied as recently as 100 years ago. Broken bits of pottery and old fire pits are very much in evidence, along with a few pieces of wonderstone (see Area D-4, Trip 6).

Jackass Flat is drained by Butler Canyon, the head of which is about one mile west of the village site. Your return is by this canyon, assisted by gravity all the way. As you enter Butler Canyon, notice the myriad of miniature pine cones littering the canyon bottom. These have come from the pinyon-dotted crown of Buck Ridge, three miles north of you and about 2000 feet higher. Buck Ridge was an important pinyon-nut-gathering area for the Cahuilla Indians.

Follow the course of Butler Canyon as it descends gently for four miles through a spectacular serpentine gorge carved out of mostly granitic rock. Beyond the mouth of this gorge you'll pick up wheel tracks leading back to your car.

Cottonwoods above Nicholias Canyon

Trip 5: Rockhouse Canyon and Valley

	Distance	25 miles
	Total Elevation Gain/Loss	4000'/4000'
	Hiking Time	16 hours
	Required Maps	USGS 7.5-min *Clark Lake NE,* *Collins Valley*
	Best Times	November through April
	Difficulty	****

Rockhouse Canyon and the broad, sloping alluvial basin drained by it—informally known as Rockhouse Valley—constitute one of southern California's truly forgotten places. As recently as 100 years ago, Indian villages thrived here. After the Indians' move to the nearby Santa Rosa Indian Reservation around the turn of the century, a few hardy prospectors made forays into the area, traveling along the ancient footpaths, and in some cases living in the old rock houses built by the Indians. Today, there is still no road beyond the lower reaches of Rockhouse Canyon. The closest inhabited place is miles away, and the only visitors are a few intrepid hikers and backpackers.

Although this grand tour of Rockhouse Canyon and Valley can be done in a single, very long day's hike (I once rushed through this way), plan to carry a backpack over a two- to three-day period so that you can enjoy the scenery at a reasonable pace.

To reach the starting point, accessible by most standard passenger vehicles, drive 9.2 miles north from Highway S-22 on Clark's Well Road and Rockhouse Truck Trail. Park near the junction of roads into Butler and Rockhouse canyons.

On foot now (unless you have a motorcycle or tough 4-wheel-drive rig to carry you three miles farther to the Rockhouse Canyon road closure), walk north into the mouth of Rockhouse Canyon and continue to Hidden Spring, four miles up-canyon. It's difficult to extract a decent supply of water from this spring, so don't depend on it. In the next 3.5 miles, Rockhouse Canyon is a narrow, rocky gorge, but you'll be on soft sand—alluvium

washed down from the valley above—most of the time.

Spectacular, near-vertical exposures of granite and gneiss embellish the canyon wall beyond Hidden Spring. A little farther on (just below the San Diego-Riverside county line) is a granite dike forming a 20-foot dry fall. In the days before this area was declared a state wilderness, jeep-club members built a road over this obstacle and used a winch to haul vehicles over it—though it's difficult to see how! Huge boulders litter the canyon floor today, a result of big flash floods in the late 1970s. Amateur road builders now would need dynamite to clear a path.

At the county line, you leave Anza-Borrego Desert State Park and enter land under the jurisdiction of the BLM. After you pass a major tributary to the east and a smaller tributary also to the east, the canyon broadens and you enter Rockhouse Valley. Here you'll spot the first junipers, an indicator of the high desert.

Next stop is the hard-to-find lower rockhouse ruins. Wandering feral cattle have obliterated any coherent trail to the ruins, so try this: follow the wash up the west side of the valley until you reach the base of a boulder-strewn ridge 0.6 mile northwest of the valley entrance; then go 0.2 mile due north to find the three rock houses spaced along a low, elongated ridge with a view of the entire valley. The largest ruin is about 15 feet square with walls four to five feet high. Mud used as chinking material still clings to the lower walls. Each house had a door and a fireplace. Though these dwellings were built by Indians over a century ago, they show a modern (rectangular) style of architecture. You can make a dry camp here, as many others have done.

The water source for this settlement was said to be a spring next to a lone cottonwood tree 0.5 mile east. Both the tree and the spring seem to have been victims of the tropical storms of the late 70s; only a dry, sandy wash is in evidence there today. (The "Cottonwood Spring" indicated on USGS topo maps northwest of the ruins is apparently an error.)

From the lower rock houses, head cross-country due northwest through sparse vegetation (mostly catclaw, agave, and golden cholla cactus) toward a low, rounded hill spur at the upper end of the valley, 2.5 miles away. This spur forms the east wall of Nicholias Canyon, your next destination. When you reach the base of the spur, swing left (west) around it and pick up a ducked trail that goes down to the creek in Nicholias Canyon. Follow either bank upstream, passing some old, rusted mining debris. The creek flows quite vigorously during the winter and spring, but even then it's quite polluted by cattle.

Up-canyon, after a bend to the right (northeast), you'll come upon a magnificent creek-hugging grove of alders and cottonwoods. These are most beautiful in mid-April when the new, delicate leaves shimmer in the breeze. Warm light floods in from the pinyon-studded, scrubby slopes surrounding the grove. On the west side of the creekbed are a few brush-free campsites on sloping ground.

Most of the water in Nicholias Canyon arises from a spring 200 yards east of the main canyon in a tributary ravine. Good water may be obtained here.

Above and south of this spring are two more rock-house ruins, even more tumbledown than those seen earlier. You can make camp on a nearby flat offering a commanding view of Rockhouse Valley, and the distant San Ysidro, Vallecito, and Laguna mountains. Massive Toro Peak, the crown summit of the Santa Rosa Mountains, looms in the north. (Adventurous climbers wishing to bag this peak can proceed up the ridge west of Nicholias Canyon. The bed of upper Nicholias Canyon, with dry falls and boulder obstacles, is a much more difficult, albeit

Rockhouse ruins above Nicholias Canyon

direct route. Plan on a full day's climb, with plenty of bushwhacking and talus scrambling.)

From the last rock-house ruins, go east to a sandy flat containing a scraggly row of cottonwoods (here again is a possible camping spot, wind-sheltered to boot). Follow the shallow drainage east of this flat; when it deepens, pick up the well-worn but partly overgrown ducked trail on the left (north) side. The trail switchbacks downward, crosses a major southward-draining ravine, then strikes a path southeast down a broad ridge. (This is one of several trails in Rockhouse Valley shown on circa-1900 topographic maps. Trampling of the valley by cattle in recent years is making it more difficult to follow these trails.)

A path straight ahead leads directly back to Rockhouse Canyon, but we'll leave it to make one more stop: the Old Santa Rosa Indian village. At about the 4000-foot contour (the same level as the base of the spur forming the east wall of Nicholias Canyon), turn east and work your way over low ridges and sharp gullies toward the two "seeps" marked on the topo map in sections 17 and

18. The first, in a canyon at 4200 feet, has had evidence of Indian use—morteros and ollas (earthen jugs), the latter removed years ago. The second seep, backed up against the rocky slopes of the Santa Rosa Mountains at 3920 feet, is the site of the old village. Two rock-house foundations are still intact here. It's hard to imagine a more wild and remote dwelling site. The seep is covered with a growth of mesquite, but no surface water seems to be present.

Obscure trails radiate from the old village to all parts of the valley. At least two, still traceable, ascend ridgelines about one mile east-southeast of the village and connect with a trail into Martinez Canyon on the east slope of the Santa Rosas. There are springs at the mouths of two canyons near the base of these trails, but I found these to be badly trampled by cattle during my last visit in 1985. Much time could be spent exploring this fascinating area.

From the old village, the last leg of this trip is straight back across the valley to the head of Rockhouse Canyon. From there you simply follow your footprints back to the starting point.

Trip 6: Box Canyon To Hidden Spring

Distance	12 miles round trip
Total Elevation Gain/Loss	2500'/2500'
Hiking Time	10 hours (round trip)
Required Maps	USGS 7.5-min *Borrego Palm Canyon, Collins Valley, Clark Lake NE*
Best Times	November through April
Difficulty	****

Hidden Spring, according to Lester Reed, author of *Old Time Cattlemen and Other Pioneers of the Anza-Borrego Area,* served as a hub for Indian trails leading to at least half a dozen destinations. Among them was a route leading to the Lower Willows of Coyote Canyon via Box Canyon. Mr. Reed, himself an old cattleman, once followed this trail on horseback from Coyote Canyon to a tributary of Box Canyon, but apparently

never returned to trace the entire route. Following general directions from his book, however, I have located significant parts of it.

The route traverses rough and isolated country, no less pristine than it was centuries ago when Cahuilla Indians passed this way on seasonal migration or food-gathering expeditions. If you haven't sharpened your skills at cross-country travel and trail-finding, you'll certainly have plenty of practice here.

It's possible to rush over this out-and-back trip in a single day, but a two-day backpack will allow you more time to look around. Campsites are abundant, but water is not. The dependable but meager supply at Hidden Spring cannot be counted on.

A one-way trip along this route is possible if you arrange to be picked up at the roadend in Rockhouse Canyon (a long, rugged drive by 4-wheel-drive vehicle). Another possibility is to continue hiking down Rockhouse Canyon and loop back through Alcoholic Pass (see Trip 3 above).

We begin our description at the point where the Box Canyon wash crosses the Coyote Canyon jeep road. This is 5.9 miles beyond the end of pavement at DiGiorgio Road (see Area D-1 introductory text). Bad road conditions or difficult fords may require that you park your car as much as two or three miles before this starting point.

Follow the sandy, boulder-choked bed of Box Canyon northeast out of Coyote Canyon. At 0.8 mile, just beyond a narrow section of canyon where the walls pinch tightly, a tributary canyon branches to the right (east). Keep left, in the main canyon. After another 0.5 mile, a second tributary canyon branches right (east). Turn right here, and in 100 yards go right again where this tributary divides. Proceed for another 0.3 mile, then leave the canyon bottom and climb to a low saddle on the ridge to the right (south).

Here you pick up a deeply worn trail, marked frequently by ducks. Apparently disused in modern times, this trail is heavily encroached by desert vegetation, including formidable thickets of teddy-bear cholla cactus. In the manner of most Indian trails, this one strikes a path on the ridgeline above the canyon, rather than following the canyon itself. Since the Indians were master pathfinders and trail builders and keen observers of nature, they knew that flash floods would frequently rearrange canyon bottoms, whereas ridge trails are affected only slightly by erosion. Having trails on ridges with clear lines of sight also facilitated easy route-

finding in a world with no maps or direction-finding instruments.

Follow trail fragments up the ridge, bearing mostly left of the ridgeline, until you pass a 2720-foot knoll. Then bear right and cross a broad 2650-foot saddle, heading northeast. A playa (undrained basin), several acres in extent, lies straight ahead. After heavy rains, a number of compact, shallow depressions in the bed hold supplies of not-very-appealing-looking water. Were these created by the local wildlife? By travelers? Or by some kind of natural slumping? The playa is fringed by a dense growth of creosote bushes and surrounded by a low wall of hills. There's a splendid sense of isolation here, and it's no wonder—the nearest road or maintained pathway lies nearly three miles away.

Cross the playa and pass over a low spot in the hills to the northeast. Continue generally northeast, following occasional ducks and a hint of trail, and negotiate a steep descent into Butler Canyon. Avoid descending directly on the nose of the ridge that divides Butler Canyon and a deeply cut western tributary; the canyon wall is undercut below.

Once in Butler Canyon, follow it north onto the vast expanse of Jackass Flat. Then head for the Indian village site on its eastern lip, just above Hidden Spring (see Trip 4). Before you reach the main village site overlooking Rockhouse Canyon, you'll notice signs of former habitation—fire pits and potsherds—on the sandy areas of Jackass Flat. Within the main village area, you'll find the top of the steep, eroded trail leading to Hidden Spring.

Area D-4: Santa Rosa Mountains

From the 8716-foot summit of Toro Peak in Riverside County, the main crest of the Santa Rosa Mountains undulates southeast past Rabbit and Villager peaks, then drops steadily to the desert floor at the edge of the Borrego Badlands. A complex of lesser ridges and promontories lies east of the main crest. Geologically, the Santa Rosas are identified as being an eastern arm of the Peninsular Ranges Province.

The northern summits of the Santa Rosa Mountains are high enough to support a variety of conifers, but the south half of the range—that part within and just north of Anza-Borrego Desert State Park and San Diego County—is, on the surface, quite desolate in appearance. The southern Santa Rosas are rugged, almost lacking in sources of water, virtually trail-less, seldom-visited, and (to the ill-prepared hiker) unforgiving. Yet it is here, more than almost any other place in San Diego County, that a person can

really get away from it all. Perched on some high peak in the Santa Rosas, you can forget all earthly cares and gaze out over hundreds of square miles of mountains and desert with the feeling that you own it all.

Other than Trip 1, beginning in Rockhouse Canyon, all hikes below start along the Borrego-Salton Seaway (County Highway S-22), northeast of Borrego Springs. Except for the area around the Calcite Mine (Trips 9 and 10), where vehicular traffic is allowed on certain roads and in certain washes, the southern Santa Rosas are classified as state wilderness. Here, as elsewhere in the state park, you're on your own—no permits are required.

Refer to John Robinson's *San Bernardino Mountain Trails* for information about hikes in the northern part of the Santa Rosas, particularly the higher, forested areas in Riverside County.

Trip 1: Peak 6582

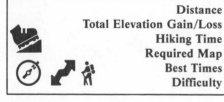

Distance	12 miles round trip
Total Elevation Gain/Loss	5800'/5800'
Hiking Time	13 hours (round trip)
Required Map	USGS 7.5-min *Clark Lake NE*
Best Times	November through April
Difficulty	*****

Peak 6582 (labelled "Dawns Peak" on some maps) is the highest point on the main Santa Rosa crest between Toro Peak (8716') and Rabbit Peak (6666'). With an average of about one visit per year over the past 15 years, it is one of the least climbed—and least accessible—peaks in the Anza-Borrego Desert. Some have passed over its summit

while traveling along the crest from Toro to Rabbit and beyond, while others have made a direct ascent from upper Clark Valley, as I'll describe here.

It takes a certain kind of determination to withstand miles of waterless, rocky terrain and thousands of feet of steady elevation gain for the privilege of standing atop a bump on a

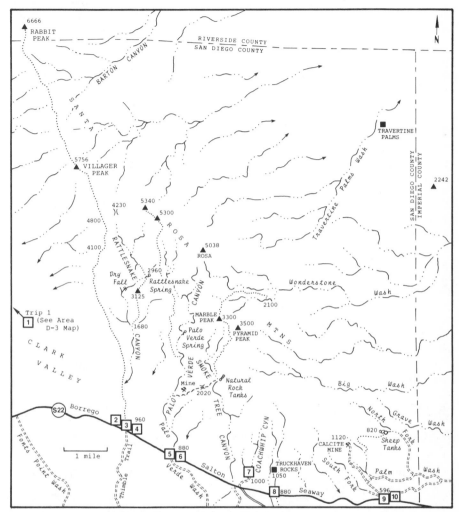

Santa Rosa Mountains

ridge barely distinguishable from others of similar stature nearby. But like many desert peaks, this one holds a special fascination. An elaborate six-foot-high pillar of stones, erected sometime before 1970, graces the summit—a monument to some unknown hiker or hikers who not only climbed the peak but also put in many hours of skilled labor.

Although this trip can be done in one long, exhausting day, a two-day trip makes more sense. A base camp established halfway up, and a quick ascent of the peak using light packs, is a method that proved success-

ful for every one of the ten people I once had the pleasure of leading on this route. The lack of water (except during rainfall or when snow is present at higher elevations) makes any trip longer than two days undesirable.

Refer to the Area D-3 introductory text for details on road access into upper Clark Valley. The place to start is anywhere between mile 6.8 and 7.3 as measured from Highway S-22, out on the sandy floor of upper Clark Valley. Find a place to park off the road in hard-packed sand, taking care not to run over vegetation. Don't forget to take a compass bearing of at least one nearby land-mark to assist in finding your car later.

About 1.5 miles north of your parking spot, a broad ridge spur descends south to meet the floor of Clark Valley. On the lower right (southeast) edge of this ridge, just below survey marker "Corp" (979'), is an impressive set of petroglyphs inscribed on the jumbled, desert-varnished boulders. Walk straight across the sandy floor of Clark Valley to reach them.

From the petroglyphs, head north-northeast and gain the narrow, rocky ridge between two canyons that leads toward peak 2700. At about the 2200-foot contour on this ridge, drop into the canyon to the right (east). Follow the rock-strewn bed of this canyon, bearing right at a major fork at 2380 feet, and continue about 0.3 mile to a large sandy flat suitable for the night's camp (3.5 miles from your car). The wash and the rocky slopes surrounding this campsite show signs of the presence of both bighorn sheep and mountain lions.

Next morning, you should set out before sunrise to bag the peak. Carrying a light day-pack, climb the steep ridge (loose rocks and cactus here) northeast of the campsite, topping out at or near peak 3489. Then go about one mile north over rolling terrain, dotted with agave and small shrubs, to the base of the ridge leading up to a point on the Santa Rosa crest 0.1 mile northwest of Peak 6582. The final mile on this ridge takes you up nearly 3000 feet of jagged terrain. Increasing numbers of pinyon pine afford welcome shade as you climb.

The view from the rounded granite boulders at the summit is magnificent. Included are most of the Santa Rosa crest, the dusky Palomar and San Ysidro mountains to the west, and long vistas south across Clark Valley to the middle and southern reaches of Anza-Borrego Desert State Park. Don't forget to sign the register hidden beneath the six-foot cairn.

By noon at the latest, you should be off the peak and retracing your footsteps back to camp. There you can pick up your backpack and start the long trudge back to the car. With luck, you'll arrive before dusk.

Winter camping at Agua Caliente Creek

Trip 2: Rabbit Peak Via Villager Peak

Distance	20 miles round trip
Total Elevation Gain/Loss	8300'/8300'
Hiking Time	18 hours (round trip)
Required Maps	USGS 7.5-min *Fonts Point, Rabbit Peak*
Best Times	November through April
Difficulty	*****

Despite their remoteness, Villager and Rabbit peaks are among the most popular destinations for peak baggers in the Anza-Borrego Desert. Several dozen people per year attain the summits of these two peaks, and bottles or tin cans containing the peak registers are often overflowing with business cards and other mementos.

Rabbit Peak has two popular routes of approach. A steep, eastern approach from Coachella Valley, beginning near sea level, is described in John Robinson's *San Bernardino Mountain Trails*. Here, I will describe the southern route, up the main crest of the Santa Rosas via Villager Peak. This is longer, more gradual, and arguably more scenic (but overall more difficult) than the eastern approach; but it begins at a point closer to San Diego County residents. A minimum of two full days is needed, with the first night's camp on or near Villager Peak. Alternatively, you can set your sights on Villager Peak only—a hike of 13 miles (11 hours).

Park in the small turnout at mile 31.8 on Highway S-22. Proceed north toward the east end of a long, sandy ridge 0.5 mile away. The north slope of this ridge is a massive scarp along the San Jacinto Fault. This is one of the largest fault scarps in unconsolidated material in North America. North of the ridge flash-flood flows in Rattlesnake Canyon have cut a series of braided washes in a swath about 0.6 mile wide. A ducked trail takes you over this dissected terrain to the base of the long, ramp-like ridge leading to Villager and Rabbit peaks.

The initial climb is very steep, but the route soon levels off to a rather steady gradient averaging about 1000 feet per mile. Stay on the highest part of the ridge to remain on route. Here and there, you'll be on fragments of trail well worn by the passage of both bighorn sheep and hikers. Creosote bush, ocotillo, and glistening specimens of barrel cactus, hedgehog cactus, and silver, golden, and teddy-bear cholla cactus grace the slopes below 3000 feet. Dense thickets of agave at 3000 to 4000 feet may slow you down a bit.

Along the lower part of the ridge you'll come upon several Indian "sleeping circles," probably used as windbreaks or the foundations of brush shelters. Some of these have been "enhanced" in modern times by hikers. At about the 3000-foot level (3.0 miles) a green patch marking Rattlesnake Spring comes into view in a tributary canyon of Rattlesnake Canyon about 1.5 miles east.

At 4100 feet (4.3 miles), you'll pass along the edge of a spectacular dropoff overlooking Clark Valley. The white band of rock prominently displayed along the face of this escarpment is marble. This is metamorphosed limestone predating the rise of the Southern California Batholith. Just beyond the 4800-foot contour (5.0 miles), the ridge descends a little to a small, exposed campsite with airy views both east and west. (This is a suitable though cramped place to spend the night if your goal is to reach Villager Peak only. From here, it's possible to descend directly into the upper reaches of Rattlesnake Canyon—this suggests an alternate return route, but not an easy one because of several dry falls in upper Rattlesnake Canyon.)

In the next mile the ridgeline becomes quite jagged. Pinyon, juniper, and nolina (a relative of the yucca) now dominate. The rounded summit of Villager Peak (6.5 miles) offers good campsites amid spreading pinyons.

A predawn start is recommended if you plan to reach Rabbit Peak, return to your packs on Villager Peak, and make the long descent back to your car all in one day. Rabbit Peak is only 3.5 miles away and 900 feet higher than Villager Peak, but the undulating ridgeline between the two adds considerable elevation gains and losses both ways—the total gain/loss for the round trip between peaks is a surprising 3300'/3300'.

Rabbit Peak lies just 0.3 mile north of the San Diego-Riverside County line. If the county line were shifted just that far north, Rabbit Peak would be the highest elevation in San Diego County.

The summit plateau of Rabbit Peak is crowned by a fairly dense cover of pinyon pine, precluding the kind of panoramic views available from more angular peaks. Still, there's a kind of restful ambience up here in this island in the sky—so aloof and remote from the rest of Southern California.

Trip 3: Rattlesnake Spring

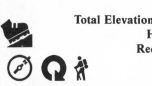

Distance	8.5 miles
Total Elevation Gain/Loss	2500'/2500'
Hiking Time	7 hours
Required Map	USGS 7.5-min *Fonts Point*
Best Times	November through April
Difficulty	***

Rattlesnake Spring is one of the few reliable sources of water in the southern Santa Rosa Mountains. Several dozen bighorn sheep depend on it for survival during periods of drought, when all other springs and waterholes within five miles may go completely dry. The spring produces a low volume—it's more like a seep. You may not want to count on it as a source for your own drinking needs. Please protect the watering rights of wildlife by camping well away from it.

On this loop hike, you'll approach the spring via one route and return via a second route comparable in difficulty. Both routes involve a fair amount of scrambling. Feel free to reverse the direction of travel from that described below.

As in Trip 2 above, park at the turnout at mile 31.8 on Highway S-22. Proceed 1.1 mile north to the base of the broad ridge leading to Villager and Rabbit peaks. Bear right around this ridge and follow the main wash into Rattlesnake Canyon. At a point about 1.3 miles farther, a major tributary will be seen to the right (east). Climb the steep slope north of this tributary and gain the ridgeline containing survey point 2971. Continue north over the top of this ridgeline (3125'); then bear northeast, avoiding some steep terrain to the north, and drop into the canyon containing Rattlesnake Spring.

Mesquite groves and a single large cottonwood tree grow in the moist area surrounding the spring. Chalky hillsides to the north of the spring have been stripped bare of vegetation by the trampling of bighorn sheep. Trails radiate in all directions to higher ridges where the bighorn spend their time when not in need of water.

The return is by way of Rattlesnake Canyon. The tributary containing Rattlesnake Spring has a set of formidable dry falls at its mouth, so the following detour is recommended: Climb northwest from the spring over a broad sloping shelf to a point in Rattlesnake Canyon below the 2960-foot contour. Then wend your way down-canyon, passing below the dry falls in the tributary.

Fallen rocks are common between the narrow walls of Rattlesnake Canyon, but several sandy stretches suitable for camping are here too. Just below the 2400-foot contour, you'll come to the top of a 20-foot dry fall—the biggest challenge on this trip.

Lower your packs on a rope and down-climb directly; or detour around the fall on the rocky, cactus-infested slopes either left or right. The latter method is less elegant but safer. From this point on, the canyon widens, and the going is quite easy over small boulders and patches of sand.

Bighorn sheep ram at Rattlesnake Spring

Trip 4: Mile-High Mountain

Distance	13 miles round trip
Total Elevation Gain/Loss	5500'/5500'
Hiking Time	10 hours (round trip)
Required Map	USGS 7.5-min *Fonts Point, Rabbit Peak*
Best Times	November through April
Difficulty	****

This unnamed, tan-colored massif, which I have dubbed "Mile-High Mountain" for the elevation of its highest summits, rivals in prominence the main south ridge containing Villager and Rabbit peaks. The unobstructed eastern and southern view from its crest is probably unequalled anywhere in the Santa Rosas; it includes the entire shoreline of the Salton Sea and virtually all of the Coachella and Imperial valleys. From here I once spotted the summits of the Sierra San Pedro Martir, 180 miles away.

The most direct route up is by way of the ridge forming the west wall of Palo Verde Canyon. Park in the turnout at mile 31.8 on Highway S-22, then head northeast across the open desert for one mile to the mouth of Palo Verde Canyon. Follow the main wash up the canyon another 1.5 miles to a sharp bend at 1900 feet elevation. Now climb the steep slope to the left (west) and gain the ridgeline. (Palo Verde Canyon itself enters a steep bowl just below the usually dry Palo Verde Spring, where further progress is blocked.)

Simply follow this ridgeline north for the next three miles or so, gaining 3000 feet. The sequence of vegetation is similar to that on the Villager/Rabbit ridge to the west, described in Trip 2.

There are four distinct, rounded summits at the top, the highest of which is farthest north, elevation approximately 5340 feet. Peak 5300 is dotted with a few scraggly pinyons, and would accommodate perhaps two or three prone bodies.

Mile-High Mountain is a good hub for routes into many remote corners of the Santa Rosas. West of Peak 5340 you can descend into Rattlesnake Canyon (warning: steep dry falls in this canyon) or into the major unnamed drainage system to the north; or you can gain the Villager/Rabbit ridge. You can also pass over survey marker "Rosa" to the southeast and descend into Wonderstone Wash. A climber's register has been placed on "Rosa," as it is considered a named peak and therefore "on the list" for peak-bagging groups from San Diego and Los Angeles.

Trip 5: Rock Tanks Loop

Distance	7.5 miles
Total Elevation Gain/Loss	1300'/1300'
Hiking Time	5 hours
Required Map	USGS 7.5-min *Fonts Point*
Best Times	November through April
Difficulty	***

Many experiences—some powerful and some merely annoying—await you on this hike: the palpable force of the desert sun's rays; the desiccated air, catching in the throat; the sharp prick of a cactus spine on the ankle, or the brittle scrape of an ocotillo wand on the elbow; the feeling of vertigo when you step to the edge of an abyss and view the shattered landscape below; and, most powerful of all, the sublime silence.

Here's how to get there: At mile 32.9 along Highway S-22 a small wash crosses the road. This is Palo Verde Wash, named for the many palo verde trees along it. (Palo verde trees are spindly in form, with a green trunk and branches. In April, they are aflame with yellow blossoms.) Park your car just off the road, taking care not to block the jeep trail going south from this point.

Begin by following the wash generally northward toward a prominent cut in the mountains ahead—Palo Verde Canyon. This contains a braided wash, consisting of multiple pathways where water has flowed during past storms. Just stay in the middle as best you can to remain on course. After about one mile you can make a short side trip to see some cottontop cacti (*Echinocactus polycephalus*), which resemble small barrel cacti but grow in dome-shaped clusters. They are rare in the Anza-Borrego area. Look for them on the low ridge spurs west of Palo Verde Wash. One specimen spans five feet.

At 1.3 miles the walls begin to close in on both sides. Walk along the wall on the right side, and in another 0.2 mile, you'll spot an obscure trail going straight up the rocky slope to the right. The base of the trail is marked by several small cairns. Ducks placed here and there will guide you over the next 1.3 miles. This trail is the beginning of an Indian route that goes over the Santa Rosa Mountains to the Rainbow Rock quarry in Wonderstone Wash (see Trip 6 below).

On your left, as you gain elevation, is an old mine tunnel sunk into a prominent vein. Woe to those who venture in more than a few feet: pack rats have secreted away a huge collection of cholla-cactus spines.

At 2.1 miles, the trail crosses a divide, then descends along a precipitous slope overlooking Smoke Tree Canyon. A big rock slide here has obliterated traces of the old trail, but frequent use by hikers has forged a new trail. When you reach the canyon bottom, make a short side trip up the narrow tributary canyon to the northeast. Here, the scouring of flash floods has worn large depressions in the rock—the Natural Rock Tanks. Pockets like these, called *tinajas*, serve as natural reservoirs of water for weeks

or months after major storms. If you're lucky, you may spot bighorn sheep here.

To continue the loop, head straight down Smoke Tree Canyon toward the highway, three miles away. The canyon becomes a narrow fissure in two places, where dark conglomerate cliffs hover menacingly overhead, seemingly subject to imminent collapse. (I once saw, two days after a mild earthquake, numerous basketball-size rocks newly fallen and embedded in the sand just below these cliffs. If you're backpacking, choose a campsite well away from these hazards.) There's a short scramble down a dry waterfall, followed by a mile or so of intermittent boulder hopping, and then it's smooth sailing on a nice bed of packed sand all the way to the highway.

Close the loop by walking along the wide shoulder of the highway. Or, if fatigued or just lazy, have one or more members of your party sprint over to pick up the car.

Trip 6: Wonderstone Trail

Distance	11 miles round trip
Total Elevation Gain/Loss	4000'/4000'
Hiking Time	10 hours (round trip)
Required Map	USGS 7.5-min *Fonts Point*
Best Times	December through March
Difficulty	****

Of the many Indian pathways crisscrossing the Anza-Borrego region, few have as much continuity of length and purpose as the one I've chosen to call the Wonderstone Trail. This is one of the routes—probably the major route—by which Indians transported wonderstone from the Rainbow Rock quarry near the Salton Sea to points west, such as Clark Valley, Rockhouse Canyon, and Coyote Canyon. Wonderstone is a milky, light purple or reddish rock used to make stone implements. Wonderstone flakes (waste material from the tool-making process) can be found in Coyote Canyon and at the old Indian village site above Hidden

Spring in Rockhouse Canyon. These flakes can also be seen, along with a multitude of broken pieces of pottery, along the Wonderstone Trail.

The reasons behind the routing of the Wonderstone Trail are clear. Rainbow Rock quarry is located about 2.5 miles west of the present State Highway 86, on the edge of Wonderstone Wash. If the Indians had tried to outflank the Santa Rosas, following a route similar to that traversed by today's Highways 86 and S-22, they would have faced a long detour across the vicious gullies of the southeastern Santa Rosas and the forbidding mud hills of the Borrego Badlands. Routes straight west toward Clark Dry Lake from the quarry would involve tedious scaling of numerous high ridges. Only a particular route which goes southwest from the upper reaches of Wonderstone Wash into Palo Verde Canyon—the route described here—offers a relatively easy way across the mountains. In accordance with the principles of modern road or trail building, the Wonderstone Trail sticks to relatively gentle terrain and avoids extremes of highs and lows.

Tracing the Wonderstone Trail is a job for those who are both agile cross-country hikers and skilled and patient navigators. The thread of the trail is there, but it is broken into snippets. The Indian signs are there, too, but only those who search carefully will find them. Day-hikers will need a full dawn-to-dusk day, with almost no breaks, to complete the trip described below. Overnight backpackers, of course, can proceed at a less hectic pace.

The route begins as in Trip 5 above. The trail from Palo Verde Canyon to Smoke Tree Canyon is only the westernmost segment of the Wonderstone Trail. From the mouth of Palo Verde Canyon, Indians could easily travel to Rockhouse Canyon, Coyote Canyon (via Alcoholic Pass), and Borrego Valley. On the other end of this trail segment, the Rock Tanks served as a dependable source of water.

When you reach the tributary containing the Natural Rock Tanks, walk up Smoke Tree Canyon 250 yards to a point just past a wall (on your right) of greenish rock. On the right (east side) is a steep little ravine with a sculpted bed of orange-banded gneiss. The Wonderstone Trail leaves the canyon bottom at this point, and follows the low curving ridge that forms the west wall of the canyon. Since it is almost impossible to trace this part of the trail very far in the uphill direction, we suggest you save this part for the return hike.

Instead, continue up Smoke Tree Canyon for 0.6 mile, passing over three dry waterfalls. When the wash divides into two equal tributaries, take the right fork and continue to the saddle at its head. A 3500-foot peak, dubbed "Pyramid Peak" by Lowell and Diana Lindsay in their book *The Anza-Borrego Desert Region*, lies 0.3 mile southeast of this saddle.

From the top of the saddle, drop directly northeast into a southern tributary of Wonderstone Wash. Follow this downward for about 1.3 miles, taking care to note your progress on the topographic map. Water seeps through the canyon after rainstorms, and tamarisk, an invading nonnative species, is already taking full advantage of what is probably a good subsurface supply. (These tamarisks probably have germinated from seeds blown in from Borrego Valley or Coachella Valley, where tamarisk trees were planted as windbreaks many years ago.) The presence of an old, dead cottonwood trunk in this canyon, along with an abundant growth of mesquite, is further evidence of subsurface water.

At 2100-feet elevation, the water trickles over a narrow defile. At this point you will leave the tributary canyon and locate the Wonderstone Trail on the ridge to your left (north). The trip back to the Natural Rock Tanks via this trail will likely take much longer than the way you came, in part because of the poor condition of the trail, and in part because of the time you'll probably spend searching for Indian artifacts.

The ruins of a small rock shelter lie on a small flat at 2060-feet elevation on the ridge. Here you can find potsherds, and evidence of more recent visits, perhaps by prospectors.

Proceed west up the ridge, following traces of trail, to a large flat at 2350-feet elevation. Here is a "portable metate", a smooth depression in a white slab of granitic rock. As all the other rocks at this site are coarse and deeply stained by desert varnish, this fresh-looking, water-polished slab must have been transported from one of the washes below. Strewn about are literally hundreds—possibly thousands—of potsherds and flakes of wonderstone. From this site you can look east-northeast and see Rainbow Rock quarry, a reddish outcrop on the north wall of Wonderstone Wash, five miles away.

Continue up-ridge, where good traces of

trail are soon found just below the ridgeline on the right (north) side. The trail is worn nearly a foot deep at one point. There are two more rock rings in this area.

Beyond a saddle at the 3000-foot contour, the trail has been rendered obscure by erosion. Continue southwest, climbing slightly all the while, and cross one major and several lesser tributaries of Wonderstone Wash. The route gradually turns south and gains a saddle just west of a marble-frosted peaklet (3300') dubbed "Marble Peak" on our map. From this high point, you can drop 0.2 mile southeast to the saddle between Marble and Pyramid peaks you crossed earlier.

Now you can attempt to follow the Wonderstone Trail as it meanders back toward the rock tanks in Smoke Tree Canyon. The general rules for following this segment are: lose elevation gradually, sel-dom climb, and avoid the bottoms of ravines. Work your way around the flank of "Pyramid Peak," where the trail is completely obliterated, and in about 0.2 mile you should spot a good trace of trail ahead of and below you. Pick this up and continue from trace to trace, all the way down to the aforementioned low, curving ridge and gneiss-bedded ravine. Ducks mark the trail at frequent intervals, but not where the trail is washed out. On the way down you'll pass two big mescal pits, each full of ashen soil.

In order that others may enjoy the same kind of experience you're sure to have, please respect the archeological integrity of this area. Move no rocks, and leave all artifacts as they lie; take home only memories and photographs. Since the ducks you see may be original trail markers, don't reconstruct or embellish them, and do not add new trail markers.

View of Salton Sea from Pyramid Peak

Trip 7: Coachwhip Canyon

Distance	1 to 4 miles
Optional Map	USGS 7.5-min *Fonts Point*
Best Times	October through June
Difficulty	*

Stark, dry, and almost barren, Coach-whip Canyon is somehow—despite these attributes—a very peaceful and appealing place. A beautiful forest of smoke trees stands at its entrance, beckoning gracefully. The wind, which can blow like the devil just outside, seldom seems to intrude within the confines of the canyon. Hidden nooks in the side canyons, each unique, invite you to pause, rest, and enjoy.

The wraithlike, gray-green smoke tree, a handsome shrub in any season, puts on quite a show in June, when it is festooned with thousands of indigo-colored blossoms. The smoke tree forest literally hums then with the wingbeats of bees gathering nectar. It is, of course, terrifically hot at that time of year, so you would want to do your hiking at dawn or dusk.

There are actually dozens of steep-walled ravines here, all draining into Ella Wash. The ravines twist and turn through soft sand-stone, each one ending abruptly at the 100- to 200-foot-high horseshoe-shaped headwall that surrounds the area.

A sandy road, suitable for most cars at its lower end, penetrates an eastern branch of Coachwhip Canyon for about 1.2 miles. (This road intersects Highway S-22 at mile 34.8, just west of the road to Arroyo Salado Primitive Camp.) Along the road are excel-lent spots for car camping; this is a good area to set up base camp in if you'll be doing a lot of day hiking in the southern Santa Rosas or Borrego Badlands.

In the Coachwhip Canyon area itself, you could walk anywhere from one to four miles, exploring one or more of the tributaries. In some, you can climb high enough up the headwall to get a good view of both the Coachwhip area and the Borrego Badlands beyond.

Borrego Badlands from rim above Coachwhip Canyon

Trip 8: Truckhaven Rocks

Distance	1.5 miles round trip
Total Elevation Gain/Loss	200'/200'
Hiking Time	40 minutes (round trip)
Optional Map	Anza-Borrego Desert State Park map/brochure
Best Times	October through May
Difficulty	*

The Truckhaven Rocks are reminiscent of the outcrops of sandstone at Garden of the Gods in Colorado Springs, Colorado. These tilted slabs of orange-tinted sandstone, which can be plainly seen from Highway S-22, are a favorite haunt of photographers.

Park on the wide shoulder of Highway S-22 at mile 35.5, then head up the wash that leads slightly east of the Truckhaven Rocks. Climbing out of this wash to reach the outcrops, you'll cross a boulder-strewn plain dotted with ocotillo. Here and there, in areas free of large rocks, are patches of "desert pavement," a common surface condition in which small pebbles of roughly uniform size form a flat mosaic. This is a result of fine particles being blown away, leaving the larger particles and pebbles to settle and pack together.

Trip 9: Calcite Mine

Distance	4 miles round trip
Total Elevation Gain/Loss	800'/800'
Hiking Time	2 hours (round trip)
Optional Map	Anza-Borrego Desert State Park map/brochure; or USGS 7.5-min *Seventeen Palms*
Best Times	November through April
Difficulty	**

Eons of cutting and polishing by water and wind erosion have produced the chaotic rock formations and slotlike ravines you'll discover in the Calcite Mine area. The highlight of this hike is, of course, the mine itself. During World War II, this was an important site—indeed the only site in the United States—for the extraction of optical-grade calcite crystals for use in gunsights. Trench-mining operations throughout the area have left deep scars upon the earth, seemingly as fresh today as when they were made.

Park in the roadside turnout at mile 38.0 along Highway S-22; then walk 0.1 mile east to the Calcite jeep road intersection. An interpretive panel here provides details about the history of the mine. Follow the jeep road as it dips into and out of the South Fork of Palm Wash, and continues northwest toward the southern spurs of the Santa Rosa Mountains. Ahead you will see an intricately honeycombed whitish slab of sandstone, called Locomotive Rock, which lies behind and to the northeast of the mine area.

About 1.4 miles from S-22, the road dips sharply to cross a deep ravine. Poke into the upper (north) end of this ravine and you'll discover one of the best slot canyons in

Anza-Borrego. (Skilled climbers can squeeze through the slot and go up a break on the right side to reach a point above and northwest of the mine area.)

At road's end numerous calcite crystals lie strewn about on the ground, glittering in the sunlight. You could probably spend a good two hours here exploring the mining trenches and the great pocked slabs of sandstone nearby. Palm Wash, a frightening gash in the earth, precludes travel to the east.

On the return, try this alternate route: Backtrack 0.5 mile to the aforementioned slot ravine. Proceed downstream along its bottom. As you pass through deeper and deeper layers of sandstone strata, the ravine narrows until it allows the passage of only one person at a time. When you reach the jumbled blocks of sandstone in Palm Wash at the bottom of the ravine, turn right, walk 0.3 mile downstream, and exit the canyon via a short link of jeep trail that leads back to the Calcite jeep road.

Smoke trees in Coachwhip Canyon

Trip 10: Palm Wash/Sheep Tanks Loop

Distance	7 miles
Total Elevation Gain/Loss	900'/900'
Hiking Time	4 hours
Required Map	USGS 7.5-min *Seventeen Palms*
Best Times	November through April
Difficulty	***

Off the beaten track, this loop hike gives access to a labyrinth of deep gorges and a bench with clear traces of ancient Indian pathways. The upper end of the North Fork of Palm Wash, about halfway around the loop, offers good camping spots for backpackers.

Begin as in Trip 9 above. At 0.8 mile from Highway S-22, leave the Calcite Mine road and drop down the jeep trail into Palm Wash. Head up-canyon (northwest) through the vertical-walled gorge, past fallen blocks of tan-colored sandstone. The walls of the canyon seem to be in a state of arrested collapse, with huge buttresses fully separated from the walls, ready to surrender to gravity during the next earthquake or flash flood.

At a point 0.6 mile up Palm Wash, a major tributary enters from the left. (This tributary goes past peak 1122 toward the Calcite Mine, and can be used to combine parts of Trip 9 with this trip. From this point you can also, if skilled at bouldering, continue up Palm Wash, climbing past sandstone blocks and huge granitic chockstones, to a point well above the Calcite Mine.) Opposite and a little beyond this tributary, on the right (east) side of Palm Wash, is an easy break through the sandstone wall. Climb this and head north along the wide bench east of Palm Wash. You'll pick up an Indian trail that leads northwest, then northeast toward the Sheep Tanks in the North Fork of Palm Wash. (The south branch of this Indian trail approaches another break in the wall of Palm Wash about one mile south-southeast.)

Due east of Locomotive Rock (see Trip 9), which you can see clearly over the gorge of Palm Wash, is a flat, cleared area with two partly collapsed cairns of desert-varnished stones. A sighting across these cairns intersects the northeastern horizon at a point within two degrees of where the sun rises over the Salton Sea on the day of the summer solstice, June 21. More cairns are in the same line farther to the northeast. It is tempting to think this is an Indian solstice marker, but the presence of test trenches nearby shows that these cairns may have had something to do with the calcite mining.

Using map and compass, work your way overland to the Sheep Tanks, an important watering hole for bighorn sheep and other wildlife. These are located in a narrow, southern tributary of the North Fork of Palm Wash that joins North Fork at 700 feet elevation. From above you can look down (very cautiously) into the slot containing several deep *tinajas*. Their capacity is estimated at some 20,000 gallons.

A series of sloping sandstone ledges leads down the south wall of the slot to the lowest tank, then out to the North Fork. You may, particularly if backpacking, want to avoid this exposed bit of downclimbing by backtracking about 0.3 mile, then going north into the upper end of the North Fork. Here, the North Fork offers expanses of flat sand suitable for camping (except during rainy periods) and no danger from unstable canyon walls.

Close the loop by walking the North Fork jeep road to Palm Wash, and the Palm Wash jeep road back to the Calcite Mine road.

Area D-5: Borrego Badlands

True to their name, the Borrego Badlands are a block of lake, stream and alluvial-plain deposits that have been severely attacked by the erosive forces of water and wind. The clay soils are so weak, and the plants which might otherwise anchor the soil are so sparse, that flash floods have carved this block into a bewildering maze of sinuous channels, razor-back ridges, and mud hills.

The most renowned point of interest here, and one of the best view spots in all of Anza-Borrego Desert State Park, is Fonts Point. Here you can stand on the edge of a receding cliff and look across many square miles of intricately carved landscape.

Relatively few plants thrive in the alkaline soil of the Borrego Badlands, but there are some surprises. Several groups of palms cling tenuously to life in areas where subsurface water is dependable; these are believed to be the tiniest remnants of a much wider distribution of palms during past, wetter periods. Small trees, such as the palo verde, desert-willow, and smoke tree line some of the sandy washes where their roots can take advantage of ephemeral flows of water. The right combination of rainfall and sunshine periodically brings forth a profusion of wildflowers, especially sand verbenas, desert asters, dune primroses, desert sunflowers, and desert lilies.

The major washes of the Borrego Badlands are laced with approved vehicle routes, and noisy vehicles are sometimes annoying, especially on weekends. Nevertheless, there are many areas within the badlands where it is possible to wander cross-country and find peace and quiet. Two such hikes are suggested below.

A canteen full of water and a good map and compass are the most important items to carry along with you. While it is almost impossible to wander very far without running into a road, it is quite easy to lose track of nearby landmarks. Use the best maps available: the entire area is covered on USGS 7.5-minute quadrangles *Fonts Point, Borrego Mountain, Shell Reef,* and *Seventeen Palms*. These maps have a contour interval ranging from 20 to 40 feet, which is enough to show a wealth of complex detail in the badlands landscape.

Borrego Badlands

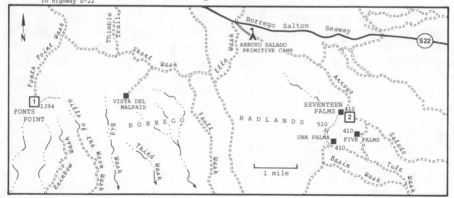

Trip 1: Fonts Point

	Distance	1 mile round trip
	Total Elevation Gain/Loss	200'/200'
	Hiking Time	40 minutes (round trip)
	Optional Maps	Anza-Borrego Desert State Park map/brochure; USGS 7.5-min *Fonts Point*
	Best Times	October through May
	Difficulty	*

Sure, it's possible to drive to within a frisbee's throw of Fonts Point Overlook and take in the famous view of mile upon mile of convoluted mud hills and sinuous washes. But no, the overlook, per se, isn't really the *best* viewing place.

Try this: Starting at the parking area, walk east along the brink of the cliffs for about 0.5 mile. Along this stretch, the drop to the badlands below is often more severe, and the pattern below assumes a more elegantly symmetrical form than that seen from the overlook itself. Bring your camera, of course. Best times for photography are one hour after sunrise and one hour before sunset.

Words of warning: Stay well back from the cliff edge while walking, and approach the brink only very cautiously. In one or two places, large blocks of cliff face are beginning to cleave. Watch those kids!

Driving to Fonts Point is a bit of an adventure in itself. Ask about road conditions first if you're operating a two-wheel-drive vehicle. From Highway S-22 turn south at mile 29.3, and follow the signs to Fonts Point, four miles away. The first hundred yards constitute a notorious sand trap. Opportunities to turn around are few and far between until you reach the end of the road. An alternative, of course, is to walk this road. This is a fine stretch for jogging, if the weather is cool.

Borrego Badlands

Trip 2: Seventeen Palms & Vicinity

	Distance	2 miles
	Total Elevation Gain/Loss	200'/200'
	Hiking Time	1½ hours
	Recommended Maps	Anza-Borrego Desert State Park map/brochure; USGS 7.5-min *Seventeen Palms, Shell Reef*
	Best Times	December through March
	Difficulty	**

Smack dab in the middle of the most desolate part of the Borrego Badlands stands a remarkable triad of palm oases. The best known of these, Seventeen Palms, is a popular destination for park visitors. The other two lie just a short distance away. They are accessible in a roundabout way via jeep trails, or overland on foot as described here.

The starting point for this hike is the Seventeen Palms parking area along Arroyo Salado. To reach it by car, turn southeast from Borrego-Salton Seaway (County S-22) at mile 34.9 onto the dirt road leading through Arroyo Salado Primitive Camp. After 0.5 mile a sign advises 4-WHEEL DRIVE RECOMMENDED. The next three miles to the Seventeen Palms parking area are usually suitable for all but low-clearance passenger vehicles if driven carefully.

An interpretive leaflet available at the Seventeen Palms parking area recounts some of the old lore associated with this famous watering place. Decades ago, prospectors and travelers used this oasis as a point to relay messages to and from. The tradition continues today, and you'll probably find hundreds of notes and business cards in an old barrel beneath the palms.

The interpretive leaflet also describes the complex web of plant and animal life that exists in this seemingly lifeless area. Because most animals dependent upon the spring are nocturnal, you are reminded not to camp in the area. Don't count on the water—if you can find it at all—for your drinking needs; it is highly saline.

Carry along a park map. If you do get lost, you'll soon intercept one of the many jeep roads in this area. These are signed at junctions and labeled on the park map.

You begin this loop hike at Seventeen Palms (410'). A hundred feet north of the northernmost cluster of palms, follow the small ravine that leads west into the mud hills. After about 100 yards, bear southwest across a low maze of washes. Continue southwest into a broad wash that bends southward toward a broad saddle. Topping this rise (510'), you'll have come about 0.5 mile from Seventeen Palms.

From the rise you can look south into a seemingly endless maze of dissected mud hills. Make an easy descent into any of the several small washes directly below. Continue downhill 0.3 mile to the Cut Across Trail (jeep trail) in Tule Wash. Turning left (east), you'll soon catch sight of Una Palma (single palm), its forlorn crown peeping above the mudhills. Head directly for it, passing a clump of mesquite along the way. Una Palma does not appear on the USGS topographic map.

From Una Palma head northeast. Topping the first hill, you'll be able to see the two living palms at Five Palms Spring, 0.5 mile away. Head directly for them east across the mud hills. If you have been scrutinizing your topo maps, you'll note a remarkable coincidence: all three oases lie at the same elevation!

Complete the loop by following the Tule Wash and Arroyo Salado jeep trails back to Seventeen Palms.

Area D-6: Grapevine Canyon/ Pinyon Ridge

This sparsely vegetated area of rounded ridges and long, linear valleys lies between Montezuma Highway (County Highway S-22) on the north, and State Highway 78 on the south. The highest elevations, about 4500 feet, feature the typical desert/mountain mix of pinyon, juniper, yucca and chaparral shrubs; while the lower elevations, hillsides and washes around 2000 feet exhibit the familiar creosote bush, cacti, agave, and desert willow of the lower desert. In moist areas willow, ironwood, and mesquite thrive.

Vehicle routes lace part of this area, but a large block centered around Pinyon Ridge is designated as state wilderness. As in all other parts of Anza-Borrego Desert State Park, no permit is required for day or overnight trips.

The longer hikes described below start and end along either Montezuma Highway or Highway 78. Also included below are three short trails in the Tamarisk Grove area off Highway 78.

Car-camping opportunities are abundant throughout the area, not only at the developed Tamarisk Grove Campground and the two primitive campgrounds near it, but also along any of the unpaved vehicle routes shown on the state park map/brochure.

Grapevine Canyon/Pinyon Ridge

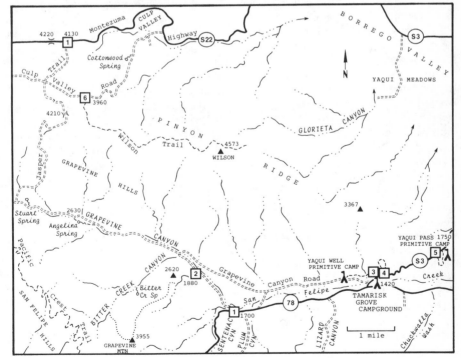

Trip 1: Jasper Trail/Grapevine Canyon

	Distance	11 miles
	Total Elevation Gain/Loss	500'/2900'
	Hiking Time	4½ hours
	Optional Maps	Anza-Borrego Desert State Park map/brochure; USGS 7.5-min *Tubb Canyon, Ranchita* (Jasper Trail not shown on 1959 *Tubb Canyon* map)
	Best Times	November through April
	Difficulty	***

This route, most often used by jeepers, motorcyclists, mountain bicyclists and equestrians, is also a worth-while one for hikers. Try it during off-days (weekdays) or during off-hours (early morning or evening) if you don't like the sound of groaning engines. Since the route is largely downhill, and almost entirely on soft sand or soft dirt, it's ideal for jogging too. A section of the old California Riding & Hiking Trail sometimes coincides with and sometimes parallels the route. The description below assumes that you stay (with a couple of exceptions) on the easier-to-follow roadways.

The starting point is the north terminus of the Jasper Trail (a jeep road), mile 6.8 on the Montezuma Highway east of Ranchita. In the first 2.4 miles, the road traverses rolling, brushy terrain, generally heading south. After passing over a rocky ridge at 2.4 miles, the road drops very sharply down a dry canyon for about 0.7 mile; then it turns north up a slope and briefly follows a ridge to avoid a narrow, rocky section of the canyon. On foot, it's easier to go down the bottom of the canyon and join the road again, saving 0.4 mile, not to mention needless elevation gain and loss.

In the next mile, the canyon is flanked by picturesque, near-vertical rock walls. After this stretch, the canyon widens, and the road swings right (west) to avoid another narrow chasm below. Don't make a short cut this time; follow the road as it crosses a flat and drops into the sandy bed of a draw leading to Grapevine Canyon.

Grapevine Canyon was one of the main routes of travel east from Warner Springs and Julian before the construction of Highway 78 through Sentenac Canyon. Several springs along the way served the needs of travelers in the early days of the automobile. Well before that, the canyon was a favorite camping area of aboriginal peoples. Bedrock morteros and other signs, especially around the springs, attest to many centuries of occupation.

Stuart Spring (0.4 mile east of the Jasper Trail junction in Grapevine Canyon) is the first source of water and a good place to fill up canteens. Angelina Spring, 1.3 miles farther, flows for several hundred feet through a tangle of willows. The road rises onto a bluff to the north; but it is more interesting to walk right along the riparian strip on a parallel horse trail.

At a point 2.3 miles beyond Angelina Spring (below the mouth of Bitter Creek Canyon), Grapevine Canyon Road bends left and then continues toward Yaqui Well and Tamarisk Grove Campground. Continue straight; Highway 78 lies ahead, two miles away. Arrange to be picked up here—mile 74.1 on Highway 78, just below the mouth of Sentenac Canyon.

Trip 2: Grapevine Mountain/Bitter Creek

Distance	6 miles
Total Elevation Gain/Loss	2400'/2400'
Hiking Time	5 hours
Recommended Maps	USGS 7.5-min *Tubb Canyon, Earthquake Valley*
Best Times	November through April
Difficulty	***

This is a good hike to get acquainted with cross-country desert travel and "peak bagging." You'll make intimate visual contact (but I hope not physical contact) with cholla, hedgehog, beavertail, barrel, and fishhook cacti; in addition you'll see agave, catclaw, and mesquite—all thorny or prickly to one degree or another. There are boulders to scramble over on occasion and faint game trails to follow through the low brush.

Winter months bring invigorating cool air to Grapevine Mountain, but the best months are March and April. This is the time to catch the cactus and the succulent blooms. You'll see everything from the pearl-like flower of the diminutive fishhook cactus to the showy magenta and red blossoms of the hedgehog and beavertail cacti.

A convenient starting point for this hike is along the dirt road connecting Highway 78 and Grapevine Canyon Road. This road intersects the highway at mile 74.1, just below the mouth of Sentenac Canyon. Drive 1.3 miles northwest on this road to reach a parking spur on the left. (High water in San Felipe Creek may block the way; if so, you can park, ford the creek on foot, and walk the extra mile to the starting point.

The parking spur is just east of a prominent unnamed canyon that leads southwest toward the highest slopes of Grapevine Mountain. Follow the sandy wash leading up to the mouth of this canyon. Around the corner is a formidable granite dike blocking direct progress up the canyon. Climb up and over on either the right or left side, through dense thickets of teddy-bear cholla.

Stay with the canyon for another 0.3 mile, then veer right toward a saddle just south of Peak 2620. (If you continue in the canyon, you'll run into a second and more formidable dry fall.) The first twisted junipers appear on the saddle; junipers will be a familiar feature from now on.

From the saddle, head generally south, following the top of the ridge all the way to the summit of Grapevine Mountain. Several minor summits are topped, after which you must lose a small amount of elevation. At one point you can look down into Bitter Creek Canyon and spot the lone cottonwood tree at Bitter Creek Spring.

Fallen survey stakes and ribbons are all that mark the summit, but the view is impressive. To the west and south, the broad trough of the San Felipe and Earthquake valleys shimmers at the foot of a backdrop of dark ranges—the Volcan, Cuyamaca, and Laguna mountains.

Continue by descending west into Bitter Creek Canyon. In the first 300 vertical feet, the going is slippery on decomposed rock, with little worthwhile to hold on to other than a few small manzanita shrubs. Footing becomes easier as you take to a narrow ridge bearing northwest. Drop into Bitter Creek, and follow the sandy bed for as long as it stays open. Small pools of water may be found here after rainy periods.

Soon you'll encounter a tangle of willow, mesquite, and tamarisk in the creek bed. Don't fight it. Instead climb up to the gentle slopes on the east bank. Easy-to-follow animal trails will guide you for about a mile to a point where the creek bed is open again.

Near this point, look for the lone cottonwood, mentioned earlier, that marks Bitter

Creek Spring. You'll find it in a nook about 100 feet above the creek bed. True to their names, both Bitter Creek and its nearby spring feature slightly bitter tasting, mineral-rich water. Old broken pipes lead from the spring to an empty bathtub downslope. The spring is a mecca for local wildlife; trails and tracks (including those of mountain lions and bighorn sheep) radiate from it in every direction.

All that remains is an easy stroll down the broad wash of Bitter Creek Canyon, and a short walk back to the starting point via the dirt road.

Trip 3: Yaqui Well Trail

Distance	1.5 miles
Total Elevation Gain/Loss	100'/100'
Hiking Time	45 minutes
Optional Map	Anza-Borrego Desert State Park map/brochure
Best Times	All year
Difficulty	*

Follow the yellow painted footprints from Tamarisk Grove Campground to the beginning of the Yaqui Well Trail. This is a self-guiding nature trail with interpretive signs posted beside several representative desert wash plants. The trail climbs slightly, skirts a hillside covered with dense growths of cholla cactus, and then descends to Yaqui Well, an important desert water hole.

Yaqui Well is one of the premier bird-watching sites in San Diego County. The presence of surface water and fine growths of ironwood, mesquite, and desert-willow have created a micro-environment cooler, more damp, and much richer in food sources than the surrounding arid hills. The well has been used by Indians, prospectors, and cattlemen, and is now surrounded by drive-in campsites. A fenced area keeps humans away from the seeps and allows wildlife undisturbed use of the water.

Stroll back to Tamarisk Grove Campground by way of either Grapevine Canyon Road or the bed of San Felipe Wash.

Receding cliff near Fonts Point

Trip 4: Cactus Loop Trail

	Distance	1 mile
	Total Elevation Gain/Loss	200'/200'
	Hiking Time	40 minutes
	Optional Map	Anza-Borrego Desert State Park map/brochure
	Best Times	All year
	Difficulty	*

The trailhead for this short but somewhat steep and rocky path is directly opposite the entrance to Tamarisk Grove Campground. On the first part of the trail, you'll find interpretive signs for a half dozen or so common desert plants. But the real story here concerns the ubiquitous teddy-bear cholla (also called Bigelow cholla and jumping cholla) cactus, which grows to exceptional size (6 feet high) and density along this trail.

The teddy-bear cholla has a well-deserved, fearsome reputation. Its thousands of glistening spines, like soft bristles, invite tactile exploration, but woe be to those who prick themselves even lightly with a single "bristle." Concealed beneath the straw-colored and innocent-looking papery sheath covering each spine is an incredibly sharp, barbed point. The spiny joints of the cholla can detach at the slightest brush by shoe or clothing, often seeming to jump at and "bite" unwary hikers.

E. Yale Dawson writes this about cholla cactus in his book *Cacti of California:*

> The vegetable kingdom has not produced anything else so fearfully armed. But in the desert one thing is worse than any pain of spine in the flesh. It is thirst. I have seen emaciated, dreadfully dehydrated cattle, deprived of water for months in the blistering heat, so mad from thirst that they eat the terrible cholla. They munch these awful morsels of moisture until their lips are pinned together with the spines, and their throats are a veritable pincushion. The spines eventually cause their death.

Incredible as it may seem in light of the above, there are reliable reports of bighorn sheep browsing on cholla cactus. On occasion you may come across a cholla, hedgehog, or other similarly armed cactus plant broken open with fresh teeth marks in the green pulp.

Barrel and teddy-bear cholla cacti

Trip 5: Bill Kenyon Trail

	Distance	1 mile round trip
	Total Elevation Gain/Loss	150'/150'
	Hiking Time	30 minutes
	Optional Map	Anza-Borrego Desert State Park map/brochure
	Best Times	All year
	Difficulty	*

Walk this easy trail in the early morning or late afternoon, when warm lighting and long shadows soften the landscape. You'll find the marked trailhead along Highway S-3 at the top of Yaqui Pass, the broad saddle in the mountains between Borrego Springs and Tamarisk Grove. The trail is named in honor of Bill Kenyon, a former Anza-Borrego park supervisor.

Vegetation is varied but sparse around the windswept pass area. Most varieties of indigenous cactus are represented. The best attraction, though, is the marvelous view from the two overlook points along the trail. Dominating the scene is Mescal Bajada, a vast, sloping sheet of alluvial deposits. The Pinyon Mountains, the source of the deposits, brood in the background.

A clear sequence of steps in the process of erosion is observed here in freeze-frame: Wind and water and heat and cold tear at the face of the Pinyon Mountains, opening up ravines and canyons. Great loads of sand and boulders wash out of these openings during floods and build alluvial fans. The fans coalesce to form a sloping skirt (*bajada*) extending outward from the base of the mountains. Material on the lower edge of the bajada is picked up by flood waters in San Felipe Creek. This debris-laden water flows through one channel and then another, dropping its load gradually and creating a braided pattern of smooth, sandy washes and rubble-strewn "islands" in the bed of the creek.

Flat and uninteresting-looking by midday, Mescal Bajada comes alive with texture and color under the grazing illumination of the low sun. The color gray-green seems to predominate, in part because of the heavy growth of "mescal" (agave, or century plant) on its surface.

Sandstone formation in Lycium Wash

Trip 6: Pinyon Ridge

Distance	8.5 miles round trip (from Old Culp Valley Road to "Wilson" peak)
Total Elevation Gain/Loss	1400'/1400'
Hiking Time	4 hours (round trip)
Recommended Map	USGS 7.5-min *Tubb Canyon*
Best Times	November through May
Difficulty	***

Dry Pinyon Ridge stands just high enough on the desert rim to support a sparse growth of pinyon-pine trees. Like other similar "islands in the desert sky" such as the Pinyon Mountains and Whale Peak to the southeast, this ridge offers expansive views of distant mountains and valleys framed by a picturesque foreground of eroded granitic boulders and gnarled pinyons.

Happily, the Wilson Trail, an old jeep trail along the crest of the ridge, has been closed to off-road vehicles. It is now a hiking route into the heart of an extensive state wilderness not otherwise penetrated by roads.

To reach the trailhead, turn west on Culp Valley Road (also known as Old Culp Valley Road) from mile 10.4 on Montezuma Highway. The road becomes progressively more difficult to negotiate in a conventional auto, especially if the surface has not been freshly graded. Bear right at the fork of a spur road after 0.4 mile. (To the left is a pleasant picnic spot at the base of a ravine.) At 1.1 miles from Montezuma Highway, a turnout near Cottonwood Spring (easily identified by three tall cottonwoods) offers the last easy place to turn around and park if you decide to drive no farther.

Whether you decide to drive or walk at this point, go another 1.6 miles to the intersection of the Wilson Trail, marked by an old lettered post. There is parking for perhaps two cars here.

The Wilson Trail's eroded track meanders south and east over and around a series of rocky knolls on the crest of Pinyon Ridge. Common vegetation seen along the way includes chamise, sage brush, mountain mahogany, scrub oak, sugar bush, man-

zanita, Mojave yucca, buckhorn cholla cactus, juniper, and, of course, pinyon pine. After about four miles you'll pass north of "Wilson" peak (4573') (let your topographic map be your guide). This is as good a view spot as any in the area. Scramble up over the rocks, discover the bench mark, and admire the view. In the west are the Palomar Mountains, with the white dome of the Hale 200-inch telescope clearly visible. The broad sweep of the Santa Rosa Mountains in the northeast serves as a backdrop for Borrego Valley and Coyote Mountain. Far to the east are the Salton Sea and the Chocolate Mountains of Imperial County. The Pinyon Mountains and Whale Peak rise to the southeast; and the Laguna and Cuyamaca Mountains stand to the south and southwest.

Several flat areas suitable for camping are passed along this hike. It is not necessary to go all the way to Wilson Peak to enjoy some fine views, although the eastward vistas are better here.

Sacred datura below Pinyon Ridge

Area D-7: Borrego Mountain

The isolated peaks and eroded ravines of Borrego Mountain lie between the Borrego Badlands on the north and Lower Borrego Valley on the south. The area is laced with a network of dirt roads, some suitable for ordinary passenger cars, others suitable only for off-road vehicles. In the adjacent Ocotillo Wells State Vehicular Recreation Area, vehicles may travel cross-country, but here (in Anza-Borrego Desert State Park) they are confined to designated roadways.

Car camping is popular in this area, especially at Hawk Canyon on the southeast side of Borrego Mountain's West Butte. At West Butte jeep roads merely encircle but do not penetrate the slopes, so this is a relatively quiet place to hike. Along the west side of West Butte are deeply eroded ravines and slot canyons that can be explored only on foot.

Borrego Mountain

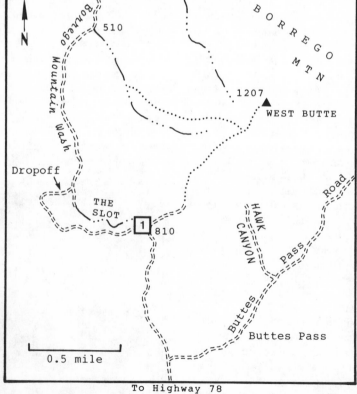

Trip 1: Borrego Mountain (West Butte)

Distance	3.5 miles
Total Elevation Gain/Loss	700'/700'
Hiking Time	3 hours
Recommended Map	USGS 7.5-min *Borrego Mountain*
Best Times	November through April
Difficulty	**

This is a fun place to get slightly lost—if only for an hour or two. The west slope of this butte is like a maze, with sheer-cut ravines that wind tortuously into soft sedimentary deposits. The most striking feature of all is called, ominously, The Slot. We'll save its exploration until the end of this hike.

To reach the starting point, turn north on Buttes Pass Road from State Highway 78 at mile 87.2. (This point is 1.5 miles east of Borrego Springs Road and 5.2 miles west of Split Mountain Road in Ocotillo Wells.) After 1.0 mile there is an intersection. Stay left, following the sign to the "Lookout"; then drive an additional 0.9 mile over an increasingly rough road to the parking area overlooking The Slot.

On foot now, follow wheel tracks 200 feet east until they end at the top of a ridge. Follow this ridge north, then northeast, directly to the summit of the West Butte (1207'), the highest point within a radius of about six miles. The summit offers excellent views of the Borrego Badlands and the Santa Rosa Mountains to the north, the Salton Sea to the east, and the Vallecito Mountains to the south.

The summit area is covered with crumbling piles of granitic rock, deeply stained by desert varnish, but there are some pegmatite exposures too: thousands of white crystals lie glittering in the sun. To the west are deep layers of soft sandstone, siltstone, and conglomerate. These layers, pushed up long ago by the granitic mass now exposed at the summit, are in the throes of rapid erosion.

Backtrack about 300 yards on the same ridge used for the summit approach. Then turn west and find a faint trail leading west,

then northwest, along the north wall of the deepest westward-draining ravine (take care not to descend to the north, an easy mistake). This trail takes you down to a point where you can drop into the ravine at its lower end; you can then walk out to the jeep trail in Borrego Mountain Wash.

Many fascinating hours can be spent tracing out the maze of ravines in this area. In fact, it's possible to descend the above-mentioned ravine all the way through its bottom, though not without great difficulty at one sheer 15-foot dropoff. The rock is absolutely untrustworthy, sometimes crumbling at the very touch.

Turn south on the jeep trail in Borrego Mountain Wash and pass an area of wind caves and small arches on the left. Here is yet another diversion to soak up the time!

Continue on, admiring the sandstone bluffs and colorful clay hills around you. You'll soon spot a scarred hillside on your right. This is the "Dropoff," a one-way jeep route into Borrego Mountain Wash from the flatlands above. Stay with the canyon as it narrows and turns east.

You now enter the portals of The Slot. The walls are fashioned from layer upon layer of dark gray siltstone, convoluted into bulbous parapets and spires. The Slot narrows as you move into it. Tilted parapets and giant chockstones lie wedged above you, seemingly subject to imminent collapse. The Slot narrows even more. You may have to remove your day pack in order to wedge through. When The Slot widens, there's a fork. Take the right branch, and in just 200 yards you'll be back at your car.

Area D-8: Pinyon Mountains

The Pinyon Mountains anchor the northwest corner of a much larger group of mountains, the Vallecito Mountains, in the geographic center of Anza-Borrego Desert State Park. Pinyon Mountain Valley separates the Pinyon Mountains from the highest summits of the Vallecito Mountains, including Whale Peak, lying to the south. Area D-9 includes Whale Peak and points west.

For the purpose of dividing this book into discretely mapped areas of reasonable size, I have lumped into this area other parts of the

Pinyon Mountains

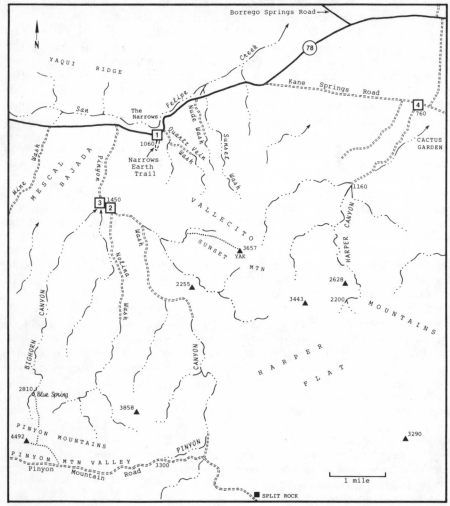

Vallecito Mountains northeast of the Pinyon Mountains, notably Sunset Mountain and Harper Canyon. Parts of the Vallecito Mountains still farther east, near Split Mountain, are covered in Area D-10.

Although the Pinyon Mountains are within state wilderness boundaries, vehicle use is permitted for some distance up several wide washes on the lower slopes. Most of these cross Mescal Bajada and Highway 78. Beyond the upper ends of these roads, travel is strictly by foot in terrain that becomes progressively rougher as elevation is gained. Besides the hikes suggested below, there are other possibilities for exploration, including many canyon tributaries and ridges that have probably never felt the impact of boot or moccasin.

The existence of a herd of nearly 100 bighorn sheep in the Vallecito and Pinyon mountains is a mystery. In 1971 at Blue Spring, and again in 1983 near Harper Flat, water-collection systems consisting of tanks and guzzlers were installed to enhance the bighorn habitat. Before these improvements were made, however, there were no known year-round sources of water. Perhaps in the course of wandering about these mountains, you may stumble upon a natural spring, solving this mystery.

Trip 1: Narrows Earth Trail

Distance	0.3 mile
Total Elevation Gain/Loss	50'/50'
Hiking Time	15 minutes
Optional Maps	Anza-Borrego Desert State Park map/brochure; USGS 7.5-min *Borrego Sink*
Best Times	All year
Difficulty	*

Stop at the Narrows Earth Trail for a brief lesson in geology. Most of the northern slopes of the Vallecito Mountains consist of granitic rock pushed up fairly recently from the interior of the earth. But here, in an area fractured by faults, it is possible to view some much older metasedimentary rock in close proximity to the granitic rock. These metamorphosed layers of sand and mud represent the oldest rock type exposed in the Anza-Borrego Desert.

The interpretive leaflet for this trail is helpful, if not essential to the lesson. Leaflets are usually present in a box at the trailhead, and also available at the nearby Tamarisk Grove Campground and the Visitor Center in Borrego Springs.

You'll find the trailhead at mile 81.6 on Highway 78, just above "The Narrows" of San Felipe Creek. The canyon behind the trail is designated Powder Dump Wash on topographic maps. For those interested in further exploring, nearby Quartz Vein Wash offers a direct way to climb into the Vallecito Mountains toward Sunset Mountain.

Trip 2: Sunset Mountain

Distance	6 miles round trip (direct route to summit)
Total Elevation Gain/Loss	2200'/2200'
Hiking Time	5 hours (round trip)
Recommended Map	USGS 7.5-min *Whale Peak*
Best Times	November through April
Difficulty	***

Sunset Mountain stands lofty and some-what isolated from the main Vallecito mountain chain. From Borrego Springs and other points in Borrego Valley, it appears smooth and rounded in profile and seems to glow with a warm light whenever low sunlight strikes the deeply varnished rocks on its surface. From the west and south it appears more pyramidal and jagged, abruptly rising above the broad, sandy expanses of Mescal Bajada and Pinyon Wash.

The easiest and most direct way to climb Sunset Mountain is by way of Pinyon Wash. Jeeps can navigate to a point less than two miles south of the summit, but standard cars probably will get no farther than the intersection of Pinyon and Nolina washes—about three miles west of the summit. To reach this latter starting point, turn south at mile 81.0 on Highway 78 onto the Pinyon Wash jeep trail and proceed 1.6 miles to the intersection of the Nolina Wash jeep trail. Park off the road on the normally smooth, hard-packed bed of sand in Pinyon Wash.

On foot now, follow the Pinyon Wash jeep trail east and southeast for about one mile. Soon the entire west slope of Sunset Mountain comes into view, and you can picture one or more routes to the top. Among the plethora of possibilities is the broad ridge west of the summit (the summit is marked on the topographic map as "Yak"—3657').

Cross the the small *bajada* at the base of the mountain, and begin the route of your choice. In any event, it will be an arduous climb—a gain of almost 2,000 feet over desert-varnished boulders, loose pebbles, and sinister patches of agave and cactus. The view from the top is worth the trouble,

though. Especially striking is the Salton Sea; on a clear day its surface mirrors the blue sky so effectively that its color resembles that of Lake Tahoe.

If you're going to combine an overnight backpack with a climb of Sunset Mountain, a good place to set up a dry camp is the small wash that passes south of the mountain and north of Peak 2255. East of Peak 2255 this wash broadens into a shallow, sandy bowl, marvelously insulated from the outside world and protected from the wind to boot. There are at least two obvious routes up Sunset Mountain from here.

Prospectors' post office at 17 Palms

Trip 3: Pinyon Mountain—North Approach

Distance	14 miles
Total Elevation Gain/Loss	3100'/3100'
Hiking Time	10 hours
Required Map	USGS 7.5-min *Whale Peak*
Best Times	November through April
Difficulty	****

Best done as a two-day backpack, this loop trip is still within the scope of an ambitious day hike. Only about ten percent of the distance covered involves difficult terrain, and most of this is encountered in the first half.

Several dozen bighorn sheep make the Pinyon Mountains their home, and you may surprise one, as I did recently, in Bighorn Canyon. Rounding a sharp bend in a narrow section of the canyon, I heard a clattering noise ahead. Forty feet away, a ewe was frantically trying to gain traction on a buttress in the near-vertical canyon wall. (When threatened, bighorn sheep prefer this "escape terrain"—steep, rocky slopes on which they are more nimble than any other large animal.) The ewe was slipping uncontrollably, her soft hooves grating against the granite. She almost lost her balance, barely avoiding a 15-foot topple to the canyon floor. While I retreated tactfully, the ewe arrested her slide and started a second, and successful, climb to the ridgeline.

A good place to start this hike is along the Pinyon Wash jeep trail. This road intersects Highway 78 at the 81.0 mile marker, and runs south across Mescal Bajada. Drive south 1.6 miles (standard passenger vehicles usually OK) to the intersection of the Nolina Wash jeep trail. Park on hard-packed sand next to the road.

Begin by hiking about 0.3 mile west to pick up one of the washes that drain Bighorn Canyon—the prominent cut in the mountains to the southwest. Don't confuse the mouth of Nolina Canyon, due south, with that of Bighorn Canyon. The going is easy over mostly hard-packed beds of sand for the next three miles; then the canyon steepens and

there are some short scrambles over small boulder piles. Water may trickle through this section of the canyon for several weeks following a heavy rain.

Blue Spring, at 4.0 miles, is the site of a sophisticated water-storage-and-delivery system for bighorn sheep and other wildlife in the area. Water is drawn from a silted-in catch basin and piped to a series of three 1600-gallon tanks. From there it flows to an open guzzler. Don't count on this as a source for your drinking needs, especially in a dry year.

Huge outcrops of quartz pegmatite surround and seem to hover menacingly over Blue Spring. Eroded into grotesque shapes by wind and water, they make a long stay here somewhat uncomfortable, particularly after the sun goes down. (In deference to the watering rights of local wildlife, you should not camp here anyway.)

(Should you decide not to climb to the top of the Pinyon Mountains, there's a shortcut option at this point: From the spring, simply go east over a low pass into a tributary of Nolina Wash, then descend back to the car.)

The canyon above Blue Spring becomes very steep and rugged, so we'll avoid it. From the spring, traverse east for about 100 yards, then go up the ridge leading to the Pinyon Mountain summit, a climb of 1700 feet. You'll be in the pinyon-juniper belt all the way, with plenty of opportunities for rest stops in the shade.

On and near the summit, there are many small campsites, and enough pinyon, nolina and other vegetation to cut the wind. During an overnight stay here, you can watch the twinkling lights in Borrego Valley, gaze at the stars above, and truly feel as if you're "king (or queen) of the mountain."

From the summit, your return is entirely gravity assisted, though you will cover nine miles instead of the five so far. Descend 500 feet to the jeep road in Pinyon Mountain Valley and follow it eastward as it descends down the head of Pinyon Canyon. After about two miles, the road diverges south from the canyon bottom and then parallels it for about one mile. Rock scramblers will prefer the moderately difficult but nontechnical descent over polished bedrock slabs in this narrow canyon section; others can follow the road. The road drops back down to join the canyon bottom after one mile.

Continue north across the west edge Harper Flat, then drop through the next narrow section of Pinyon Canyon. Finally, pick up the Pinyon Wash jeep trail and stroll four miles back to the starting point.

Lower Cougar Canyon

Trip 4: Harper Canyon

Distance	9 miles round trip
Total Elevation Gain/Loss	1500'/1500'
Hiking Time	6 hours (round trip)
Recommended Maps	USGS 7.5-min *Borrego Mountain, Harper Canyon*
Best Times	November through April
Difficulty	***

Formerly accessible to off-road vehicles, the four-square-mile expanse of Harper Flat now lies within a recently declared state wilderness area, and thus is open only to hikers. Jeep roads approach it from the west and south, but a more interesting route for foot travelers is by way of Harper Canyon on the north.

A patchwork of unmarked access roads at the mouth of Harper Canyon complicates things, so follow these directions carefully in order to avoid taking a wrong turn: Drive south from Highway 78 on the dirt road intersecting at mile 87.2.Go 1.6 miles south to a T-intersection with the old Kane Springs Road. Turn right here, drive 0.2 mile west, then veer left on a dirt road trending southwest. (The "jeep trail" marked on the 1959/60 *Harper Canyon/Borrego Mountain* topographic maps no longer leads to the mouth of Harper Canyon; instead it leads to a small canyon a mile to the west.)

Those with standard cars should find a place to park no farther than 0.5 mile up this southwest-trending road, or back along Kane Springs Road. With four-wheel-drive you can proceed 1.5 miles to the road's end at the mouth of Harper Canyon. Hiking mileages in this description refer to Kane Springs Road as the starting point.

In the first mile, you skirt the Cactus Garden, an area where most common species of cactus on the Colorado Desert are represented, but especially barrel cactus. Some specimens near the road are seven feet tall.

Beyond the roadend, the walls of Harper Canyon narrow, then widen again as tributary canyons split off on both sides. A good

descriptive name for the canyon would be "Ironwood Canyon." Hundreds of specimens of this slow-growing tree line it for three miles, providing welcome, if somewhat partial, shade during the middle of the day. Desert lavender also grows quite abundantly here. Starting about February, its tiny purple blossoms exude a perfumelike aroma.

At about 3.5 miles the canyon narrows, and you climb over the base of some sharply eroded fins of granitic rock that soar skyward along the canyon wall. Smoke trees and desert willow begin to appear in the canyon bottom. At 4.5 miles you reach the head of Harper Canyon, and emerge upon a vast basin—Harper Flat. Harper Flat is only partly drained by Harper Canyon.

If you're backpacking and make camp here, there are several options for further exploration. Peak 2628 lies directly to the north (scramble up 400 vertical feet on its south side), offering superb views of both Harper Flat and landmarks to the north, including the Santa Rosa Mountains and the Salton Sea. Harper Flat itself is rich in archeological evidence of Indian use (fire pits, tools), and is easily covered on foot. Other possibilities are point-to-point backpacking routes to exit points at Blair Valley or Split Mountain.

Area D-9: Granite Mountain/Blair Valley/Whale Peak

Nestled between the rounded summits of Granite Mountain and Whale Peak is Blair Valley, a focal point of recreational activity along the central part of the west edge of Anza-Borrego Desert State Park. Nooks in the rock-strewn ridges surrounding the valley serve as popular primitive campsites, and roads and trails radiate out to nearby attractions such as the Marshal South cabin and a well-known pictograph site. Motivated hikers can go beyond these familiar areas to summits affording some of the best views in Anza-Borrego.

At 2600 feet elevation, Blair Valley gives a taste of the transition zone between high and low desert. Its floor is covered by dense stands of agave (century plant), which in April or May send up a riot of tall, yellow-flowered stalks. A few hundred feet higher, in the bouldered canyons and on the ridges, juniper, Mojave yucca, ephedra (Mormon tea), jojoba, creosote bush, catclaw, desert apricot, cholla cactus, and white sage are common. Still higher, toward the summits of Granite Mountain and Whale Peak, pinyon pine, nolina, scrub oak, and manzanita flourish.

County Highway S-2, the long, lonely road that follows or closely parallels the Southern Emigrant Trail and the Butterfield Stage route of the mid-1850s, provides easy access to hikes in the Blair Valley area. The main entrance to Blair Valley itself is 6.0 miles south of Scissors Crossing (the intersection of Highways S-2 and 78).

Granite Mountain/Blair Valley/Whale Peak

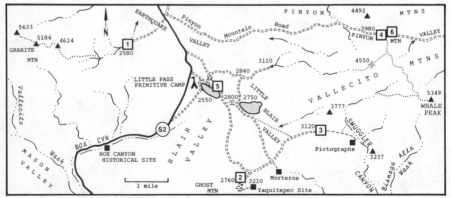

Trip 1: Granite Mountain

Distance	6.5 miles round trip (to highest summit)
Total Elevation Gain/Loss	3200'/3200'
Hiking Time	7 hours (round trip)
Required Map	USGS 7.5-min *Earthquake Valley*
Best Times	November through April
Difficulty	***

Although there is no trail to the summit of Granite Mountain, it is possible to climb the mountain from nearly every direction. The new Pacific Crest Trail alignment across the north and west slopes should enhance these options. Climbing up Granite Mountain can be a bit of a bore, especially if you stick with the same ridge or slope all the way, so the following route incorporates some variety. Try to do this on a crystal-clear day; the view is the main reward.

The starting point for this trek lies 1.1 miles down a dirt road (slightly rutted, but usually suitable for standard passenger cars) that goes southwest from Highway S-2 at mile 21.5.Drop into the wash north of the road, and follow it west through a narrow portal. Intricate complexes of granitic and metamorphic rock are seen in the walls and on the floor of this canyon. Desert apricot grows along the wash bottom, and the upper slopes are thickly covered with brittlebush, a big producer of yellow, daisylike flowers in March and April. In the wet season, mosses and green grass thrive in shady areas along the south side.

After 0.2 mile the canyon divides. Take the left (major, south) fork, passing over several interesting, but easy dry falls. At 0.9 mile the canyon splits into three forks. Go about 100 yards into the right (northwest) fork, and veer north to climb the ridge between the northwest and west forks. You climb moderately at first through sparse growths of cacti and small shrubs. Set your sights on the rocky shoulder 600 feet below and southeast of Peak 4624. After attaining this shoulder, work your way steeply upward to Peak 4624 over large boulders and past scattered pinyons and junipers.

Good campsites are found on the table-like top of Peak 4624, itself a worthy destination for those who don't wish to go on. There's a fine view of Earthquake Valley and the many summits of the Vallecito Mountains to the east.

Descend west a little to cross a saddle, and make your way up a difficult slope of brush and boulders to Peak 5184.Then follow the easy ridgeline west toward Peak 5633, tracing tracks of both deer and mountain lion. After a short, brushy climb, you reach the topmost boulder pile—with a spectacular view. On the far horizons are Old Baldy in the San Gabriel Mountains (seen just above the head of San Felipe Valley); San Jacinto Peak; a sliver of San Gorgonio Mountain; the Salton Sea; and, just over a low spot between the Cuyamaca and Volcan mountains (the Julian area), Santa Catalina and San Clemente islands!

San Felipe Valley from Granite Mountain

Trip 2: Marshal South Cabin Trail

Distance	2 miles (round trip)
Total Elevation Gain/Loss	400'/400'
Hiking Time	80 minutes (round trip)
Optional Maps	Anza-Borrego Desert State Park map/brochure; USGS 7.5-min *Earthquake Valley*
Best Times	October through May
Difficulty	*

The California desert has been home to many an eccentric, but possibly none so audacious as Marshal South. From 1931 until the mid-40s, Marshal and his poetess wife, Tanya, lived atop what was then a very remote mountaintop in the Vallecito area, depending in large part on natural desert resources for food, water, and shelter. Here, they built an adobe cabin, "Yaquitepec"; fashioned an ingenious rainwater collection system; raised three children; and tried to emulate, as completely as possible, the life of the prehistoric Indians.

The ruins of Yaquitepec are today one of Anza-Borrego's noted attractions—and quite easy to reach. At mile 22.9 on Highway S-2, turn east into Little Pass Campground and the Blair Valley area. Follow the dirt road around the eastern side of Blair Valley for 2.7 miles, then turn right (southwest) toward the roadend at the foot of Ghost Mountain. The trail ahead climbs in switchbacks to the top of the ridge, then bears east to the Yaquitepec site. Little remains of the dwelling except some of the walls and the water cistern, but the view from the site is magnificent.

South's writings on his family's experiment in primitive living appeared frequently in *Desert Magazine* during the 1940s. These articles are well worth looking up in the local library.

Marshal South cabin

Trip 3: Pictograph Trail

Distance	2.4 miles round trip (to Pictographs and Overlook)
Total Elevation Gain/Loss	500'/500'
Hiking Time	90 minutes (round trip)
Optional Maps	Anza-Borrego Desert State Park map/ brochure; USGS 7.5-min *Whale Peak*
Best Times	October through May
Difficulty	*

The Kumeyaay Indians who made camp in Blair Valley well over a century ago left more than bedrock morteros and potsherds. They also left some impressive pictographs—red and yellow painted designs—on the face of a large boulder in nearby Smuggler Canyon. Generations of archeologists have puzzled over the meaning of these and other pictographs and petroglyphs (etched designs) which appear not only in the Anza-Borrego region but throughout the Southwest. The diamond-chain motif at the Smuggler Canyon site has been linked to puberty rites, but the real purpose of these rock inscriptions may never be known.

Drive into Blair Valley as described above in Trip 2, but make a left turn (northeast) at 2.7 miles. (At 3.5 miles, a fork goes right—southeast—toward a cluster of large boulders. Walk over, and you'll find Indian morteros on several of the flatter slabs. Note, also, how several of the tallest boulders are pocked with dozens of shallow depressions—called cupules. Their use may have been associated with fertility ceremonies or puberty rites.)

At 3.6 miles, a road to Little Blair Valley branches to the left. Stay right (northeast) and continue another 1.5 miles to the end (the topo map shows a nonexistent "Petroglyphs" site here).

Continue on foot over the low pass to the east. Once over the top, bear right and stay along the west side of Smuggler Canyon—a wide, sandy wash at this point. You'll find the pictographs on the face of a very large boulder to your right, 0.8 mile from your starting point.

If it's a clear day, you won't want to miss the spectacular view of the surrounding desert from the top of a nearby overlook. Continue southeast down the wide bed of Smuggler Canyon another 0.4 mile to the lip of a dry waterfall. This frames a view of Vallecito Valley to the south. Climb the knoll east of you (Peak 3237) for a much more inclusive view.

Buckhorn cholla cactus in Blair Valley

Trip 4: Whale Peak—North Approach

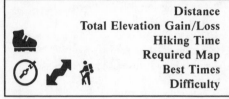

Distance	4 miles round trip
Total Elevation Gain/Loss	1500'/1500'
Hiking Time	3½ hours (round trip)
Required Map	USGS 7.5-min *Whale Peak*
Best Times	October through May
Difficulty	***

Whale Peak is probably the most visited major summit in Anza-Borrego Desert State Park. Perhaps 200 people every year day-hike or backpack into this serene, wooded island in the desert sky to enjoy a bit of solitude. Like Granite Mountain, Whale Peak yields readily to approaches from nearly every direction. The area around it, however, can prove distressing from a navigational point of view. The higher elevations consist of a series of similar-looking hogback ridges and gentle valleys, and the peak itself remains hidden from view until you are almost upon it. Excepting rain or snow, there are no sources of water.

The easiest way to hike up Whale Peak is from the north at Pinyon Mountain Valley (described here). A long drive on a primitive dirt road is required, however. A more difficult but equally interesting route, without the long approach by car, is described in Trip 5 below.

At mile 21.4 on Highway S-2, turn east on the signed Pinyon Mountain Road (low-clearance vehicles not recommended; four-wheel drive helpful). Stay right (east) at the fork in 0.1 mile, and continue up the alluvial fan. The road is never very steep, but there are patches of soft sand and occasional protruding rocks. At 5.7 miles the road tops a watershed divide at 3980 feet in the middle of Pinyon Mountain Valley. Find a place to park in one of the turnouts or spur roads nearby. In his *Anza-Borrego Desert Guide Book,* Horace Parker describes Pinyon Mountain Valley as being "caressed by some of the most invigorating air found anywhere in the world . . . it has the tang and coolness of the high mountains and the warmth and dryness

of the deserts." His comments apply equally to the pinyon-clad slopes you will soon be climbing.

Head directly up the small canyon to the south. A little hand-and-foot climbing is required to negotiate some large boulders. The canyon soon widens into a sandy flat just below 4400 feet. You can now pick up an informal ducked trail trending southeast over and around several rocky summits. Keep track of your position by map and compass in case you lose the trail. Flat areas for camping are quite abundant in small valleys near the trail.

The mature pinyon pine, juniper, scrub oak, manzanita, yucca, and nolina on these north slopes of Whale Peak are San Diego County's best example of the pinyon-juniper woodland community. This rather small community is similar to a much larger expanse of pinyon-juniper woodland on the vast Sierra Juarez plateau just below the Mexican border.

A little over one mile from the sandy flat, you come to a small valley west-northwest of Whale Peak. From this point scramble diectly up the slope to the flattish 5349-foot summit. More small campsites lie amid the scattered pinyons here.

Much time could be spent reading through the climbers' register, but don't ignore the view. In addition to the usual landmarks (the Santa Rosa Mountains, the Salton Sea, etc.), there's a good panorama to the south, including the Sierra Juarez, Signal Mountain, and the Laguna Salada—Baja's counterpart of California's Salton Sea.

Trip 5: Whale Peak—West Approach

	Distance	13 miles
	Total Elevation Gain/Loss	3200'/3200'
	Hiking Time	9 hours
	Required Maps	USGS 7.5-min *Earthquake Valley, Whale Peak*
	Best Times	November through April
	Difficulty	****

A pleasing mix of experiences await you on this trek: a stroll down an old stagecoach path, meandering passages up and down boulder-strewn canyons, even the crossing of a dry lake. Don't forget to take along plenty of water.

You begin at Little Pass Primitive Campground in Blair Valley (entrance at mile 22.9 on Highway S-2). Park in the camping area tucked up against a rocky ridge 0.5 mile east of Highway S-2. Walk north past a campfire circle and climb over the saddle ahead. This is Foot and Walker Pass, separating Blair Valley from Earthquake Valley. Passengers on the Butterfield Overland Stage, which operated along this route in 1858–61, had to walk and sometimes help push the coaches over this rocky pass.

Just north of the pass pick up the dirt road to Little Blair Valley and go east. After 0.8 mile, bear left (east), while the main road swings south into Little Blair Valley. One mile farther, this spur road ends at the mouth of a small, rocky canyon.

Go up this canyon, taking care to bear right (southeast) at a canyon fork just 0.1 mile ahead. Using map and compass, carefully follow the drainage upstream emerging to cross a nearly flat valley and continuing into a narrow gorge. After climbing about 1000 vertical feet through this gorge, you'll reach a saddle at 4550 feet. This is one of several suitable places to make camp if you're backpacking.

Continue northeast, dropping slightly, until you come to a sandy flat just below 4400 feet. Whale Peak lies 1.5 miles southeast of here—see Trip 4 for details.

The trip back to Blair Valley is an interesting variation on the approach route. Go back down the west slope of Whale Peak to a small valley that lies 0.3 mile west-northwest of the summit. Now head generally west, losing elevation steadily, until you drop abruptly into Smuggler Canyon. Follow the canyon out to a broad valley, and turn south toward the pictograph site. (Resist the temptation to continue toward Little Blair Valley by going north of Peak 3777—you won't save time this way.) Swing west, picking up the Pictograph Trail and the dirt road leading to it. Once in the south end of Little Blair Valley, leave the road and cut straight across easy terrain to the valley's dry lakebed, about 1.5 miles away. This creosote-bush-fringed valley often comes alive with wildflowers in March and April. The lakebed itself is a muddy morass during wet periods.

Pass over a gap in the boulder-strewn ridge west of the dry lakebed, and voila!—Blair Valley and Little Pass Campground lie below.

Trip 6: Pinyon Mountain—South Approach

Distance	2 miles round trip
Total Elevation Gain/Loss	500'/500'
Hiking Time	90 minutes (round trip)
Optional Map	USGS 7.5-min *Whale Peak*
Best Times	October through May
Difficulty	**

A long, bumpy drive up Pinyon Mountain Road puts you within easy hiking distance of the Pinyon Mountain's 4492-foot high point. The hike itself is easy compared to the drive; it leads to one of the best view spots easily accessible to hikers in the Anza-Borrego Desert.

See Trip 4 for details concerning the approach via Pinyon Mountain Road. From the road summit at 3980 feet in Pinyon Mountain Valley, simply head cross-country up the ridge to the north and west. The south slope is almost bald, but good growths of pinyon and nolina are found on the summit and on north-facing slopes, where the sun's drying effect is allayed.

Whale Peak swells across the southern horizon, blocking views in that direction. Opposite, however, is a sweeping vista of the San Ysidro and Santa Rosa mountains, Borrego Valley, the Borrego Badlands, and the Salton Sea.

Wall of Split Mountain

Area D-10: Split Mountain/Fish Creek

This is the desert at its lowest, hottest, and—to the unappreciative eye—most unfriendly. To those in the know, however, it is a fascinating labyrinth of rugged canyons, twisted arroyos and mud hills, containing not only some of nature's best examples of earth sculpture, but also a complete sequence of animal fossils spanning a period of several million years. In truth, it's not unfriendly at all. Even the climate is nice—in winter.

Fish Creek is the major drainage system of the area. Numerous washes feed into the upper end of Fish Creek from the south slopes of the Vallecito Mountains and the north edge of the Carrizo Badlands. For more than two miles, Fish Creek squeezes between the near-vertical walls of Split Mountain, the dividing line between the rambling Vallecito Mountains to the west and the lower Fish Creek Mountains to the east. Fish Creek has maintained its course through this gap by cutting downward fast enough to compensate for the rise of the adjacent mountains. Exposed on the walls of Split Mountain and many of its tributaries is a layer cake of strata reflecting successive eras of invasion by the sea and reclaiming by the land. Recent faulting has offset some of these layers, creating spectacular discontinuities.

Old-timers have reported that Fish Creek was once a sluggish creek with large potholes in its sandstone and conglomerate floor, some containing desert pupfish. A big flood in 1916, it is surmised, smothered the creekbed with a thick carpet of sand and destroyed the habitat for the fish. Today's Fish Creek supports only scattered smoke trees, desert lavender, mesquite, and other shrubs. A trademark of the area is the Orcutt aster, a plant whose purple-petaled, yellow-centered, daisylike flowers bloom profusely whenever water is present.

Unfortunately for hikers, some of the most fascinating areas in the Split Mountain area are quite heavily used by some off-road and motorcycle enthusiasts for whom speed and loud noise are great goals. On the flip side, many of the beautiful tributaries of Fish Creek are closed entirely to vehicle use. Split Mountain itself seems to get most of the motorized use; however it's peaceful and quiet here on most weekdays.

Paved Split Mountain Road leads south from State Highway 78 at Ocotillo Wells, passes the Elephant Trees Area (Trips 1 and 2), and continues south to a dirt road turnoff for Fish Creek Primitive Camp and Split Mountain. Passenger cars can usually make it to the entrance of Split Mountain (starting point for Trip 3) and, if road conditions allow, all the way through Split Mountain to the bottom of the North Fork (starting point for Trip 4). Soft sand is prevalent in the upper reaches of Fish Creek; 4-wheel-drive is needed to drive as far as Sandstone Canyon (Trip 5).

Wind caves near Fish Creek

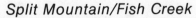

Split Mountain/Fish Creek

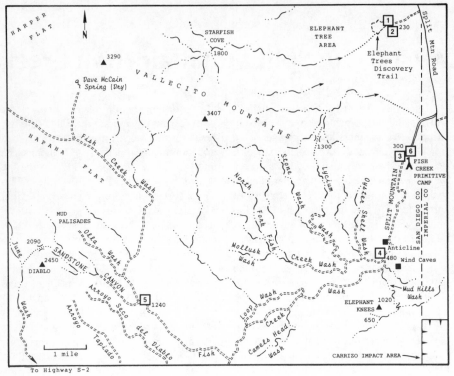

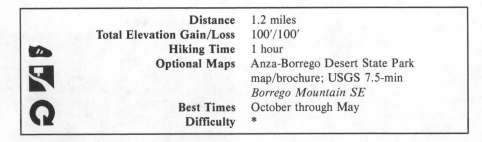

Trip 1: Elephant Trees Discovery Trail

	Distance	1.2 miles
	Total Elevation Gain/Loss	100'/100'
	Hiking Time	1 hour
	Optional Maps	Anza-Borrego Desert State Park map/brochure; USGS 7.5-min *Borrego Mountain SE*
	Best Times	October through May
	Difficulty	*

The elephant tree is one of Anza-Borrego's remarkable plants. This self-guided nature trail winds through a small group of these trees and calls attention to 20 other plants indigenous to the low, hot, alluvial-fan environment. Numbered posts along the trail are keyed to a leaflet available at the trailhead.

Long considered to be rare north of the border, the few small elephant tree (*Bursera microphylla*) specimens you see here are only a part of a group that includes at least several hundred more to the west (see Trip 2). Elephant trees are also present in scattered numbers in the south end of the state park (see Area 12). Although the leaflet states that this is the northernmost grove of elephant trees known in the United States, one old Cahuilla Indian recalled seeing elephant trees in the Santa Rosa Mountains.

The elephant tree is truly a botanical oddity. With a short, stubby trunk, puffy limbs, reddish twigs and sap, tiny green leaves, and purplish fruit, it is right at home with the wierd types of vegetation found in Baja's central deserts. Like cacti and succulents, the elephant tree is able to store water internally.

Indians believed the plant was associated with a great power capable of curing many diseases, especially skin ailments. Shamans kept the sap from the plant hidden away, as it was considered too dangerous to keep openly around a household.

To reach the Elephant Trees Discovery Trail, drive six miles south of State Highway 78 (at Ocotillo Wells) on the paved Split Mountain Road. A dirt road, negotiable with care by standard cars, goes 0.9 mile west to the trailhead.

Trip 2: Alma Wash to Starfish Cove

Distance	10 miles round trip
Total Elevation Gain/Loss	1600'/1600'
Hiking Time	7 hours (round trip)
Recommended Maps	Anza-Borrego Desert State Park map/brochure; USGS 7.5-min *Borrego Mountain SE, Harper Canyon*
Best Times	December through March
Difficulty	***

If it's solitude you want, this is your trip. I made the journey in on a cold, silent winter night, under the pale light of a first-quarter moon. I felt as if I were traveling a canyon no one had ever visited before—and that may have been close to the literal truth. In the flashlight's beam I discovered fresh, fist-sized tracks—those of a mountain lion.

By the light of dawn I discovered the densest population of elephant trees I had ever seen, north or south of the border. These trees grow on both sides of the canyon, but especially on the north wall, where the tiny leaves of the plants can soak up the maximum amount of sunshine. Some stand upright 10 or more feet tall, while others, rooted to talus slopes, have limbs that seem to slither along like stunted, battered, conifers at timberline. Once the small, wiry saplings gain a foothold in small pockets of soil on the slopes, they survive by rolling with the punches: rock slides merely train the flexible limbs to grow in new directions.

Begin this trip on the Elephant Trees Discovery Trail (Trip 1 above). At post #6, leave the nature trail and bear left into one of the many channels of Alma Wash (Alma Wash is labelled on the state park map, but not on the topographic maps. Follow the braided wash floor southwest around the left (south) side of a low dome, then continue west for about two miles up the alluvial fan that debouches from the mouth of a prominent cut in the Vallecito Mountains. The wash bottom has been extensively flooded and stripped of vegetation, most recently by tropical storms Kathleen (September 1976) and Doreen (August 1977). Note the contrast between the desert-varnished rock on the higher surfaces of the fan and the gleaming white rock in the recently scoured stream channels.

Scattered elephant trees appear on the fan as you approach the mouth of the canyon. Conglomerate rock is exposed at its portals, then big slabs of granitic rock—the bare bones of the Vallecito Mountains—as you penetrate the canyon.

The going is relatively easy: mostly on flat sandy patches, but occasionally over small boulder piles. Intermixed with the elephant trees on the slopes are creosote bushes. From a distance the two plants look similar, except that elephant tree foliage is a slightly darker (or grayer) shade of green. Up close, of course, there's no confusion.

Three miles past the portals of the canyon is a junction of several tributaries. Because of its starfish shape on the topo map, I like to call it "Starfish Cove." Campsites on flat beds of sand are abundant here.

Starfish Cove is in the heart of one of the least visited areas of Anza-Borrego. There are numerous peaks and ridges to climb in every direction. On a warm day, however, you'll be content just to relax in the sun and enjoy the splendid solitude.

Trip 3: Split Mountain/Lycium Wash Loop

Distance	12.5 miles
Total Elevation Gain/Loss	1000'/1000'
Hiking Time	8 hours
Required Maps	USGS 7.5-min *Borrego Mtn. SE*, *Carrizo Mtn. NE*, *Arroyo Tapiado*, *Harper Canyon*
Best Times	December through March
Difficulty	***

This long circle trip includes a passage through Split Mountain and a traverse over the Vallecito Mountains to the east. About three miles of this hike pass through some semirugged terrain—a scramble through a narrow ravine and down along a rocky ridgeline. The rest involves easy walking on jeep trails and along a sandy wash.

Begin at the entrance to Split Mountain (near Fish Creek Primitive Camp), about two miles south of paved Split Mountain Road. An early start will probably ensure you a measure of peace and quiet along the first few miles of jeep trail ahead. The walls of Split Mountain consist of two stacks of various sedimentary layers, including sandstones and a curious kind of conglomerate called "fanglomerate"—an aggregate of cobbles and sand originating from deposits on ancient alluvial fans. Many of these layers are tilted or folded into spectacular synclines and anticlines.

Just past Split Mountain's entrance, look for evidence of landslides along the steep cliffs left and right. Notice also the series of

vertical fault cracks in the west wall. The fresh debris at the bottom of the cliffs was the result of a 1968 earthquake centered near Ocotillo Wells. The Visitor Center in Borrego Springs has an interesting videotape of events immediately following this magnitude 6.4 quake.

At about 2.2 miles, just before the walls of Split Mountain begin to part, look for a spectacular anticline (an inverted U) of sandstone shelves on the west side.

When the walls fully part, bear right (west) on the jeep road through the North Fork of Fish Creek. Continue one mile through a landscape dominated by clay hills (also called "mud hills" for their consistency when wet) strewn with sparkling chips of gypsum crystal.

Turn right (north) into Lycium Wash, named after the shrub *Lycium,* or boxthorn, which flourishes here and in other badlands washes. Follow Lycium Wash on a meandering course through more mud hills to the end of the jeep trail, 2.5 miles past North Fork.

Continue up-canyon through a picturesque layer of fanglomerate. Avoid a narrow trench filled with deep *tinajas* (pools) by climbing up and over on the right (east side). Fanglomerate soon yields to tilted sandstone layers sculpted by water into fantastic shapes. After scrambling over three low dry falls, you'll come to a big, boulder-choked defile that can be detoured by climbing up and over to the right.

Now make your way north over easier terrain, staying in the biggest drainage as tributaries separate left and right. You'll soon reach a high point along a rounded ridge frosted with darkly varnished granitic rocks.

An old cairn of crumbling rocks marks the summit.

Go north from the summit, passing down along a rocky ridge dividing two north-flowing canyons that later join. At any convenient place, drop into either of these (caution: loose rocks here) and proceed down the sandy wash ahead.

A short-cut across the rocky alluvial fan toward the mouth of Split Mountain is tempting, but not a time-saver, as the plain is cut by too many small washes and ravines. Instead simply follow the main wash as it curves east, then southeast toward the road that leads into Split Mountain.

Greatly folded anticline in sandstone wall of Split Mountain

Trip 4: Mud Hills Wash

Distance	5 miles round trip
Total Elevation Gain/Loss	300'/300'
Hiking Time	2 hours (round trip)
Recommended Map	USGS 7.5-min *Carrizo Mtn. NE*
Best Times	November through April
Difficulty	**

This hike will put you within easy reach of ancient fossil shell reefs so dense that fossils and fossil fragments outweigh the very matrix in which they lie.

You can combine this walk with a stroll through Split Mountain if road conditions block passage by automobile through the Split itself. This would involve an additional five miles round trip. We'll assume a starting point at the south end of Split Mountain, where parking is available on hard-packed sand.

Before or after your hike, be sure to check out the "wind caves" on the slope to the east of Fish Creek—just past the south end of Split Mountain. At least three informal trails lead up to several sandstone outcrops, where sandblasting by the wind has hollowed out chambers and skylights. This type of formation is quite common in the Fish Creek watershed and around Borrego Mountain.

Just beyond (south of) the starting point, bear left, staying in the main Fish Creek Wash, as the North Fork veers to the right. In another 0.3 mile Mud Hills Wash comes in from the left (south). Walk past the vehicle closure signs and make your way along the smooth bed of this wash. If the wash bottom is wet from rains, you'll accumulate about two inches of mud on your shoes, but that's all part of the fun.

To the right is a spectacular undulating landscape of mud hills, glistening with chips of gypsum. Above this is a flat-topped butte with the formation known as Elephant Knees along its north flank.

About 1.5 miles up meandering Mud Hills Wash, there's a major split. Take the right (southwest) fork, and swing around the south side of the Elephant Knees butte. Here you'll find, scattered along the wash and imbedded within the butte, the fossilized remains of oysters and pectens (scallops) which thrived in a northern extension of today's Gulf of California several millions of years ago.

Further exploration in the immediate area is rewarding, but be sure to keep track of your bearings, especially if you travel over-land into the mud hills. Take care not to stray into the Carrizo Impact Area, which is strictly off limits to the public.

Elephant Knees

Mud Hills

Trip 5: Sandstone Canyon and Tributaries

👢	**Distance**	up to 7 miles for any single out-and-back excursion
🧭	**Required Maps**	USGS 7.5-min *Arroyo Tapiado, Harper Canyon*
🥾	**Best Times**	November through April
	Difficulty	* to ***

Sandstone Canyon has been called the most spectacular small wash in Anza-Borrego Desert State Park. After exploring the main canyon, and any of its many tributaries, it would be hard to argue with that assertion.

For the purposes of this description, a starting point at the mouth of Sandstone Canyon is assumed. Four-wheel drive is usually needed to reach this point, 10.5 miles up Fish Creek from Fish Creek Primitive Camp. Jeeps can navigate about two miles up

Sandstone Canyon, but its tributaries can be explored only on foot. The uppermost reaches of Sandstone Canyon can be reached from the southwest via June Wash (see Trip 6).

The walls of Sandstone Canyon consist of horizontally stacked layers of tan and dark brown sandstone. In some places the sheer walls soar almost 200 feet, but are only 10 feet or so apart at their bases. The canyon bottom is filled with granitic sand and boulders, washed down from the southern flanks of the Vallecito Mountains, a largely granitic body. A few large smoke trees inhabit the canyon, along with catclaw, desert lavender, locoweed, and other small shrubs.

At a point 1.2 miles up from the confluence of Fish Creek, a major tributary enters Sandstone Canyon from the right (north). Up this canyon a short distance is a small *tinaja* below a narrow, almost unclimbable dry fall. In your wanderings about the area, take care not to descend this wash from above in the hopes of reaching Sandstone Canyon.

At 1.7 miles another major tributary enters from the left (west). This narrow slot canyon may be followed for 0.5 mile to the top of the gently sloping plateau above and to the south of Sandstone Canyon. A complex of Indian trails radiates into the Arroyo Tapiado and Arroyo Seco del Diablo drainages, and along the south wall of Sandstone Canyon. Excellent if somewhat frightening views of bottom of Sandstone Canyon can be seen along the latter trail.

At 2.1 miles a third major tributary enters from the right (north). This is your access to the top of the Mud Palisades overlooking Olla Wash: Go up this canyon one mile, bearing right at all forks, then climb the slope to the right. Technically, the Mud Palisades are a receding cliff, one of several similar features along the south flank of the Vallecito Mountains. The view from the brink encompasses most of the upper Fish Creek drainage and extends to the Imperial Valley and Mexico.

Past the third major tributary, you can go another 1.3 miles to reach the head of Sandstone Canyon—a saddle overlooking June Wash. A good side trip from here is the short, steep climb up peak "Diablo" to the southeast. From the top there's a nice overview of the entire Carrizo Badlands.

Trip 6: June Wash to Split Mountain

Distance	18.5 miles
Total Elevation Gain/Loss	1050'/1800'
Hiking Time	9 hours
Required Maps	USGS 7.5-min *Agua Caliente Springs, Arroyo Tapiado, Carrizo Mtn. NE, Borrego Mtn. SE*
Best Times	December through March
Difficulty	****

This grand tour across the Carrizo Badlands traces attempts by early prospectors and travelers to find a short cut between the Vallecito Creek corridor (the Southern Emigrant Trail and Butterfield Stage route) and Lower Borrego Valley. Legend says that some of these travelers went "in" and failed to come "out." In the days before accurate maps were available, it was easy to become disoriented in the maze of washes that carry flood waters in three directions.

Plan this as a day-long day hike, or an overnight backpack with light equipment. Since nearly all of the route is on hard-packed or soft-sand surface, it is ideal for jogging. Regardless of your method of travel, be sure to take along sufficient water. A car shuttle of roughly 55 miles, via Highways S-2 and 78 and Split Mountain Road, is required to tie both ends of this trip together.

We'll assume that you begin the hike at the intersection of the jeep road up June Wash, mile 41.5 on Highway S-2. (You can also begin at points near Agua Caliente Springs and travel cross country toward upper June Wash.) The road up June Wash is negotiable by 4-wheel-drive vehicles, and sometimes conventional autos, for about four miles. Sparse growths of smoke trees and mesquite dot the floor of this wide wash. Be sure to keep left (west) as major tributaries diverge at 1.5, 2.4 and 3.3 miles from S-2.

At mile 4.5, June Wash passes west of peak "Diablo." There, bear right into a small drainage, leaving June Wash, and continue northeast around Diablo over a short stretch of rocky, cactus-studded terrain toward a broad saddle.

The saddle is a major divide between areas that shed water toward Vallecito and Carrizo creeks, and those that drain into Fish and San Felipe creeks. Runoff from the southeast slope of Diablo goes into Arroyo Tapiado and Arroyo Seco del Diablo. Diablo is thus a "triple divide peak."

Pass over the saddle and descend, steeply at first, then gradually, into the cool depths of Sandstone Canyon. It's now a simple matter of following the wash bottom, mostly on a jeep trail, all the way (13.7 miles from the saddle) out to the mouth of Split Mountain, a point easily accessible to automobiles. If you have time, many side trips beckon in Sandstone Canyon (Trip 5), in the Mud Hills area (Trip 4), or in any of several other tributaries of Fish Creek.

Running the Pacific Crest Trail

Area D-11: Agua Caliente Springs

Take in a deep breath of clean, dry air. Bask in the larger-than-life brilliance of the desert sun. Sink into the womblike comfort of warm spring water. At Agua Caliente Springs you can have your cake and eat it too—hike first, then enjoy a relaxing soak in the hot springs.

A county park has been established here in the midst of state park lands on the edge of the Tierra Blanca Mountains. The big campground and nearby store, along with the bathing pools, have made Agua Caliente Springs a focal point of activity in the south half of the Anza-Borrego area, with something for everybody.

A splinter of the Elsinore Fault is responsible for the upwelling of 98°F, mineral-rich water. This is the same fault that passes through Lake Elsinore, 70 miles northwest, where hot springs are also present.

There are three options for soaking at Agua Caliente Springs: a large indoor jacuzzi (open 9–3 except Tuesday), where the water temperature is boosted to a steaming 100+ degrees; a shallow, outdoor pool (open daylight hours) at a temperature averaging about 95°; and the tiny "Indian Pool" (always open) fed by the decidedly chilly waters of an ordinary spring.

Two short trails out of Agua Caliente Springs, described below, penetrate the stark hills to the west and south.

Agua Caliente Springs lies 27 miles northwest of Interstate 8 at Ocotillo, and 22 miles southeast of Highway 78 at Scissors Crossing, both by way of County Highway S-2. Driving time is about the same along either route from San Diego and South County areas. The northern route (Highway 78) is faster from North County areas.

Agua Caliente Springs

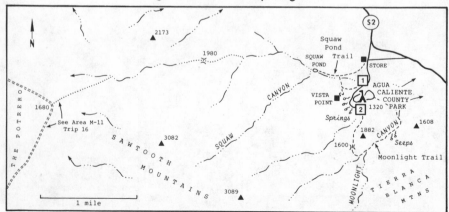

Trip 1: Squaw Pond Trail

	Distance	1.4 miles round trip (to Squaw Pond)
	Total Elevation Gain/Loss	200'/200'
	Hiking Time	50 minutes (round trip)
	Optional Map	USGS 7.5-min *Agua Caliente Springs*
	Best Times	October through May
	Difficulty	*

You can pick up this trail at the campfire circle near the county park's entrance. You wind over a low ridge, passing a spur trail leading to an overlook point a little higher on the ridge, then descend to the bed of Squaw Canyon. Turn left and make your way past thickets of mesquite—vibrant green when leafing out in March, and festooned with creamy yellow-green flower spikes in April through June.

The nutritious pealike pods of the mesquite ripen in September, and are eaten by numerous mammals, including man. The 19th century American botanist C. C. Parry, who is commemorated in the scientific names of several important native plants, wrote this about early Cahuilla Indian usage of mesquite:

> A due mixture of animal and vegetable diet is also secured in the mesquite bean, the pods of which are largely occupied with a species of weevil. The whole pod and its contents are pounded into a fine powder, only the woody husk of the seed being rejected. The process of baking is equally primitive. A squaw takes, generally from her head, a cone-shaped basket of close texture; the meal, slightly sprinkled with water is packed in close layers into this hat or pot as the case may be; when full it is carefully smoothed off and then buried in the sand exposed to a hot sun. The baking process goes on for several hours, till the mass acquires the consistency of a soft brick, when it is turned out, and the hat resumes its proper position on the head. The solid cake so made (if we could forget the process) is sufficiently palatable, containing a gummy sugar which dissolves in the mouth and is unquestionably nutritious.

While pondering the value of native plants, you'll soon come to Squaw Pond—a small spring in a marshy area with several large willow trees and a single palm tree. At least one diamondback rattlesnake makes a living on the small furry creatures that come here to drink. Coyotes and bobcats also frequent this little oasis. On the nearby hillsides you can admire the natural gardens of barrel and teddy-bear-cholla cactus— without a doubt of no nutritive value to any creature but the bighorn sheep.

Just beyond the spring, in a jagged ravine to the south (the main Squaw Canyon), is a tiny cave, a *tinaja,* and a usually dry waterfall. Further exploration is possible up any of the several branches of the canyon.

Trip 2: Moonlight Trail

	Distance	1.5 miles
	Total Elevation Gain/Loss	350'/350'
	Hiking Time	1 hour
	Optional Map	USGS 7.5-min *Agua Caliente Springs*
	Best Times	October through May
	Difficulty	*

This well-marked but somewhat steep and rugged trail climbs over a rock-strewn saddle, drops into a small wash mysteriously named Moonlight Canyon, descends past some seeps and a little oasis of willows in the wash bottom, and finally circles back to Agua Caliente Springs. You'll find the trailhead near the shuffleboard court at the south end of the campground. Although moonlight treks on this trail are possible, a good flashlight wouldn't hurt after dark.

True to their name, the Tierra Blanca ("white earth") Mountains are composed of generally light-colored granitic rock that seems not very likely to develop desert varnish. The rock fractures easily, and readily breaks down into small, irregular chunks and coarse sand particles.

From the high point on the trail, 300 feet above the campground, you can climb an additional 250 feet to reach Peak 1882, offering a superb view of Carrizo Valley and the Vallecito Mountains.

Another, much longer side trip may be made up-canyon (south) in Moonlight Canyon to a point overlooking the Inner Pasture, an isolated valley ringed by the Tierra Blanca and Sawtooth mountains. This is one way to reach a vast chunk of BLM-managed public land lying along the west edge of Anza-Borrego Desert State Park (see Area D-12, Trip 7 for more on this area).

Indian Pool at Agua Caliente County Park

D-12: Bow Willow/ In-Ko-Pah Mountains

The area between County Highway S-2 in the south end of Anza-Borrego Desert State Park and the BLM-managed McCain Valley Resource Conservation Area constitutes some of the most wild, beautiful and serene territory in San Diego County. Here, the Tierra Blanca and In-Ko-Pah mountains serve as a bridge between the hot sands of the low desert and a vast stretch of chaparral-dotted tableland southwest of the Laguna Mountains. Amid the tortured folds of these mountains are fan-palm oases, hidden waterfalls, and many species of plants that would seem more at home in places hundreds of miles to the north or south. Here, for example, water-loving trees like cottonwood and bay are found only a few miles from stands of elephant trees, which are common in the most arid parts of Baja California.

Bow Willow Campground (entrance at mile 48.3 on Highway S-2), the only semi-developed camping area in Anza-Borrego's south end, is a good staging area for hikes into the Tierra Blancas and the eastern In-Ko-Pahs. There is ready access from here into Bow Willow and Rockhouse canyons. Dirt roads lead to the Mountain Palm Springs area (turnoff at mile 47.1) and Indian Gorge (turnoff at mile 46.1), starting points for trips to numerous side canyons, desert valleys and peaks.

Topside, there's McCain Valley Road, a well-graded dirt road that runs some 14 miles north and west from Old Highway 80 near the town of Boulevard. (To reach it, leave Interstate 8 at the Highway 94/Boulevard exit, go 0.5 mile south, then go 1.9 miles east on Old Highway 80.) This road is the only public access into the McCain Valley

Resource Conservation Area, managed for multiple uses by the BLM. Most areas west of this road are open for restricted and unrestricted off-road vehicle use, while most areas east of the road have now been declared off-limits for vehicles in order to protect the habitat of the bighorn sheep. With the exception of hunters and target shooters, who seldom travel more than a mile or two from the main road, the east margins of the Resource Area are essentially hikers' domain. Cottonwood Campground, in the northern part of the Resource Area, is a good place to car-camp, and serves as a jumping-off point for hikes into the "de facto" wilderness areas north and east.

Several interesting but rugged one-way hikes may be undertaken between McCain Valley and the desert floor. One such hike is specifically described below (Trip 7), and others are suggested (see Trips 5, 6 and 8). The route by car between the starting and ending points, via Interstate 8 and Highway S-2, can take as long as 90 minutes, however.

Ocotillo at sunset

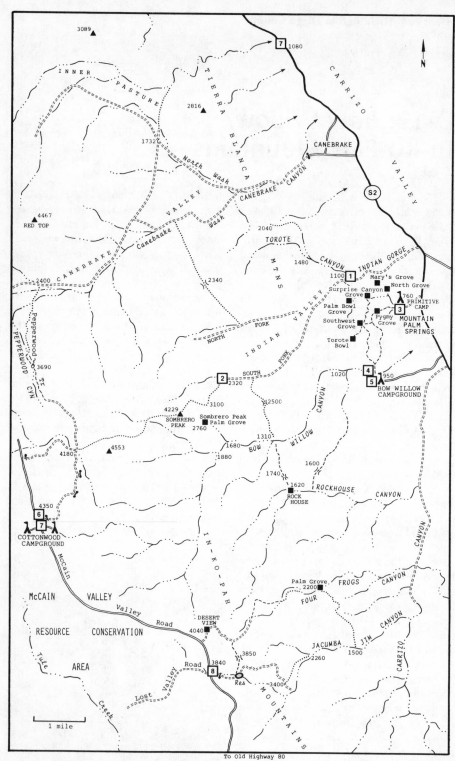

3089 ▲

INNER PASTURE

TIERRA BLANCA

2816 ▲

7 1080

CARRIZO

CANEBRAKE

S2

VALLEY

1732

North Wash

CANEBRAKE CANYON

VALLEY

Canebrake Wash

4467
RED TOP

2040

TOROTE MTNS

CANYON

INDIAN GORGE

2400

CANEBRAKE

2340

1480

1100 1

Mary's Grove
North Grove
Surprise Canyon
Grove
760 PRIMITIVE
CAMP
3
MOUNTAIN
PALM
SPRINGS

Pepperwood

PEPPERWOOD CYN

3690

NORTH FORK

INDIAN VALLEY

Palm Bowl
Grove
Southwest
Grove
Pygmy
Grove

Torote
Bowl

2

SOUTH
2320

FORK

1020

4
5 950
BOW WILLOW
CAMPGROUND

4229
SOMBRERO
PEAK
Sombrero Peak
Palm Grove
2760

3100

2500

1310

BOW

WILLOW

CANYON

4553 ▲

4180

1680
1880

1740

1600

4350

6
7

COTTONWOOD
CAMPGROUND

1620
ROCK
HOUSE

ROCKHOUSE

CANYON

CANYON

IN-KO-PAH

McCAIN

VALLEY

Valley

Road

RESOURCE CONSERVATION

AREA

Tule

DESERT
VIEW
4040

3850

3840

8

Res

3400

Palm Grove
2200

FROGS CANYON

FOUR

JACUMBA
2260

1500

JIM CANYON

CARRIZO

CANYON

McCain

Valley

Road

Lost

Creek

1 mile

To Old Highway 80

Bow Willow/In-Ko-Pah Mountains

Trip 1: Torote Canyon

Distance	4 miles round trip
Total Elevation Gain/Loss	1000'/1000'
Hiking Time	2½ hours (round trip)
Optional Maps	USGS 7.5-min *Sweeney Pass, Arroyo Tapiado, Agua Caliente Springs*
Best Times	November through April
Difficulty	**

Dozens of elephant trees cling to the walls of this interesting canyon. In Mexico, this tree is called *torote,* which means "twisted," in reference to the haphazard way in which the limbs twine upward. (Refer to Area D-10, Trips 1 and 2, for more on this fascinating botanical oddity).

A series of secluded valleys, each seemingly cut off from the rest of the world, lie up-canyon a mile or two. A broad expanse of sand, a few sparse shrubs, cobbled walls in the distance, and the vault of sky overhead: an hour spent quietly contemplating such purity and simplicity can bring on a feeling of profound peace.

Drive up the road into Indian Gorge (turnoff at mile 46.1 on Highway S-2), and proceed 1.8 miles to the mouth of Torote Canyon on the right (north), where it is possible to pull off the road onto what is usually hard-packed sand. On foot, scramble up the rock-strewn bed of the canyon, passing the elephant trees that seem to cling tenaciously to the steep walls.

After 0.8 mile you enter the first valley, an almost-flat, sand-drowned expanse stretching nearly half a mile. Within this valley the canyon divides, with the main branch (Torote Canyon) climbing sharply up a bouldered crease on the left (northwest). Keep right, in what seems to be the main part of the valley, and proceed north into a small, narrow canyon, a tributary of Torote Canyon. Within 200 yards this broadens into a second valley, similar to the first. Continue northwest to the second valley's end, and climb to the low pass that appears straight ahead. Reaching it, you'll discover a canyon just below that drains east toward the desert

floor. To your left (west) you can contour over rocks into this canyon, and within 200 yards reach the east end of still another sand-drowned valley. This one is richly endowed with desert vegetation, and hosts a lively population of jackrabbits.

This is as good a place as any to turn back and retrace your steps. If you do go on, though, you can make your way west over a divide, descend a rocky canyon, and reach the big valley above Canebrake Canyon.

Smoke tree in Torote Canyon

Trip 2: Sombrero Peak—East Approach

Distance	3 miles round trip
Total Elevation Gain/Loss	1900'/1900'
Hiking Time	3½ hours (round trip)
Recommended Map	USGS 7.5-min *Sombrero Peak*
Best Times	November through April
Difficulty	***

Cone-shaped Sombrero Peak rises head and shoulders above the east lip of the McCain Valley plateau, overlooking a hundred-square-mile expanse of rock-strewn mountains and gorges, sun-baked valleys, and distant badlands. Conversely, the peak itself is a prominent and familiar landmark widely observed from the desert below.

There is but one relatively easy way to climb to the summit from the desert side, involving a long approach by car up Indian Gorge and Indian Valley. (Another way to climb this mountain is from the west—see Trip 6.)

As in Trip 1 above, turn off Highway S-2 and drive through Indian Gorge. After 2.0 miles, the walls of the gorge part, and you enter Indian Valley. In another 0.7 mile, the road splits, with branches going into the north and south forks of Indian Valley. Keep left at this junction and drive into the south

fork about three more miles to the road's end near the mouth of a deep canyon (a few palms can be found up this canyon).

From the roadend, climb straight up the ridge to the south until you reach a flat at elevation 3100 feet. (Side trip suggestion: Sombrero Peak Palm Grove, a dense cluster of palms below this flat, is more easily reached from here than by way of Bow Willow Canyon.) Proceed west, then southwest up the ridgeline to the summit—fairly easy scrambling over modest-sized rocks all the way.

The view is best toward the east, where Bow Willow Canyon and its tributaries yawn open to the blazing sun. On your return to Indian Valley, don't be tempted to drop off the east side of the peak toward Sombrero Peak Palm Grove; house-sized boulders and scrub oak will stop you!

Trip 3: Mountain Palm Springs

Distance	2.5 miles (to Southwest Grove and Palm Bowl Grove)
Total Elevation Gain/Loss	350'/350'
Hiking Time	90 minutes
Optional Map	USGS 7.5-min *Sweeney Pass*
Best Times	October through May
Difficulty	*

The Mountain Palm Springs area boasts, without a doubt, the most charming palm oases south of Borrego Palm Canyon. The palms here are gregarious, growing in thick clusters, often with pools of water at their

feet. Many have never been burned: they still hold full skirts of dead fronds around their trunks, the better to serve the local population of rodents and snakes. In late fall and early winter, the sticky, sweet fruit of the palms hangs in great swaying clusters, sought after by birds and the sleek coyotes that prowl up and down the washes.

The palm groves are distributed along several small washes that drain a roughly one-square-mile area on the east side of the Tierra Blanca Mountains. As at Agua Caliente Springs to the north and Bow Willow to the south, water lies close to the surface here. A primitive camping area sits on the alluvial fan just below the point where the washes come together. A short dirt road leads to this campground from mile 47.1 on Highway S-2.

Consider the loop hike described here as a fairly complete tour of the area; but do be enticed to extend your explorations in the form of side trips or extended loop trips if the spirit moves you.

Begin by walking up the small canyon southwest of the primitive camp. Past some small seeps you'll come upon the first groups of palms—Pygmy Grove. Some of these small but statuesque palms grow out of nothing more than rock piles.

A long pause is in order at Southwest Grove, a restful retreat shaded by a vaulted canopy of shimmering fronds. A rock-lined catch basin fashioned for the benefit of the local wildlife mirrors the silhouettes of the palms. One or two elephant trees cling to the slopes just above the grove, but for a better look at these curious plants, you can climb a spur trail to Torote Bowl, where a bigger group of elephant trees will be found. Further travel (cross-country over boulders) can take you to a single huge specimen, perhaps 15 feet tall and 20 feet wide, 0.6 mile west-southwest of Torote Bowl—0.4 mile south of peak "Palm."

From Southwest Grove, pick up the well-worn, but obscure trail that leads north over a rock-strewn ridge to Surprise Canyon Grove in Surprise Canyon. Up-canyon from this small grove lies Palm Bowl, filled with tangled patches of mesquite and fringed on its western edge by more than a hundred palms. On warm winter days, the molasses-like odor of ripe palm fruit wafts upon the breeze, and phainopepla hoot and flit among the palm crowns, their white wing patches flashing.

Northwest of Palm Bowl Grove, an old Indian pathway leads over a low pass into Indian Gorge—another tempting diversion. To conclude our loop hike, however, we return to Surprise Canyon Grove and continue down-canyon to the campground. On the way, we pass North Grove and Mary's Grove, hidden in a side drainage on the left.

Spring at Southwest Grove

Trip 4: Bow Willow/Rockhouse Canyon Loop

Distance	7.5 miles
Total Elevation Gain/Loss	1100'/1100'
Hiking Time	4½ hours
Recommended Maps	USGS 7.5-min *Sweeney Pass, Sombrero Peak*
Best Times	November through April
Difficulty	***

A simple shack fashioned of rock, cement and corrugated metal might be unremarkable anywhere else, but in the midst of thousands of acres of wild desert, it becomes a point of interest. The old cattlemen's line shack in Rockhouse Canyon is a case in point: hikers routinely travel overland three or more miles just to see it. (Note: another canyon named Rockhouse Canyon lies 50 miles north of this one—see Area D-3.)

This rather popular if somewhat rugged hike includes some stretches of well-worn but poorly marked trails. Ducks and wooden stake markers are of some help in following the route. Topographic maps are very handy if you do go off course.

From the starting point, Bow Willow Campground, walk 0.5 mile up-canyon; on your left (south) is a small alluvial fan leading up to a rocky draw in the mountains. Clamber upward through this draw, passing a single palm tree (whose source of water is mysterious), gaining about 200 vertical feet. You'll come up to a sandy wash that winds upward to a gently sloping plateau area of broken rock formations. Hardy desert plants, like cholla cactus, ocotillo and creosote bush, cover the area. After you stay with the wash for about a mile, ducks and wooden markers guide the way generally south-southwest over an almost imperceptible divide (1600'), then down more steeply onto the broad floor of Rockhouse Canyon.

The jeep road shown on the topo map is gone now; simply head up-canyon 0.5 mile to an elliptical valley thickly covered with cholla and ocotillo. Nestled against the rocky hillside on the south side of this valley is the line shack, which leans against the face of a

large boulder. The decrepit interior of the shack houses the remains of a fireplace and the usual rusty bedsprings. This is still a good place, however, to take refuge during inclement weather.

East of the shack, at the mouth of a canyon, is a watering trough and the remains of a pipeline to a seasonal spring and waterfall 0.4 mile up-canyon. A pleasant hour or two can be spent exploring this canyon and the next canyon to the west.

The line shack marks the halfway point of this hike. Return by going directly over the low pass to the north into Bow Willow Canyon. An old cattle trail—probably once an Indian trail—traverses this pass. Once in Bow Willow Canyon, the walking is very easy over mostly hard-packed sand.

Palms at Surprise Canyon Grove

Trip 5: Bow Willow Canyon

Distance	7.5 miles round trip (to palms)
Total Elevation Gain/Loss	750'/750'
Hiking Time	4 hours (round trip)
Optional Maps	USGS 7.5-min *Sweeney Pass, Sombrero Peak*
Best Times	November through April
Difficulty	***

The intriguing name "Bow Willow" seems to be associated with the supple wood of the desert willow, used by Indians to fashion hunting bows. Hundreds of these fragrant, bushy trees are scattered along Bow Willow Canyon's lower end. A small spring at the mouth of the canyon serves a modest campground and a seasonal ranger station.

Vehicles were allowed on the sandy bed of Bow Willow Canyon until the early 1980s, when flash flooding obliterated the road and half the campground. Thereafter, park officials decided to keep the canyon vehicle-free. In 1985 several new campsites, replacing those washed away, were built on a gentle slope nearby.

The now-silent lower canyon is perfect for cool-weather hiking. Its white ribbon of sand winds, fjordlike, some three miles between sheer walls heaped with desert-varnished boulders. In the upper canyon, the terrain is much more rugged: the canyon divides into several branches that cut deeply into the In-Ko-Pah plateau.

A 1.5-mile-long graded dirt road, intersecting Highway S-2 at mile 48.5, leads in to Bow Willow Campground, where hiking begins. Walking in the canyon wash is easy since the sand is made up of rather large crystals deriving from easily decomposed granitic rocks above. As you stroll along, look for elephant trees—a few cling inconspicuously to the south wall. The canyon bends abruptly south, then gradually resumes a western course. The massive east flank of Sombrero Peak can be seen ahead, resplendent in early morning sunshine.

After 2.7 miles, a low pass over the ridge to the south-southeast can be seen. This is the route from Rockhouse Canyon (see Trip 5). On the opposite (north) side, a faint trail up and over the north wall leads to the South Fork of Indian Valley—a vigorous climb for the adventurous.

Our way straight ahead (west) now becomes increasingly choked with obstacles—low brush, rocks, and, during most of the year, a bubbling stream. The first scraggly palms appear at about 3.0 miles; but much finer specimens are seen farther on. The year-round supply of water in this canyon over the past several years has resulted in dense growths of mesquite, catclaw, willow and tamarisk in or near the streamcourse. Detour around this tangle of vegetation by staying high on the banks.

At about 3.7 miles (1680'), a dry tributary comes in from the northwest. (This tributary can be used as a route to the Sombrero Peak Palm Grove, an enigmatic, solitary cluster of palms on the flank of Sombrero Peak.) This junction is as good a place as any to while away some time or have lunch before returning. Listen for the sound of falling water, and you'll be drawn to one of the secret grottos nearby.

A major fork lies upstream (1880'), with V-shaped branches going west and southwest. The right fork is steeper, with less water, while the left fork enjoys a nearly perennial flow of water over massive boulders. In both branches, scattered cottonwood and alder trees lend a touch of softness to the harsh glare of naked granite.

Trip 6: Sombrero Peak—West Approach

Distance	9 miles round trip
Total Elevation Gain/Loss	1300'/1300'
Hiking Time	6 hours (round trip)
Required Map	USGS 7.5-min *Sombrero Peak*
Best Times	October through May
Difficulty	***

Dust off your route-finding skills—you'll need to use them on this approach to Sombrero Peak via the gently rolling McCain Valley plateau. The peak remains hidden behind growths of chaparral and intervening ridges. To make matters more difficult, many of the roads and jeep trails shown on the most recent (1975) topo map are totally overgrown and some new roads have appeared in the interim.

A good place to begin is Cottonwood Campground, 12.7 miles northwest of the McCain Valley Road/Old Highway 80 intersection. It's nestled in a pleasant strip of oak woodland along an upper tributary of Bow Willow Creek. Bedrock morteros nearby show that the Indians liked this area too.

Pick up the hiking and horse trail (a disused dirt road) 0.1 mile north of the campground entrance. Heading east at first, the trail soon swings generally north, crossing two small tributaries of Bow Willow Canyon. After about one mile, a 0.3-mile-long public easement begins, taking you through a corner of a private inholding within the BLM lands.

At 2.0 miles from the campground you should leave this trail (which continues north into Pepperwood Canyon) and swing east over a gentle divide north of peaklet 4553. Once over the divide, faint traces of an old jeep trail (marked on the topo map) may be followed east toward a north fork of Bow Willow Canyon. The conical summit of Sombrero Peak pops into view from time to time toward the east-northeast.

After a while, make your way northeast toward the rolling ridge directly west of Sombrero Peak, choosing the easiest route through the maze of tall, widely spaced chaparral shrubs. Now Sombrero's summit is clearly visible ahead. A short, tough scramble up a heap of boulders puts you on the summit.

Using a variation of the approach just described, expert hikers can drop down either major fork of Bow Willow Canyon to reach the desert floor, with a possible pick-up at Bow Willow Campground. These canyons are boulder-strewn and rugged, graced with palms and cottonwoods, and, of late, permanent streams.

Sombrero Peak

Trip 7: Pepperwood Trail to Canebrake

	Distance	14.0 miles (to mile 41.0 on Highway S-2)
	Total Elevation Gain/Loss	450'/3700'
	Hiking Time	8 hours
	Required Maps	USGS 7.5-min *Sombrero Peak, Agua Caliente Springs*
	Best Times	November through April
	Difficulty	***

On a cool day this is one of the most delightful downhill hikes in the county. Except for a two-mile scramble down the eroded and overgrown remnants of the Pepperwood Trail in Pepperwood canyon, little effort is required to keep moving. Below Pepperwood canyon, the route traverses the lonely reaches of Canebrake valley and the Inner Pasture; these two form a U-shaped alluvial plain about six square miles in area surrounded by the stark, boulder-strewn slopes of the Tierra Blanca and Sawtooth mountains. These valleys lie along the east edge of the BLM's Sawtooth Mountains Wilderness Study Area.

The riparian area along the upper part of Pepperwood canyon is a worthy enough destination of itself, as a trail of footprints attests. As of this writing, however, traffic down the lower end of the Pepperwood Trail is virtually nil. Few people visit Canebrake valley and the Inner Pasture either, save the few ranchers who have been granted grazing allotments here. If the BLM acts on a long-standing proposal to reconstruct and extend the Pepperwood Trail and develop camping facilities for hikers and horse riders, more people will surely be drawn this way.

As in Trip 6 above, we begin at Cotton-wood Campground and proceed generally north on the main hiking route toward Pepperwood canyon. At 2.0 miles and 2.7 miles, roads diverge left and right, respectively. Stay on the main route, which veers northwest over a divide and begins a steep descent between two tributaries of Pepperwood canyon.

As you descend, the trail becomes steeper and more obscure, until finally it is only a narrow path kept recognizable through occasional use by hikers and wildlife. Frequent periodic maintenance would be necessary to maintain a trail that met modern standards because the soil is a loose, decomposed granite that flows downslope with your every step.

Before long, there's a pungence in the air that brings a sense of *deja vu* to those familiar with the Coast Ranges of Northern California and Oregon: this is the unmistakable fragrance of the pepperwood tree (California bay, or bay laurel). When crushed and sniffed, the leaves give off an odor that is pleasant but, if overdone, the cause of a headache. The line between pleasure and pain is a fine one, yet who can resist going the limit?

Stumbling down past the first pepper-woods, you reach the canyon bottom and a stretch of flat sand (4 miles, 3720'). A seasonal waterfall is just upstream, shaded by pepperwoods and cottonwoods. Down-stream about 200 yards is a year-round spring in the flat bed of the creek. This area is a good place to turn around if you wish to go no farther.

Beyond the spring, faint trails lead down the steep walls of both sides of the canyon. Try to follow the trace of the original foot trail, as plotted on the *Sombrero Peak* topo map (1975), on the ridge east of the canyon bottom. This leads, after some moderate scrambling over loose rocks and through low brush, to the floor of Canebrake valley.

A search of the south side of the valley would turn up, among the strangely eroded granitic rock formations, several Indian mortero sites and a recently discovered ceremonial site related to fertility rites. Without lots of time to spare, however, we continue north to pick up the dirt road that takes us, after several miles, to Inner Pasture.

Strangely enough, Inner Pasture is drained by two major washes—North Wash, which flows through Canebrake Canyon, and another, unnamed wash that cuts through the Tierra Blanca Mountains to the northeast. It seems only a matter of a short time, geologically, before one or the other wash captures the entire drainage.

This unnamed wash is our exit and we reach mile marker 41.0 on Highway S-2 after a walk of some three miles. The easy stroll down this wash is a fitting climax to a long day's (or weekend's) hike. In the late afternoon sun, the shattered walls of granite on either side glow softly, offering a silent benediction.

There are at least two alternative ways to reach Highway S-2. From a south arm of Canebrake valley, it is possible to reach Indian Valley's north fork via a rocky pass; this is the BLM-proposed route for the lower end of the Pepperwood Trail. From Indian Valley one can walk out to S-2 or get a pre-arranged ride. Another, more obvious, route is right through Canebrake Canyon itself but private lands within the canyon make this route inadvisable without permission.

Trip 8: Four Frogs/Jacumba Jim Loop

Distance	9 miles
Total Elevation Gain/Loss	3200'/3200'
Hiking Time	8 hours
Required Maps	USGS 7.5-min *Sombrero Peak, Sweeney Pass*
Best Times	November through April
Difficulty	****

The palm-lined canyons known informally as "Four Frogs" and "Jacumba Jim" lie in the heart of the BLM's Carrizo Gorge Wilderness Study Area, a region whose east boundary abuts a large expanse of state wilderness in adjacent Anza-Borrego Desert State Park. The area supports a sizable herd of bighorn sheep most of the year. During the springtime lambing season, the sheep cross Carrizo Gorge and take up residence in the Jacumba Mountains. The strenuous, cross-country loop hike described here touches both canyons and gives a good overview of this rugged area.

Unlike most long trips in this book, this one starts "at the top," with most of the work—a 2400-foot elevation gain over gut-wrenching terrain—at the end. You'll dip deeply into your energy reserves for this one.

Do it in a single long day, or take your time and backpack in.

A good place to begin is the intersection of McCain Valley and Lost Valley roads. Drive 8.0 miles north of Old Highway 80 to reach this unmarked road, turn east, and find a place to park before reaching the permanent steel gate.

Past the gate, the abandoned road takes you 0.5 mile east to an overgrazed meadow and a storm-breached reservoir. Above the reservoir, cross a flood-torn gully, proceed north on traces of a jeep trail over a viewful summit (0.9 mile), and continue down a slope into a wide draw. Stay in the draw (northeast) as roads intersect from the left. At 1.9 miles a good trace of jeep trail detours you up and across the slope to the north, avoiding a sharp dropoff. After returning to the draw, pick your way down along the bottom for another mile. A thin stream of water flows here about half the year.

At 3.5 miles easy walking ends as you come to a spectacular abyss at the head of the canyon. Negotiate a route downward over the tops of the truck-sized boulders, and you will soon see clusters of palms below. Little or no surface water is present at the biggest grove (2200'), but it's nice to stop here for shade.

A good two thirds of the trip, in terms of effort, remains ahead. Head due east from the grove, first contouring, then climbing obliquely, to a small flat (2450') on the ridgeline above. Now, taking the path of least resistance, proceed generally south-southeast 0.5 mile across the glaring slopes to a flattish area, again at 2450 feet, covered with scattered low shrubs. This can be used as an excellent dry campsite, with a panoramic view of Carrizo Canyon and its many tributaries. Bighorn sheep "beds" (scuffed areas) and scats are common in this area; so too is evidence of feral cattle, which in recent years have roamed unfettered throughout the Jacumba Jim drainage.

Next continue generally south-southeast,

descending sharply into Jacumba Jim canyon. A low wall of stones, possibly an Indian hunting blind, may be seen on the way down. Upon reaching bottom, turn west and make your way up toward the first set of palms. The springs in this canyon are among the most dependable in the In-Ko-Pahs, and a vigorous supply of water cascades over the polished rock following wet periods. Above the first palms, however, the canyon becomes choked with vegetation, and it is necessary to clamber over the rocks on slopes north of the creek to make decent progress. Water trickling over numerous small falls can be heard below.

Many more palms are found above 2260 feet, where a tributary canyon comes in from the right (west). At this point it's time to begin climbing in earnest. Swing southwest onto the ridge between the two forks and climb up the sandy slope. Make your way through large and small semidesert shrubs (scrub oak, juniper, sugarbush, mountain mahogany) and a few palms. After about 0.7 mile, past an obstacle course of large rocks, you'll reach an old jeep road that leads northwest and west toward the washed-out reservoir and the meadow east of your car.

Inner Pasture

Area D-13: Coyote Mountains/ Carrizo Badlands

The Coyote Mountains and the Carrizo Badlands are located generally east and north of County Highway S-2 in the south end of Anza-Borrego Desert State Park and west of the BLM's Yuha Desert Recreation Area. Spectacular examples of badlands erosion in soft claystones, mudstones and sandstones are found throughout the area. These include clay hills, mud caves, small arches and windows, receding cliffs, sinuous washes, and deep-cut ravines.

Five million years ago, today's badlands were nothing but ooze at the bottom of a shallow sea that occupied the southeastern corner of California. The same geological forces that built up the Peninsular Ranges to the west raised and tilted these soft sedimentary deposits. Erosion has acted almost as quickly to tear them down. The forces of wind and gentle rainfall, acting slowly, have done their part to smooth a few rough edges; but it is the catastrophic events—the rare flash floods and earthquakes—that have played and will continue to play the major roles as shapers of this chaotic landscape.

The Coyote Mountains, a long east-west trending ridge, have a core of ancient granitic and metamorphic rocks overlain by marine sediments. Along much of this ridge, erosion has cut down through the softest sediments, leaving harder sandstones and fossil-shell reefs exposed. Fossil Canyon and Painted Gorge on the east end of the range (not discussed here) and the "Domelands" in the mid-part are prime examples. On the west end of the range, much older metamorphic and granitic rocks are exposed in places such as Canyon Sin Nombre.

In the western Carrizo Badlands, centered on Arroyo Tapiado, many fossils of land creatures, dating back one to two million years, have been found, including bones of mammoth, sabertooth cat, rhinoceros, camel, and dire wolf.

County Highway S-2, the road that finally opened up southern Anza-Borrego to easy access by conventional automobiles in the early 60s, is still the only way to reach the areas described here. Most San Diego County residents will find it easier to come by way of the south end of Highway S-2—from Ocotillo along Interstate 8.

Off-road vehicles can travel more than a hundred miles of approved routes in the area. There is much to see and do for hikers, too, both on and off the roads. The trips below will introduce you to some of the most fascinating areas.

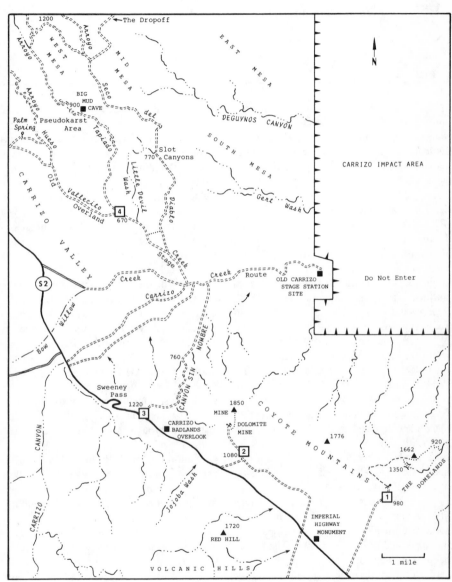

Coyote Mountains/Carrizo Badlands

Trip 1: The Domelands

Distance	6 miles
Total Elevation Gain/Loss	1200'/1200'
Hiking Time	5 hours
Required Map	USGS 7.5-min *Carrizo Mountain*
Best Times	December through March
Difficulty	***

Rich beds of marine fossils are common throughout the Coyote Mountains, a fact well-known among collectors. Here in the Domelands, however, the fossils lie relatively undisturbed. The moderately strenuous hike in is discouraging to most souvenir hunters.

The unmarked turnoff to the trailhead is 7.1 miles northwest on Highway S-2 from Interstate 8 at Ocotillo, and 1.1 miles southeast of the Imperial Highway Monument at the San Diego-Imperial county line (mile 56.2 on Highway S-2). Drive 2.0 miles northeast on a dirt road (suitable for all vehicles if driven slowly) to an old quarry in some yellowish clay hills.

On foot, go uphill (north) on an eroded jeep road, closed to motorized vehicles. At 0.5 mile the road passes over a small summit. At 0.8 mile veer right (east) on a more obscure road that follows a small wash. Shell fragments and sand dollars are imbedded in the broken sandstone and clay deposits on either side of the wash. At about 1.3 miles the road climbs to the north bank of the wash, and at 1.6 miles it deadends against a hillside just west of peak 1662.

Turn south, passing over a series of sharp little ravines, and after about 0.2 mile drop southeast down some steep clay slopes into the upper end of a major ravine. The ravine becomes a deep gorge, with a hodgepodge of geological features including yellow and gray clay deposits, desert-varnished granitic boulders, and sandstone walls tinted various shades of tan and orange. At one point huge chunks of sandstone have fallen from the walls, creating a fat man's misery situation. Sandy patches in the canyon bottom serve as

fine campsites—except, of course, during heavy rain.

When you've traveled about 1.2 miles through the canyon, to a point just above the 920-foot contour, a clay butte with a sandstone cap comes into view up ahead on the right. On the left (west) side of the canyon you'll discover a small tributary blocked by a 35-foot dry fall. Just above the top of the fall is a delicate natural bridge: a sandstone shelf seven feet long, three feet wide, and just eight inches thick.

Climb up the rocky slope to the left of the dry fall (or if this is too difficult, go down-canyon a bit farther and find another way up) and drop down the sculpted ravine to examine the natural bridge first-hand.

From the bridge, make your way west or northwest over the convoluted landscape to the high ridge topped by Peak 1662. To the south are spectacular views of the domelike features above the walls of the canyon you just hiked through. These are the namesakes of the Domelands.

Follow the high ridge toward Peak 1662, examining the abundant pecten, sand dollar, mollusk, urchin, and coral fossils. These date from the Pliocene epoch, about four million years ago. You can also work your way south toward a group of wind caves, one of which could serve as comfortable wind-and-rain-sheltered cocoon for two people.

Passing south of Peak 1662, you'll pick up a well-worn trail that leads west down the slope to the roadend just west of Peak 1662. Return to your car, as you came, by way of this road.

Trip 2: Mine Peak

Distance	2.5 miles round trip
Total Elevation Gain/Loss	700'/700'
Hiking Time	2 hours (round trip)
Optional Map	USGS 7.5-min *Sweeney Pass*
Best Times	November through April
Difficulty	**

Mine peak (1850') is the highest point on the west end of the Coyote Mountains. On a clear day the view from the summit seems to go on forever, with the wrinkled Carrizo Badlands in the north, the cobbled Tierra Blanca, In-Ko-Pah, and Jacumba mountains to the west through south, and the flat, hazy Yuha Desert and Salton Sink to the southeast and northeast.

Turn east at mile 53.4 on Highway S-2 onto the West Dolomite Mine Trail. Drive 0.7 mile, then turn sharply left (north). Go 0.2 mile to a large parking area and stop. After this, the road sharply deteriorates.

On foot now, cross a wash and continue up the road 0.6 mile to an abandoned dolomite mine. From here it's a simple matter of scrambling straight up the ridge, due north, to the rounded summit of Mine peak.

Trip 3: Canyon Sin Nombre

Distance	5 miles round trip
Total Elevation Gain/Loss	550'/550'
Hiking Time	3 hours (round trip)
Recommended Map	USGS 7.5-min *Sweeney Pass*
Best Times	November through April
Difficulty	**

One of the best examples of a slot canyon in Anza-Borrego's south end is off of Canyon Sin Nombre (Canyon without a Name). Canyon Sin Nombre serves as a route for off-road vehicle travel between Highway S-2 above Sweeney Pass and Carrizo Creek, but is seldom busy. Hiking down this canyon, especially when a low sun brings out the variegated colors of its walls, is pure delight.

Park in the small turnout at mile 51.3 on Highway S-2, and begin by following the vehicle tracks that descend steeply down a sandy slope toward the head of Canyon Sin Nombre. As you near the head of the canyon, admire the beautiful barrel cacti on the flats and slopes nearby: many grow to heights of five feet or more. Notice how they lean south—toward the sun at its brightest.

The entrance walls are only a foretaste of the hodgepodge of shapes and colors to come. The twisted brown and gray layers are Julian Schist, a metasedimentary rock commonly found around Julian, where it is associated with gold-bearing ore. Pieces of petrified wood are found around here. Just beyond this, granitic rock is exposed. On the right (east) wall, about 0.3 mile farther, is a crumpled swirl of sedimentary layers—both synclines and anticlines are seen here.

After this, the canyon broadens somewhat, and the walls are fashioned from a more uniform-textured mudstone and sandstone. At a point 1.3 miles into the canyon—at the 760-foot contour—a tributary cuts deeply into the clifflike left (west) wall. This becomes a narrow slot canyon, with walls perhaps 150 feet high. A squeeze through, climbing all the while, brings you to the top of the cliffs overlooking Canyon Sin Nombre.

The easiest way to return is the same way you came. Further exploration in this area might include a trek up the trace of an Indian trail running southwest along the hills west of Canyon Sin Nombre in the direction of Sweeney Pass; this trail can be picked up above the slot canyon. You might also try poking into one of the many concretion-littered tributaries east of Canyon Sin Nombre and north of Mine peak.

Concretions in tributary of Canyon Sin Nombre

Trip 4: Arroyo Tapiado/Arroyo Seco Del Diablo Loop

	Distance	16.5 miles
	Total Elevation Gain/Loss	600'/600'
	Hiking Time	8 hours
	Optional Map	USGS 7.5-min *Arroyo Tapiado*
	Best Times	December through March
	Difficulty	****

This is one of the longest hikes described in this book, but one of the most relaxing—relaxing, that is, if you pick the right day or days. Avoid weekends, particularly holiday weekends, if you can. Otherwise you'll share these arroyos with too many noisy all-terrain vehicles and motorcycles. The terrain, except for side trips, is smooth and virtually flat.

After a heavy rainfall, these meandering washes are muddy and impassable to all but foot travelers. Otherwise they're fully accessible to 4-wheel-drive vehicles, and partly accessible to standard automobiles. It is only by walking, however, that the otherworldly beauty of this area can really be appreciated. Plan on one very long day, or a two-day backpack, to take advantage of the many side trips and adventures along the way. Secluded campsites can be found in the upper reaches of both Arroyo Tapiado and Arroyo Seco del Diablo.

The highlight of the trip comes early: the Arroyo Tapiado cave formations. Some of the caves are pitch dark; bring at least two flashlights (per person) and a hard hat or a rock-climbing helmet if you intend to explore them.

To reach the starting point, find the signed Palm Spring turnoff at mile 43.0 on County Highway S-2. This is opposite (east of) Canebrake Canyon. Go east, bypassing the spur road to Palm Spring, and continue (if road conditions allow) down Vallecito Wash. Park at the intersection of the road into Arroyo Tapiado, 4.5 miles from S-2.

On foot, proceed north in the wash of Arroyo Tapiado (translation: "mudwall wash"). After 2.0 miles you reach the beginning of a deep, twisting gorge. The next two miles will take you through what geologists call *pseudokarst* topography. Like the *karst* topography found in many parts of the world, *pseudokarst* contains caves, subterranean drainage systems, sinkholes, and blind valleys that end in swallow holes. Unlike *karst* topography, which results from the dissolution of limestone or similar material by water, this topography is the result of an unusual process: First, flood waters gouge out slotlike tributaries in the soft claystone walls of the main arroyo (Arroyo Tapiado). Second, landslides fill in the slots. Third, flood waters dig tunnels through the bottom levels of the landslide debris.

Some of the caves (subterranean stream channels) in the area are over 1000 feet long, with rooms up to 80 feet high and 30 feet wide. Others are tall and narrow, much like a meandering slot canyon with a roof overhead. Some have multiple levels, and one contains a 45-foot-high subterranean dry fall. Sinkholes (skylights) illuminate the interiors of some caves. Most cave passages eventually lead upstream through a swallow hole to a blind valley.

The bigger and more mature caves are quite stable, with ages on the order of thousands of years. Except during an earthquake or flood, the hard-packed floors of these caves should offer safe passage. It is very dangerous, however, to wander around topside in the *pseudokarst* valleys (those with sinkholes) and blind valleys (those ending in swallow holes). There would be no exit if one were to fall into some of these holes—or incipient holes. (This may explain the reported dissappearance of travelers in the last century who tried various shortcuts across the Carrizo Badlands.)

Several tributaries on the left, just past 2.0 miles in Arroyo Tapiado, are worth investigating. Huge berms of slumped debris lie across most of them; climb these berms and cautiously peer into frightening pits 40 or more feet deep; these lie at the foot of dry falls.

A small grove of mesquite on the left at 2.7 miles is the clue to finding the entrance to one of the longer caves. Halfway through this cave is a tiny skylight, 50 or more feet up. Another cave entrance on the left at 2.9 miles offers an easy passage of several hundred feet to a wide swallow hole. This cave also features a large sinkhole in the roof of its midsection, and a curious oxbow, or alternate passage.

On the right at 3.1 miles is the entrance to the "Big Mud Cave," the collapsed remnants of a former cave passage. It's an easy and worthwhile side trip, and you don't need a flashlight: Walk through the huge punctured cavern at the front and continue up the narrow wash bridged by many arches. After about 0.5 mile, on the left, you can climb out of the wash for a look at the mazelike terrain topside. Stay on the ridgeline, don't wander through the valleys, and keep track of your footprints—you *must* re-enter the same wash to get back safely!

Other passage entrances penetrate the walls of Arroyo Tapiado and some of its tributaries. So do "pipes," or upper-level conduits, which create spectacular waterfalls during rare flash floods.

Arroyo Tapiado widens after 4.0 miles and sets a straighter course northwest. The canyon divides at 6.3 miles; take the right fork, following the sign indicating the jeep road cutoff to "Arroyo Diablo" (sic). At 6.7 miles, the road goes up the slope to the right and meanders southeast to join Arroyo Diablo at 9.0 miles. (The "Dropoff" jeep route to Fish Creek intersects nearby, offering a direct connection to the Split Mountain area of the Carrizo Badlands.)

Shallow at first, Arroyo Diablo deepens steadily between golden-colored walls of sandstone—quite unlike the gray-green claystone walls you saw in Arroyo Tapiado.

Sandstone concretions, most shaped like balls or bullets, lie half-imbedded in the water-polished walls. Others have completly weathered out and lie on the ground. Between 11.0 and 13.0 miles, there are many interesting tributaries to explore if you have time; the one at 12.3 miles (west side) divides into a maze of narrow slot canyons chockfull of concretions, each one a unique sculpture. (Leave 'em as they lie; even rocks are protected in the state park.)

Down near the mouth of Arroyo Diablo are some mesquite groves, and a small seep in the floor of the canyon. When you emerge out onto the flatlands just beyond the mouth, save some time and distance by leaving the wheel tracks and turning west to pick up the jeep road in Vallecito Wash.

Big Mud Cave in Arroyo Tapiado

Area D-14: Jacumba Mountains/ Carrizo Gorge

A north-south trending fault zone is responsible for the series of ridges and canyons at the southern tip of Anza-Borrego Desert State Park. The great gash of Carrizo Gorge is the most spectacular of the north-south canyons, and it forms the dividing line between the Jacumba Mountains to the west and the In-Ko-Pah Mountains (Area D-12) to the east.

Carrizo Gorge is best known for the railroad that threads along its eastern wall: the San Diego & Arizona Eastern. Built between the years of 1907 and 1919, the railroad carried freight, and for a time passengers, between San Diego and the Imperial Valley. The gorge section features 11 miles of twisiting track, 17 tunnels, and numerous wooden trestles. The spectacular Goat Canyon trestle, completed in 1933 as part of a realignment of the original route, is a noted county landmark. Hurricane Kathleen badly mangled the line in 1976, and cut off traffic through the gorge for five years. After reopening in 1981, the line was quickly severed again, this time by a fire that burned out several smaller trestles. Today (1985) the Carrizo Gorge section is still out of service, but repairs continue. The current owners are negotiating for its reopening.

Hiking along the SD&AE tracks through Carrizo Gorge is expressly forbidden. The route is posted and patrolled daily. The railroad also owns a strip of land on either side of the tracks. It is the opinion of Anza-Borrego rangers, however, that hikers are permitted to cross the tracks at right angles within the state park.

The remote canyons and ridges of the Jacumba and In-Ko-Pah mountains are home to a herd of perhaps 100–200 bighorn sheep. These sheep migrate back and forth across Carrizo Gorge as the seasons progress. Surprisingly, mule deer share the same habitat at times.

Jacumba Mountains/ Corrizo Gorge

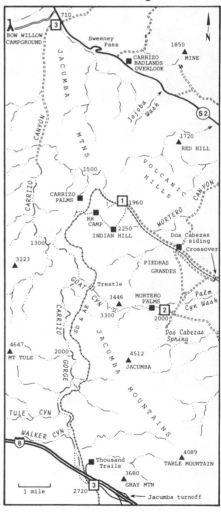

Except for a network of jeep roads on the south and east side of the Jacumbas, a sandy track leading up to the mouth of Carrizo Gorge, and of course the railroad, the Jacumba Mountains and Carrizo Gorge are isolated and pristine. Ancient Indian sites, palm groves, and hidden springs beckon to the hardy hiker.

Goat Canyon Trestle

Trip 1: Indian Hill/Carrizo Palms Loop

Distance	6.5 miles
Total Elevation Gain/Loss	900'/900'
Hiking Time	4½ hours
Required Map	USGS 7.5-min *Sweeney Pass*
Best Times	November through April
Difficulty	***

A variety of interesting cultural, historical, botanical and geological features are seen along this route. Even if you don't want to attempt this entire loop, there's enough interesting sightseeing here that shorter hikes in the area are worthwhile.

The hike begins at a point along the San Diego & Arizona Eastern Railroad tracks near Dos Cabezas siding. Do not take the Mortero Wash and Jojoba Wash jeep trails to reach this point in your conventional auto! A route on much firmer ground—the so-called Dos Cabezas Road on the state park map— goes along Palm Canyon Wash westward from Ocotillo. From Interstate 8, drive 3.8 miles up Highway S-2 to a dirt road which

slants to the left (west-southwest). Go 6.7 miles to Dos Cabezas siding (marked by an old water tank), staying north of the tracks always—do not take the short cut across the north-bulging loop of tracks. From the siding, continue driving 2.2 miles on the north side of the tracks until you reach road's end, overlooking a wash.

On foot, backtrack about 200 yards, cross the tracks (west of here the tracks are posted against trespassing and patrolled daily—don't walk along them or loiter around them), and head south-southwest across a broad alluvial plain dotted with cacti and small shrubs. Several rocky hills consisting of desert-varnished granitic boulders punctuate the surface of the plain. Go past the one incorrectly labelled "Indian Hill" on the topographic map, and continue to a smaller promontory 0.25 mile south made up of boulders the size of small houses—the true Indian Hill.

Indian Hill is considered one of the most significant aboriginal sites in the Colorado Desert. On the northeast side of the hill you'll find a fire-blackened rock cave with a four-foot-high ceiling. Several morteros pock a rock surface just outside the cave. Swing around to the southeast side and climb up about 15 feet to discover a shallow cave, facing south, embellished with what are probably the finest Indian pictographs in Anza-Borrego. Circles and radial patterns (sun symbols) rectangular hatchings (rain symbols) and other figures abound.

Next point of interest is the remains of a circa-1912 railroad camp used during the construction of the San Diego & Arizona Eastern Railroad. The ruins are located 0.7 mile northwest of Indian Hill, 0.1 south of the center of section 20. Use your topo map as a guide. Here you'll find the walls of an old shed constructed of mortar and blasting-powder cans.

Back up about 0.1 mile and follow the obscure bed of an abandoned jeep trail west toward a hillside overlooking the railroad tracks. Cross the tracks and descend over a rugged slope into a tributary of Carrizo Canyon; then go north in the sandy bed of the canyon past several seeps and small palm groves. There's good camping here and there in flat, sandy areas sheltered from the wind.

The seep and large grove of palms at the 1720-foot contour is one of the spots labelled "Carrizo Palms" on the topo map. During 1912 through 1919 railroad workers installed a pump here to boost water up to the camp.

After one more mile, you'll come to a major confluence. Go right (east, upstream) into this colorful narrow canyon, and begin scrambling over a series of bedrock exposures and easy dry falls. After 0.5 mile the bed becomes sandy again; continue one more mile south to the tracks. Don't follow the tracks; instead cross them, continue south, and drop into an east-draining wash. Pass under the tracks and you'll soon arrive at the point just below your parked car.

Trip 2: Mortero Palms To Goat Canyon

Distance	4 miles round trip (to camp sites in Goat Canyon)
Total Elevation Gain/Loss	1500'/1500'
Hiking Time	4 hours (round trip)
Required Map	USGS 7.5-min *Jacumba*
Best Times	November through April
Difficulty	***

Along the crest of the Jacumba Mountains lies several hidden bowls, surrounded by austere, rock-strewn peaks. To spend a night here on a bed of sand, immersed in an achingly profound silence, with nothing but a sky filled with stars overhead is to experience the desert in all its wonder and simplicity.

Not far away from one of these bowls is a landmark revered by railroad buffs the world over. This is the 200-foot-high, 600-foot-long trestle over Goat Canyon on the San Diego & Arizona Eastern line. It has been called the longest curved railroad trestle and the highest wooden trestle in the world.

The starting point for this hike is the

mouth of the canyon containing Palm Canyon Wash and Mortero Palms. The approach by car is via Dos Cabezas Road (see Trip 1). At a point 5.3 miles from S-2, however, go south across the tracks on the paved crossover. After continuing on the other side of the tracks for about 100 yards, turn left (southeast) and proceed 1.0 mile to a road fork. Bear left (south) and drive past an old cattleman's line shack at the base of an isolated rocky hill. After another 0.3 mile turn right (west) and go 0.4 mile to the end of the road overlooking Palm Canyon Wash.

Take care to hike up the main (Mortero Palms) canyon to the west, not the tributary canyon to the south. A small trail follows the south bank for a while, avoiding the vegetation-choked streambed. Soon you begin climbing over granitic boulders. Look for a half-dozen morteros, namesakes of the palm grove, in the center of the drainage 100 yards below the beginning of the palms.

The palm grove is one of the densest in Anza-Borrego, arising from seeps amid a jumble of huge boulders reminiscent of the rock formations at Joshua Tree National Monument. On most warm days this is a seductively cool and breezy spot, and it takes some will power to get moving again to tackle the rugged and difficult stretch of canyon ahead.

At the 2440-foot contour it's easier to leave the canyon bottom temporarily and go up on the slope to the north through stands of teddy-bear cholla. Drop back in at about 2750 feet, but leave the canyon again at the 2840-foot contour. Proceed west and southwest across a small saddle and continue west over a divide into the Goat Canyon drainage.

Descend to a delightful juniper-dotted bowl at about 3200 feet, a good place to spend the night. Further exploration in the area might include a visit to Peak 4512 (Jacumba survey station) south along the crest of the Jacumba Mountains, or a descent down Goat Canyon for a look at the famous trestle. At about 2700 feet in Goat Canyon, there's an excellent—if not at all close-up—

view of the bridge, framed by the steep walls of the canyon. Keep in mind that it is illegal to loiter around the railroad line. Viewing is best done from afar.

Mortero Palms

Trip 3: Carrizo Gorge

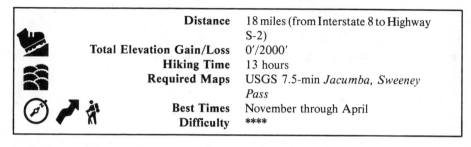

	Distance	18 miles (from Interstate 8 to Highway S-2)
	Total Elevation Gain/Loss	0'/2000'
	Hiking Time	13 hours
	Required Maps	USGS 7.5-min *Jacumba, Sweeney Pass*
	Best Times	November through April
	Difficulty	****

The trek down the length of Carrizo Gorge is long, rugged, difficult, and memorable. It is one to be undertaken cautiously, with the right equipment and clothing. Essential are long pants and sturdy, waterproofed boots.

This trip is best done as a two-day backpack, though one very long day is sufficient for speed demons who travel lightly. The last six miles, on jeep tracks in the sand, may be comfortably done at night. If you're backpacking, keep the weight of your pack to a minimum. Consider leaving your stove, tent, and other luxury items behind. Several roomy rock caves may be used for shelter in the midsection of this hike. Parts of the gorge have experienced year-round flows since about 1976. But carry drinking water anyway, or in lieu of that, a good water-purification filter. The creek is heavily polluted by cattle.

Although the San Diego & Arizona Eastern tracks along the east wall of Carrizo Gorge seem an easier alternative to the rugged, twisting bed of Carrizo Canyon, it is important to keep in mind that the railroad is posted against trespassing. Heavy fines have been levied against those caught on the tracks in recent years.

You'll have to arrange a car shuttle or drop-off and pick-up arrangement to do this hike in the recommended one-way direction. The starting point is reached by taking the Jacumba exit off Interstate 8. Go west on the frontage road (Carrizo Gorge Road) 1.5 miles, but do not cross under Interstate 8. (There is no access to Carrizo Canyon

through the Thousand Trails trailer park on the north side of I-8.)

Staying south of I-8, walk across the SD&AE tracks, and parallel the freeway for 200 yards until you reach the Interstate 8 bridge over Carrizo Creek. Go north under I-8, then go west along the north side of the freeway for about 250 yards until you reach the edge of Section 32 on the topo map, where you will find an ill-defined fence line marking the boundary of Thousand Trails. Go north until you drop into Carrizo Creek again.

The creek carries a respectable flow of water during the wet season, and you'll be up on the banks most of the time in an effort to avoid getting your boots filled with water. At 2.0 miles, the creek drops over a tumble of car-sized boulders; you may have to detour over the jagged rocks on the left (west) side, a climb of 150 feet, class 3 rock climbing. This is the only really serious obstacle on the trip. Carrizo Gorge now lies ahead.

The next 10 miles offer bushwhacking, boulder-hopping and mud-stomping in abundance. The sharp thorns of mesquite and catclaw; the needlelike tips of a particularly wicked type of bunch grass; dense thickets of *carrizo*, or cane, a bamboolike reed; and slippery rocks will all conspire to slow your progress. Mercifully, however, there are also many easy stretches across sand and dry rock. The feet of feral cattle, hikers and undocumented aliens have beaten down trails in these areas.

The gorge has served as a trap for railroad debris which has tumbled off the slopes, and for flotsam and jetsam washed down from the Jacumba area during past floods. At about 4.0 miles, four sets of railroad wheels and axles lie in the canyon. Signs of recent fire are apparent at this point, and you can look up to see rails drooping over two of the ravines like limp clotheslines, their underpinnings burned completely away.

At about 6.0 miles, above a landscape of rusted tin cans from a former railroad camp, there is a beautiful teddy-bear-cholla forest with specimens up to 10 feet tall. Tall barrel cacti, eight or more feet high, are also seen a short distance down the gorge.

Goat Canyon, a tributary, enters from the right (east) at 8.5 miles. Climb 200 feet up the ridge to the north of this canyon for a great view of the famous curved trestle. Several rock caves are nearby, some with signs of Indian occupation, and nearly all

with evidence of more recent visits by undocumented aliens.

The bed of Carrizo Gorge (now called Carrizo Canyon) widens out past Goat Canyon, though it is not until about 12.0 miles that you can walk continuously on a smooth bed of sand. Occasionally, four-wheel-drive vehicles can make it to the official road closure here, but recent heavy flows in the creek have made this difficult most of the time. Carrizo Canyon is a notorious sand trap, so you should not count on anyone in a vehicle picking you up short of the Highway S-2 dip through Carrizo Creek (mile 48.6 on S-2).

Another possible endpoint for this trip is Bow Willow Campground. To reach it, leave Carrizo Canyon about one mile short of the highway and head directly northwest toward the dirt road into Bow Willow Canyon.

Giant cholla cactus in Carrizo Gorge

Area D-15: Jacumba Outstanding Natural Area

Five to ten miles east of the old resort town of Jacumba, pressed against the California-Baja California border, is a series of scenic peaks and valleys affording vistas of mountain and desert landscapes in two nations. The BLM calls this the "Jacumba Outstanding Natural Area," and manages the area for wildlife protection and primitive recreation. Vehicle access is officially restricted or impractical in much of the area, but camping and backpacking are encouraged.

Although American mapmakers consider this rugged area to be a part of the Jacumba Mountains, it is more closely associated with the hundred-mile-long Sierra Juarez, Baja's northernmost link in the chain of Peninsular Ranges. Like the Sierra Juarez high country, the western edges of the Natural Area are high desert, with pinyon pines clinging to the windswept, granite-bouldered crags. The eastern margins are low desert, with rock-strewn ridges separating valleys that have typical growths of ocotillo, agave, cholla cactus, mesquite and brittlebush. Clusters of fan palms grace some of the midelevation drainages.

Each of the three trips below is within Imperial County, just beyond the San Diego County line. They are included in this book because they are easily accessible from San Diego (about 90 minutes by car) and because the area is practically adjacent to Anza-Borrego Desert State Park.

To reach the starting point for both Trips 1 and 2, exit Interstate 8 at In-Ko-Pah Park Road (east of Jacumba). Drive southwest 0.2 mile along the frontage road, Old Highway 80, then turn left (away from Interstate 8) on an unmarked dirt road. Standard passenger

vehicles should park no farther than 0.8 mile up this road, at a large turnout. Sturdy four-wheel-drive vehicles may continue farther, prudently, up the steep road toward the patchwork of jeep trails and primitive campsites. The hiking descriptions below assume that you park in the turnout at 0.8 mile.

A nice alternative (or complement) to the USGS topographic map listed below for Trips 1 and 2 is the Mexican government "La Rumorosa—I11D63," 1:50,000 scale map. Unlike the USGS map, which is blank below the border, the Mexican topo shows features on both sides. It is not legal, of course, to cross the border into Mexico except at official ports of entry.

Jacumba Outstanding Natural Area

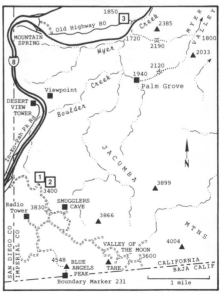

Trip 1: Blue Angels Peak

Distance	5 miles round trip
Total Elevation Gain/Loss	1300'/1300'
Hiking Time	3 hours (round trip)
Recommended Map	USGS 7.5-min *In-Ko-Pah Gorge*
Best Times	October through May
Difficulty	**

Blue Angels Peak, one of several crags of roughly equal height along a high north-south ridge spanning the two Californias, happens to be the highest point in "Alta" California within six miles of the international border. The peak is surely one of the windiest spots in southern California—especially in spring, when hot air rising up from the low desert to the east draws in a strong flow of cooler air from the coastal regions.

From the parking area 0.8 mile from Old Highway 80, walk up the road to a saddle at 3830 feet. A jeep trail branches left to Smuggler's Cave, an old hideout of bandits and smugglers, now a fire-blackened, grafitti-emblazoned wreck. Proceed another 0.1 mile south and bear right (west). Continue south and finally east to the roadend, staying left at two road junctions at 1.1 and 1.4 miles. An old mining prospect lies at the end of the road.

Blue Angels Peak is to the southeast, hidden behind a false peak capped by a massive block of granite seemingly poised to roll. Scramble up over lichen-encrusted boulders and past scraggly pinyons to find the bench mark on the summit.

On the return trip, make a short detour to discover International Boundary Marker 231, a handsome ten-foot-high steel obelisk, in the middle of a flat south and a little west of the peak. These markers are numbered consecutively along the border from #1 at the Gulf of Mexico shoreline east of Brownsville-Matamoros to #258 at the Pacific shoreline (see Area B-4, Trip 1). A barbed-wire fence parallels the true border sixty feet north of the border, delineating a strip of land in the U.S. and under the jurisdiction of the U.S. International Boundary Commission. This buffer is also apparent at the border crossings in San Ysidro-Tijuana and Tecate.

There seems to be some movement of undocumented aliens across this part of the border, but not a lot, as the terrain south of here is quite rugged. Keep in mind that, while you are welcome on this side of the border, you are responsible for staying out of Mexico.

Border marker south of peak

Trip 2: Valley Of The Moon

Distance	7 miles round trip
Total Elevation Gain/Loss	900'/900'
Hiking Time	4 hours (round trip)
Recommended Map	USGS 7.5-min *In-Ko-Pah Gorge*
Best Times	October through May
Difficulty	**

Strolling along jeep roads in the informally but appropriately named Valley of the Moon, you would almost think that a square-mile chunk of Joshua Tree National Monument had been transported here—minus, of course, the famous Joshua trees. Huge granitic outcrops, seamed with horizontal and vertical cracks, ring the valley.

Begin this hike as in Trip 1 above, but bear left at the intersection 0.1 mile beyond the saddle. Descend sharply and bear southeast toward a small peak ("Tahe") containing the Elliot Mine, an abandoned amethyst mine. Keep straight, avoiding spur roads to campsites tucked up against coves in the rocks, but turn left (east) just before the main road continues sharply uphill to the mine. Bend east and south around the base of "Tahe," then veer east and enter the Valley of the Moon.

The sandy floor of the valley is dotted with Mojave yucca, catclaw, Mormon tea and buckwheat. You can continue toward an old water tank in the northeast corner of the valley, or follow any of the jeep roads that wind around the statuesque boulder heaps to the south. Photographers should be here early or late in the day, when the sun bathes the stone battlements in a warm light, and sharply defined shadows march across the valley.

In the Valley of the Moon

Trip 3: Myer Valley/Boulder Creek

Distance	4.0 miles
Total Elevation Gain/Loss	1000'/1000'
Hiking Time	3 hours
Required Map	USGS 7.5-min *In-Ko-Pah Gorge*
Best Times	November through April
Difficulty	***

Have you ever driven down Interstate 8 east of Jacumba, and, eyeing the immense boulder piles that rise on both sides, wondered what it would be like to clamber over them? Here's your chance. Follow these directions, and in just a few minutes you can be safely parked off the freeway, and on your way into a primeval landscape visited only by an occasional adventurer like yourself.

Exit I-8 at Mountain Spring. At a point midway in the "island" between the eastbound and westbound lanes of the freeway, turn east on a rough dirt road. In 0.2 mile this road joins the abandoned concrete ribbon of old U.S. Highway 80. Drive east, dodging fallen boulders on the roadway, for an additional 1.3 miles and park near the road's end—just before the brink of a road cut made for the eastbound lanes of I-8.

Scramble down the slope (this is probably the most difficult part of the hike!) about 100 feet to the sandy bed of Myer Creek. Pass under the lanes of I-8 through the large culvert to the west and continue 0.1 mile in the wash until you come to the base of a rocky gully on the left (east). Scramble up the coarse-grained granitic boulders in this gully; after 400 feet of elevation gain you join a sandy wash. Continue east and top a saddle—this is 0.2 mile south of peak 2385. Pass over the saddle, and descend an easy drainage leading to Myer Valley. The half-square-mile valley gently slopes to the north. It is so thickly grown with cresote bush, ocotillo, and other plants whose color intensifies after periods of rainfall that it can look from a distance as if it were covered by a verdant carpet. There is a maze of old jeep roads in the valley, but vehicles aren't often seen here. Access by motorized vehicles is controlled by special permit from the BLM, and the vehicle approach route via Myer Creek is often blocked by flash-flood debris.

Upon reaching the edge of the valley, you can turn south and skirt the west edge of the valley, following a minor wash. Pick up traces of an old jeep trail about 0.3 mile southwest of peaklet 2033. Follow this west-southwest to the top of a broad divide, then drop into a ravine that leads west into a north-flowing tributary of Boulder Creek. After some moderate scrambling, you'll arrive at a beautiful palm oasis, complete with a year-round spring. A sculpted dry fall and a nice set of Indian morteros are nearby.

From the palm oasis, it's an easy 1.2 miles back to the culvert under I-8, via Boulder and Myer creeks downhill in wash bottoms all the way. Several small groups of palms provide welcome shade if needed.

At 0.3–0.4 mile below the palm oasis, two canyons come in on the left, inviting side trips. The first of these, a rugged tributary to the south, is fascinating, with immense boulders, hidden cottonwoods and palms, and secluded campsites. Some difficult scrambling is required to fully explore it. The second of these, upper Boulder Creek canyon to the southwest, is vegetation-choked and unremarkable.

APPENDIX 1: BEST HIKES

BEST BEACH HIKE
La Jolla Shores to Torrey Pines Beach (Area B-2, Trip 1). Here the primeval southern California coastline survives more or less intact.

BEST SUBURBAN HIKES
Torrey Pines State Reserve (Area B-2, Trip 2). Breathtaking views of the coastline, eroded landforms, and the rare Torrey Pine.

Penasquitos Canyon (Area C-3, Trips 2 & 3). Largest undeveloped canyon system close to San Diego. Rolling hills, meadows, and a delightful, tree-lined stream.

Cowles Mountain (Area C-5, Trips 1 & 2). The summit has the best view of metropolitan San Diego.

BEST MOUNTAIN HIKES
Lower Doane Valley/Lower French Valley (Area M-2, Trip 4). Trickling streams, dark forests, and sunny meadows.

Azalea Glen Trail (Area M-9, Trip 6). Oak and conifer forests and a trickling stream.

BEST DESERT HIKES
Borrego Palm Canyon Nature Trail (Area D-2, Trip 1). Discover a fan palm oasis in a magnificent setting of soaring canyon walls.

Mountain Palm Springs (Area D-12, Trip 3). A half dozen palm groves secreted in boulder-strewn hills.

BEST CANYON HIKES
Noble Canyon (Area M-11, Trip 14). A year-round mountain stream in a narrow, shaded canyon.

Pine Valley Creek (Area M-13, Trip 1). Beautiful rock exposures, lots of water in winter and spring.

Sheep Canyon (Area D-1, Trip 3). Palms, sycamores, lush vegetation, and waterfalls.

BEST WATERFALLS AND SWIMMING HOLES
Cedar Creek Falls (Area M-7, Trip 3). San Diego County's most spectacular waterfall; deep "punchbowl" beneath.

Cougar Canyon (Area D-1, Trip 5). Waterfalls and deep pools in a pseudo-tropical desert setting.

BEST PEAK CLIMBS
Stonewall Peak (Area M-9, Trip 8). Easy trail; good overview of Cuyamaca and Laguna mountains from the pointed summit.

Garnet Peak (Area M-11, Trip 3). Easy climb; fabulous view on the Laguna escarpment.

Villager Peak and Rabbit Peak (Area D-4, Trip 2). Long, rugged, desert peak climb; views across half the width of California and deep into Mexico.

BEST WILDFLOWERS
Torrey Pines State Reserve (Area B-2, Trip 2). Nearly all varieties of wildflowers common to the coastal region are represented here.

East Mesa Loop (Area M-9, Trip 13). Wildflowers of the mountain meadows and chaparral.

Laguna Lakes (Area M-11, Trip 8). Wildflowers of the mountain meadows and pine forest.

Borrego Palm Canyon Nature Trail (Area D-2, Trip 1). Most common varieties of desert wildflowers bloom here.

BEST AUTUMN COLORS
Fry Creek Trail (Area M-2, Trip 6). Conifer and oak forest.

Kelly Ditch Trail (Area M-9, Trip 1) Conifer and oak forest; trickling streams.

West Mesa Loop (Area M-9, Trip 14). Conifer and oak forest; meadows.

Indian Creek Loop (Area M-11, Trip 4). Black oak and pine forest.

BEST BIRD AND WILDLIFE WATCHING
Tijuana River Estuary (Area B-4, Trip 2). Local as well as migrant bird life.

Penasquitos Canyon (Area C-3, Trips 2 & 3). Deer, coyotes, and (rarely) mountain lions have been seen here.

Barker Valley (Area M-3, Trip 2). Deer, bobcats, mountain lions, and bald eagles are common in this area.

Dyar Spring/Juaquapin Loop (Area M-9, Trip 11). One of the largest deer herds in San Diego County roams this area unmolested.

Lower Willows Loop (Area D-1, Trip 1). Birds, small mammals, and insects thrive in the jungle-like growth. (Area closed in summer to protect the watering rights of bighorn sheep.)

Borrego Palm Canyon Nature Trail (Area D-2, Trip 1). Bighorn sheep commonly seen here in summer.

Yaqui Well (Area D-6, Trip 3). Good birding in this small desert oasis.

Squaw Pond Trail (Area D-11, Trip 1). Desert oasis draws coyotes, bobcats, birds, bats and rattlesnakes.

BEST RUNNING TRAILS (• indicates routes also suitable for mountain bicycling)

La Jolla Shores to Torrey Pines Beach (Area B-2, Trip 1). Beach all the way except for a few cobbled areas. Recommended during low tide only.

Lake Poway Loop (Area C-2, Trip 1). Pleasant loop around a small lake. One steep and several mild grades.

• **Penasquitos Canyon** (Area C-3, Trips 2 & 3). Mostly flat dirt road. Pleasant scenery, cool breezes, peace and quiet.

• **Rose Canyon & San Clemente Canyon** (Area C-4, Trips 1 & 2). String these together and close the loop on city streets. Shaded dirt roads.

Cowles Mountain (Area C-5, Trips 1 & 2). The quintessential mountain workout in the San Diego area. Superb views.

Sweetwater Trail (Area C-7, Trip 1). A classic California landscape of golden,

rolling hills. Narrow trail with some short, steep grades.

Oak Grove to High Point (Area M-3, Trip 1). To the highest point on Palomar Mountain via road and trail. Experts only.

Cuyamaca Peak (Area M-9, Trip 7). Paved road all the way, but steep.

Stonewall Creek/Soapstone Grade Loop (Area M-9, Trip 9). Mostly gentle fire roads, some steep grades on trails.

West Mesa Loop (Area M-9, Trip 14). Pleasant, shady route on fire roads.

• **Mason Valley Truck Trail** (Area M-10, Trip 1). Run from the mountains to the desert on an old dirt road.

Noble Canyon Trail (Area M-11, Trip 14). Narrow, but mostly smooth trail. Downhill direction preferred. One long, steep stretch.

• **Otay Mountain** (Area M-15, Trips 1 & 2). Steady ascent on good dirt roads. Unusual cypress groves, good views all the way.

• **Jasper Trail/Grapevine Canyon** (Area D-6, Trip 1). High desert to low desert on mostly smooth, sandy jeep trails.

• **June Wash to Split Mountain** (Area D-10, Trip 6). Traverse across the badlands. Mostly on jeep trails in soft or hard-packed sand, but one-half mile over a rocky pass.

• **Arroyo Tapiado/Arroyo Seco del Diablo** (Area D-13, Trip 4). Through the badlands washes on flat, smooth jeep trails.

APPENDIX 2: RECOMMENDED READING

Hiking, Backpacking, and Mountaineering

Fletcher, Colin, *The New Complete Walker,* Knopf, 1976.
Ganci, David, *Desert Hiking,* Wilderness Press, 1983.
Manning, Harvey, *Backpacking One Step at a Time,* Vintage Books, 1980.
Peters, Ed (ed.), *Mountaineering, the Freedom of the Hills,* 4th edition, The Mountaineers, 1974.
Winnett, Thomas, *Backpacking Basics,* Wilderness Press, 1979.

San Diego Area Guidebooks

California Coastal Commission, *California Coastal Access Guide,* University of California Press, 1982.
Lindsay, Diana and Lowell, *The Anza-Borrego Desert Region,* revised edition, Wilderness Press, 1985.

McKinney, John, *Day Hiker's Guide to Southern California*, Capra Press, 1981.

Mendel, Carol, *San Diego!... City and County*, Carol Mendel, 1985.

Mendel, Carol, *San Diego On Foot*, Carol Mendel, 1985.

Parker, Horace, *Anza-Borrego Desert Guide Book*, revised edition, Anza-Borrego Desert Natural History Association, 1979.

Peik, L. and R., *Campers Guide to San Diego County Campgrounds*, Peik Enterprises, 1981.

Robinson, John W., *San Bernardino Mountain Trails*, revised edition, Wilderness Press, 1986.

Ruland, Skip, *Backpacking Guide to San Diego County*, revised edition, Calif. Backpacking Co., 1984. (Includes log of Pacific Crest Trail in San Diego County.)

Schad, Jerry, *Backcountry Roads & Trails, San Diego County*, revised edition, Touchstone Press, 1983.

Schaffer, Jeffrey P., *et al. The Pacific Crest Trail, Volume 1: California*, Wilderness Press, 1982. (Includes log and maps of Pacific Crest Trail in San Diego County.)

History and Natural History

Bailey, H. P., *The Climate of Southern California*, University of California Press, 1966.

Chase, J. Smeaton, *California Desert Trails*, Houghton Mifflin Co., 1919. (Out of print)

Ellsberg, Helen, *Mines of Julian*, La Siesta Press, 1972.

James, George Wharton, *The Wonders of the Colorado Desert*, Little Brown, & Co., 1906. (Out of print)

Jaeger, Edmond C. and Smith, Arthur C., *Introduction to the Natural History of Southern California*, University of California Press, 1971.

Larson, Peggy, *A Sierra Club Naturalist's Guide: The Deserts of the Southwest*, Sierra Club Books, 1977.

Lindsay, Diana E., *Our Historic Desert: The Story of the Anza-Borrego Desert*, Copley Books, 1973.

Pourade, Richard F., *Anza Conquers the Desert*, Copley Books, 1971.

Pourade, Richard F., *Ancient Hunters of the Far West*, Copley Books, 1966.

Pryde, Philip R., *San Diego: An Introduction to the Region*, 2nd ed., Kendall/Hunt Publishing Co., 1984.

Reed, Lester, *Old Time Cattlemen and Other Pioneers of the Anza-Borrego Desert Area*, Desert Printers, Inc., 1963. (Out of print)

Rensch, Hero Eugene, "Fages' Crossing of the Cuyamacas," in *California Historical Society Quarterly*, Vol. 34, March 1955.

Rensch, Hero Eugene, "Wood's Shorter Mountain Trail to San Diego," in *California Historical Society Quarterly*, Vol. 36, June 1957.

Stein, Lou, *San Diego County Place-Names*, Tofua Press, 1975.

Geology

Abbott, P. (ed.), *Geologic Studies of San Diego,* San Diego Association of Geologists, 1982.

Kennedy, M. P., and Peterson, G. L., *Geology of the San Dieqo Metropolitan Area, California,* Bulletin 200, California Division of Mines and Geology, 1975.

Kuhn, Gerald G. and Shepard, Francis P., *Sea Cliffs, Beaches, and Coastal Valleys of San Diego County,* University of California Press, 1984.

Sharp, Robert P., *Coastal Southern California* (geology guide), Kendall/ Hunt Publishing Company, 1978.

Weber, F. H., *Geology and Mineral Resources of San Diego County, California,* County Report 3, California Division of Mines and Geology, 1963. (Contains large-scale geological map of San Diego County.)(Out of print)

Biology

Bean, L. J. and Saubel, S. S., *Temalpakh: Cahuilla Indian Knowledge and Usage of Plants,* Malki Museum Press, 1972.

Beauchamp, R. Mitchel, *A Flora of San Diego County, California,* Sweetwater River Press, 1986.

Belzer, Thomas J., *Roadside Plants of Southern California,* Mountain Press Publishing Co., 1984.

Dawson, E. Yale, *Cacti of California,* University of California Press, 1971.

Jaeger, Edmond C., *Desert Wild Flowers,* revised edition, Stanford University Press, 1969.

Jaeger, Edmond C., *Desert Wildlife,* Stanford University Press, 1961.

Johnson, Paul, *Cacti, Shrubs and Trees of Anza-Borrego,* Anza-Borrego Desert Natural History Association, 1982.

Munz, Philip A., *California Spring Wildflowers,* University of California Press, 1961.

Munz, Philip A., *California Desert Wildflowers,* University of California Press, 1962.

Munz, Philip A., *California Mountain Wildflowers,* University of California Press, 1963.

Peterson, P. Victor, *Native Trees of Southern California,* University of California Press, 1966.

Raven, Peter H., *Native Shrubs of Southern California,* University of California Press, 1966.

Unitt, Philip, *Birds of San Diego County,* San Diego Society of Natural History, 1984.

Yocom, Charles and Dasmann, Ray, *Pacific Coastal Wildlife Region,* revised edition, Naturegraph Publishers. No date.

APPENDIX 3: LOCAL ORGANIZATIONS

(all telephone numbers are area code 619)

Anza-Borrego Desert Natural History Association
P.O. Box 311
Borrego Springs, CA 92004
(Activities associated with Anza-Borrego Desert State Park)

Adventure 16 Wilderness Outings
4620 Alvarado Canyon Road
San Diego, CA 92120
283-2374
(Basic mountaineering instruction and backpacking trips in San Diego County)

Audubon Society of San Diego
4536 Park Blvd.
San Diego, CA 92116
291-8271
(Nature and bird walks, and operates the Silverwood Wildlife Sanctuary and Nature Education Center)

Cuyamaca Rancho State Park Interpretive Association
12551 Highway 79
Descanso, CA 92016
(Activities associated with Cuyamaca Rancho State Park)

Laguna Mountain Volunteer Association
3348 Alpine Blvd.
Alpine, CA 92001
(Activities associated with the Descanso Ranger District of Cleveland National Forest)

Los Penasquitos Cultural and Natural Resource Center
c/o San Diego Ecology Center
430 Olive Street
San Diego, CA 92101
294-2926
(Interpretive walks at Los Penasquitos Canyon Preserve)

San Diego Backpacking Club
31308 Highway 94
Campo, CA 92006
478-5985
(Day hikes and backpacking trips throughout San Diego County)

San Diego Society of Natural History
(Natural History Museum, Balboa Park)
P.O. Box 1390
San Diego, CA 92112
232-3821
(Interpretive outings throughout San Diego County)

Sierra Club, San Diego Chapter
1549 El Prado, Balboa Park
San Diego, CA 92101
233-7144
(Hiking and backpacking outings throughout the San Diego region, plus a basic mountaineering training course in winter-spring.)

Southwest Wetlands Interpretive Association
P.O. Box 575
Imperial Beach, CA 92032
   (Nature walks in the coastal wetlands of San Diego County)
Walkabout International
P.O. Box 6540
San Diego, CA 92106
223-9255
   (Walks throughout metropolitan San Diego)

APPENDIX 4: INFORMATION SOURCES

(all telephone numbers are area code 619)

Anza-Borrego Desert State Park
P.O. Box 428
Borrego Springs, CA 92004
767-5311

Border Field State Park
c/o Frontera District, California Dept. of Parks and Recreation
3990 Old Town Avenue 300-C
San Diego, CA 92110
237-6766

Bureau of Land Management
El Centro Resource Area Office
333 South Waterman Avenue
El Centro, CA 92243
352-5842

Cabrillo National Monument
Point Loma
293-5450

Cleveland National Forest
   Wilderness and remote camping permits available from:
   Forest Supervisor
   880 Front Street (Federal Building)
   Room 5-N-14
   San Diego, CA 92188
   232-3769
   Descanso Ranger District
   3348 Alpine Blvd.
   Alpine, CA 92001
   445-6235/473-8824
   (24-hour recreation recording: 445-8341)
   Palomar Ranger District
   332 South Juniper Street, Suite 100
   Escondido, CA 92025
   745-2421

Cuyamaca Rancho State Park
12551 Highway 79
Descanso, CA 92016
765-0755

Palomar Mountain State Park
Palomar Mountain, CA 92060
742-3462

Lake Poway Recreation Area
c/o City of Poway Recreation Dept.
13202 Poway Road
Poway, CA 92064
748-2224

La Jolla Indian Reservation Campground
742-1297

Los Coyotes Indian Reservation
Los Tules Road
Warner Springs, CA 92086
782-3269

San Diego County Parks (includes all county parks)
5201 Ruffin Road, Suite P
San Diego, CA 92123
565-3600

Silverwood Wildlife Sanctuary
13003 Wildcat Canyon Road
Lakeside, CA 92040
443-2998

Torrey Pines State Reserve
P.O. Box 38
Carlsbad, CA 92008
755-2063

Map Sources

Adventure 16
4620 Alvarado Canyon Road
San Diego, CA 92120
283-2374
   (topographic maps)

Map Centre
2611 University Avenue
San Diego, CA 92104
291-3830
   (topographic maps of San Diego County and Baja California; geological
   maps)

Bureau of Land Management
1695 Spruce Street
Riverside, CA 92507
   ("surface management status" maps showing distribution of public lands
   in San Diego County)

Cleveland National Forest—see above
   ("recreation" and other maps)

Miscellaneous

Project Hug-a-Tree
(send SASE)
6465 Lance Way
San Diego, CA 92120

San Diego County Sheriff
(Emergencies—dial 911)
565-5200

California Division of Forestry
(To report fires—442-1615)
588-0364

INDEX